Czechs, Germans, Jews?

Czechs, Germans, Jews?
National Identity and the Jews of Bohemia

Kateřina Čapková

Translated by Derek and Marzia Paton

berghahn
NEW YORK · OXFORD
www.berghahnbooks.com

Published by
Berghahn Books
www.berghahnbooks.com

English-language edition
©2012, 2015 Berghahn Books
First paperback edition published in 2015

Czech edition
©2005, *Češi, Němci, Židé? Národní identita Židů v Čechách, 1918-1938*
Prague: Paseka Publishing House.

All rights reserved. Except for the quotation of short passages
for the purposes of criticism and review, no part of this book
may be reproduced in any form or by any means, electronic or
mechanical, including photocopying, recording, or any information
storage and retrieval system now known or to be invented,
without written permission of the publisher.

Library of Congress Cataloging-in-Publication Data

Czechs, Germans, Jews : national identity and the Jews of Bohemia / Kateřina Čapková ; translated by Derek and Marzia Paton.
  p. cm.
Includes bibliographical references and index.
  ISBN 978-0-85745-474-4 (hardback) — ISBN 978-1-78238-679-7 (paperback) — ISBN 978-0-85745-475-1 (ebook)
  1. Jews—Czech Republic—Bohemia—Identity. 2. Jews—Czech Republic—Bohemia—Social conditions—20th century. 3. Jews—Czech Republic—Bohemia—History—20th century. 4. Bohemia (Czech Republic)—Ethnic relations—History—20th century. I. Čapková, Kateřina.
DS135.C95 C3713 2012
305.892/404371

2011051708

British Library Cataloguing in Publication Data

A catalogue record for this book is available from the British Library

Printed on acid-free paper.

ISBN: 978-0-85745-474-4 hardback
ISBN: 978-1-78238-679-7 paperback
ISBN: 978-0-85745-475-1 ebook

To my parents

Contents

List of Illustrations	viii
Acknowledgments	xi
A Note on Personal and Place Names	xiv
Abbreviations	xv
Map of Czechoslovakia and the Bohemian Lands	xvi
Introduction	1
Chapter 1. The Basic Features of the Jewish Community in Prague and in Bohemia	14
Chapter 2. Jews as a National Minority in the New Republic	26
Chapter 3. German Jews	56
Chapter 4. Czech-Jews	92
Chapter 5. Zionists	169
Conclusion	241
Bibliography	254
Index	271

Illustrations

Maps

Map of Czechoslovakia and the Bohemian Lands   xvi

Figures

1.1. Hana Blasková, a Shoah survivor, seen here in a photograph from 1925, dressed as an angel. Courtesy of Židovské muzeum, Prague.   21

2.1. August Stein and Josef Popper meeting with President Masaryk on his 80th birthday, 1930. Courtesy of Židovské muzeum, Prague.   35

2.2. Max Brod. Courtesy of Archiv hlavního města Prahy, Prague.   39

2.3. Bohumil Bondy. Courtesy of Památník národního písemnictví, Prague.   51

3.1. The editors of the *Prager Presse*. Courtesy of Památník národního písemnictví, Prague.   72

3.2. Presidents of the Grand Lodge of B'nai B'rith in central Europe, at the Carlsbad conference, 23 August 1924. Courtesy of Židovské muzeum, Prague.   75

3.3. A short statement by Sigmund Freud on the importance of the B'nai B'rith Order. Courtesy of Židovské muzeum, Prague.   80

3.4. The programme of an evening organised by the B'nai B'rith lodges Bohemia and Praga on 28 April 1920. Courtesy of Židovské muzeum, Prague.   81

4.1. An invitation from the Czech-Jewish Students' Society. Courtesy of Archiv University Karlovy, Prague. 95

4.2. Jakub Scharf. Courtesy of Židovské muzeum, Prague. 101

4.3. August Stein. Courtesy of Židovské muzeum, Prague. 147

4.4. and 4.5. Rare photographs from the congress of the Association of Czech-Jews, 29 January 1938. Courtesy of Archiv ČTK, Prague. 161

5.1. Inscription of the Bar Kochba Society, commemorating members who died in World War I. Courtesy of Archiv hlavního města Prahy, Prague. 186

5.2. Max Brod visiting Moscow as a journalist, 1935. Courtesy of Archiv ČTK, Prague. 205

5.3. Swimmers from Hagibor. Courtesy of Židovské muzeum, Prague. 226

5.4. Footballers from Hagibor before a match against Slavia, 1937. Courtesy of Židovské muzeum, Prague. 229

5.5. A girls' athletics team from Hagibor at a meet in Kolín, 1932. Courtesy of Židovské muzeum, Prague. 231

5.6. The departure for Palestine of Jewish refugees from the Reich. Photographed at Wilson Station, Prague, 1934. Courtesy of Archiv ČTK, Prague. 236

C.1. Eva Pokorná, a Shoah survivor, shown here in her Sokol uniform. Courtesy of Židovské muzeum, Prague. 249

Graphs

1.1. Changes in Jewish population (according to religion) in Bohemia, Moravia, Silesia and Prague, from 1890 to 1930. 23

2.1. The languages of everyday communication (according to the 1910 census) and nationalities (according to the 1921 and 1930 censuses) of people of the Jewish religion in Bohemia. 54

2.2. The national composition of people of the Jewish faith in Bohemia, Moravia and Silesia, Slovakia and Subcarpathian Ruthenia, according to the 1930 census. 55

3.1. Jewish communities in Bohemia with more than a thousand people of the Jewish faith according to the 1930 census. 62

Table

3.1. Jewish children and youth (according to religion) and their attendance in Czech-speaking and German-speaking educational institutions. 60

Acknowledgements

I sincerely thank everyone who has assisted me in the researching and writing of *Czechs, Germans, Jews?*. The book is based on my doctoral work at Charles University, Prague, and I thank my supervisor, Robert Kvaček, whose thorough knowledge of Czechoslovak history proved invaluable to me. I owe a debt of gratitude to David Rechter, Oxford University, who was my supervisor during a year's stay in England. He opened up modern Jewish history for me, a field which was still taboo at Charles University in the 1990s. I am extremely grateful to him for the many discussions we had about my topic, Jewish history in general, and also methodology. They were crucial to my work, including aspects going far beyond this project. I thank him also for his support and encouragement through all the years, for his thorough reading of several drafts of the English manuscript and for his many useful comments and suggestions. My great thanks also go to Otto Dov Kulka at the Hebrew University of Jerusalem, with whom I was able to discuss on the structure and content of my work during my study stay in Israel.

Michal Frankl, my friend and fellow-historian in Prague, also deserves my sincere thanks. Drawing on his profound knowledge of antisemitism in the Bohemian Lands, he provided me with numerous useful ideas. Since several years have passed since I finished the Czech version of this book, I would like to add thanks to Michal for his excellent collaboration while we were working together on a book about Czechoslovak refugee politics in the 1930s.

Since I continued to develop my thesis after having successfully defended it, I owe a debt of gratitude also to the specialists who were willing to read it and provide their comments and opinions. I greatly appreciate the suggestions and input of Hillel Kieval, whose book *The Making of Czech Jewry* is rightly regarded as a pioneering work in the historiography of the Jews of the Bohemian Lands and provided the basis for my own research on the roots of the different national movements among the Bohemian Jews before 1914. I also appreciate the encouragement he has given me over the years. I am similarly indebted to Wilma Iggers, the author of important works on the flexibility of the national identity of the Jews of Bohemia, for her detailed reading of the English manuscript and for providing me with numerous useful suggestions. For his remarks on my chapter about the German Jews, I thank Kurt Krolop, who has written widely on German-Jewish literature. Moreover, he lent me rare publications from the period I was researching. To Jerzy Tomaszewski of the Jewish Historical Institute, Warsaw, I am very grateful for the identifying of some imprecise points, which he mentioned in his review of the Czech version of my book in the *Kwartalnik Historii Żydów*, and for his subsequent advice. In particular, his detailed knowledge of the legal standing of the Jewish minorities of various European countries in the interwar period was of great benefit to me. I would also like to thank my friends Monika Báar, the author of an excellent book on historians and nationalism in East-Central Europe, and Malcolm Haslett, a BBC Russia and Eastern Europe analyst, for reading the manuscript and providing me with a number of helpful suggestions. With gratitude I also accepted the comments of Arno Pařík, the leading art historian at the Jewish Museum in Prague.

I am also most grateful for the assessment of my work provided by the late Jan Havránek, who sat on the dissertation committee. Professor Havránek, who died suddenly in August 2004, was among the most knowledgeable people on the history of the Jews of the Bohemian Lands. It is a great pity that he did not manage to pass his knowledge on to future generations in the form of a large monograph. I also owe special thanks to Petr Brod, a freelance journalist, formerly the head of the Czech section of the BBC in Prague. Despite his very busy schedule, he helped me greatly with the final version of my manuscript. In a number of places he compelled me to express myself more clearly and, thanks to his encyclopaedic knowledge of the history of European Jews, he drew my attention to many places where it was useful to say more. I should also like to express my gratitude to the late Viktor Fischl (Avigdor Dagan), whose conversations with me were of key importance to my work and whose remarks on the manuscript were highly valuable. Along the way many individuals have shared with me their own experience with the interwar life in Czechoslovakia as well as during the Shoah. I would like to single out Anna Hyndráková, Toman Brod and Eva Dušková, whom I have the honour to call my friends.

The assistance of archivists was of course also extremely important to me in my research. I wish to mention at least those who helped me above and beyond the call of duty: Marek Lašťovka and Tomáš Rataj at the Prague City Archives; Vlasta Měšťánková of the National Archives, Prague, and Jaroslava Milotová, the head of the Institute of the Terezín Initiative; and Kateřina Bobková and Jana Ratajová at the Archive of Charles University, Yvetta Dörflová at the Literary Archive of the Museum of Czech Literature, Pavlína Kořínková of the Shoah History Department at the Jewish Museum, Prague, and Rochelle Rubinstein of the Central Zionist Archives, Jerusalem. I also thank Alena Jelínková and her colleagues at the library of the Jewish Museum, Prague, for their selfless assistance in finding booklets and periodicals from this period.

For funding my research I owe a debt of gratitude to the Memorial Foundation for Jewish Culture, New York, which helped me to cover costs connected with my stay in Israel and my research in the archives there. I am greatly indebted also to the Rothschild Foundation (Europe) for funding the translation of the book into English. And I thank Derek and Marzia Paton for their painstaking, well-informed approach to the translation of the book and for their excellent suggestions for ways to make the subject matter more comprehensible to readers who may want additional historical background. I am grateful to Petr Čížek of the Paseka publishing house, who prepared the pictures for publishing and who granted me those for the English version.

Finally, my special thanks go to my family. This book is dedicated to my parents who brought us up in a loving and open-minded household and who were always supportive and very interested in our activities. I owe particular thanks to my husband Jakub without whom not only this book, but everything else I have accomplished would have been impossible. It is also hard to believe that I started this project before our children were born. In the meantime, we were blessed with David, Zuzana, Adam and Hana, and we are very thankful for them.

Berlin, February 2011

A Note on Personal and Place Names

In works about Central Europe, local place names can present problems since they can exist in several forms (in Bohemia, for example, German and Czech). Except for the names of towns with an established English version (like Prague, Pilsen and Vienna) I have used the names for places that can be found on recent maps. After the primary name, I have added the other names in brackets. The other names of places discussed in the book are also listed in the index.

For names of people and organisations in Hebrew, I have chosen the transcription used in *The YIVO Encyclopedia of Jews in Eastern Europe* (2008).

Abbreviations

AHMP   Archiv hlavního města Prahy
AKPR   Archiv Kanceláře prezidenta republiky
AUK   Archiv Univerzity Karlovy
AÚTGM   Archiv Ústavu Tomáše G. Masaryka
AŽMP   Archiv Židovského muzea v Praze
CAHJP   Central Archives for the History of the Jewish People
ČTK   Česká Tisková Kancelář
CZA   Central Zionist Archives
JNUL   Jewish National & University Library
NA   Národní archiv (Prague)
PNP   Památník národního písemnictví
ŽMP   Židovské muzeum v Praze

Map of Czechoslovakia and the Bohemian Lands

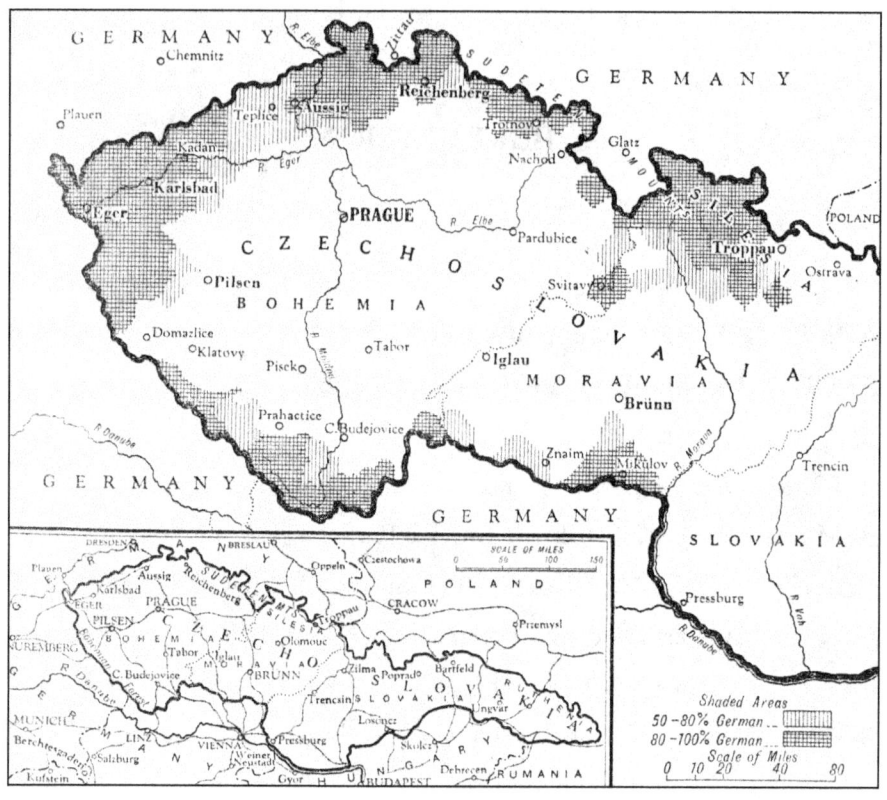

Source: *The Observer*, 4 September 1938.

INTRODUCTION

> There are many kinds of Jewishness and everyone has the right not only to define one's Jewishness as one feels is correct, but also to be accepted as a Jew by others just as one is a Jew according to one's own definition and not according to the clichés of others.
> — Marcel R. Marcus[1]

In the modern history of the Jews of central Europe the question of identity holds a key position. The debate about the character of Jewishness runs throughout the nineteenth and twentieth centuries like a red thread. Are Jews an ethnicity, a nation, a *Schicksalsgemeinschaft* (community formed by fate) or a 'mere' confession? Various answers to this question have divided Jews, and continue to divide them, into several often antagonistic groups.

One finds this variety of assessment of the character of Judaism in the scholarly literature as well. Historians disagree over whether Jewish religious tradition also contains nationalist elements.[2] Interpretations vary from the assumption that Jews were the first nation and are therefore an exception among other communities which did not become nations until the modern period. Hans Kohn, for example, claims that three funda-

---

[1] Marcel R. Marcus, '"Der Jude" - gibt es ihn eigentlich? Über die Arten, Jude zu sein', in *'Judenklischees' und jüdische Wirklichkeit in unserer Gesellschaft*, ed. Jörg Albertz (Berlin, 1989), 43.
[2] For a discussion of the different positions, see Aviel Roshwald, 'Jewish Identity and the Paradox of Nationalism', in *Nationalism, Zionism and Ethnic Mobilization of the Jews in 1900 and Beyond*, ed. Michael Berkowitz (Leiden, 2004), 11-24.

mental features of modern nationalism first emerged among the Hebrews: the idea of a chosen people, the emphasis on a common memory of the past and hope in the future, and national messianism.[3] At the other end of the scale is the idea that even the concept of a Jewish identity is an illusion, because there is no authentic or essential 'Jewish self'; instead, according to this view, there is an 'undesignatable field of difference' which cannot be 'summarized by a descriptive identity category such as religion, ethnicity, or nationality'.[4] In this range of approaches, David Biale's path-breaking work, *Cultures of Jews*, offers an innovative, balanced alternative. In his introduction, Biale asserts that, on the one hand, 'Jewish identity changed according to differing historical contexts', which is why one should speak about Jewish cultures in the plural. On the other hand, he emphasizes that a key aspect of Jewish culture is the 'continuity of both textual and folk traditions throughout Jewish history and throughout the many lands inhabited by the Jews. The multiplicity of Jewish cultures always rested on the Bible and – with the exception of the Karaites and the Ethiopian Jews – on the Talmud and other rabbinic literature.'[5]

The central European (and therefore Bohemian) Jews' identification with Judaism remained unquestionable until the emancipation period. Because of their distinct legal position in an otherwise Christian society, Jews were united not only by common religion, but also by their particular education and laws, based on the Talmud. And yet the modernization process, which had led the central European communities to establish national narratives, operated precisely the other way round amongst the Jews. Emancipation, which placed Jews on the same level as the rest of the population, led to their cultural, political and economic integration into the surrounding population. Actually, the emancipation was preconditioned by their acceptance of the national narrative of the dominant population.[6] When, however, Jewish autonomist and Zionist movements began gaining strength in the late nineteenth century, they could easily develop a Jewish national narrative based on the distinct Jewish experience before emancipation.

---

[3] Hans Kohn, *Nationalism: Its Meaning and History* (Princeton, NJ, 1955), 11.
[4] Laurence J. Silberstein, 'Mapping, Not Tracing: Opening Reflections', in *Mapping Jewish Identities*, ed. Laurence J. Silberstein (New York and London, 2000), 1–36. The quotation comes from p. 13, where Silberstein bases his theory on definitions by Judith Butler, a feminist philosopher.
[5] David Biale, 'Preface: Toward a Cultural History of the Jews', in *Cultures of the Jews: A New History*, ed. David Biale (New York, 2002), xxiii–xxiv.
[6] Detlev Claussen, *Grenzen der Aufklärung. Die gesellschaftliche Genese des modernen Antisemitismus.* 2nd ed. (Frankfurt am Main, 1994), 52.

Nationalist interpretations of history generally used to emphasize, and often still do, the claim that ethnos and nation were equivalent. They consider the nation a historical constant tied to a common language, culture and customs – in other words, to the ethnicity of a certain community. The concept of a modern nation did not, however, universally relate to any precisely determined group of people with shared cultural and historical features. It came into being as a political construct, based mainly on a linguistic, cultural definition of a certain community.[7]

This idea is demonstrated well using the example of Bohemia, where the first Czech patriots in the early decades of the nineteenth century could agree amongst themselves only on one thing – namely, that Czechs are not Germans. This fundamental Czech-German antagonism left open a number of questions. Are Czechs, these patriots asked, part of a pan-Slav nation? Are Czechs and Slovaks one nation? Is it reasonable to include Moravians, with their slightly different traditions, in the Czech nation? Moreover, local communities such as the Chods (chiefly inhabiting the Bohemian areas of Domažlice, Tachov and Přimda), the Moravian Wallachians, and the people of the Haná region of central Moravia had preserved their own special identities with their own customs and traditions.[8] The strength of local identity, which in the course of the nineteenth century had to give way to the political pressure of nationalist conflict, has been persuasively demonstrated, for example, by Jeremy King in his work on the inhabitants of České Budějovice (Budweis), south Bohemia.[9]

Historians of nationalism mostly agree on the leading role of social élites in the process of the construction and implementation of a national programme.[10] This was no different among the Bohemian Jews. The three

---

[7] See, for example, Benedict Anderson, *Imagined Communities: Reflections on the Origin and Spread of Nationalism*, 2nd ed. (London, 1991); Eric J. Hobsbawm, *Nations and Nationalism since 1780: Programme, Myth, Reality*, 2nd ed. (Cambridge, 1990); Anne-Marie Thiesse, *La création des identités nationales* (Paris, 1999).

[8] See Otto Urban, 'Zur Fragen der Formierung der neuzeitlichen nationalen Gesellschaft: Die Modellsituation der tschechischen Gesellschaft', in *Formen des nationalen Bewußtseins im Lichte zeitgenössischer Nationalismustheorien*, ed. Eva Schmidt-Hartmann (Munich, 1994), 255-62. See also Gary B. Cohen, 'From Bohemians to Czechs and Germans', in *The Politics of Ethnic Survival: Germans in Prague, 1861–1914*, 2nd ed. (West Lafayette, IN, 2006), 16-40.

[9] Jeremy King, *Budweisers into Czechs and Germans: A Local History of Bohemian Politics, 1848–1948* (Princeton, NJ, and Oxford, 2002).

[10] Ernest Gellner, *Nations and Nationalism*, 2nd ed. (Oxford, 2007); Hobsbawm, *Nations and Nationalism since 1780*; Miroslav Hroch, *Social Preconditions of National Revival in Europe* (Cambridge, 1985); Ronald Grigor Suny and Michael D. Kennedy, eds., *Intellectuals and the Articulation of the Nation* (Ann Arbor, MI, 1999).

leading narratives about the Jews of Bohemia being Germans, Jews or Czechs were developed and spread by Jewish intellectuals (lawyers, writers, doctors, journalists, university students and professors). The core of my book is an analysis of these narratives. I therefore confine my discussion to the organized national movements of the Jews in Bohemia – the Czech-Jewish and the Zionist movements as well as the German-speaking Jews, though this last group did not form an equivalent movement in the interwar period.

Only a small fraction of the Jewish population of Bohemia was involved in Czech-Jewish and Zionist organizations. But the conflict between Zionists and Czech-Jews largely influenced the lives of all Jews in the country. For example, Zionists and Czech-Jews owned the most widely read Jewish periodicals – *Židovské zprávy* (Jewish News), *Selbstwehr* (Self-defence) and *Rozvoj* (Development). The discord between the Zionists and the Czech-Jews also importantly affected the way the Jews were thought of by the majority society and politicians.

In contrast to some radical constructivists, I am confident that the élite did not pull the national narrative, discourse, or myth (to use the most widespread terms for national ideology) out of thin air. We need not claim that nations evolved from ethnic groups, a thesis which would be close to primordialism, where ethnicity is defined as a specific set of characteristic features that a person inherits.[11] And though it is generally accepted that not all ethnic groups developed into nations, the concept of ethnicity usually does not allow any plurality or change. But it is obvious that the élite had to have some 'building blocks' to begin to construct their national (and ethnic) myth.[12] In this respect I would adopt Anthony Smith's term 'usable past'.[13] There must have been something in the history of that group of people, which they were willing to accept as a common experience. The intellectuals surely chose the key milestones carefully when constructing their national past. Moreover, documents that should have demonstrated the ancient history of the nation (the 'foundational

---

[11] Jeremy King, 'The Nationalization of East Central Europe: Ethnicism, Ethnicity, and Beyond', in *Staging the Past: The Politics of Commemoration in Habsburg Central Europe, 1848 to the Present*, ed. Maria Bucur and Nancy M. Wingfield (West Lafayette, IN, 2001), 112–52; see also Albert Reiterer, *Die unvermeidbare Nation: Ethnizität, Nation und nachnationale Gesellschaft* (Vienna, 1988). For a different conception of ethnicity, which is rehabilitating the term in a very enriching way, see Richard Jenkins, *Rethinking Ethnicity: Arguments and Exploration*, 2nd ed. (London, 2008).

[12] The term 'building blocs' in this context was introduced by Karl F. Bahm, 'Beyond the Bourgeoisie: Rethinking Nation, Culture, and Modernity in Nineteenth-Century Central Europe', *Austrian History Yearbook* 29 (1998): 19–35.

[13] Anthony Smith, 'The "Golden Age" and National Renewal', in *Myths and Nationhood*, ed. Geoffrey Hosking and George Schöpflin (London, 1997), 59.

myth'[14]) were often forged. Still, in order to persuade people to believe the national narrative, they had, in the words of Hobsbawm, to 'mobilize certain variants of feelings of collective belonging which already existed'.[15] Smith argues that at least the 'golden age' of a nation ('the zenith in the master narrative'[16] of every nation) has to be to some point 'historically verifiable'.[17]

On the other hand, there were, and surely still are, more communities that could claim to have some 'usable pasts' than there are national movements (with or without a state). A key argument in my book is that communities with the potential to become a nation can overlap. This is clear where people with different languages or religions live on the same territory. On this point I differ with Smith, who mentions the possibility that several communal pasts can be invoked on one territory, for example, Palestinians and Israelis.[18] But he considers these pasts as parallel, since he believes in the ethnic basis of a national community.

Here is the central argument of my book and I shall return to it in the conclusion. Though Zionism and the Czech-Jewish movement were competing conceptions of nationalism among Bohemian Jews in the interwar period (there was no equivalent of the organized German-Jewish movement at that time), we can still legitimately point to many similarities in their argumentation. Their narrative is constructed with the same 'building blocks'; they point to the same past experiences. Neither the Zionists nor the Czech-Jews deny sharing the experiences of other Bohemian Jews or other Czechs. What is decisive is the interpretation and emphasis.

This thesis has two consequences. First, we have to ask what made Jews, who were part of the Zionist or Czech-Jewish organizations, choose one narrative over another. I would argue that social ties with Jews as well as non-Jews were more important than any linguistic or political matters.[19] Second, the parallel narratives enabled the Jews to switch from one na-

---

[14] Hall uses the terms 'foundational myth' and 'myth of origin' and emphasizes the importance of such a myth in the invention of a nation. Stuart Hall, 'The Question of Cultural Identity', in *Modernity: An Introduction to Modern Societies*, ed. Stuart Hall et al. (Cambridge and Oxford, 1996), 614 ; see also Anne-Marie Thiesse, *La Création des identités nationales* (Paris, 1999).
[15] Hobsbawm, *Nations and Nationalism since 1780*, 46. Hobsbawm calls these bonds 'protonational'.
[16] Monika Báar, *Historians and Nationalism: East-Central Europe in the Nineteenth Century* (Oxford, 2010), 224. Báar analyzes and compares the 'Golden Ages' of five east-central European nations, including the Czechs (see 224–55).
[17] Smith, 'The "Golden Age" and National Renewal', 59.
[18] Ibid., 38.
[19] The crucial role of social ties for national identification is stated also by Cohen, *The Politics of Ethnic Survival*, passim, most explicitly 11–12.

tional identity to another without making any changes in their daily lives. Alternatively, they could remain undecided or claim to have several identities, since there were overlaps in the Czech, German and Zionist social networks.

The complex network of Prague inhabitants of different national and linguistic identities has recently been thoroughly analysed by Ines Koeltzsch in her excellent dissertation, 'Geteilte Kulturen'.[20] The high degree of indifference to nationality among Bohemians and Moravians is persuasively demonstrated in Tara Zahra's *Kidnapped Souls*. Zahra provides many unique examples of ordinary people who were unhappy enough with the pressure from above to opt for one national identity only.[21] Chad Bryant has convincingly demonstrated that during World War II even the Nazis had problems defining who was Czech and who was German. Czech nationalists faced the same problem after the war.[22]

I have chosen to use the term 'national identity' in the title of my work. Like Richard Jenkins, I understand identity not as a 'fixed, immutable or primordial' concept, but as one that is 'utterly socio-cultural in its origins' and is 'negotiable and flexible'.[23] In contrast to some critics of the very concept of identity and identification,[24] I also share Jenkins's view on the importance of this term.

> Public concern about identity may wax and wane, but the perpetual bottom line is that we can't live routine lives as humans without identification,

---

[20] Ines Koeltzsch, 'Geteilte Kulturen: Eine Geschichte der tschechisch-jüdisch-deutschen Beziehungen in Prag (1918–1938)', PhD thesis, Freie Universität Berlin, 2010. For the pre-war period, see Dimitry Shumsky, 'Introducing Intellectual and Political History to the History of Everyday Life: Multiethnic Cohabitation and Jewish Experience in Fin-de-Siècle Bohemia', *Bohemia* 46, no. 1 (2005): 39–67.
[21] Tara Zahra, *Kidnapped Souls: National Indifference and the Battle for Children in the Bohemian Lands, 1900–1948* (Ithaca, NY, and London, 2008). See also Peter Judson, *Guardians of the Nations: Activists on the Language Frontiers of Imperial Austria* (Cambridge, MA, and London, 2006). Judson compares the multilingual daily life experience of rural border regions of south Bohemia and in Styria with the image of these regions portrayed in the nationalist propaganda. Even though most of the inhabitants of these border regions were nationally indifferent, the concept of 'language frontiers' played a crucial role in the nationalist political propaganda and border regions were presented as the current battlegrounds of the neighbouring national communities.
[22] Chad Bryant, *Prague in Black: Nazi Rule and Czech Nationalism* (Cambridge, MA, 2007); Bryant, 'Czech, or German? Nazi Occupation, Postwar Expulsions, and the Origins of the Central European Nation-State'. *European Studies Forum* 31, no. 1 (Spring 2008): 37–42.
[23] Richard Jenkins, *Social Identity*, 3rd ed. (Abingdon, NY, 2008) 19.
[24] See the frequently quoted Rogers Brubaker and Frederick Cooper, 'Beyond "Identity"', *Theory and Society* 29 (2000): 1–47.

without knowing – and sometimes puzzling about – who we are and who others are. This is true no matter where we are, or what our way of life or language. Without repertoires of identification we would not be able to relate to each other meaningfully or consistently. We would lack that vital sense of who's who and what's what. Without identity there could simply be no human world, as we know it.[25]

The term 'identity' is fitting for the title of my book for two reasons. First, when talking about the national identity of an individual, I am considering which national community the individual identified with more or I am trying to envision the plurality of his or her national identification. I am, then, inquiring into the individual's own, subjective opinions. It would, I believe, be misleading in many cases to define the nationality of an individual according to some universal criteria, for example, his or her language, as was done in the census.

The dreadful consequences of the allegedly objective determination of nationality according to language were experienced by the German-speaking Jews after World War II in Czechoslovakia. Despite having just returned from concentration camps or safe countries to which they had managed to emigrate in time, they were automatically declared Germans by the Czechoslovak authorities. In unclear cases, the person's choice of nationality in the last census in 1930 was checked. If he or she had not yet been born in 1930, the choice that his or her parents had made was applied. The Jews who had been considered Germans by nationality could now regain their Czechoslovak citizenship only with great difficulty. Many of them were denied the right to the restitution of property taken from them by the Nazis and some of them were even deported together with the Germans who were expelled from the Bohemian Lands, often violently, after the war.[26]

The second advantage of the term 'identity' is that it admits of plurality and flexibility. Even though I have focused on Jews who were active in organizations that explicitly favoured one or the other national narratives, I did come across many individuals who either had no problem in joining associations of different national orientations or who changed their

---

[25] Jenkins, *Social Identity*, 27.
[26] For the situation after World War II, see esp. Peter Meyer, 'Czechoslovakia,' in *The Jews in the Soviet Satellites*, ed. Peter Meyer et al. (Westport, CT, 1971), 49-206; and Petr Brod, 'Die Juden in der Nachkriegstschechoslowakei', in *Judenemanzipation – Antisemitismus – Verfolgung in Deutschland, Österreich-Ungarn, den Böhmischen Ländern und in der Slowakei*, ed. Jörg K. Hoensch et al. (Essen, 1999), 211-28; for a case study, see Monika Hanková, 'Klara Fischer-Pollak (1899-1970): (Po)válečné osudy židovské lékařky z Karlových Varů', in *Židé v Čechách 2: Sborník příspěvků ze semináře konaného v září 2008 v Nýrsku*, ed. Vlastimila Hamáčková, Monika Hanková and Markéta Lhotová (Prague, 2009), 50-70.

preference of national identity.[27] One example is the well-known thinker Alfréd Fuchs (1892–1941), who at first sympathized with Zionism, but later became an active member of the Czech-Jewish movement. In 1922 he converted to Roman Catholicism and became an expert on Christian mysticism. Fuchs was tortured to death in Dachau concentration camp.[28] Another example is Karel Fleischmann (1897–1944), an artist and physician, who worked closely with Czech artists and was a member of Budivoj, a society of university students in south Bohemia, which favoured the Czech national programme and stood 'against the expansion of German culture'.[29] Fleischmann was also member both of the Theodor Herzl Society in Prague, which was the leading student organization of young Zionists, and of the Makkabi, a Zionist sports organization.[30] In the Theresienstadt ghetto, Fleischmann depicted daily life in his paintings and worked as physician. He was killed in Auschwitz.[31]

Geographically, I am considering the Jews of Bohemia. I often discuss Moravia as well, because of the many similarities and contacts, but my book has Bohemian Jews as its primary focus because I am also aware of the many differences between Bohemia and Moravia and Austrian Silesia, the other historic parts of the Bohemian Lands.

In terms of period, my book is concerned with the national identities of the Jews in the interwar years. I have of course had to look back to the nineteenth century in order to explain the roots of many of the interwar phenomena. But even though I did extensive archival research on the period before World War I in order to understand the changes after 1918, I was fortunate to be able to rely on the research of Hillel Kieval, whose book about Bohemian Jews before World War I is now a classic. I understand my book as a continuation of the research done by Kieval in *The Making of Czech Jewry*.[32]

One term appears particularly often in the historical documents and needs to be commented on here: 'assimilation'. As Shulamit Volkov argues,

---

[27] See also Wilma Iggers, 'The Flexible National Identities of Bohemian Jewry', *East Central Europe* 7, pt 1 (1980): 9–48.
[28] Hillel J. Kieval, *Languages of Community: The Jewish Experience in the Czech Lands* (Berkeley, 2000), 217–29; Ctibor Mařan, *Kniha o Alfredu Fuchsovi* (Prague, 1946).
[29] Hana Housková, *Česlicí času: Život a dílo Karla Fleischmanna* (Prague, 1998), 31.
[30] CZA, Bar Kochba / Barissia Collection, A 137/5, 'Mein Lied wird gehört werden'.
[31] See also Markéta Petrášová and Jarmila Skochová, *Karel Fleischmann: Life and Work* (Prague, 1987), exhibition catalogue.
[32] Hillel Kieval, *The Making of Czech Jewry: National Conflict and Jewish Society in Bohemia, 1870–1918* (New York and Oxford, 1988).

the term underwent dynamic development in the nineteenth and early twentieth centuries. It was first used in a positive sense by Jews as well as by Christians to describe the social and cultural integration process of Jews into the majority society, which accompanied and actually preconditioned their emancipation. It was only in reaction to Zionism in the late nineteenth century that the term acquired negative connotations: 'Assimilation conjured up a picture of people who were ready and willing to eradicate their own self, foolishly and blindly thereafter facing a hostile world.'[33]

There are other reasons for discomfort with the concept of 'assimilation'. For German Jews, who were often seen as the most successfully 'assimilated', David Sorkin convincingly argued back in the 1980s, first of all, that German Jews did not lose their Jewish identity but produced a 'subculture' together with their own public sphere, by means of periodicals and associations, and, second, that Jews were not passive consumers of the dominant culture in this process but actively shaped their own cultural outlook and social relations.[34] The concept of 'subculture',[35] though an important step towards a better understanding of the social process that accompanied the emancipation of Jews, can also be misleading. It presupposes a hierarchy of cultures and underestimates Jewish influence on Gentile culture. The flourishing of the world of art and ideas in *fin de siècle* Vienna and Prague, for example, was a cultural phenomenon that is unimaginable without the Jews but it is understood as a European phenomenon of far-reaching cultural impact in general.[36]

In my book, I discuss the different concepts of 'assimilation' which were held by the Czech-Jewish movement and were seen as the culmination of the Czech-Jewish narrative. For a long time I sought in vain for another term to describe those Jews who called themselves 'assimilationists'. In the English-language literature the term 'integrationists', coined by Ezra Mendelsohn, has caught on.[37] But in Bohemia, not only 'assimilationists', but also Zionists and German Jews were integrated into the Bohemian society, so the term 'integrationists' also would be misleading. Moreover, the term 'integrationists', I would argue, actually accepts the Zionist narrative that

---

[33] Shulamit Volkov, *Germans, Jews, and Antisemites: Trials in Emancipation* (Cambridge, 2006), 202.
[34] David Sorkin, *The Transformation of German Jewry, 1780–1840* (Oxford, 1987).
[35] Another defender of this concept is Trude Maurer, *Die Entwicklung der jüdischen Minderheit in Deutschland (1790–1933): Neuere Forschungen und offene Fragen* (Tübingen, 1992).
[36] See Klaus Hödl, 'Zum Wandel des Selbstverständnisses zentraleuropäischer Juden durch Kulturtransfer', in *Kulturtransfer in der jüdischen Geschichte*, ed. Wolfgang Schmale and Martina Steer (Frankfurt and New York, 2006), 60.
[37] Ezra Mendelsohn, *On Modern Jewish Politics* (New York, 1993), 16.

sees Jews as being apart from the societies in the Diaspora. The history of the Bohemian Zionists shows, however, that despite their propaganda, they were an integral part of the social networks in Bohemia. Most of the Zionists who managed to leave Bohemia before the outbreak of World War II did so only after the Munich Agreement (September 1938), like the other Jews of the Bohemian Lands.

Aware of the difficulties of using the term 'assimilationist', I have chosen to write it here in inverted commas. When I discuss Jews who consciously sought to integrate culturally into the Czech nation and became involved in Czech-Jewish organizations, I am discussing them as Czech-Jews (*Čechožidé*). Czech Jews without the hyphen, then, are all Jews who preferred to use the Czech language, even though they had declared, for example, Jewish nationality in the census; among them were also people who did not actively participate in the organized Czech-Jewish movement.

A proper analysis of the different national narratives of the Bohemian Jews has to start with contextualization. Chapter 1 offers the basic historical background to the social, cultural and religious development of the Bohemian Jews. To understand the specific features of the Jewish community in Bohemia, I discuss the circumstances in neighbouring regions, especially Moravia and Germany, for comparison. Another aim of the chapter is to suggest the reasons that led to the Jews' high rate of integration into the Czech or German milieu (or both) in Bohemia.

Chapter 2 focuses on the factors that contributed to the codifying of Jewish nationality and appear in an explanatory statement to the Czechoslovak Constitution. They need to be discussed in order to illustrate the legislative setting of the Jews of Czechoslovakia. The Jews of Bohemia, particularly those who were active in one of the national movements, actively sought to understand the nationality policies of the Czechoslovak government and the role that the government wanted the Jews to play in this complex matter. Moreover, as research on the public discussion about the codifying of Jewish nationality reveals, different Jewish associations and individuals played an active role in this discussion, and willingly or less willingly formed coalitions with different parts of the Czechoslovak public which supported or opposed the proposal, often for very different reasons. In this chapter, I also analyse the census results and the limits of what they can usefully tell us.

Chapter 3 focuses on the German-speaking Jews of Bohemia. Though there was no organized German-Jewish movement in the Bohemian Lands in the interwar period, I discuss German-speaking Jews here for the simple reason that the forebears of those Jews who in interwar Czechoslovakia declared themselves Czech-Jews or Zionists had still mostly identified with German culture and language in the first half of the nineteenth century. Kieval consequently calls the Bohemian Jews' integration into Czech culture 'secondary acculturation' (primary acculturation being integration into German culture).[38] This chapter therefore considers the reasons for this primary identification and also the special features of the German-speaking Jewish community of Bohemia in the late nineteenth and early twentieth centuries and in the First Republic. I would stress, however, that the claims in the chapter about German Jews do not relate only to Jews who would have identified with the German nation. Since there was no organized German national movement among the Jews of Bohemia, in this chapter I discuss Jews from the German milieu, that is, all the Jews of Bohemia who preferred to use German. I also consider the factors that help to explain why there was no organized 'German-Jewish movement' in the interwar period.

Chapter 4 analyses the roots and character of the Czech-Jewish movement in comparison with other such movements in Austria and Germany. It also considers the important and, in central Europe, unique projects of the Czech-Jews and the revival initiatives of the young Czech-Jewish students. It remains a paradox that even though most of the Jews of Bohemia decided to adopt the Czech national narrative and to integrate into Czech-speaking society in the interwar period, the Czech-Jewish movement experienced a decline in membership and in political prestige at that time.

Chapter 5 is devoted to the Jewish national movement, which, unlike the Czech-Jewish movement, managed to occupy leading positions in negotiations with the Czechoslovak politicians on questions related to the Jewish population. The chapter analyses the unique character of cultural Zionism developed by the Bar Kochba association and the ideological changes after the war. Even though the spiritual questions of Zionism were subdued during the interwar period because of the unique opportunities for political agitation, some common features remained (at least for most Bohemian Zionists) – particularly the moderate political programme and the criticism of radical and revisionist Zionism.

In the conclusion I return to the theoretical framework drawn out in the introduction, using the results of my research.

To be truly comprehensive my work should have considered Jews in the Communist movement, because their cosmopolitan views did not correspond with the views discussed in the three basic chapters about Czech,

---

[38] See Kieval, *The Making of Czech Jewry*, 4, 8, 198–203.

German and Zionist Jews. An analysis of the concept of nation among Communists of Jewish origin would certainly have enriched my work. It would indeed be interesting to have discovered the extent to which the Communists observed the conflicts over national identity within the Jewish community and whether they expressed an opinion on these questions. The Communist movement between the two world wars, moreover, was influenced by a great many eminent Jewish figures, whose own importance grossly distorts the importance of Jews in the Communist movement. Their participation in Communist activity was minimal. I have not included Communists of Jewish origin in my analysis. From the accessible records related to members of the Communist Party it appears that the Communists considered Jewish origin irrelevant; the membership forms of Communist organizations contain no categories like 'confession' or 'nationality'. To focus on 'Jewish-sounding names', as was recommended to me by a renowned Czech historian, seems to me a thoroughly unscholarly approach. Also, the compiling of family trees of individuals in order to determine who had a Jewish background has negative connotations, and is therefore unacceptable. That does not change the fact that the Communist leanings of people of Jewish origin should be researched: one can analyze the political careers both of people who made no secret of their Jewish origin and of those who were called Jews during the Communist show trials of the 1950s. That topic, however, is beyond the scope of this book.

Some of the results of my research have previously been published in individual articles. I originally published the introductory essay on the Jewish national minority in Czechoslovakia in *Český časopis historický* (2004).[39] In the chapter about German Jews, I use some of the results of my research on B'nai B'rith, which were published in full in *Judaica Bohemiae* 36 (2000).[40] The chapter about the Zionist movement was published in an expanded form in *Judaica Bohemiae* 38 (2002).[41] In the conclusion, I use the thesis about the similarity between the arguments of advocates of Czech-Jewish assimilation and advocates of Zionism that I first used at the conference 'Germans – Jews – Czechs: The Case of the Czech Lands,'

---

[39] Kateřina Čapková, 'Uznání židovské národnosti v Československu 1918-1938', *Český časopis historický* 102, no. 1 (2004): 77-103.
[40] Čapková, 'Jewish Elites in the 19th and 20th Centuries: The B'nai B'rith Order in Central Europe', *Judaica Bohemiae* 36 (2000): 119-42.
[41] Čapková, 'Specific Features of Zionism in the Czech Lands in the Interwar Period', *Judaica Bohemiae* 38 (2002): 106-59.

held in Munich in December 2003.[42] The current publication includes parts of my essay that was published in the conference volume *Praha-Prag 1900-1945*, edited by Peter Becher and Anna Knechtel (2010).[43]

---

[42] Čapková, 'Czechs, Germans, Jews – Where Is the Difference? The Complexity of National Identities of Bohemian Jews, 1918-1938', *Bohemia* 46, no. 1 (2005): 7-14; in German: 'Tschechisch, Deutsch, Jüdisch – wo ist der Unterschied? Komplexität von nationalen Identitäten der böhmischen Juden 1918-1938', in *Juden zwischen Deutschen und Tschechen: Sprachliche, literarische und kulturelle Identitäten*, ed. Marek Nekula and Walter Koschmal (Munich, 2006), 73-84.
[43] Čapková, 'Raum und Zeit als Faktoren der nationalen Identifikation der Prager Juden', in *Praha-Prag 1900-1945*, ed. Peter Becher and Anna Knechtel (Passau, 2010), 21-30.

Chapter 1

THE BASIC FEATURES OF THE JEWISH COMMUNITY IN PRAGUE AND IN BOHEMIA

Until the middle of the nineteenth century, the Prague Jewish community was one of the numerously most important communities in central Europe. Before the First Partition of Poland in 1772, Prague had the largest Jewish community in Cisleithania, the Austrian part of the Habsburg Monarchy. There were more Jews in Prague than in Berlin even in the 1830s.[1] At the end of the nineteenth century, however, Prague was, in comparison with Berlin, Vienna, Budapest and Warsaw, only a provincial city and its Jewish community was insignificant in size. Even more striking are the figures from the interwar period, when the number of Jews in these metropolises grew into hundreds of thousands and Prague, with its 35,000 Jewish inhabitants, lagged behind.[2]

This paradox stems from two features particular to Jewish settlement in Prague and Bohemia in general. First, Prague, unlike most central and western European cities, had continuous Jewish settlement with only two short interruptions, one in the middle of the sixteenth century, the other in the middle of the eighteenth. The demographic growth of the Jewish

---

[1] There were 6,842 Jews in Prague in 1834 and 4,969 in Berlin in 1831. See František Friedmann, 'Pražští Židé', *Židovský kalendář* 10 (1929/1930): 150-151, 165.

[2] *Sčítání lidu v republice Československé ze dne 1. prosince 1930. Československá statistika*, vol. 98 (Prague, 1934), 82-83.

population had been limited by the legislation known as the *Familianten Gesetz* since the early eighteenth century.³ Despite all this, the situation in Prague was far better than in Berlin, Vienna and other European cities where the settlement of Jews was either forbidden or highly restricted for many years (in Vienna, for example, until the middle of the nineteenth century).

Second, the paradoxical development of the Jewish population of Prague in the nineteenth century was the result of Prague's not having been a destination for Jews fleeing from territories that had belonged to Poland before 1772. This phenomenon, which had far-reaching consequences for Jewish settlement in Bohemia, had several causes. One was that Prague was outside the migration routes both to Vienna and to the ports of Germany, Holland and Belgium. Another was that in the last third of the nineteenth century Prague City Hall was in Czech hands and so Yiddish-speaking Jews may well have feared the language barrier and also, very likely, the antisemitism of a Slav nation. Also, as William O. McCagg has noted, Jews from Russia and Galicia avoided Prague because, unlike Budapest, Vienna and Pressburg, Prague lacked an important Orthodox Jewish community with a sufficient infrastructure.⁴

Before World War I, the Jews of Bohemia therefore had only limited experience of eastern European Jewish immigration. In 1911, for example, a theatre company from L'viv (Lemberg or Lwów) in Galicia arrived in Prague. Whereas the company had met with success in Berlin and other German and Austrian towns, their performances in Prague were a failure. One important reason was probably that in the western capitals, unlike in Prague, their performances were attended mainly by eastern European Jewish immigrants, whose mother tongue was Yiddish. Another reason was that the theatre company and the Prague audiences each had completely different conceptions of Jewishness. The Galician actors' ardour for Judaism and their knowledge of Jewish traditions and religious texts, as well as their uncouth behaviour, shocked the Prague audiences. Even for Zionists from the Bar Kochba student association the performances were a disappointment. And yet it was these young Zionists who had latched on to Martin Buber's ideas about eastern Jewry bringing salvation to the western Jews and being a great source of inspiration to them. After watching a play by Abraham Goldfaden (1840–1908), the first important

---

³ For more on the *Familianten* Laws in the Bohemian Lands, see Michael Laurence Miller, *Rabbis and Revolution: The Jews of Moravia in the Age of Emancipation* (Stanford, CA, 2010), 35–40.

⁴ William O. McCagg, 'The Jewish Position in Interwar Central Europe: A Structural Study of Jewry in Vienna, Budapest and Prague', in *A Social and Economic History of Central European Jewry*, ed. Yehuda Don and Victor Karady (New Brunswick, NJ, 1990), 54.

Yiddish playwright, even these young Zionists could not help feeling that the actors were part of the uneducated rabble with whom they, as intellectuals, had nothing in common. For Franz Kafka (1883-1924), who almost never missed a performance, the encounter with Yiddish-speaking actors provided, on the other hand, the impulse to search for his own Jewish identity.[5]

A large number of refugees did not reach Prague and other Bohemian towns until 1914-1916, when the Austrian-Russian front had temporarily come to a halt in Galicia. Most of them, however, left Bohemia even before the end of the war. The Galician refugees who remained were ordered out of the country by the government of the new state of Czechoslovakia in 1918-1919. According to the estimates of the Ministry of the Interior from December 1919, 1,428 Jewish war refugees lived in Bohemia (515 in Prague) and the Ministry planned to reduce their number with continuous 'repatriation' in the following months.[6] The Prague Jewish community thus, paradoxically, became 'more western'[7] than the Jewish communities of Berlin, London, Paris and Vienna, where eastern European refugees became an integral part of local Jewish society.

In Bohemia, where Jews mostly had a lukewarm attitude to religion, the situation was not changed even by the many traditional Jews who had come to Prague from Subcarpathian Ruthenia between the two world wars.[8] They may have been among those who most conscientiously attended the Alt-Neu Synagogue,[9] but they did not substantially influence the nature of the Prague Jewish Community, tending to adapt themselves to the way of life of the society around them.

---

[5] Iris Bruce, *Kafka and Cultural Zionism: Dates in Palestine* (Madison, WI, 2007), 34-56; Scott Spector, *Prague Territories: National Conflict and Cultural Innovation in Franz Kafka's Fin de Siècle* (Berkeley, Los Angeles and London, 2000), 86-92; Kateřina Čapková, 'Kafka un der yidisher teater: di mizrakh-eyropeyishe yidn in di oygn fun proger yidn', *yerusholaymer almanakh* 28 (2008): 362-71.

[6] See Švehla, Antonín. 1920. Odpověď ministra vnitra k dotazu členů Národního shromáždění Frant. Zeminové, Rud. Laubeho a spol. (tisk č. 1848), kdy budou tak zvaní haličští uprchlíci donuceni navrátiti se do svých domovin. http://www.psp.cz/eknih/1918ns/ps/tisky/t2204_00.htm, Společná česko-slovenská digitální knihovna, Tisk 2204. Accessed 28 May 2010.

[7] For the concept of 'western' and 'eastern' types of Jewish communities, see Mendelsohn, *The Jews of East Central Europe between the World Wars*, 6-7.

[8] According to Vobecká, the Jewish population in Bohemia increased by 662 people between 1921 and 1930; they had most probably come from Subcarpathian Russia and Poland. Jana Vobecká,'Populační vývoj Židů v Čechách v 19. a první třetině 20. století: Společenské a hospodářské souvislosti', *Studie Národohospodářského ústavu Josefa Hlávky* 3 (2007): 80.

[9] This was the experience of the Zionist journalist Tsvi Hirsh Waksman, a frequent visitor to Prague. See his *In land fun maharal un masaryk* (Warsaw, 1936).

Returning to the period before World War I, we see that Prague and Bohemia as a whole did *not* experience a growth in Jewish population as a result of 'eastern Jewish' immigration. As Jana Vobecká has recently shown, even the natural growth of the Bohemian Jewish population between 1857 and 1900 was declining and she estimates the number to be 28,000 people.[10] It is generally assumed that the most frequent destination of Bohemian Jews was Vienna,[11] and that they also left for Germany and the United States.

And yet, even though almost no Jews immigrated to Bohemia, and in fact the Bohemian Jewish population was on the decline, the Jewish community in Prague doubled in size in the second half of the nineteenth century as a result of internal migration. The statistics of 1900 reveal a surprising phenomenon: 91 per cent of the Jews who settled in Prague were born in Bohemia (25 per cent in Prague and 66 per cent in predominantly Czech areas of Bohemia).[12] By contrast, only 3 per cent of the Jews of Moravia and Silesia felt drawn to Prague; most Moravian Jews preferred Vienna.[13]

But not only Prague became a magnet for members of the numerous small Jewish communities in central Bohemian villages and towns. Immediately after the restrictions on mobility and settlement had been lifted in 1849, new Jewish communities were established in border regions in north and west Bohemia, where the population was predominantly German-speaking. Jews, like many Czechs at that time, moved to places known for rapid development of industry, especially Liberec (Reichenberg), Děčín (Tetschen), Most (Brüx) and Teplice (Teplitz) and also spa towns like Mariánské Lázně (Marienbad) and Carlsbad. The number of Jews who decided to leave for these new communities was similar to the influx of Jews into Prague.

Jewish immigrants came to Prague at the peak of the period of national conflict between Czechs and Germans, which culminated in the unrest of 1897, sparked by the Badeni language ordinances.[14] Most Jewish immigrants to Prague came from predominantly Czech-speaking parts of Bohemia. After moving to Prague, however, they were confronted with

---

[10] Vobecká, 'Populační vývoj Židů v Čechách v 19. a první třetině 20. století', 80.
[11] Rauchberg suggests that in 1900 around 28,000 Jews from Bohemia and Moravia settled in Vienna. Heinrich Rauchberg, *Der nationale Besitzstand in Böhmen* (Leipzig, 1905), 303, 391.
[12] Friedmann, 'Pražští Židé', 152. See also Gary Cohen, 'Ethnicity and Urban Population Growth: The Decline of the Prague Germans, 1880-1920', *Studies in East European Social History*, no. 2 (Leiden, 1981): 11; Kieval, *Languages of Community*, 138.
[13] See also Miller, *Rabbis and Revolution*, 320-322.
[14] Jan Křen. *Konfliktní společenství: Češi a Němci 1780-1918* (Prague, 1990), 257-79.

an overwhelmingly German-speaking Jewish community. Because of the key social position of the German-speaking Jews in Prague, many newcomers tried to be part of this higher-ranking society and so sent their children to German schools. This was true, for example, of the families of Kafka, Bergmann, Kohn and Weltsch. Despite the thousands of newcomers from predominantly Czech regions, the German-speaking Jewish élite held all the important social positions in Prague until the foundation of the Czechoslovak Republic after the war. Soon afterwards, however, this situation changed.

Urbanization played an important role in the secularization of the Jews of Bohemia. Nineteenth and twentieth-century urbanization there led to a striking difference between Jews living in villages and Jews living in cities. Jews in the country, whether in a German or Czech milieu, had a highly traditional way of life.[15] The difference between the traditional countryside and the secularized urban milieus is evident also in numerous memoirs and belles-lettres. The best known examples are probably the works of fiction by Vojtěch Rakous (born Adalbert Österreicher, 1862–1935), a leading proponent of Czech-Jewish assimilation. His stories about two characters, Modche and Rezi, provide unique, though surely idealized, testimony to the symbiosis of Christians and Jews in the Bohemian countryside. His writing also provides evidence that the rural Jews maintained Jewish traditions. Similarly, some Zionists remark in their memoirs that they owed their Jewish consciousness to their childhood in rural Bohemia. The philosopher and leading Zionist activist Samuel Hugo Bergmann (1883–1975), for example, wrote in his 1958 birthday greetings to Karel Pacovský, a member of the Theodor Herzl Society, who came from the village of Zálužany, south Bohemia:

> I'd have to write a whole essay if I wanted to explain here to the young generation what these small Czech villages meant to Jewishness. In Israel we now talk a lot about 'Jewish self-confidence' and how such self-confidence should be grafted on here to the young generation. We don't really know how to do that. There, in a small village, Jewish self-confidence wasn't a problem. In each village there was usually only one Jewish family, at most two or three. And what a Jewish life it was, even though it was far removed from Orthodoxy![16]

---

[15] Ruth Kestenberg-Gladstein, 'The Internal Migration of Jews in 19th Century Bohemia', *The Field of Yiddish* (1969): 308.
[16] Hugo Bergmann, 'Pacovsky – 70 Jahre', *Bar Kochba Zirkular* (February 1958), 2. The parents of Arthur and Hugo Bergmann (two of the first Zionists in Bohemia) came from a similar rural environment. See 'Nekrolog Arthura Bergmanna', *Bar Kochba Zirkular* (13 November 1958), 2.

Even though we lack serious research on the rural Jews of Bohemia, these and other testimonies suggest that the situation here hardly differed from that of rural Jews in Germany. Though the number of Jews in villages shrunk from the second half of the nineteenth century onwards, those Jews who remained did not share the same problems with their coreligionists in the big cities. As Steven Lowenstein argues for Germany, '[m]uch of the picture we have of German Jewry overall – its cultural contributions, identity problems, far-reaching assimilation – was not true of rural Jewry.'[17] Like rural Jews in Germany (mainly in the south of the country), Bohemian rural Jews were often well rooted locally, proud of having lived in the same place for generations. Jews became an integral part of the social and economic infrastructure of villages and small towns. And because they had co-existed with their Christian neighbours for generations, they took their own Jewishness for granted.

The decline of small rural communities was, however, rapid. In 1872, for example, there were 327 Jewish communities in the Bohemian Lands, but by 1890 there were only 247.[18] According to the 1921 census, 69 per cent of all people of the Jewish faith lived in towns with populations of more than 10,000.[19] Urbanization continued in the First Republic as well. Whereas in 1921 there were 205 Jewish communities in Bohemia and Moravia, their number declined to 170 over the next ten years.[20]

It is truly startling that although Prague was an important European centre of Jewish religious learning until the end of the eighteenth century, the local Jewish community was one of the most secularized in Europe by the beginning of the twentieth century. Most Jews were 'three-day' Jews, attending synagogue only on the High Holidays. Before World War I they were called 'four-day' Jews, because they went to synagogue also to celebrate the birthday of Emperor Francis Joseph.[21]

One of the best-known, eloquent accounts of the lukewarm attitude of the Jews of Bohemia to the Jewish religion is Kafka's *Brief an den Vater* (1919). In this 'letter' Kafka reproaches his father for having been unable, or simply unwilling, to communicate anything of what it meant to be a

---

[17] Steven M. Lowenstein, 'Decline and Survival of Rural Jewish Communities', in *In Search of Jewish Community: Jewish Identities in Germany and Austria, 1918–1933*, ed. Michael Brenner and Derek J. Penslar (Bloomington and Indianapolis, IN, 1998), 236.
[18] Arno Pařík, 'Z dějin židovských náboženských obcí v Čechách a na Moravě', in *Židovské památky v Čechách a na Moravě*, by Jiří Fiedler (Prague, 1992), 21.
[19] *Československá statistika*, vol. 9, series VI (Sčítání lidu, sešit 1), pt I (Prague, 1924), 93*, table 108.
[20] Rudolf M. Wlaschek, *Juden in Böhmen: Beiträge zur Geschichte des europäischen Judentums im 19. und 20. Jahrhundert*, 2nd ed. (Munich, 1997), 91.
[21] Wilma Iggers, *Zeiten der Gottesferne und der Mattheit: Die Religion im Bewußtsein der böhmischen Juden in der ersten tschechoslowakischen Republik* (Leipzig, 1997).

Jew. He then enumerates his experiences connected with the synagogue, which are all negative.[22] And the journalist and script-writer Willy Haas (1891-1973), for instance, writes:

> Nothing remained in us of the faith of our forebears . . . . We were neither Jews nor Christians, and yet we were believers. Our faith was of a dual character: first we believed in Original Sin, about which we knew more than many Christians; second, we believed in the veiled nature and absolute unattainability of God, who manifested Himself only in the brutality, corruption and malicious glee of some petty officials, a God, who shaped our fate much in the way our grammar-school teachers did. That was our world, about which we debated day and night in our rooms, in parks and nightclubs. It was the world of one man, whom we hardly really knew back then: Franz Kafka.[23]

The interviews that the researchers Anna Lorencová and Anna Hyndráková conducted with Shoah survivors and recorded for the Jewish Museum in Prague frequently reveal a lax approach to Judaism in Bohemian Jewish families before World War II.[24] Here a striking difference between Bohemia and Moravia is evident. Moravian Jews lived mostly in small towns, where they constituted large communities. They maintained much closer ties among themselves than did the Jews of larger towns. Throughout Moravia, in great contrast to Bohemia, there were only seven Jewish village communities.[25] The chief reason was the expulsion of the Jews from all Moravian royal towns between 1426 and 1514, which radically changed the demographic and social structure of the Jewish population. Jews could freely settle in these towns only after the revolutionary year of 1848.[26] Except for the more than 2,000 members of the Jewish community of Mikulov (Nikolsburg), most Moravian Jews lived in fifty-two communities that numbered 500 Jews or less.[27] It was only in the second half of the nineteenth century that Jewish communities were established in Brno (Brünn), Jihlava (Iglau), Znojmo (Znaim), Moravská-Ostrava (Mährisch-Ostrau) and Olomouc (Olmütz). Brno quickly became the

---

[22] Franz Kafka, *Brief an den Vater* (Prague 1919); for an English edition, see *Letter to His Father*, trans. Ernst Kaiser and Eithne Wilkins (New York, 1996).
[23] Willy Haas, *Die literarische Welt: Erinnerungen* (Munich, 1958), 30.
[24] The recordings of the interviews and their transcripts are deposited in the Shoah History Department of the Jewish Museum, Prague. See also Anna Lorencová and Anna Hyndráková, 'Die tschechische Gesellschaft und die Juden in den Erinnerungen von Zeitzeugen', *Theresienstädter Studien und Dokumente* (1999): 156-59.
[25] Fiedler, *Židovské památky v Čechách a na Moravě*, 39.
[26] For more on this, see Miller, *Rabbis and Revolution*, 16-22.
[27] Ibid., 3.

Figure 1.1. Hana Blasková, a Shoah survivor, seen here in a photograph from 1925, dressed as an angel; her brother is dressed as Saint Nicholas.

largest Jewish community in Moravia and its renown eventually overshadowed that of Mikulov.[28] The cohesion of many old Moravian communities was strengthened by their having been granted political autonomy.[29] Even after the Jews had been granted equal rights in the Bohemian Lands in 1867, the Jews of many Moravian towns could influence affairs in their own autonomous communal administrations with their own elected officials and police departments.[30] Twenty-seven Moravian towns, including Boskovice (Boskowitz), Prostějov (Proßnitz) and Holešov (Holleschau), therefore had dual government until the end of World War I.[31] Most were merged with the Christian parts of the towns in 1919 and 1920, though two did not merge until 1924.[32] The fact that the Jews of Moravia could take advantage of communal autonomy also after their emancipation is unique in the history of western and central Europe.

Jews in Bohemia were far more secularized than in Moravia. This parallels the situation in the dominant society: the number of practising Christians in Bohemia was far lower than in Moravia.[33] The statistics about the number of mixed marriages also illustrate well the extent of religious observance in the different parts of Czechoslovakia. Of new marriages in Czechoslovakia between 1928 and 1933 in which at least one of the partners declared the Jewish religion, about 19 per cent were mixed. In Bohemia, however, this proportion was 43.8 per cent, in Moravia 30 per cent, in Slovakia only 9.2 per cent and in Subcarpathian Ruthenia a negligible 1.3 per cent.[34]

---

[28] Ibid., 320–22.
[29] For the genesis of these Moravian Jewish Quarters, see ibid., 29–35, 274–87.
[30] Ibid., 331.
[31] Other towns with Jewish self-government were Uherský Brod (Ungarisch Brod), Břeclav (Lundenburg), Bzenec (Bisenz), Hranice (Mährisch Weißkirchen), Dolní Kounice (Kanitz), Kyjov (Gaya), Ivančice (Eibenschitz), Jevíčko (Gewitsch), Lednice (Eisgrub), Lipník nad Bečvou (Leipnik), Lomnice (Lobnig), Mikulov (Nikolsburg), Miroslav (Mißlitz), Uherský Ostroh (Ungarisch Ostra), Písečné (Piesling), Podivín (Kostl), Pohořelice (Pohrlitz), Přerov (Prerau), Rousínov (Raussnitz), Slavkov (Austerlitz), Strážnice (Straßnitz), Šafov (Schaffa), Třebíč (Trebitsch) and Veselí nad Moravou (Wessely an der March). See the Bill of 12 December 1918, proposed by members of the Czechoslovak National Assembly, including Jan Pelikán, Alois Konečný and Julius Kopeček, for the disbanding of Jewish political communities in Moravian towns, document no. 212, Společná česko-slovenská digitální parlamentní knihovna, http://www.psp.cz/eknih/1918ns/ps/tisky/t0212_00.htm (accessed 25 January 2010).
[32] Peter Urbanitsch, ‚Die politischen Judengemeinden in Mähren nach 1848', in *Moravští Židé v rakousko-uherské monarchii (1780-1918). XXVI. Mikulovské sympozium* (Brno, 2003), 50.
[33] Ján Mišovič, *Víra v dějinách zemí koruny české* (Prague, 2001), 78, 83.
[34] Peter Meyer, 'Czechoslovakia', in *The Jews in the Soviet Satellites*, ed. Peter Meyer et al. (Westport, CT, 1971), 54–55. Meyer even gives the percentage differences between men and women. From his comparison it is clear that, except for Subcarpathian Ruthenia, a larger percentage of men than women decided to marry someone of a different religion.

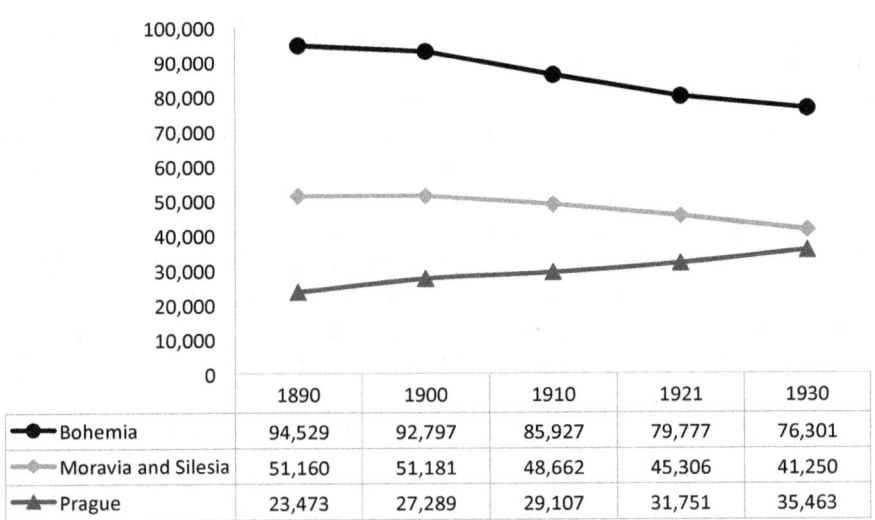

Graph 1.1. Changes in Jewish population (according to religion) in Bohemia, Moravia, Silesia and Prague, from 1890 to 1930.
Source: František Friedmann, Einige Zahlen über die tschechoslovakischen Juden (Prague, 1933), 6-7.

Orthodoxy in Bohemia had been on the decline since the mid-nineteenth century. By the 1840s the Prague *yeshiva* was closed and Prague could no longer offer rabbinical training, and yet not even a reform rabbinical seminary was established there, unlike in Germany. In general it is fair to say that not even the Reform movement in Bohemia enjoyed any great success. The synagogue in Dušní ulice (Geistgasse) in Prague, today the Spanish Synagogue, became the centre of the movement. Here, the Verein für geregelten israelitischen Gottesdienst (Society for the Reformed Service in the Mosaic Faith) was responsible for the rules of the service. The reforms in the synagogue in Dušní ulice, however, tended to be concerned with external matters like the introduction of organ music, sermons in German, or rabbis' vestments adopted from the Protestants. Unlike in neighbouring Germany, however, the reforms were not concerned with articles of faith.[35] The Reform movement in Germany, by contrast, constituted a kind of middle path between Orthodoxy and secularization and enabled those Jews who wanted to integrate into German society to have a religious life adapted to new social circumstances.[36]

The limited role of religion among Prague Jews is well illustrated by an episode from 1926. At a meeting of the council of the Prague Jewish Com-

---

[35] Kieval, *Languages of Community*, 160-61.
[36] Iggers, 'The Flexible National Identities of Bohemian Jewry', 40.

munity in the centre of town, one of its members, Maxim Reiner, from the Czech-Jewish movement, was astonished at the amount of money being spent on the maintenance of synagogues that were directly or indirectly run by the community. There were seven such synagogues: three Orthodox – the Alt-Neu, the Klausen and the Hohe synagogues; two Reform – the Jerusalem and the Maisl; and two run by private societies – the Orthodox Pinkas synagogue and the Reform synagogue in Dušní ulice. Reiner proposed, 'during the year, when all the synagogues are empty, except on the High Holidays, limiting the number of open synagogues to one or two, and opening all of them only on High Holidays'.[37] The proposal was followed by a heated debate, in which no one denied that the synagogues were empty during the rest of the year. The arguments for and against were centred solely on economics. The boards of the synagogues that would be open only three days a year could hardly rent out seats for money. It would also have been difficult to dismiss long-serving wardens of synagogues.[38] And yet, in the same period, synagogues in Prague districts with predominantly Czech-speaking populations – particularly Královské Vinohrady (Königliche Weinberge) and Smíchov (Smichow) – were attended regularly and became centres of social networks.[39]

The Prague community had few Orthodox Jews. The council of the Jewish Community in the Prague centre, which numbered about thirty members, had during most of the First Republic only two Orthodox members – Salomon Hugo Lieben (1881–1942), the founder of the Jewish Museum; and Berthold Jeiteles (1872–1958), a pharmacist and Talmudist.

The social structure of the Jews of Bohemia, their concentration in the large towns where they constituted only a negligible proportion of the total population, and also their attitude to religion were all factors that supported their integration into the surrounding society. The dominant society, moreover, created conditions favourable to this. The secular character of Bohemian society certainly did not make religious differences more acute. Particularly in the First Republic antisemitism became politically untenable and for most Czech intellectuals unacceptable.[40] The

---

[37] AŽMP, the minutes of board meetings of the Prague Jewish Community, session of 18 April 1926.
[38] Ibid.
[39] Čapková, 'Raum und Zeit als Faktoren der nationalen Identifikation der Prager Juden', 21–30.
[40] For a more critical approach to Czech antisemitism in the interwar Prague, see Ines Koeltzsch, 'Antijüdische Straßengewalt und die semantische Konstruktion des "Anderen" im Prag der Ersten Republik', *Judaica Bohemiae* vol. 46, part 1 (2011): 73–99.

key to understanding the low degree of antisemitism in Czech society in the interwar years is not so much secularization as it is the fact that the national ambitions of the Czechs were completely satisfied by the creation of the Czechoslovak state. The antisemitism that came to the surface with unexpected speed during the six months from the Munich Agreement to the German occupation, in a Czech society disappointed by its allies France and Great Britain during the period known as the Second Republic, suggests antisemitism was proportionate to Czech national frustration. Otto Dov Kulka also analyses the striking similarities in the anti-Jewish behaviour of German society in the period 1933-1939 and Czech society during the six months of the Second Republic.[41] A considerable role in shaping the attitudes of Czech politicians and intellectuals towards Jews was also played by the first president of the country, Tomáš Garrigue Masaryk (1850-1937), who sought to enshrine the recognition of Jewish nationality in an explanatory statement to the Czechoslovak constitution. His well-known involvement in the Hilsner Affair contributed to the fact that any attack on the Jews was understood also as an attack on the ideology of Masaryk and his supporters. Martin Schulze-Wessel argues that Masaryk's conception of the Czech nation was from the beginning tied to the idea of western democracy, in which antisemitism is unacceptable. Masaryk was aware that only such a concept of a nation could find support among western European and American politicians.[42] The linking of Masaryk with his support for the Jews also had its sordid side, as is evident from the press in the Second Republic, World War II, and, in a different form, the years of Communist rule. In each case, Masaryk was cursed as a politician who had led the republic astray and it was more or less explicitly stated that he was aided and abetted in this by the Jews.[43]

---

[41] See Otto Dov Kulka, 'History and Historical Consciousness: Similarities and Dissimilarities in the History of the Jews in Germany and the Czech Lands, 1918-1945', *Bohemia* 46, no. 1 (2005): 77-81.
[42] Martin Schulze-Wessel, 'Die Politik gegenüber den Juden in der Ersten Tschechoslowakischen Republik: Entwürfe und Wirklichkeiten (1918-1938)', in *Zwischen großen Erwartungen und bösem Erwachen: Juden, Politik und Antisemitismus in Ost- und Südosteuropa 1918-1945*, ed. Dietmar Dahlmann and Anke Hillbrenner (Paderborn, 2007), 130.
[43] See also Michal Frankl, 'Tschechien', in *Handbuch des Antisemitismus: Judenfeindschaft in Geschichte und Gegenwart*, ed. Wolfgang Benz, vol. 1, *Länder und Regionen* (Munich, 2008), 364-69; Bedřich W. Loewenstein, 'Überlegungen zum tschechischen Antisemitismus', in *Wir und die anderen: Historische und kultursoziologische Betrachtungen*, by Bedřich Loewenstein (Dresden, 2003), 399-412.

Chapter 2

JEWS AS A NATIONAL MINORITY IN THE NEW REPUBLIC

In the census, Jews were given different criteria than the other citizens of Czechoslovakia. Czechs and Slovaks (as Czechoslovaks), Germans, Poles, Hungarians and members of other nationalities in the 1921 and 1930 censuses each had to declare their nationality based on the language that they considered their mother tongue and were fluent in. Their decisions could be checked by the authorities, and in some cases were. Apart from choosing a nationality according to language, the Jews were the only group of Czechoslovak citizens who could also declare themselves to be of Jewish nationality yet did not have to demonstrate proficiency in Hebrew or Yiddish or even be members of a Jewish Community. What had led the legislators of Czechoslovakia to make such an exception for them?

The attitude of the Czechoslovak authorities towards the question of Jewish nationality needs to be considered more broadly, that is, in the context of both the domestic politics and international relations of Czechoslovakia. In the international context, the debate on Jewish nationality at the Paris Peace Conference of 1919 was decisive. It was there, at Versailles, that the demand for the recognition of the Jewish nation first made it onto the agenda of the top-level representatives of the states of the new, post-war Europe. That is not to suggest, however, that the representatives of the Jewish national movement had not sought the recognition of Jewish nationality before. Several decades earlier, in fact, they had demanded a special minorities policy for Jews in Russia and Austria-Hungary, countries where Jews lived in large homogeneous communities. Particularly in the Pale of Settlement and in Galicia, in Cisleithania, the Jews preserved their Jewish identity thanks not only to religion, but also to Yiddish and other social and cultural traditions. Moreover, as both Russia and the Habsburg Monarchy were multinational states, Jews had ample opportunity to learn from the example of other nationalities, who had struggled for their right to self-determination. The results of the Jews' pre-war efforts, however, were modest. In Russia, Jewish nationalists temporarily achieved rights they had demanded when the first Duma was convened in 1906. Five Jews with programmes oriented to the rights of the Jewish nation managed to win seats in the Duma elections.[1] In Austria, in the 1907 general elections, four 'Jewish national' deputies formed a 'Jewish parliamentary group',[2] which would 'favor national-democratic policies, and would particularly exert itself to secure the full recognition of the Jewish nationality'. Its statement also says that the group would push for the protection of national minorities.[3]

The Balfour Declaration of 1917 is a milestone in the history of Zionism. In this formal statement of policy, the British Government promised Jews the right to a national home in Palestine. Two years later, at the Paris Peace Conference, it was decided that the British would be entrusted with the mandate for Palestine. The British promise shifted the plans for the creation of a Jewish state in the Near East from the realm of speculation to the realm of serious international diplomacy.

American encouragement of the Zionists was also important in this respect. The right to national self-determination, as set out by President Woodrow Wilson in the Fourteen Points of his address of 8 January 1918, meant a great deal not only to Czech politicians; Jewish nationalists also saw it to as being in their favour. Even before the end of the war they established Jewish National Councils in the individual states of Europe to represent the Jews and to promote the rights of the Jewish minorities there. In Bohemia the Jewish National Council (Židovská národní rada)

---

[1] Oscar Janowsky, *The Jews and Minority Rights, 1898–1919* (New York, 1966) (orig. pub. 1933), 89.
[2] One of the four deputies was Arthur Mahler, Docent of Archaeology at the German University of Prague. See CZA, Bar Kochba / Barissia Collection, A 317/c 8, Arthur Bergmann's history of Bar Kochba, manuscript, 16; Marsha L. Rozenblit, *Reconstructing a National Identity: The Jews of Habsburg Austria during World War I* (Oxford, 2001), 37. For more on the campaign of the Jewish nationalists and Zionists to recognize Jewish national autonomy in Austria, see David Rechter, 'A Nationalism of Small Things: Jewish Autonomy in Late Habsburg Austria', *Leo Baeck Institute Year Book*, vol. 52 (2007): 87–109.
[3] Janowsky, *The Jews and Minority Rights*, 143–44. A long debate between Czech-Jewish and Zionist functionaries about whether to establish a Jewish curia in the forthcoming elections to the Reichstag appears in a police report of 29 January 1906, AHMP, SK XXI/51.

was founded in Prague on 22 October 1918. Its chief demands are set out in its manifesto of 23 October – namely, the recognition of Jewish nationality and the freedom of the individual to declare Jewish nationality as his or her own; full civil rights; national minority rights; and the democratization of Jewish communities, which were meant to come together under the leadership of a centralized Jewish organisation.[4]

On October 28, the day Czechoslovak independence was declared, the chairman of the Jewish National Council, Ludvík Singer (1876-1931), achieved a diplomatic coup that was intended to make Czech politicians more amenable towards the demands of the Jewish nationalists. Only several hours before the declaration of independence, representatives of the National Committee in Prague[5] received three representatives of the Jewish National Council – Ludvík Singer, Max Brod and Karl Fischl. The three men presented the National Committee representatives with a memorandum in the name of the Jewish nation, containing demands repeated from its manifesto.[6] Singer congratulated the members of the National Committee for having achieved Czechoslovak independence. He also pointed out that the 'Jewish club' of four deputies to the Austrian Reichstag had always also sought to support the endeavours of other nationalities in the monarchy.[7] Some Zionist officials interpreted Singer's prompt actions as a fundamental step towards gaining the confidence of the first 'revolutionary' Czechoslovak government in order to get legislation passed that would recognize Jewish nationality.[8] On the other hand, as Frank Hadler has pointed out, Czech politicians probably did not attach any importance to the reception of the Jewish National Council representatives. Not one of the documents of 28 October mentions this visit, nor does František Soukup (1871-1940), a Social Democrat and the first Minister of Justice in the new republic, mention it in his two-volume *28 říjen 1918* (28 October 1918), published in 1928.[9]

Representatives of European Jewish Councils, together with representatives of American Jewry, then established the Comité des délégations juives auprès de la Conférence de la paix, which sought the recognition of

---

[4] Rozenblit, *Reconstructing a National Identity*, 144.
[5] Namely, Antonín Švehla, František Soukup, Jiří Stříbrný and Otakar Srdínko.
[6] The memorandum is published in full in *Židovské zprávy*, nos. 14-15 (1918): 3-6.
[7] Koloman Gajan, 'Masaryk a Max Brod: Židovská otázka v ČSR v letech 1918-1920', *Židovská ročenka* (2000-01): 31-32.
[8] See, for example, the opening address of Josef Rufeisen, chairman of the Zionist Organization in Czechoslovakia, given at the Twelfth Zionist Congress, Moravská Ostrava, March 1938, in *Zprávy-Nachrichten*, no. 6 (7 March 1938): 1.
[9] Frank Hadler, '"Erträglicher Antisemitismus"? Jüdische Fragen und tschechoslowakische Antworten 1918/19', *Jahrbuch des Simon-Dubnow-Instituts*, 1 (2002): 182-83.

Jews as a national minority.¹⁰ It was the diplomatic efforts of the Americans, in particular Louis Brandeis (1856-1941), Associate Justice of the U.S. Supreme Court, and Rabbi Stephen Wise (1874-1949), which had far-reaching influence on the talks about the minority rights of the Jews of Europe. Jewish members of the British and French delegations, by contrast, came out against recognition of Jewish nationality in the treaties on the protection of national minorities (the 'minority treaties'). They were represented by the Joint Foreign Committee and the Alliance Israélite Universelle (established in 1860), which tended to push for the conception of Jewry as a religious group. Their members considered themselves British or French, and were against the efforts of the Zionists and Jewish nationalists. The attitude of the British and French delegates, however, also reflects a profound contradiction: they may have come out against Jewish minority rights in western Europe, but they recognized the necessity of resolving the precarious situation of the many Jewish communities in eastern Europe.¹¹

The result was a compromise, which appears also in the minority Treaty of Saint-Germain-en-Laye, between Czechoslovakia and the Allies, of 10 September 1919. The treaty does not explicitly mention Jews as a 'national minority', but it does recognize the same rights for all members of 'racial, religious and linguistic minorities'.¹² This vague formulation need not have been interpreted, however, as a demand for the recognition of Jewish nationality.

The treaty with Poland, moreover, contained 'Jewish clauses' (articles 10 and 11 in the treaty with Poland), which were explicitly intended to defend the rights of the Jewish minorities in matters of education and the keeping of the Sabbath.¹³ The representatives of the Jewish National Council in Bohemia firmly believed that the Jewish clauses should be included in the treaty with Czechoslovakia. A meeting was meant to take place in late August 1919 between Singer of the Jewish National Coun-

---

¹⁰ Carole Fink, *Defending the Rights of Others: The Great Powers, the Jews, and International Minority Protection, 1878-1938* (Cambridge, UK 2004), 196. For the context of the formation of the Jewish delegation that went to the Paris Peace Conference, see also Mark Levene, 'Nationalism and Its Alternatives in the International Arena: The Jewish Question at Paris, 1919', *Journal of Contemporary History*, 28 (1993): 511-31. The Czechoslovak Jews were represented at the Paris Peace Conference by Hugo Bergmann, Ludvík Singer, Markus Ungar, Oswald Freund, Norbert Adler and Hans Kohn. See Josef Tenenboym, *Tsvishn milkhome un sholem: Yidn oyf der sholem konferents noch der ershter veltmilkhome* (Buenos Aires, 1956), 93.
¹¹ Fink, *Defending the Rights of Others*, 193-202.
¹² Kurt Stillschweig, 'Nationalitätenrechtliche Stellung der Juden in der Tschechoslowakei', *Historia Judaica* I (1938-1939): 41-42.
¹³ Władysław Józef Zaleski, *Międzynarodowa ochrona mniejszości* (Warsaw, 1932), 129-30.

cil and Edvard Beneš (1884-1948), the Czechoslovak foreign minister. Instead of Beneš, however, Singer met only with Beneš's secretary, who gave him the Foreign Minister's written statement. Beneš sought to justify their non-inclusion mainly by arguing that the Jewish clauses would imply the Allies' lack of confidence in Czechoslovakia's intention to uphold the rights of national minorities in Czechoslovakia:

> Our state and nation generally enjoy the sympathy and confidence of all the Allies in this respect. Furthermore, we have met all our obligations, and shall continue to meet them, and we are more liberal than anyone else in the matter of the nationality question. I rejected a clause that would have cast doubt on this moral relationship between our state and the Allies.[14]

The inclusion of articles 10 and 11 in the Minority Treaty would also have meant getting involved in the debate between the Zionists and the Jewish assimilationists, while the rights of the nationally-minded Jews were ensured by the general protection of national minorities, and, similarly, the rights of Jews as a religious group (including the observance of the Sabbath) were also guaranteed. Beneš's last argument was rather a warning that it was in the interest both of the Czechoslovak Jews and of the Republic not to stir up the Jewish question:

> Speaking for our republic, I consider it a better tactic, in the interest of Jewry and in the interest of the Republic, not to emphasize this problem. There are justified complaints and reproaches made against Jewish circles in the country. To raise the problem now would mean to emphasize the question and again to call forth recriminations from one party or another. It is in the interest of us all not to raise the problem in theoretical terms, but to solve it practically, on the basis provided by the treaty. That will provide the foundation for good, level-headed coexistence. I have worked on this matter according to my conscience, in the interest of that good coexistence and good collaboration, and my standpoint is dictated only by this feeling and this endeavour.[15]

The statement of the Czechoslovak foreign minister filled most members of the Jewish delegation at the Paris Peace Conference with indignation. Instead of Singer, it was Nahum Sokolow (1859-1936), the chairman of the international Jewish delegation, who attempted to apply further diplomatic pressure. According to Hugo Bergmann's diary, only Singer agreed from the beginning with Beneš's standpoint. Like Beneš, Singer

---

[14] AÚTGM, fond TGM - R, kr. 453, církve, složka židé 1918-1919, letter from Edvard Beneš, 25 August 1919.
[15] Ibid.

continuously tried to assess the impact that the adoption of the Jewish clauses could have on the Jews of Czechoslovakia. Bergmann considered this attitude narrow-minded, as if Singer were unable to see the problem from a 'pan-Jewish' point of view. Singer, he wrote, had long been against Sokolow's taking the matter into his own hands.[16]

Sokolow met Beneš on 28 August, and made no secret of his disillusionment with Beneš's attitude. He explained to Beneš that the adoption of articles 10 and 11 in the treaty with Czechoslovakia was important mainly in the context of the status of the Jews of central and eastern Europe, and argued that the articles would help to protect Jewish minority rights. Sokolow admitted that the Jews could consider Beneš and Masaryk a sufficient guarantee that the Jews of Czechoslovakia would be protected. That could change radically, however, once these two politicians were no longer in office. The Jewish clauses were meant to ensure the protection of the Jews of Czechoslovakia well into the future.

Beneš's response to this urging, however, was also highly pragmatic. He tended to see articles 10 and 11 as a 'yellow badge', suitable only for Poland or Romania. Austria, Yugoslavia and Czechoslovakia, he argued, did not need special Jewish articles in the treaties. Sokolow managed to convince Beneš to ask Masaryk to state his position.[17] In this way he sought to gain time, and hoped that Masaryk would support the Zionist position. That, however, did not happen; to the great disappointment of the Jewish delegation, the Jewish clauses did not appear in the treaty with Czechoslovakia. Moreover, the treaty did not mention any recognition of the three million German citizens of Czechoslovakia or make any provision for the Magyars in Slovakia, who numbered about 650,000. Carole Fink has attributed this to Beneš's outstanding diplomatic abilities, 'his astute propaganda campaign portraying the Prague government as a paragon of western liberalism', and his 'vow to create a "little Switzerland"'.[18] That Masaryk and Beneš were well aware of the power of propaganda and used it consciously for the Czechoslovak state throughout the interwar years is persuasively demonstrated in Andrea Orzoff's *Battle for the Castle*.[19]

In retrospect one may wonder whether the hectic activity of the Jewish National Council representatives and of Sokolow himself was truly necessary. Did they not overestimate the importance of these articles for the

---

[16] Hugo Bergmann, *Tagebücher und Briefe, 1901–1948*, ed. Miriam Sambursky, vol. 1 (Königstein, 1985), 125.
[17] Aharon Moshe Rabinowicz, 'The Jewish Minority', in *The Jews of Czechoslovakia: Historical Studies and Surveys*, vol. I (New York, 1968), 174–77.
[18] Fink, *Defending the Rights of Others*, 268–69.
[19] Andrea Orzoff, *Battle for the Castle: The Myth of Czechoslovakia in Europe, 1914-1948* (Oxford, 2009).

Jews' standing in society? No clauses prevented Polish universities, for example, from introducing a quota system for Jewish students. And despite article 10 of the Minorities' Treaty, the Polish state refused to subsidize schools that taught in Yiddish or Hebrew.[20]

The history of the origin of article 7 on minorities of the Treaty of Saint-Germain-en-Laye is well worth considering. Jewish nationalists wanted more than merely the rights generally provided for in this article. They demanded a special Jewish clause. Yet article 7 originated from extending to the Jews guarantees given to all national minorities. That is evident in the report delivered by the Agrarian Party deputy František Hnídek (1876–1932) to the Czechoslovak National Assembly: 'At the peace conference, when the great pogroms took place in Poland, it was initially believed first and foremost that the Jews should be protected by these laws. Then, it was realized that it was impossible, after all, to defend only one confession or one nationality, and so a whole new article related to the protection of minorities in general emerged from this. All citizens, regardless of nationality, should have equal rights in Czechoslovakia; they are citizens equal before the law.'[21] So, even though article 7 on the protection of minorities actually originated in reaction to the antisemitic attacks in Poland, it was as if Jewish nationalists did not believe that it would be universally applied and so demanded a special clause with explicit reference to Jewish nationality.

Unlike the Treaty of Saint-Germain-en-Laye, the 1920 Constitution of Czechoslovakia contains the term 'nationality' not directly in the law itself but in the explanatory memorandum to article 128.[22] Article 128 states generally: 'All citizens of the Republic of Czechoslovakia are fully equal before the law, and enjoy the same civil and political rights regardless of race, language or religion' (article 1) and 'Difference in religion, belief, confession, or language shall . . . constitute no obstacle to any citizen of the Czechoslovak Republic particularly in regard to entry into the civil service and public office . . . or in regard to the exercise of any trade or occupation' (section 2). Articles 130 to 132 refer to the rights and du-

---

[20] Ezra Mendelsohn, *The Jews of East Central Europe between the World Wars* (Bloomington, IN, 1983), 39.
[21] Zpravodaj posl. dr. Hnídek, řeč v Národním shromáždění československém, 89. schůze, pátek 7. listopadu 1919, Společná česko-slovenská digitální parlamentní knihovna, accessed 25 January 2010, <http://www.psp.cz/eknih/1918ns/ps/stenprot/089schuz/s089002.htm>. See also Fink, *Defending the Rights of Others*, 171–208.
[22] For a thorough discussion of the terms 'nationality' (*národnost*) and 'nation' (*národ*) in the Czechoslovak Constitutions, see Jaroslav Kučera, 'Politický či přirozený národ? K pojetí národa v československém právním řádu meziválečného období', *Český časopis historický* 99, no. 3 (2001): 548–68.

ties of national minorities, though not enumerating them specifically. The explanatory memorandum to section 128, however, states:

> The Constitution does not specify national minorities, because it would then be up to it also to resolve questions that were academically moot. After all, the very term 'nation' [národ] has not yet been precisely defined. . . . The question, for example, of whether the Jews are a nation is moot. The Constitution, adopting the phrase 'regardless of race, language, or religion' (*race, langage ou religion*) leaves it up to everyone to decide what they perceive the determinant of nationality to reside in, and to decide freely according to that. If, consequently, one considers the Jews to be a separate nation [národ], one is entitled to declare oneself to be a Jew by nationality, even if, for example, by religion one were non-denominational and one's mother tongue were Czech or German, and so forth. During the taking of the census, elections, and so forth, Jews are therefore not required to declare themselves to be members of any ethnic-national [ethnická národnostní] minority other than Jewish.[23]

One could therefore choose Jewish nationality for oneself without any restrictions. The choice did not, as we have seen, depend even on knowledge of a Jewish language or on membership of a Jewish community. In the 1921 census 239 people of a religion other than Jewish also declared Jewish nationality: 100 declared no denomination, 74 Roman Catholic, 23 Uniate, 19 Protestant, 12 Eastern Orthodox, 1 the Czechoslovak Church, 4 declared other confessions, and 6 did not state any religious affiliation. In 1930, 352 people of a religion other than Jewish declared Jewish nationality; of them, however, 335 were non-denominational, only 12 Roman Catholic, and 4 Protestant, as well as 1 woman who was a member of the Eastern Orthodox Church.[24]

What exactly it was that led Czech politicians to adopt the explanatory memorandum, on the basis of which Jewish nationality was exempted from the general criteria, remains an open question. An important role was definitely played here by Masaryk. In particular his having come out in defence of Leopold Hilsner in the blood libel case ensured Masaryk's

---

[23] Zasedání Národního shromáždění československého roku 1920. Tisk 2421. Zpráva ústavního výboru k ústavní listině Československé republiky, usnesené ústavním výborem podle § 14. a 7. jednacího řádu. O ochraně menšin, Společná česko-slovenská digitální parlamentní knihovna, http://www.psp.cz/eknih/1918ns/ps/tisky/t2421_03.htm (accessed 25 January 2010).
[24] See *Československá statistika*, vol. 37, řada VI (Sčítání lidu, sešit 6), part III (Prague 1927), 3–4, tab. 1; *Československá statistika*, vol. 98, řada VI (Sčítání lidu, sešit 7), part II (Prague, 1934), 104–07, tab. 12.

popularity among Jews all over the world.[25] His attitude in the Hilsner Affair, 1899-1900, later helped Masaryk in diplomatic talks in the United States during World War I, because it ensured him the support of American Jews.[26] That is evident also from a letter he wrote to Beneš in Geneva in late October 1918: 'Hilsner has been of great help to us now: Zionists and other Jews have openly accepted our programme.'[27]

American Jews, at the same time, urged Masaryk to recognize Jewish nationality in Czechoslovakia. In September 1918, in response to greetings from the American Zionist organisation to the Czechoslovak National Council in Washington, D.C., Masaryk wrote them a long letter. In it, he expresses his gratitude for Zionist support for the endeavours of the Czech nation to achieve political independence, and promises that equality before the law would be guaranteed to all minorities in the new state. And, he writes:

> As regards Zionism, I can only express my sympathy with it and with the national movement of the Jewish people in general, since it is of great moral significance. I have observed the Zionist and national movement of the Jews in Europe and in our own country, and have come to understand that it is not a movement of political chauvinism, but one striving for the moral rebirth of its people. . . . You may be sure that I will try to the best of my ability to do what I deem just and right not only for my own nation but for all other nations as well.[28]

As is clear from the letter, Masaryk's positive attitude towards Jewish nationalism had deep roots. Long before World War I he had been interested in the ideas of Aḥad Ha'Am (born Asher Hirsch Ginsberg, 1856-1927), the father of 'Cultural Zionism', which most Czech Zionists were proponents of. Aḥad Ha'Am understood the Zionist movement as the spiritual revival of the Jewish nation, particularly in the arts and educa-

---

[25] Stölzl writes cogently that the Hilsner Affair became the 'key point' in the relationship between Masaryk and the Jews. See Christoph Stölzl, 'Die "Burg" und die Juden: T. G. Masaryk und sein Kreis im Spannungsfeld der jüdischen Frage: Assimilation, Antisemitismus und Zionismus', in *Die 'Burg': Einflußreiche politische Kräfte um Masaryk und Beneš*, vol. II, ed. Karl Bosl (Munich and Vienna, 1974), 88. For Hilsner Affair, see Michal Frankl, '*Emancipace od židů*': *Český antisemitismus na konci 19. století* (Prague and Litomyšl, 2007); Kieval, *Languages of Community*, 181-97; Jiří Kovtun, *Tajuplná vražda: Případ Leopolda Hilsnera* (Prague, 1994).
[26] See Tomáš Garrigue Masaryk, *Světová revoluce* (Prague, 1930), 272.
[27] Frank Hadler, ed., *Weg von Österreich! Das Weltkriegsexil von Masaryk und Beneš im Spiegel ihrer Briefe und Aufzeichnungen aus den Jahren 1914 bis 1918: Eine Quellensammlung* (Berlin, 1995), 539.
[28] Masaryk's letter is published in full in Rabinowicz, 'The Jewish Minority', 165-66. A copy of the letter is deposited in the AÚTGM, fond TGM - R, kr. 453, církve, složka židé 1918-1919.

Figure 2.1. August Stein, chairman of the Jewish Community in Prague, and Josef Popper, vice-chairman of the Jewish Community in Prague and president of the Grand Lodge of B'nai B'rith, meeting with President Masaryk on his 80th birthday, 1930.

tion. Masaryk read Aḥad Ha'Am's works and found inspiration in them for his own ideas about the revival of the Czech nation.[29]

Particularly during World War I, but also after, Masaryk made no secret of the fact that he had greater understanding for the Zionist movement than for the Czech-Jewish movement.[30] This was largely because of his

---
[29] Kieval, *Languages of Community*, 209–10.
[30] Drawing on Masaryk's pre-war writings, Kieval demonstrates that Masaryk kept a distance from the Czech-Jews even before this period. Kieval, *Languages of Community*, 198–216.

belief in the ethnic character of Judaism. Like Czechs, Jews should, he thought, be 'reborn' morally and develop their own unique national identity.[31] Masaryk must therefore have found it particularly distasteful that some Czech-Jewish ideologues in the First Republic considered the aim of the Czech-Jewish movement to be not just the integration of the Jews into the Czech nation, but also their complete merging with the majority society, in other words, assimilation in the original sense of the word. Well into the 1930s, however, he continued to meet with Jindřich Kohn (1874–1935), a leading Czech-Jewish thinker. Kohn never pushed for complete assimilation and was open to discussion with Zionists, whose ideology he considered as legitimate as the idea of integration.

The Czech philosopher Emanuel Rádl (1873–1942) had the same attitude to the Czech-Jews as Masaryk did.[32] In his article 'České židovství' (Czech-Jewishness), published in the Czech-Jewish periodical *Rozhled*, Rádl expresses his sympathies with Zionism, which supported the existence of an independent Jewish state, religious and national consciousness, and *Humanität*, an idea crucial to Masaryk's conception of the Czech nation. Rádl was in favour of 'assimilation', but only the kind that did not lead to homogenization. He was thus reacting to the then prevailing tone in the Czech-Jewish press, which promoted radical assimilation.[33]

Supporters of the organised Czech-Jewish movement did not look favourably upon Masaryk's sympathies for Zionism. The lawyer and writer Otakar Guth (1882–1943) sent Masaryk a letter, shortly after Masaryk had returned to Prague from exile in December 1918, in which he complains about the anti-Jewish pogroms in Bohemia and Moravia. He finishes the letter with the words: 'The Zionists belabour us Czech-Jews, in your name and on your authority. It is said you sympathize with them, not with us. I don't know how much of that is true, but I feel that my Czechness is such an essential part of my being that no power on Earth could take it away from me.'[34]

A few days later, Masaryk received a delegation of the Jewish National Council – Brod and Singer together with the chairman of Poale Sion, Ru-

---

[31] Michael A. Riff, 'The Ambiguity of Masaryk's Attitudes on the 'Jewish Question', in *T.G. Masaryk (1850–1937). Vol. 2. Thinker and Critic*, ed. Robert B. Pynsent (London, 1989), 85.

[32] For more on Rádl, see Bedřich Loewenstein, 'Ein tschechischer Denker der Krise Emanuel Rádl (1873–1942)', *Bohemia* 46, no. 1 (2005): 135–51, and also Tomáš Hermann and Anton Markoš, eds., *Emanuel Rádl – Scientist and Philosopher: Proceedings of the International Conference Commemorating the 130th Anniversary of the Birth and 60th Anniversary of the Death of Emanuel Rádl* (Prague, 2004).

[33] Emanuel Rádl, 'České židovství', *Rozhled*, no. 23 (1918): 4.

[34] AÚTGM, fond TGM – R, kr. 453, církve, složka židé 1918–1919, letter from Otakar Guth to T. G. Masaryk, 21 December 1918.

dolf Kohn. The Jewish nationalists informed Masaryk of a memorandum that the Jewish National Council had sent to the Czechoslovak National Committee (Národní výbor československý) on the day independence was declared, 28 October 1918; the committee had also stated its intention to write another memorandum to the National Assembly. The main part of the memorandum is a request for the legal recognition of Jewish nationality, and then a cautiously formulated query whether the National Assembly might not be planning also to welcome representatives of the Jewish nation into its ranks.[35]

Some Czech-Jewish officials reacted to the Jewish National Council representatives' meeting with Masaryk in a long letter to Masaryk. In it they write about antisemitism in the Czech Progressive Party (Česká strana pokroková) during World War I, antisemitism in Czech society in the first months of the Republic, and, more generally, they criticize the Zionists. The letter states, among other things:

> In this country Zionism is mostly the refuge of Jews whose sense of belonging to a nation has been neutered, who live according to the principle 'bissl böhmisch, bissl deutsch [a bit Bohemian, a bit German]'. The exceptions only prove the rule. The movement is inwardly 99 per cent German. Culturally in Bohemia there was always a kind of mixture of Orthodoxy (one need only look at the Bohemian Zionists' position on free-thought) and atheism.
>
> The orthodox are middle class; young people indulge in atheism. Zionism in Bohemia overlaps with the well-known great international movement, with which, however, it has only the name in common. Recently, Zionists in this country have been agitating to have the Jewish nationality recognized here as being distinct.
>
> We Czech Jews are calmly, but emphatically, taking a stand against this propaganda: in the days of the self-determination of nations, individuals must be granted self-determination. We Czech Jews feel completely Czech, and cannot be forced by any nationalities law to accept some other nationality – even Jewish. We therefore see in Bohemian Zionism a cultural and national danger, and refute it not as Jews, but as Czechs who know what its essence is.[36]

The Jewish nationalists, however, never tried to compel Jews who were linguistically German or Czech to declare Jewish nationality. Masaryk probably knew more about the character of Zionism in Bohemia than many Czech-Jews. In contrast to the orientation expressed in the Czech-

---

[35] Ibid., memorandum of 31 December 1918.
[36] AÚTGM, fond TGM – R, kr. 453, církve, složka židé 1918–1919, letter from the Czech-Jewish organisations to the president, 3 January 1919.

Jewish organisations' letter, the cultural orientation of the Bohemian Zionists was much closer to Masaryk's way of thinking than the politically or even militant Zionists of Poland or other eastern European countries. The Zionists of the Bohemian Lands put forward a truly moderate national programme. This is not surprising, because they did not have to face any militant antisemitism or defend the Orthodox way of life (for example, observance of the Sabbath), since most of them were secularized. They were essentially concerned only with being able to declare Jewish nationality openly and, as a recognized national minority, to have a right to financial support from the state for Jewish institutions of the arts and education. By contrast, in Poland, where three and half million Jews lived between the two world wars, the Zionists also demanded, for example, proportional representation of Jewish deputies in the Sejm and the establishment of the institution of an adviser to the Polish government on Jewish affairs, who would be appointed by the Jewish National Council in Poland. Whereas the Czech politicians accepted the moderate demands of the Czech Zionists without difficulty, talks in Poland between the government and the local Jewish National Council broke down. The only things that the Polish government recognized were special schools for Jews and the observance of the Sabbath, which the Allies had demanded of Poland.[37]

Compared to Poland, Czechoslovakia tried to be on good terms with the Allies. The recognition of Jewish nationality was meant to be evidence of the democratic character of Czechoslovakia. After all, the Czechoslovak National Assembly adopted the explanatory memorandum to article 128 without being required to do so by the Treaty of Saint-Germain-en-Laye.[38] Similarly, during the antisemitic riots that attended the declaration of Czechoslovak independence, most Czech politicians spoke out against the riots, arguing that the way Czech society behaved towards the Jewish minority would be judged by people abroad as the measure of Czechoslovak democracy.[39]

In 1918-1919 Masaryk kept in touch with Zionists mainly through Max Brod, a member of the Jewish National Council.[40] Brod became the unofficial chief adviser to Masaryk on questions related to the Jews of

---

[37] Mendelsohn, *The Jews of East Central Europe between the World Wars*, 34-35.
[38] Ladislav Lipscher, 'Die soziale und politische Stellung der Juden in der ersten Republik', in *Die Juden in den böhmischen Ländern*, ed. Ferdinand Seibt (Munich and Vienna, 1983), 272.
[39] See, for example, the speech by Premier Karel Kramář to the Chamber of Deputies, 20 December 1918, Společná česko-slovenská digitální parlamentní knihovna, http://www.psp.cz/eknih/1918ns/ps/stenprot/012schuz/s012012.htm (accessed 25 January 2010) .
[40] See Gajan, 'Masaryk a Max Brod'.

Figure 2.2. Max Brod, a writer and translator, made not only Kafka internationally known, but also Hašek and Janáček and was a leading adviser to Masaryk on matters related to the Jews of the Bohemian Lands.

Czechoslovakia. Evidence of Masaryk's full confidence in him is provided by the many handwritten letters of recommendation, requests and statements on individual matters related to the Jews.[41] Brod explained to Masaryk problems linked, for example, to Jewish schools, and brought specific cases of antisemitism to his attention. He used his friendly relations with Masaryk also to the benefit of the activities of the Jewish nationalists. For example, he turned to Masaryk to get Alfred Engel (1881–1944) transferred to Brno, where he was needed as the headmaster of a local Jewish school, or to ensure that Angelo Goldstein (1889–1947), the secretary general of the Jewish National Council, would not be called up for military service.

In September 1919 Brod asked President Masaryk whether he could intervene to get Brod's employer, the director general of the Czechoslovak Post Office, to grant him a leave of absence of several months. He wanted time off to campaign in Slovakia. Masaryk immediately granted Brod's request and, moreover, summoned him to a special meeting.[42] This took

---

[41] See AÚTGM, fond TGM – R, box 453, církve, složka židé 1918–1919.
[42] Gajan, 'Masaryk a Max Brod', 37–38.

place several months before the adoption of the Czechoslovak Constitution and the explanatory memorandum to article 128. The minister of the Post and Communications, Alois Staněk, notified Masaryk that he had immediately granted Brod a three-month leave of absence 'to take part in organisational work aimed at getting the Jews established as a special nation and to educate them in understanding the interests of the republic'. In the same letter Staněk states that he had decided of his own accord to grant the poet Petr Bezruč (born Vladimír Vašek, 1867–1958), whose poems are full of antisemitic stereotypes, a leave of absence for an undetermined amount of time, to promote the young Czechoslovak Republic in Moravian Silesia.[43] The Masaryk Papers also contain a copy of a document with the heading 'Židovská otázka' (The Jewish Question), which expresses the view of the President and his recommendation to the Cabinet and the National Assembly. The copy, unfortunately, is undated and unsigned. The document states:

> It is desirable that the Government support this politically mature Jewish movement. In practice this means that Jewish nationality should be officially recognized. But because the so-called 'assimilationists' are against the movement, some caution is recommended. After careful consideration and having reached agreement with the interested parties, I recommend the following approach: let the enumeration of national minorities be omitted from acts of the National Assembly, so that the Jews need not be expressly mentioned; but the commentary [of the laws] can (in the language law or in the basic rights) contain the following provisions about the Jews: 'The Jews of the Czechoslovak Republic shall not be forced in the census, elections, or other political or official proceedings, even in instances concerning cultural and social institutions mentioned in the minority treaty (education, religious proceedings, social welfare) to declare themselves part of any ethnic (national) minority other than Jewish, regardless of what language of everyday communication they use.'[44]

The recommendation contained in the document was in essence enacted in article 128 and in its explanatory memorandum. If the text is indeed Masaryk's proposal to the government, it is further evidence of how

---

[43] AÚTGM, fond TGM – R, box 453, církve, složka židé 1918–1919, letter from the Minister of the Post and Communications to Masaryk, 20 September 1919. Bezruč was among the first Czech poets who focused on the social injustice in the Ostrava region and he often depicted Jews as the exploiters of the hard-working local Christian population. Despite his antisemitism, his poems were popular also among the writers of the Prague Circle and Brod translated some Bezruč works into German.

[44] AÚTGM, fond TGM – R, box 453, církve, složka židé 1918–1919, copy of an undated document titled 'Židovská otázka' (The Jewish Question).

he pushed in a fundamental way for the recognition of Jewish nationality under Czechoslovak law.

Masaryk was not, however, the only Czech statesman with a positive attitude towards the efforts of the Zionists. Other important supporters were, for example, the psychologist and positivist philosopher František Krejčí (1858–1934) and the philosopher Emanuel Rádl. Krejčí, as a Social Democrat deputy, presented a proposal for the recognition of Jewish nationality to a plenary session of the Chamber of Deputies of the National Assembly. The National Assembly, however, passed the bill on the recognition of Jewish nationality for purely pragmatic reasons. The whole debate seems somewhat paradoxical. Those opposed to the inclusion of Jewish nationality in the list of national minorities correctly argued that, among other things, the Jewish population of Czechoslovakia was not united by knowledge of any particularly Jewish language. Yet it was this 'shortcoming' of the Jewish nation that tipped the balance in their favour. Only in this way could the recognition of Jewish nationality reduce the numbers of other minorities, mainly German and Hungarian, in the statistics. The tactic was successful both in the census and in the application of the language law.

The Census

Neither the Treaty of Saint-Germain-en-Laye nor the Constitution contains any definition of nationality. The explanatory memorandum merely points out the problematic nature of the term. What guidelines, then, could one follow in deciding which nationality one belonged to? What does nationality (*národnost*) consist of? These questions were to be dealt with by special regulations related to the census.[45] The first such regulation was passed on 30 October 1920 and remained law until 1930. Under section 3, apart from sex, marital status, age, country of origin, religion and occupation, nationality was also to be declared. Section 8 then defines this more precisely: 'Nationality is understood as belonging to a people [*kmenová příslušnost*], whose chief external feature is usually one's mother tongue. Jews can declare Jewish nationality.'[46]

---

[45] A more detailed analysis of these special regulations and of discussions related to them has recently been offered by Ines Koeltzsch, 'Geteilte Stadt', 30–95.
[46] NA, fond Státní úřad statistický, 1931–1939, box 45, inv. č. 144, sign. P 3541/1. Quoted in Jaroslav Bubeník and Jiří Křesťan, 'Zjišťování národnosti a židovská otázka', in *Postavení a osudy židovského obyvatelstva v Čechách a na Moravě v letech 1939–1945*, ed. Helena Krejčová and Jana Svobodová (Prague, 1998), 13.

Whereas in the 1921 census Jews could declare Jewish nationality without having to demonstrate their Jewish identity in any way, the drafts of the new government regulation of late 1929 and early 1930 tended to suggest that this would not be possible in the 1930 census. A problematic point of the 1920 government regulation was 'the clear vacillation between the conception of nationality as an objectively given category and . . . its conception as a subjectively chosen matter of each individual or the lack of clarity in the relations between the two'.[47] Although section 20 states that the nationality which people 'themselves declare' (the possibility of subjective choice) is decisive, a census commissioner had the right to question people who were suspected of having given false information, or in order to instruct them or even to fill in the section on nationality 'according to their mother tongue' (the empirical criterion).[48]

A debate on the definition of nationality was started among the general public by Emanuel Rádl and Antonín Boháč (1882–1950), a docent of demographics at Prague, who was also an official at the State Office of Statistics (Státní úřad statistický). Rádl, whose book *Národnost jako vědecký problém* (Nationality as a Question for Scholars) was published in 1929,[49] defended the subjective conception. For him, the declaration of nationality was a matter of 'one's own free choice', and should be as free from external influences as possible. Boháč, by contrast, in an article in the *Československý statistický věstník* (Czechoslovak Bulletin of Statistics) advocated the view that in determining nationality one had to respect objective factors. Only in this way, he argued, could credible results be achieved, which could in most cases be verified. Furthermore, concerning objectively given factors in determining nationality, for the people filling in the census it would minimize the pressure exerted on them by nationalist movements or directly by the census commissioners.[50]

Amongst German-speaking academics the debate was carried on in the *Prager Tagblatt*, the largest liberal-democratic German-language daily newspaper in Bohemia. In the 16 June 1929 edition, the journalist Gustav Peters (1885–1959) clashed with the statistician Heinrich Rauchberg (1860–1938). Peters held a view similar to Rádl's. Nationality, he argued, should be a question of free will, and the question about nationality should be asked as in a secret ballot in a general election (and he recommended

---

[47] Jan Steiner, 'Národnost při sčítání lidu v roce 1930 a její zjišťování na Ostravsku,' *Slezský sborník* 85, no. 2 (1987): 114.
[48] Ibid.
[49] Emanuel Rádl, *Národnost jako vědecký problém* (Prague, 1929).
[50] Antonín Boháč, 'Rádlův sociologický rozbor naší národnostní statistiky', *Československý statistický věstník*, nos. 1–2 (1930): 1–22.

the term 'Bekenntnisdeutsche', that is, a sense of belonging to the German nation). Rauchberg, who originally taught statistics at Vienna University and then at the German university in Prague, was, on the other hand, in favour of language as the chief distinguishing feature.[51] As in the debate between Rádl and Boháč, in this debate too there is a clear difference in approach, one philosophical, the other pragmatically statistical.

Because of the great muddle in nationality questions a subcommittee of the statistics committee was eventually established to solve the problem before the coming census. The position of some members of the subcommittee was clear from the start. František Weyr (1879-1951), another statistician, lawyer and philosopher, and Krejčí were intent on the subjective conception of nationality, whereas Josef Mráz (1882-1934), Jan Auerhan (1880-1942), Emil Schönbaum (1882-1967), Boháč and Rauchberg proposed the objective conception. Similarly, the members of the subcommittee were divided over the question of Jewish nationality. Rauchberg, in particular, insisted on the criterion of language and consequently came out against the 'construct' of a Jewish nationality 'because Hebrew is a dead language and that so-called jargon [Yiddish] is a dialect of German, not a language in its own right'.[52] When Rauchberg was notified in the debate that Yiddish truly was of the nature of a Jewish national language, he admitted the legitimacy of Jewish nationality for those Jews who spoke Yiddish. Krejčí and Weyr then insisted: 'Jews are an exceptional phenomenon among nations. For them an exceptional provision should therefore hold, and even those Jews who do not speak Yiddish should have the right to declare Jewish nationality.'[53]

In a summary report for the general public, Boháč listed the individual proposals and reactions to them.[54] The last proposal was adopted on 9 January 1930. It contains the conception of the pragmatic statisticians, which won over the other views – namely, that nationality should be determined according to mother tongue, and that Jews too should conform to this criterion. The respondent could state Yiddish and also Hebrew as Jewish languages.

The proposal naturally filled the Jewish nationalists with indignation. In early February 1930, two members of parliament for the Jewish Party, Julius Reisz (1880-1976) and Ludvík Singer, presented a memorandum to František Tomášek (1871-1938), the chairman of the parliamentary group of the Czechoslovak Social Democratic Party, of which both Reisz

---

[51] Boháč, 'Národnost při druhém sčítání lidu', *Statistický obzor* 12, nos. 1-2 (1931): 15.
[52] Ibid., 17.
[53] Ibid., 18.
[54] Ibid., 14-30.

and Singer had been members. The memorandum mentions the decision of the constitution committee of the Czechoslovak Republic of 20 February 1920, where Jews in the new state would not be forced to declare themselves members of any nationality other than Jewish, even if they were without denomination or their mother tongue was Czech, German or some other language. A copy of the memorandum was sent by the Jewish Party deputies also to the Head of the Czechoslovak President's Office. In the cover letter Singer wrote:

> We are well aware that we are greatly indebted to the President of the Republic for that decision. We therefore ask you, sir, to be so kind as to bring to the President's attention the extremely unfavourable proposal of the State Office of Statistics and our memorandum. We are asking this favour of you because a government decision along the lines of the proposal of the State Office of Statistics would be a great blow to our whole movement, primarily in the moral sense.[55]

In his letter of 13 February, the Head of the President's Office replied:

> Whether nationality, for the purpose of the census and for the civil service, is a purely subjective matter or whether it can be determined from its objective features is a matter of dispute for scholars. One would be ill advised to become involved in this academic question. The admittance of Jewish nationality in the last census went beyond the basic idea upon which the definition was built and which judged nationality primarily according to language. That happened for political reasons, in order to weaken the Hungarian and German nationalities, but it created a new, sixth nationality in the state, and to a certain extent weakened the Czechoslovak nationality. These political aspects were overestimated as is evident from the fact that the current change was proposed by nationalist Czech members of the Office of Statistics. . . . If petitioners argue that the whole world considered our position progressive, that fact has to be appreciated, even though it is largely, or almost entirely, a matter of the Jewish public. This reputation of ours will not suffer, because, as has already been said, Jewish-speaking [meaning Hebrew or Yiddish-speaking] people continue to retain the right to be counted in the census as Jews. It could not have a bad effect on world public opinion, if we got rid of an aberration that in the last census we created only for the Jews by our basing nationality solely on a subjective conviction. As far as I know, we were the only ones in the world to do that.[56]

---

[55] AKPR, D 1274/30, letter from Ludvík Singer to the Head of the President's Office, 10 February 1930.
[56] Ibid., letter from the Head of the Czechoslovak President's Office to Singer, 15 February 1930.

As is clear from this reply, the Czech statisticians noted in 1930 that there were more and more Czech-speaking Jewish nationalists, who, by choosing Jewish nationality, were weakening the Czechoslovak camp. As we shall see, this was indeed the case. The last claim of the report from the Office of the Czechoslovak President, that Czechoslovakia was the only country in the world to recognize a citizen's choice of Jewish nationality, is, however, untrue. The Jews of Poland, Lithuania (for a while) and the Ukraine could also declare Jewish nationality.[57]

Other reactions to the decision of the State Office of Statistics may be usefully divided into those that supported the proposal and insisted on the criterion of language and those, on the other hand, that demanded recognition of Jewish nationality without any objective criterion. The Czech-Jews, who sought to have Jews included among the Czech nation,[58] and liberal German Jews were naturally satisfied with the proposal of the statistics subcommittee.[59]

The opponents' camp was bigger, but the arguments of those in it differed radically from each other. Various people reached similar conclusions by considerably different arguments. Rádl addressed the matter again in *Právo lidu*, the daily newspaper of the Social Democrats. He argued that nationality was a matter of conscience, and that no one had a right to force anyone else to make a decision or even to simplify the decision-making. But even the German antisemites of Czechoslovakia were in favour of the subjective conception of nationality. In the *Sudetendeutsche Tages-Zeitung* they wrote that they 'did not consider Jews members of the German nation' and would therefore welcome German-speaking Jews declaring Jewish nationality. The position of the Zionists was also supported by some Czech newspapers, particularly the press of the National Democratic Party and the Agrarian Party – for example *Národní listy* (National Mail), *Národ* (The Nation), *Národní politika* (National Politics), *Večer* (Evening) and *Samostatnost* (Independence). They justified their position by stating that many Jews who declared Jewish nationality weakened the other national minorities, particularly the German and Hungarian.[60]

The fact that the same aim brought together groups of people of opposing views runs like a red thread throughout the history of the Jews of Bohemia in the interwar years. As we shall see, coalitions of various

---

[57] See, Henry Abramson, *A Prayer for the Government: Ukrainians and Jews in Revolutionary Times, 1917–1920* (Cambridge, 1999); Sarunas Liekis, *A State within a State? Jewish Autonomy in Lithuania 1918–1925* (Vilnius, 2003).
[58] 'Sčítání', *Rozvoj*, no. 7 (1930): 3.
[59] Civis judaeus [Jacob Joel Braun], 'Die neue Volkszählung', *Jüdische Presse*, 15 February 1930.
[60] Boháč, 'Národnost při druhém sčítání lidu', 23–27.

kinds were formed. Quite often, however, participants in the debate were divided into two opposing camps very much as in the debate about the means of determining Jewish nationality. Zionists, emphasizing national identity, were a thorn in the side both of Czech-Jews (who otherwise came out energetically against the German-speaking Jews) and of German Jews. The Zionists could find support from a number of liberal figures among the Czechoslovak politicians. Often, however, their aims at least partly overlapped also with those of the spiteful antisemites.

The debate on determining nationality in the forthcoming census was ended by the Ministry of the Interior, which presented the final definition of nationality in *Národní listy* and the *Prager Tagblatt* on 27 May 1930. Arguing that the matter had become political, the Ministry, regardless of the proposals of the special section of the State Office of Statistics, pushed through the following version: 'Nationality is to be understood as ethnic affiliation, whose main external feature is mother tongue. A nationality other than what corresponds to one's mother tongue may be stated only if the person filling out the census form does not speak his mother tongue either with his family or at home, and has completely mastered the language of that nationality. Jews may, however, declare Jewish nationality. Only one nationality may be stated.'[61] Jews could therefore again declare Jewish nationality without having to demonstrate knowledge of one of the Jewish languages or membership of a Jewish Community. The involvement of the Ministry of the Interior therefore only demonstrates the claim of the historian Jaroslav Kučera that the preparation of the rules and regulations of the statistics of nationality in interwar Czechoslovakia was not a 'highly scientific affair', but rather 'some sort of cross-section of the administrative needs of the State and the requirements of the discipline of statistics, and also of political motivations and aims'.[62]

Though Jews were recognized as a national minority in the First Republic, they were not a linguistic minority. Under the special language law of 29 February 1920, which was related to section 129 of the Czechoslovak Constitution, the 'Czechoslovak' language was declared the official language of the republic. Linguistic communication, however, was meant to be facilitated in all spheres for linguistic minorities where, in the last census, people speaking the same language, other than Czechoslovak, constituted at least twenty per cent of the population. As we have seen, however, the state could properly estimate the language of the population only from the information about nationality (in other words, in the oppo-

---
[61] Ibid., 28–29.
[62] Kučera, 'Politický či přirozený národ?', 555.

site way done in the Monarchy, when the size of a national minority was judged from the number of people speaking a certain language). Nowhere in Czechoslovakia did the Jews manage to achieve the twenty per cent minimum. Compared to Poles, Germans and Hungarians, Jews could not therefore claim the right to use Yiddish in communication with government offices (a right that some Slovak Jews and particularly Jews from Subcarpathian Ruthenia would have liked to have).

Though they did not help themselves in this way, the Jews could harm other national minorities, for example in the Košice (Kaschau) region of Slovakia, where Hungarians constituted, according to the 1921 census, 19.03 per cent of the population. Since part of the Jewish population had declared Jewish nationality, though it spoke Hungarian, the advantages stemming from the language law did not apply to the Hungarian minority of Košice.[63]

The Pitfalls of Statistics

The institution of the census played a key role for the Czechoslovak state. First, as Benedict Anderson has shown, the census (in addition to maps and museums) was the most important institution of power in helping to create the illusion of a national community.[64] The census forced the population to think of nationalities as separate communities, each based mostly on a different language. As Anderson rightly puts it: 'The fiction of the census is that everyone is in it, and that everyone has one – and only one – extremely clear place.'[65] Second, for multinational states like Czechoslovakia and Poland, the census results were meant to strengthen the authority of the ruling nation (the state-nation). This goal influenced the choice of the categories that were meant to constitute nationality.

On the other hand, concerning the Jewish population, another factor was whether Jews were compatible with the 'master narrative' of the state-nation. This thesis should be illustrated by a comparison of census categories and their interpretation in Poland and Czechoslovakia. The Republic of Czechoslovakia, like Poland, adopted the concept of nationality from Austria-Hungary. Before World War I the Austrian authorities estimated the size of the national minorities with the help of a part of the census, which asked the respondent to state his or her language of everyday communication (*obcovací řeč*, in Czech, or *Umgangsprache*, in German). Later,

---

[63] Stillschweig, 'Nationalitätenrechtliche Stellung der Juden in der Tschechoslowakei', 45-46.
[64] Anderson, *Imagined Communities*, 163-85.
[65] Ibid., 166.

in both Poland and Czechoslovakia, one's mother tongue became the basis for determining one's nationality. The reason for this change, at least in Czechoslovakia, was the assumption that many adults whose mother tongue was Czech nevertheless used German because of its former importance in the Habsburg Monarchy. In Czechoslovakia, however, the census formulas asked each respondent to state his or her nationality (*národnost*); the word was followed immediately by the term 'mother tongue' (*mateřský jazyk*) in brackets. In Poland, the authorities did not add the word 'nationality' to this question and the size of the national minorities was ultimately assessed according to the replies to the question about mother tongue (in Polish, *język ojczysty*, that is, the language of the father). In contrast to the Habsburg monarchy, where it was considered a dialect of German, Yiddish, together with Hebrew, was accepted in interwar Poland as a language of the Jewish people.

In Czechoslovakia, as we have seen, adding the term nationality to this question enabled the state authorities to offer Jews Jewish nationality even if they did not have Yiddish or Hebrew as their mother tongue. Jews would then be helping to increase the authority of the Czechs and Slovaks over the Germans of the country. In the census, many people of Jewish nationality would have otherwise had to state a nationality other than Czechoslovak. On the other hand, no one forced them to do so and many Czech and Slovak-speaking Jews thus directly strengthened the position of the Czechoslovaks.

In Poland, the statistical data from the census were immediately challenged. All the national minorities – Germans, Ukrainians, Jews, Belorussians, Lithuanians and Russians – disagreed with the numbers stated by the Polish Central Statistics Office.[66] Regarding the Jewish population, a discrepancy between the political aim of underestimating the national minorities and the concept of a Polish nation is obvious. In 1931, for example, there were, according to the census, 3,113,900 people of the 'Mosaic faith' in Poland. Of them, 2,489,000 claimed to have Yiddish as their mother tongue, 243,500 Hebrew and 371,800 Polish. According to the concept of one's mother tongue being the chief criterion for defining a nation, more than 371,000 of Poland's Jews were of Polish nationality. By interpreting these data, the Polish politicians as well as the Jewish nationalists struggled between the linguistic and the religious criteria as being the basis for a Jewish nationality.[67] Irena Hurwic-Nowakowska claims that

---

[66] Stephan Horak, *Poland and Her National Minorities, 1919–39* (New York, 1961), 80.
[67] See, e.g. 'Kwestja narodowościowa w programie drugiego powszechnego spisu ludności Rzeczypospolitej Polskiej. Wywiad z Generalnym Komisarzem Spisowym p. Dr. Rajmundem Buławskim', *Sprawy narododościowe* VI, no. 1 (1932): 1–27; 'Interpelacja koła żydowskiego i odpowiedź p. Ministra spraw wewnętrznych w sprawie rubryki „narodowość" na

in contrast to other national minorities, Jews in Poland were rather defined by religion. She writes: 'A Pole of the Mosaic faith, as well as a Pole without confession but with Jewish origin, was . . . a meaningless concept in the contemporaneous reality of the official administration, as well as in the social reality of daily life [in the interwar period].'[68]

To identify nationality with language would in many ways be bad scholarship. The changes in 'mother tongue' and 'language of everyday communication' in the course of several generations is well illustrated, for example, by the history of the Brod family, as described by the journalist Petr Brod (b. 1951), for it shows the change in linguistic identity of many Jews of Bohemia in the course of the nineteenth and twentieth centuries. He writes that in the last four generations of the Brod family 'the family's mother tongue was different in each generation, and, to add to the confusion, it was not always the language of the mother'.[69] Petr Brod's great-grandfather grew up in a household where Yiddish was probably spoken. His grandfather, living in rural Bohemia made Czech his language. His father grew up in Prague, attending German schools, and in Petr Brod's time the family again returned to Czech.

Although from the beginning of the twentieth century the Jews of Bohemia increasingly preferred to speak Czech rather than German, it was true also during the First Republic that a high proportion of the Jewish population was bilingual. This phenomenon was particularly striking in Prague, where people fluent in both Czech and German began to be called 'utraquists' (humorously alluding to the moderate faction of the Hussites, who maintained, against Roman Catholic practice, that the Eucharist should be administered 'in both kinds', as bread and wine, to the whole congregation). Dimitry Shumsky therefore recommends not differentiating between Czech and German Jews in Bohemia and he instead promotes the term 'Czecho-German Jewry', which, he argues, better describes the cultural mosaic of the Jews of Bohemia in the period before the fall of the Habsburg Monarchy.[70] Robert Luft also questions the results of the censuses to determine the nationality structure of the population of Bo-

---

formularzu spisowym ludności oraz naruszania praw języka żydowskiego w instrukcji spisowej', *Sprawy narododościowe* VI, no. 1 (1932): 91–93. I thank Stephan Stach for recommending this Polish journal to me.

[68] Irena Hurwic-Nowakowska, *Żydzi polscy (1947–50): Analiza więzi społecznej ludności żydowskiej* (Warsaw 1996), xiii.

[69] Peter Brod, 'Židé v Československu', in *Židé v Sudetech* (Prague, 2000), 281.

[70] Dimitry Shumsky, 'Historiografia, leumiut ve-du-leumiut: yahadut czecho-germanit, zionei prag u-mekorot ha-gisha ha-du-leumit shel Hugo Bergmann', *Zion* 69, no. 1 (2004): 45–80; idem, 'Introducing Intellectual and Political History to the History of Everyday Life: Multiethnic Cohabitation and Jewish Experience in Fin-de-Siècle Bohemia', *Bohemia* 46, no. 1 (2005): 39–67.

hemia in Austria-Hungary and points to the bilingualism of a significant part of the population.[71]

Because of their fluency in both languages Jews contributed immeasurably to Czechs' and Germans' learning about each others' cultures. This was true as early as in the nineteenth century. For example, Siegfried Kapper (1820-1879) was, in 1844, the first to translate the Romantic verse tale *Máj* (May, 1836) by Karel Hynek Mácha (1810-1836) into German, a work which was fiercely criticized when first published, but which later became a prominent Czech national poem. In the early twentieth century and the interwar years, the role of Bohemian Jews as intermediaries became particularly clear. Among the important proponents of Czech culture and translators of Czech and German literature, one would name at least Friedrich Adler (1857-1938), Otokar Fischer (1883-1938), Pavel (Paul) Eisner (1889-1958), Rudolf Fuchs (1890-1942), Otto Pick (1887-1940), Camill Hoffmann (1878-1944) and Max Brod (who brought the writer Jaroslav Hašek [1883-1923] and the composer Leoš Janáček [1854-1928] to the attention of western Europe).[72]

When Jews were deciding what language or nationality they should choose, a great role was also played by how comfortable or uncomfortable they felt in their society. A good example is Hermann Kafka, the father of Franz Kafka, who, after moving to Prague, preferred to use German, the language of the Prague middle classes. He brought up his children speaking German and sent them to German schools. In the 1890 and 1900 censuses, however, probably under social pressure, he declared his language of everyday communication as Czech, as did all the other members of the Kafka family.[73]

---

[71] See Robert Luft, 'Nationale Utraquisten in Böhmen: Zur Problematik "nationaler Zwischenstellungen" am Ende des 19. Jahrhunderts', in *Allemands, Juifs et Tchèques à Prague 1890–1924*, ed. Maurice Godé, Jacques Le Rider and Françoise Mayer (Montpellier, 1996), 37-51. Concerning the problems of stating nationality in the censuses of 1921 and 1930, particularly in Teschen/Cieszyn, Silesia, see Jerzy Tomaszewski, 'Spisy ludnosci w Czechosłowacji w 1921 i 1930 r. jako zródło do badania stosunków narodowosciowych', *Slezský Sborník. Acta Silesiaca* 96, vol. 2 (1998): 95-105. The limits of the census in revealing national identity in Prague are discussed in Ines Koeltsch, 'Die gezählte Stadt. Tschechen, Juden und Deutsche im Prager Zensus (1900-1930)', in Peter Becher, *Praha–Prag 1900–1945: Literaturstadt zweier Sprachen, vieler Mittler*, 9-20.

[72] For the Bohemian Jews' (mostly from Prague) role as mediator, see, in particular, Koetzsch, 'Geteilte Stadt', 201-34; Hillel J. Kieval, 'Choosing to Bridge: Revisiting the Phenomenon of Cultural Mediation', *Bohemia* 46, no. 1 (2005): 15-27; Peter Becher and Anna Knechtel, eds., *Praha-Prag 1900-1945. Literaturstadt zweier Sprachen* (Passau, 2010). For Max Brod, see Barbora Šrámková, *Max Brod und die tschechische Kultur* (Wuppertal, 2010), and Gaëlle Vassogne, *Max Brod in Prag: Identität und Vermittlung* (Tübingen, 2009).

[73] Kurt Krolop, 'Zu den Erinnerungen Anna Lichtensterns an Franz Kafka', *Acta Universitatis Carolinae – Philologica*, no. 5 (1968): 56. See also Marek Nekula, 'Česko-německý bil-

Another fundamental problem regarding national identity was that whereas officially the declaration of one's language of everyday communication was connected with an ethnic identity, many Jews as well as Christians often tended to understand language solely as a means of communication. They were therefore satisfied with the fully geographical-cultural term 'böhmisch', which was, until World War I, used in official documents as a synonym for Czech.[74] From the 1880s, however, the pressure to decide between the Czech and German peoples became increasing acute. It was impossible not to belong to one or the other camp. Great importance therefore began to be attached to which language of everyday communication one stated in the census. Gary Cohen has convincingly demonstrated that some Jews had difficulty stating their language of everyday communication, and he cites the example of the family of Bohumil Bondy (1832–1907). Bondy, a Jewish industrialist, was a devoted proponent of the Old Czech Party, and in 1880 and 1890 stated Czech as the language of everyday communication used by himself, his children and

Figure 2.3. Bohumil Bondy, Kaiserlicher Rat, a member of the Czech Chamber of Commerce, an Old Czech deputy to the Bohemian Diet, and an honorary member of the Czech-Jewish Students' Society.

---

ingvismus', in Češi a Němci: Dějiny – kultura – politika, ed. Walter Koschmal, Marek Nekula, and Joachim Rogall (Prague and Litomyšl, 2002), 152–57; and Marek Nekula, Franz Kafkas Sprachen: '. . . in einem Stockwerk des innern babylonischen Turmes . . .' (Tübingen, 2003).

[74] See Tilman Berger, 'Böhmisch oder Tschechisch? Der Streit über die adäquate Benennung der Landessprache der böhmischen Länder zu Anfang des 20. Jahrhunderts', in Franz Kafka im sprachnationalen Kontext seiner Zeit: Sprache und nationale Identität in öffentlichen Institutionen der böhmischen Länder, ed. Marek Nekula, Ingrid Fleischmann and Albrecht Greule (Cologne, Weimar and Vienna, 2007), 167–82.

his servants. His wife, who came from Vienna, declared German as her language of everyday communication. Bondy's response, explains Cohen, 'signified his social and political identification with the Czechs even if he may have spoken a considerable amount of German each day. In all likelihood, Mrs. Bondy's statement indicated simply that she did not speak Czech, not that she wanted to affirm a German identity at a time when her husband sat in the Old Czechs' highest councils'.[75]

The problem in the census, however, was not only in the ambiguity of the criterion of mother tongue. Jewish nationality was not determined by anything apart from the will of the person choosing or rejecting it. This possibility was something new for the Jews of Czechoslovakia. In the period before World War I the national feeling also of the most ardent Zionists was not at all reflected in the statistics. In the first census, conducted in 1921, almost 54 per cent of the Czechoslovaks who declared themselves as being of the Jewish religion also declared Jewish nationality.[76]

Choosing Jewish nationality, however, did not automatically mean supporting the Zionist movement and it would therefore often be misleading to interpret this census data as a mirror of the national identities of the Jewish population. One has to be cautious in interpreting these data, because they were often misinterpreted by the state as well as by the Jewish nationalists themselves.[77] In contrast to the census, which was a key political question (and many Jews understood it as such), national identity, as I see it, was a subjective category that was largely dependent on social ties. In essence only a small proportion of those who in the Czechoslovak census declared Jewish nationality were active Zionists. Evidence of this is the number of payers of the shekel, the obligatory financial contribution of each Zionist to the coffers of the world Zionist Organization. In 1921 there were 8,685 of them throughout Czechoslovakia. That is a mere 4.5 per cent of the 180,855 Jews who declared Jewish nationality. In 1930, when 186,642 Czechoslovaks declared their nationality as Jewish, the Zionist statistics show 15,472 payers of the shekel.[78] There was, then, a marked growth in the number of politically conscious Zionists, that is, 8.3 per cent of all people of Jewish nationality. Nevertheless, a large disproportion remained between the number of people declaring Jewish nationality and the number of active Zionists.

Most of the Jews declaring Jewish nationality were in Subcarpathian Ruthenia and Slovakia. As Rebekah Klein-Pejšová has convincingly dem-

---

[75] Cohen, *The Politics of Ethnic Survival*, 67–68.
[76] *Československá statistika*, vol. 37, 2*, tab. 3.
[77] For a detailed analysis of the misuse of census results by Jewish nationalists, see Lichtenstein, 'Making Jews at Home', 72–123.
[78] Oskar K. Rabinowicz, 'Czechoslovak Zionism: Analecta to a History', in *The Jews of Czechoslovakia*, vol. II (Philadelphia and New York, 1971), 124.

onstrated, the concept of Jewish nationality offered a unique opportunity to unite otherwise distinct parts of the Jewish community in Slovakia.[79] This, again, did not automatically mean that they were Zionists. In Subcarpathian Ruthenia most of the Jews who declared Jewish nationality were Hasidim, and most of them were highly critical of Zionism. Moreover, it took several years before a network of Zionist organisations was established in Subcarpathian Ruthenia. In Slovakia, on the other hand, Agudas Yisroel (or Agudat Yisra'el), an organisation of Orthodox Jews, was strong, and it was also an uncompromising opponent of Zionism.[80]

But also in Bohemia and Moravia Jews who did not support Zionism often chose Jewish nationality. They did so either simply because they wanted to avoid having to choose other nationalities or wanted to express their loyalty to the Czechoslovak state: many understood what the young Czechoslovak Republic expected from them. Rather than add their voices to the Germans or Hungarians, they opted for the new alternative. When we compare the number of people of Jewish religion who spoke German or Hungarian before World War I with the numbers from the statistics of the First Republic, it is clear that many of them declared Jewish nationality after the war. To illustrate this I cite the figures for Bohemia, even though this trend is much clearer in the other parts of the republic. In Bohemia in 1910, 51.5 per cent of the people of Jewish religion declared Czech as their language of everyday communication and 48.4 per cent declared German. In 1921 almost 14 per cent fewer Jews declared German nationality, less than two per cent fewer Jews declared themselves Czechoslovak and 14.8 per cent Jewish.[81]

For many people, the choice of Jewish nationality also meant a welcome opportunity to declare their Jewish identity in more than a merely religious sense. Many people realized that Judaism meant more to them than membership of the Church meant to Christians.

---

[79] Rebekah Klein-Pejšová, '"Abondon Your Role as Exponents of the Magyars": Contested Jewish Loyalty in Interwar (Czecho)Slovakia', *Association for Jewish Studies Review* 33, no. 2 (November 2009): 359-62. See also idem, 'Among the Nationalities: Jewish Refugees, Jewish Nationality, and Czechoslovak Statebuilding', PhD thesis, Columbia University 2007, 214.

[80] For more about this organisation, see Gertrude Hirschler, 'The History of Agudath Israel in Slovakia (1918-1939)', in *The Jews of Czechoslovakia*, 155-72. For the establishment and development of the Agudat Israel movement, see Alan L. Mittleman, *The Politics of Torah: The Jewish Political Tradition and the Founding of Agudat Israel* (Albany, 1996).

[81] *Československá statistika*, vol. 37, 2*, tab. 4. The case was similar in Prague. In 1900, 54 per cent of the Prague Jews declared their language of everyday communication to be Czech; 44.4 per cent declared German. In 1921, 53.6 per cent of the Prague Jews declared Czechoslovak nationality, 25.4 per cent German, and 20.1 per cent Jewish. See František Friedmann, *Mravnost či opportunita? Několik poznámek k anketě akad. spolku "Kapper" v Brně* (Prague, 1927), 25.

Similarly, we may question the information value of the statistics of people of the Jewish religion who declared their nationality as Czechoslovak or German. Not all Czechoslovak Jews of course were Czech-Jews, that is to say, supporters of the organised Czech-Jewish movement. This is important to note, because as part of their propaganda Czech-Jews often interpreted the census results to mean that everyone of the Jewish religion of Czechoslovak nationality was among their supporters.

Further evidence that the national identity of the Jews in the First Republic can hardly be discerned by looking only at columns in a census form is provided by the number of votes won by the Jewish Party. This party was only loosely connected to Zionist organisations, partly so that it could claim the right to represent a large proportion of the Jewish population. Nonetheless, supporters of Zionism ran the Jewish Party headquarters. The party set itself the task of defending the interests of the Jewish population in the broadest sense – namely, in questions of religion, national interests and protection against antisemitism. The main points that Jewish Party deputies were concerned with were ultimately the problems of the Jews in Subcarpathian Ruthenia and east Slovakia – in particular the questions of Hebrew schools and Czechoslovak citizenship for Jews originally from Romania or the Ukraine.

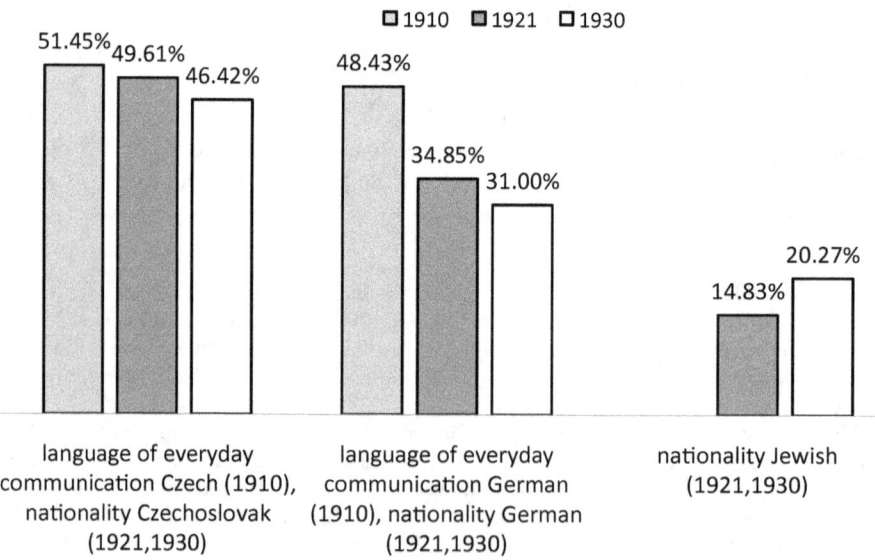

Graph 2.1. The languages of everyday communication (according to the 1910 census) and nationalities (according to the 1921 and 1930 censuses) of people of the Jewish religion in Bohemia.

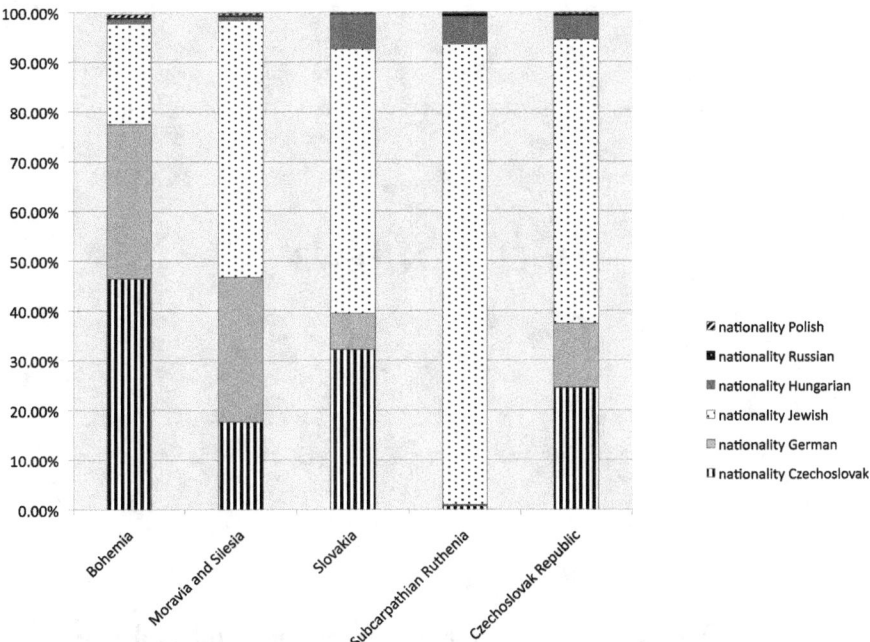

Graph 2.2. The national composition of people of the Jewish faith in Bohemia, Moravia and Silesia, Slovakia and Subcarpathian Ruthenia, according to the 1930 census.

It is safe to assume that the Jewish Party won support chiefly from Jews in Slovakia and Subcarpathian Ruthenia. Many of the Jews of Slovakia and Subcarpathian Ruthenia, who considered Jews a national community, had no intention of voting for the Jewish Party, simply because it was led by Zionists. In Bohemia, on the other hand, the Jewish Party won, for example, 22,317 votes in 1925, yet in Bohemia in 1921, only 11,156 people declared Jewish nationality. Furthermore, the voting age was 21 years, whereas the census includes even babies. The Jewish Party must therefore have received votes from a relatively large percentage of people of the Jewish faith, who in the census declared Czechoslovak and German nationality.[82] They were, then, people for whom being rooted in Czech or German culture meant so much that they declared Czechoslovak or German nationality in the census. In the elections, however, they preferred to vote for a party that defended the minority rights of Jews and emphasized the national character of Judaism.

---

[82] Friedmann, *Mravnost či oportunita?*, 29–30.

Chapter 3

GERMAN JEWS

The Adoption of the German Language and Culture in the Nineteenth Century

In the first half of the nineteenth century, the period of Jewish emancipation, by far most Bohemian Jews used German as the language of everyday communication and adopted German culture in general. Almost no work on the topic fails to mention that the rapid integration of the Bohemian Jews into the German cultural community was brought about by the reforms of Emperor Joseph II. His decree establishing, in particular, Jewish schools with German as the language of instruction had far-reaching influence on the cultural orientation of the Jewish population. An examination in German-language proficiency also became a condition for many occupations, including that of rabbi. To a large extent, however, the reforms of Joseph II suited the young Jewish scholars of the time. They had been influenced by the ideology of the Haskalah (the Jewish Enlightenment). Adherents of the Haskalah, called Maskilim, had also strongly objected to the original Jewish education in cheders (elementary schools) and yeshivot. The curriculum of those schools consisted primarily of knowledge of the Torah, the Talmud and other key religious texts. The language of instruction was Yiddish or at least *Judendeutsch*, a Jewish dialect of German.[1] Maskilim, on the other hand, influenced especially by the teaching

---

[1] According to Kestenberg-Gladstein, most of the Jews of Bohemia in the first half of the nineteenth century spoke *böhmisch-mährisches Judendeutsch*, a Jewish dialect of German,

of the Berlin philosopher Moses Mendelssohn (1729-1786), promoted schools of a secular nature, with an emphasis on the natural sciences and the humanities. In the new schools the language of instruction was to be German, not Yiddish, a language the Maskilim held in contempt as the jargon of the ghetto, and the teaching of biblical Hebrew was to be kept to a minimum. The pupils (including – in a break with tradition – girls) were now to learn western languages, particularly French.

This linking of the decrees of an absolute monarch to the ideology of the Haskalah probably enabled the strong union of the Jews not only of Bohemia, but also of all Cisleithania, with German culture. The reforms of Joseph II and the endeavours of the Maskilim stemmed, however, from various impulses. Joseph II was led to reform particularly by a desire to establish the legal standing of his subjects so that they were most directly subject to him. He then pushed for German at Jewish schools and elsewhere because he wanted to establish it as the administrative language of the Monarchy.

The Maskilim, on the other hand, pushed for German secular education because they considered it a recipe for 'extricating' themselves from the backward, unhealthy life of the ghetto. It was mostly Maskilim who became enthusiastic teachers at the newly established state-run Jewish schools. The best ones then taught at what was known as the 'Hauptschule' in Prague, a college for future teachers at Jewish schools. Among the most important figures of the Jewish Enlightenment in the Bohemian Lands were Naftali Herz Homberg (1749-1841) of Libeň (Lieben, now part of Prague) and Peter Beer (1758-1838) of Nový Bydžov (Neu-Bydžov), both of whom were in close touch with the centre of the Haskalah, Berlin.[2] The Germanization of the Jews of Bohemia did not proceed as quickly as the Maskilim had imagined. In an article in *Sulamith* (the first Jewish monthly in German), in 1809, Beer complains that despite the introduction of German Jewish schools most Jews still did not speak German well and used a Bohemian version of *Judendeutsch* instead.[3]

---

which differed from other countries by expressions derived from Czech. See Ruth Kestenberg-Gladstein, *Neuere Geschichte der Juden in den böhmischen Ländern: Das Zeitalter der Aufklärung 1780-1830*, vol. I (Tübingen, 1969), 358.

[2] Homberg compiled a handbook of the Jewish religion and morals in German, *Ein religiösmoralisches Lehrbuch für die Jugend israelitischer Nation* (1812). Knowledge of its contents was required, for example, of all Jews about to get married and they did not receive state permission to marry until successfully passing an exam in the subject. For Beer, see Louise Hecht, *Ein jüdischer Aufklärer in Böhmen: Der Pädagoge und Reformer Peter Beer* (1758-1838) (Cologne, 2008). See also Iveta Cermanová, 'Židovské osvícenství v Praze', *Židovská ročenka* 5768 (2007-08), 42-63.

[3] Kestenberg-Gladstein, *Neuere Geschichte der Juden*, 164. More focused research on Prague Jewish German has been carried out by Leopold Schnitzler, *Prager Judendeutsch: Ein Beitrag zur Erforschung des älteren Prager Judendeutsch in lautlicher und insbesondere in lexikalischer Beziehung* (Gräfling bei München, 1966).

It was typical of Bohemia that the ideas of the Haskalah that were connected also with moderate change in the Jewish liturgy were quickly taken up despite initial resistance. The chief rabbi of Bohemia, Ezechiel Landau (1713-1793), readily accepted the creation of Jewish schools. On the other hand, he ensured that the study of the Torah and Talmud, unlike in the German lands, would not be limited in the school curricula here.[4] Perhaps because of the relatively quiet beginnings of the Jewish Enlightenment in the Bohemian Lands, and later because of the small number of Orthodox Jews, the Jewish community did not split into Orthodox and Reform wings in Bohemia and Moravia. In Prussia, in the second half of the nineteenth century, by contrast, the Jewish community split into two independent congregations with their own independent administration, and in Hungary it split into three.[5]

Ruth Kestenberg-Gladstein, the author of a large work about the Haskalah in Bohemia, argues that it had another particular feature. The Maskilim in Bohemia, according to her, put far more emphasis on ethnic features of Jewishness. Though they spoke out in favour of Jewish integration into majority society, they also emphasized the solidarity and special nature of the Bohemian Jewish community. These elements of the Jewish Enlightenment in Bohemia may, according to Kestenberg-Gladstein, also be considered the germ of the later Jewish national movement.[6] Hillel Kieval disagrees with Kestenberg-Gladstein's conception of the national character of the Jewish Enlightenment in Bohemia. Referring to a text by Israel ben Ezechiel Landau, son of the Chief Rabbi, he clearly demonstrates that the ideas of the Prague Maskilim were not particularly different from those of their German colleagues.[7]

The adoption of German culture, particularly the language, by the Jews of Bohemia was the result not only of the reforms of Joseph II and the ideology of the Haskalah. Another important factor was the Jews' gratitude to Joseph II for having radically improved their legal and social standing. The Jews in the mid-nineteenth century were also grateful to the German liberals, who managed to have included in the new constitution of the Austrian half of the Dual Monarchy, which was established with the Ausgleich of 1867, full equality of the Cisleithanian population regardless of confession. This happened in the absence of the Czech politicians, who

---

[4] Kieval, *Languages of Community*, 54-56.
[5] See Steven M. Lowenstein, 'Das religiöse Leben', in *Deutsch-jüdische Geschichte in der Neuzeit*, vol. III, *Umstrittene Integration 1871-1918*, ed. Steven M. Lowenstein et al. (Munich, 1997), 101-22; Jacob Katz, *A House Divided: Orthodoxy and Schism in Nineteenth-Century Central European Jewry* (Hanover and London, 1998).
[6] Kestenberg-Gladstein, *Neuere Geschichte der Juden*, 284-89.
[7] Kieval, *Languages of Community*, 51-52.

were disappointed by the Dual Monarchy solution and therefore boycotted the sessions of the Austrian Parliament.

Until 1867, the language of instruction at Jewish schools that had been established in the reign of Joseph II could not change either. Even if the Jews had wanted to change it, they could not do so, because the administration of German Jewish schools was in the hands of the state authorities. They insisted on the maintenance of the German character of the schools. Those in charge, for example, of the German-Jewish school in Kostelec nad Černými lesy (Schwarzkosteletz), just east of Prague, attempted to introduce Czech as the language of instruction, but the school then forfeited its right to state funding and was closed.[8]

An important factor in the Bohemian Jews' inclination to German in the first half of the nineteenth century and part of the second half was that Czech was only gradually becoming the language of the middle and upper classes and the educated.[9] It is important to recall that if the Czechs wished to continue their education, the only secondary and post-secondary schools available to them were, until the 1850s, German. In this regard, the historian Otto Urban makes an interesting comparison: whereas basic educational institutions had been established quickly in most countries of central Europe by the end of the eighteenth century, 'Czech education developed very slowly and on the fringes or even outside the institutionally recognized school system. Several generations of educated Czechs received their education in German. They thus contributed in essence to the expansion of the ranks of the German-speaking intellectuals (*Bildungsbürgertum*). With a bit of exaggeration one could say that these patriots, at first few in number, were "dissidents" of German education and enthusiastic amateurs in developing the Czech educational system.'[10]

The watershed year, Urban argues, is roughly 1880. As early as 1869 there was a Czech polytechnic in Prague, but Prague University was not divided into its Czech and German parts until 1882. Even more important, according to Urban, is the development of secondary schools. Whereas in 1850 Czech was the language of instruction at only two grammar schools (*gymnasia*) in the Bohemian Lands, in 1875 it was used at eight, and in 1910 at thirty-seven. In 1890 the Czech Academy of Arts and Sciences was

---

[8] Guido Kisch, 'Linguistic Conditions among Czechoslovak Jewry: A Legal-Historical Study', *Historia Judaica* 8 (1946): 28.
[9] The importance of education and the school system for formation of a national community is emphasized especially by Ernest Gellner, *Nations and Nationalism*, 2nd ed. (Oxford, 2007).
[10] Otto Urban, 'Bürgerlichkeit und das tschechische Bildungsbürgertum am Ende des 19. Jahrhunderts', in *'Durch Arbeit, Besitz, Wissen und Gerechtigkeit': Bürgertum in der Habsburgermonarchie*, vol. II, ed. Hames Stekl et al. (Vienna, Cologne and Weimar, 1992), 205.

founded. Only after 1880 therefore did the Czech intelligentsia emerge as a 'clearly defined socio-cultural segment' of Czech society.[11]

Also closely connected to this shift in the development of the Czech school system, and to the improved standing of Czech culture as well, is the Bohemian Jews' attitude to the Czech language. It was not by chance that the organised Czech-Jewish movement emerged in the second half of the 1870s. It was started by the first graduates of Czech grammar schools chiefly from south and east Bohemia. The number of Jews who in the census declared Czech as their language of everyday communication (*obcovací jazyk*) rapidly increased from the 1880s onwards.

This trend then continued until World War II. It may be traced in the First Republic thanks mainly to the statistics of children of the Jewish faith (*israelské vyznání*) at Czech schools. This aspect is lucidly explained by Bruno Blau. The data, presented here, relate to the whole Czechoslovak Republic.

Table 3.1. Jewish children and youth (according to religion) and their attendance in Czech-speaking and German-speaking educational institutions.

	Academic year	1926/27	1935/36	1936/37
University				
	Czech	1 157		1 669
	German	1 034		552
Polytechnics				
	Czech	338		221
	German	963		223
High schools (Mittelschulen)				
	Czech	3 200		5 694
	German	3 042		2 051
Secondary schools (Bürgerschulen)				
	Czech	3 468	7 254	
	German	708	758	
Business academies				
	Czech	798		610
	German	735		410
Primary schools				
	Czech	12 943	19 649	
	German	3 369	1 504	

Source: Bruno Blau, 'Nationality among Czechoslovak Jewry', *Historia Judaica* X (1948), 152.

---

[11] Ibid., 205–06. For a thorough analysis of Czech secondary education before World War I, see Kateřina Řezníčková, *Študáci a kantoři za starého Rakouska. České střední školy v letech 1867–1918* (Prague, 2007); for an overview of the growth of Czech education on all levels, see Kieval, *Languages of Community*, 138–41.

The greater number of children at Czech schools can probably be explained not only by the Jews' inclination to the Czech language, but also by the antisemitic atmosphere at many German schools after Hitler's coming to power in Germany. According to Wilma Iggers, however, from 1930 to 1932, that is, even before the Nazis came to power in Germany, most German-speaking Jews had already begun to send their children to Czech schools.[12]

The process of the integration of the Jews of Bohemia into Czech culture is also well illustrated by the situation at the Czech and German universities in Prague. At the medical school of the German University of Prague until 1937 about a quarter of the students were Jews (not only from Bohemia, but also from countries where the *numerus clausus* was used to restrict Jewish admissions).[13] The total number of students at the German university declined, however, in the interwar years. At the Czech part of the university, by contrast, where the number of students continuously increased, the percentage of Jewish students continuously increased from the 1919/20 academic year onwards. Whereas at the beginning of the First Republic they constituted 3.7 per cent, in 1931/32 that proportion rose to 14.7 per cent. Apart from Jews from countries with the *numerus clausus*, an increasing number of Jews from the Bohemian Lands applied to the Czech part of the university.[14] From 1931 onwards more Jewish students from Bohemia enrolled at the Czech University in Prague, even though it was only in 1937 that the pro-Nazi students and professors dominated the German University.[15] This trend increased even more after Hitler came to power.

Nonetheless, one factor must be borne in mind, for it considerably slowed down the Bohemian Jews' trend to adopt Czech. As pointed out by Kestenberg-Gladstein, this trend is linked with Jewish migration in the second half of the nineteenth century. Until 1848, Jews in the Bohemian Lands were not permitted to change their place of residence. This ban had been in force since the beginning of the eighteenth century. The number of Jews was fixed also because of the *Familianten Gesetz*, which permitted only the eldest son to marry and get a residence permit (*incolat*).

---

[12] A letter from Wilma Iggers to the author, 24 December 2002. Her statement is based on the experience of her parents, other relations and acquaintances from Horšovský Týn.
[13] Jiří Pešek, Alena Míšková, Petr Svobodný and Jan Janko, 'Německá univerzita v Praze v letech 1918-1939', in *Dějiny Univerzity Karlovy 1918-1990*, vol. IV, ed. Jan Havránek and Zdeněk Pousta (Prague, 1998), 185.
[14] Jan Havránek, 'Univerzita Karlova, rozmach a perzekuce 1918-1945', in *Dějiny Univerzity Karlovy 1918-1990*, vol. IV, 28.
[15] Jiří Pešek, 'Jüdische Studenten an den Prager Universitäten, 1882-1939', in *Franz Kafka im sprachnationalen Kontext seiner Zeit: Sprache und nationale Identität in öffentlichen Institutionen der böhmischen Länder*, ed. Marek Nekula, Ingrid Fleischmann and Albrecht Greule (Weimar and Cologne, 2007).

If the demographic distribution of the Jews of Bohemia had remained as it was in the first half of the nineteenth century, it is reasonable to assume that at the end of the nineteenth century most Bohemian Jews would have integrated into Czech society. After the lifting of the ban on migration in 1848, however, there was a large shift in the Jewish population of Bohemia and Moravia. Jews moved from predominantly Czech villages and little towns to industrial centres. Industrialization at the time continued, however, particularly in the towns of the German-speaking borderlands in north and northwest Bohemia and many Jews therefore moved there. They were not alone. A similar trend took place among the Czech working class.[16]

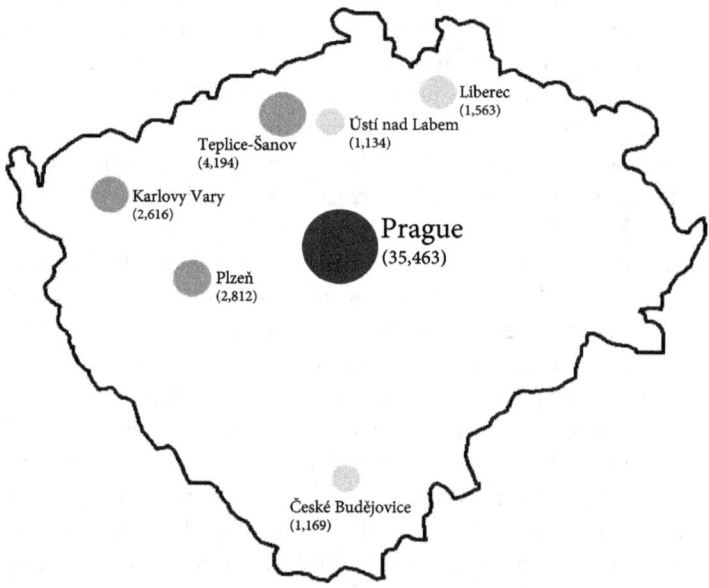

Graph 3.1. Jewish communities in Bohemia with more than a thousand people of the Jewish faith according to the 1930 census.

The largest Jewish communities in the First Republic were therefore in the towns of Teplice-Šanov (Teplitz-Schönau), Pilsen, Carlsbad, Liberec (Reichenberg), Ústí nad Labem (Aussig), České Budějovice (Budweis), Žatec (Saaz) and Jablonec nad Nisou (Gablonz).[17] Apart from Pilsen and

---

[16] Kestenberg-Gladstein, 'The Internal Migration of Jews in 19th Century Bohemia', 308.
[17] At eleven per cent, the proportion of the Jewish population was higher in Teplice-Šanov (Teplitz-Schönau) than in any other town in the Bohemian Lands. The other towns in which Jews constituted more than five per cent of the population in 1890 were Carlsbad and Žatec (Saaz), 9 per cent; Kolín (Kolin), Náchod (Nachod), Prostějov (Proßnitz) and Třebíč (Trebitsch), 8 per cent; Brno (Brünn), 7.5 per cent; Prague and its suburbs,

Budweis, each with a large German minority, all these towns were in Bohemian border areas with mostly German-speaking populations.

Jewish migration from predominantly Czech villages and small towns to the German-speaking borderlands or to towns with a considerable German minority markedly contributed to the inclination of these Jews to adopt the German language and culture in general. Whereas Jews from Czech villages did not stop using Czech to communicate with their Czech neighbours even after the reforms of Joseph II, many of the next generation living in the borderlands often were no longer able to do so. Rarely did Jewish families in the German-speaking borderlands communicate in Czech.[18] One must therefore differentiate between the situation of the Jews in Prague and in the German borderland towns on the one hand, and the situation in Czech, largely agrarian areas on the other. This distinction has not only a linguistic dimension, but also economic and social ones. Jews from Prague and the borderlands soon became involved in industry and business, and thus naturally became part of the local German middle and upper classes. Jews from preponderantly Czech areas remained in commerce and crafts connected with farming, and often competed with the Czech lower middle classes. Only gradually did they change their orientation to some branch of industry.[19]

Tensions between Prague and the Borderlands

One must, however, also bear in mind the difference in the atmosphere in Prague and that in the German-speaking borderlands. A special feature of the German minority in Prague was, among other things, that it had no working class. Most of the German-speakers of Prague were white-collar workers, shop-keepers, industrialists, landed gentry or nobility, and they tended to be among the richer residents of Prague.[20] Politically, most were liberal. Because of the minority status of the Prague Germans and their political orientation, the integration of Jews into Prague German society was uniquely successful. German political parties frequently nominated

---

Moravská Ostrava (Mährisch Ostrau) and Tábor (Tabor), 7 per cent; Olomouc (Olmütz), 6.5 per cent; and Kroměříž (Kremsier) and Mladá Boleslav (Jungbunzlau), 6 per cent. See A. L. Hickmann, *Geographish-statistischer Taschen-Atlas von Österreich-Ungarn* (Vienna, 1900), tables 50–52.

[18] For Ústí nad Labem (Aussig), for example, Kaiser mentions the family of a Jewish doctor Libický and a textile merchant Pick. See Vladimír Kaiser, 'Židovská komunita v Ústí nad Labem v 19. a 20. století', in *Židé v Sudetech* (Prague, 2000), 218, 232 n. 5.

[19] Wolfdieter Bihl, 'Die Juden', in *Die Habsburgermonarchie 1848–1918*, vol. III, pt 2 (Vienna, 1980), 912.

[20] Hans Tramer, 'Die Dreivölkerstadt Prag', in *Robert Weltsch zum 70. Geburtstag von seinen Freunden*, ed. Hans Tramer and Kurt Loewenstein (Tel Aviv, 1961), 140.

Jewish candidates in Prague, whereas their candidates in the borderlands were openly antisemitic.

In the borderlands, in contrast to Prague, German nationalism and modern forms of racial antisemitism were thriving. Amongst the chief disseminators of antisemitism there in the late nineteenth and early twentieth century was Georg Schönerer (1842–1921).[21] His ideology was a direct inspiration to Hitler and also to Karl Hermann Wolf (1862–1941), who achieved popularity among German nationalists particularly after he protested sharply against the Language Ordinances of the Austrian Prime Minister, Casimir Badeni, in 1897. As the chairman of the Deutschradikale Partei (German Radical Party), Wolf achieved success in north and west Bohemia in the first decade of the twentieth century. Many people at the time considered him the natural leader of the Austrian Germans.[22] A thread runs from Wolf to the Deutsche Arbeiterpartei in Österreich (German Workers' Party in Austria, DAP), which was founded in Trutnov (Trautenau), north Bohemia, in 1904, all the way to the Deutsche Nationalsozialistische Arbeiterpartei (German National Socialists' Workers Party, DNSAP), founded in 1918, about six months before Czechoslovakia declared its independence. On the political spectrum of the First Republic, the DNSAP was the only party with antisemitism explicitly in its programme. After the DNSAP was banned in 1933, its voters went over to the party of Konrad Henlein (1898–1945).[23]

In April 1938, Leo Herrmann (1888–1951), a former chairman of the Bar Kochba Zionist organisation, whose family came from the German-speaking borderlands, noted: 'There is a very strong connection between the Sudeten Germans and the Nazis. The radical nature of the racial theories and practice of Nazi power-politics truly has its origins in that witch's caldron (*Hexenkessel*), because Czech and German life, together and apart, was like a bomb with a slow-burning fuse.'[24]

The clash of the attitudes of the liberal Prague Germans with those of the German nationalists from the borderlands is well illustrated by events at the German part of Prague University. By far most of its students came

---

[21] For Schönerer's position within the German nationalist movement in the late Austrian Empire, see Pieter M. Judson, *Exclusive Revolutionaries: Liberal Politics, Social Experience, and National Identity in the Austrian Empire, 1848–1914* (Ann Arbor, MI, 1996), 226-36.
[22] See Michael Wladika, *Hitlers Vätergeneration. Die Ursprünge des Nationalsozialismus in der k.u.k. Monarchie* (Vienna, 2005).
[23] Alena Míšková, 'Od Schönerera ke genocidě?', in *Židé v Sudetech* (Prague, 2000), 52-54.
[24] Herrmann, 'Erinnerungen eines sudetendeutschen Zionisten', 8. Concerning collaboration between the Henlein party and the Nazis, see Volker Zimmermann, *Die Sudetendeutschen im NS-Staat: Politik und Stimmung der Bevölkerung im Reichsgau Sudetenland (1938–1945)* (Essen, 1999).

from Bohemia. German-speaking students from Moravia and Silesia preferred the University of Vienna. Consequently, it was mostly students from the northwest border areas – Poohří (Böhmisches Mittelgebirge), dolní Polabí (Elbeland), the area of Česká Lípa (Böhmisch Leipa) and Liberec (Reichenberg) – that met with German-speaking people from Prague at the university. From the end of the nineteenth century into the 1930s tensions arose between these two groups, from time to time erupting in open conflict. The authors of a book on the German part of Prague University thus describe the situation:

> Students from the Prague agglomeration were . . . in many respects alien to their own colleagues from the border areas. The atmosphere in Prague, tending to be liberal, with many German-Jewish individuals, families, businesses and groups, was almost incomprehensibly remote from what was known to the poor German-nationalist youths from little towns in the border areas, who preferred action to long consideration. In several respects they thus remained foreigners even in little German Prague, whose character was determined chiefly by the rich aristocratic, business or white-collar and intellectual strata.[25]

The conflicts first erupted in 1891, when German nationalists decided to introduce the 'Aryan clause' (*Arierparagraph*) into the statutes in order to refuse entry to Jews in the Lese- und Redehalle der deutschen Studenten in Prag, the most popular student society. But the liberals won with 634 votes to 566,[26] and the nationalists established their own 'Aryan' society called Germania, Verein deutscher Hochschüler. The dominant founding member of Germania was Wolf, still a student of the German university.[27]

At the German university tensions between liberal and Social Democrat groups on the one hand and the nationalists on the other lasted right into the First Republic. And the antisemitic rhetoric of the German nationalist radicals grew stronger.[28] The best known event that increased tensions at the German university only a few years after World War I was the Steinherz Affair. In 1922 Samuel Steinherz (1857–1942), a well-known Jewish historian, was elected rector. In Austria-Hungary it was customary that a Jewish candidate voluntarily resigned if elected. Steinherz did not do this,

---

[25] Jiří Pešek, Alena Míšková, and Ludmila Hlaváčková, 'Německá univerzita v Praze 1882–1918', in *Dějiny Univerzity Karlovy 1802–1918*, vol. III, ed. Jan Havránek (Prague, 1997), 311–13.
[26] Ibid., 316.
[27] Herrmann, 'Erinnerungen eines sudetendeutschen Zionisten', 2.
[28] Pešek, Míšková, Svobodný and Janko, 'Německá univerzita v Praze v letech 1918–1939', 185.

confident that he had the backing of the democratic system of the First Republic. His refusal met with great resistance from German nationalist students. The Deutsche Studentenschaft, a society of Aryan German nationalists, organised a boisterous strike. They were soon supported by students in Vienna, and a petition was organised against Steinherz in towns of the German border areas. Representatives of about fifty towns and villages, predominantly from north and west Bohemia, sent statements protesting against the election of the Jewish rector, and in some places public demonstrations were held. Steinherz therefore handed in his resignation, but the Ministry of Education did not accept it. Consequently, the antisemites did not get their way in 1922.[29] German students from the border areas continued, however, to be a growing source of support for markedly nationalist and antisemitic societies at the German university. After graduating from Prague, fortified by student life in the Burschenschaften, they were actively involved in spreading antisemitic and anti-Czech sentiment in the border areas.

The conflict between the German border areas and Prague was also a matter of interest among German intellectuals at the time. In January 1935, for example, a debate was held in the Urania society on the topic 'Prag und die sudetendeutsche Provinz' (Prague and the Sudeten-German Provinces), with Emil Hadina of Opava (Troppau), Walter Seidl of Prague and Frank Matzke of Liberec (Reichenberg). The participants stated: 'Prague is a centre without provinces, and the Sudeten-German provinces lack a centre. Neither understands the other.' In an effort to find a conciliatory way out, they argued, Prague would have 'to be concerned with the needs of the Sudeten-German provinces, rather than arrogantly rejecting everything that comes from there as being Nazi. The provinces, on the other hand, must not label as "alien to the people" (*volksfremd*) all the movements that the metropolis is naturally full of.'[30] Julius Mader, writing in the Prague journal *Die Wahrheit* in 1935, however, noted that although the debate at the Urania society was interesting, the real differences were not openly discussed there: 'Not a word was said about the gulf between the Sudeten-Germans and Prague being mainly in their totally opposed outlooks on life and social differences. They could not be surmounted even by putting pressure on Prague or the provinces, or even by an organised exchange of spiritual values.'[31] Despite the different conditions in the German-speaking borderlands and in Prague, one finds a common denominator for the German-speaking Jews of Bohemia. Both in the in-

---

[29] Ibid.; Mišková, 'Od Schönerera ke genocidě?', 54–55.
[30] Julius Mader, 'Prag und die sudetendeutsche Provinz', *Die Wahrheit*, no. 3 (1935): 9.
[31] Ibid., 10. For further evidence of tensions between the borderlands and Prague, see Koeltzsch, 'Geteilte Kulturen', 129–30.

dustrial centres of the borderlands and in Prague, the German-speaking Jewish community was mostly middle-class.

The German-Jewish Elite

There are many reasons why the vast majority of upper-middle-class Jews in Bohemia clung to the German language. In the area of education, the upper middle classes of the German-speaking Jews preferred German-language schools even in the 1920s. Their reasons were purely pragmatic: a much wider range of employment opportunities in the Bohemian Lands and also in Germany and Austria would open up for their children.

Proponents of Liberalism

The inclination of the Jewish upper middle classes towards German culture was, however, also connected to their adherence to Liberalism.[32] Liberalism had found its proponents among the Jews as early as in the 1830s. It was thus not by chance that the Jews played an important role on the liberal side also in the 1848 revolution. The adherence of the vast majority of the Jews in Germany and in the Habsburg Monarchy to Liberalism became firmly established in the period of the Jews' achieving full equality with the rest of the population of Austria-Hungary in 1867 and Germany in 1871. It was, after all, the liberals who managed to get freedom of confession enshrined in the new constitutions.

In Cisleithania the German liberals held the leading position in the Government from 1867 to 1879. But the Jewish upper middle classes remained true to the liberal movement in the subsequent period as well. In 1879 Eduard Taaffe became prime minister of the government in Vienna. He sought to break the influence of the German liberals. For this, he found support in his 'Iron Ring', an interest group of Bohemian and Polish deputies and the conservative Party of Law (Rechtspartei), which was led by the Austrian count Karl Hohenwart. The change in Austrian politics led to a crisis in the liberal movement. The nationalist wing, led by Schönerer, broke off from the German liberals in the late 1870s. The extension of the vote and the growth of nationalism then led to nationalist and socialist parties' coming to the fore.[33] In such a context it is un-

---

[32] For the tendency of the Prague Jewish élite towards Liberalism, see Trude Maurer, 'Juden im Prager deutschen Bürgertum', *Judaica* 58, no. 3 (September 2002): 177–81; Gary B. Cohen, 'Jews in German Liberal Politics: Prague, 1880–1914', *Jewish History* 1, no. 1 (1986): 55–74.

[33] For more see Judson, *Exclusive Revolutionaries*, 165–266.

derstandable that upper-middle-class Jews, who did not wish to support nationalist parties because of their antisemitism, nor socialist parties because of their anti-bourgeois policies, had no choice but to continue to cling tenaciously to the dying liberal movement.

Another reason, however, why upper-middle-class Jews supported liberalism was that it was essentially an élite political movement. Liberalism seeks equal rights for all but allows only capable, educated and propertied individuals to take over the leadership of society. Liberals, unlike socialists, do not think about how to support the less capable or those without property. Critics, as well as some adherents, thus claim that liberalism aims to give room to the élite in the arts and sciences, who then defend 'high' culture and the values of humanism against mass democracy.[34]

The Jews' coming together with German liberalism had more than a political dimension. It also influenced the cultural and language orientation of the Jewish élite. This aspect is observable in Poland, Hungary, Romania and the Bohemian Lands. Why were the upper-middle-class Jews inclined to German cultural and political circles even in the period of growing German nationalism? Steven Beller points out that under the Liberal government, in the 1860s and 1870s, liberalism was linked to the Germanness of its proponents to such an extent that a kind of political short-circuit occurred. Things German in central Europe were automatically considered progressive, liberal. This political cliché, however, very soon ceased to be true, when German nationalist parties came to the fore. Nevertheless, it survived long afterwards, mainly among middle-class and upper-middle-class Jews. The latter loyally defended what they perceived as 'genuine, highly cultural and progressive Germanness', often right up to World War II.[35]

Jewish Devotion to German Culture

A third important reason that upper-middle-class Bohemian Jews clung to the German language and German culture in general, often long into the First Republic, was that they had managed with surprising ease to integrate into the German middle class, not only in the period when liberalism was dominant, but also in the 1890s, when Jews in Germany were already being excluded *en masse* from societies, professional organisations and other élite spheres, on the basis of an 'Aryan clause'.

---

[34] Robert Hollinger, *The Dark Side of Liberalism: Elitism vs. Democracy* (London, 1996), 78, 80–81.
[35] Steven Beller, 'Germans and Jews as Central European and "Mitteleuropäisch" Élites', in *Mitteleuropa: History and Prospects*, ed. Peter Stirk (Edinburgh, 1994), 69. See also Judson, *Exclusive Revolutionaries*, 269.

The situation of the German Jews in Prague, which has been analyzed in particular by Gary Cohen, was unique. An important special feature of Prague German society was that Jews could integrate into the German middle and upper middle classes in Prague without losing their Jewish identity. In Vienna, for example, conversion to Christianity, or at least leaving the Jewish community, was a condition for the Jews' being able to move up the social ladder.[36] As Michael Riff has demonstrated, the number of conversions in Vienna in the second half of the nineteenth century far surpassed the number in Prague. In Vienna from 1898 to 1907, 5,730 Jews (4 per cent of the total number) decided to leave the Jewish community, whereas in Prague only 450 Jews (2.25 per cent of the total) made the same choice.[37]

Some Jewish members of the German Casino in Prague, the most prestigious German institution of its kind there, were even on the board of the Prague Jewish Community or of a B'nai B'rith lodge. Though the president of the Jewish community of the Old Town of Prague was always a Czech-speaking Jew (a Zionist or a Czech-Jew) throughout the years of the First Republic, German Jews retained their dominant position on the board of that community.[38] In the independent Prague boroughs of Královské Vinohrady, Smíchov and Libeň, which introduced more democratic electoral systems, however, Jews involved in Czech culture clearly predominated.

Why was Prague German society, unlike the upper middle classes of Vienna, so much more willing to accept Jews? It was mainly because of the smaller number of Germans in Prague. The census of 1900 show that 47 per cent of the inhabitants of inner Prague who declared German to be their language of everyday communication were of the Jewish faith.[39] In Prague, therefore, Christian German society could not set the terms and conditions under which it would accept the Jews. Quite the opposite was true: the gentile Germans of Prague needed the Jews to help them

---

[36] Cohen, *The Politics of Ethnic Survival*, 131-32.
[37] Michael Anthony Riff, 'Assimilation and Conversion in Bohemia: Secession from the Jewish Community in Prague, 1868-1917', in *Leo Baeck Institute Yearbook*, vol. 26 (1981): 78. The contrast between Vienna and Prague on the question of conversion is discussed also in Wolfgang Häusler, 'Das österreichische Judentum zwischen Beharrung und Fortschritt', in *Die Habsburgermonarchie, 1848-1918*, vol. IV (Vienna, 1985), 656.
[38] Nancy M. Wingfield, 'Czech, German or Jew: The Jewish Community of Prague during the Interwar Period', in *The Czech and Slovak Experience: Selected Papers from the Fourth World Congress for Soviet and East European Studies, Harrogate 1990*, ed. John Morison (Hondmille and London, 1992), 220, 222.
[39] After the inclusion of parts of Prague with lower social strata, Jews constituted 37 per cent of those declaring German as their language of everyday communication (*Umgangsprache*). See Antonín Boháč, *Hlavní město Praha. Studie o obyvatelstvu* (Prague, 1923), 36.

to defend the interests of the Germans in Prague. Gary Cohen convincingly demonstrates that Prague German liberals could never have permitted themselves to work with antisemitic German political parties, because any sign of such collaboration would immediately be subjected to the harsh criticism of Jewish members of these liberal groups.[40] One must also take into account the high degree of secularization of Czech society. The smooth integration of the Jews into Prague German society was made possible also by the fact that Prague basically lacked a German working class and enjoyed a higher standard of living. The lower classes of the originally German population, both Jewish and non-Jewish, mostly lived dispersed throughout the predominantly Czech milieu, and thus tended to adopt the Czech language and Czech culture in general.[41] The élite nature of the German minority in Prague is reflected, for instance, in the statistics about students at secondary schools. In the 1900/01 school year the proportion of German-speaking secondary-school pupils (Christians as well as Jews) in Prague was 26.3 per cent, in other words four times greater than that of Germans among the inhabitants of Prague.[42] Prague German Jews were so integrated into the infrastructure of the German community that they did not need to establish their own organisations, because their interests could be promoted in German institutions, where they had an important role. As Cohen has demonstrated, Jewish Germans constituted 45 per cent of all members of the German Casino in 1899 (at the time of the Hilsner Affair).[43]

Similarly, German Jews had no need to start up their own periodicals. Many journalists on German periodicals were of Jewish origin. German Jews (not only from Prague) placed advertisements, wedding announcements, and obituaries predominantly in the *Prager Tagblatt*.[44] Many Jewish journalists, including Rudolf Fuchs, Max Brod, Willy Haas, Egon Erwin Kisch (1885-1948), Theodor Lessing (1872-1933), Friedrich Torberg (1908-1979) and Joseph Wechsberg (1907-1983, who was also secretary of the

---

[40] Gary Cohen, 'Jews in German Society: Prague, 1860-1914', in *Central European History* X, no. 1 (1977): 46.
[41] Cohen, *The Politics of Ethnic Survival*, 209.
[42] Jan Havránek, 'Sociální struktura pražských Němců a Čechů, křesťanů a Židů ve světle statistik z let 1890-1930', *Český časopis historický* 93, no. 3 (1995): 478. Published in French as 'Structure sociale des Allemands, des Tchèques, des chrétiens et des juifs à Prague, à la lumière des statistiques des années 1890-1930', in *Allemands, Juifs et Tchèques à Prague 1890-1924*, ed. Maurice Godé, Jacques Le Rider and Françoise Mayer (Montpellier, 1996), 71-81.
[43] Cohen, *The Politics of Ethnic Survival*, 177.
[44] In an encyclopaedia from the late 1920s, the *Prager Tagblatt* is described as 'the German daily with the greatest circulation in the Czechoslovak Republic today, particularly with its first-class correspondents and economics section'. See B. Kočího *Malý slovník naučný*, vol. II (Prague, 1929), 1653.

Jewish Party), wrote for the *Prager Tagblatt*.[45] This daily was considered the unofficial mouth-piece of the Deutsche demokratische Freiheitspartei (the German Democratic Liberal Party) and the paper of 'Prague German intellectuals with a progressive orientation and German-minded Jews'.[46] With its liberal orientation, the *Prager Tagblatt* became the most popular daily of the Bohemian Jews. Emil Utitz (1883-1956) remarked: 'one of the journalists commented that when a Bohemian Jew dies no one was sorrier than he [the journalist], because he had just lost a subscriber to his paper; conversely, there was no greater cause for joy than a Jewish wedding, because it meant one Jewish subscriber more.'[47]

Another important German-language daily was *Bohemia*, which started as a supplement to the *Prager Zeitung* and became the official newspaper of the Deutsche Fortschrittspartei. First published in 1828, *Bohemia* increasingly became a conservative newspaper by the end of the century. Although it resisted the antisemitic propaganda of its readers from the German borderlands and the German students at the German part of Prague University, it often fell back on German chauvinism.[48] Many Jewish journalists, including Egon Erwin Kisch, Alfred Klaar (1848-1927), Emil Faktor, Friedrich Torberg and Georg Mannheimer (1887-1942), worked on *Bohemia*.[49]

A third German newspaper, the *Prager Presse*, also had many Jewish journalists as its contributors. This paper was financed by the state, and was intended mainly for readers outside the country. Its editor-in-chief of many years was Arne Laurin (born Arnošt Lustig, 1889-1945), who before World War I sympathized with the Czech-Jewish movement, and originally worked for the Czech-Jewish daily, *Tribuna*. In addition to Laurin, other journalists and writers straddling both Czech culture and German were on the *Prager Presse*, for example Pavel Eisner (1889-1958) and Otto Pick (1887-1940).

An often-overlooked German periodical that merits mention is *Die Wahrheit*. Started up in Prague in 1921, it published commentary on foreign policy, particularly of Germany and Austria, but also long articles and reviews on the arts. It was published by Adalbert Rév and Georg Mannheimer.[50] *Die Wahrheit* spoke out clearly against the ideas of the

---

[45] Tomáš Pěkný, *Historie Židů v Čechách a na Moravě*, 2nd ed. (Prague, 2001), 538-39.

[46] Karel Tauš, *Slovník cizích slov, zkratek, novinářských šifer, pseudonymů a časopisů pro čtenáře novin*, 2nd ed. (Blansko, 1947), 612.

[47] Emil Utitz, *Egon Erwin Kisch: Der klassische Journalist* (Berlin, 1956), 11-12.

[48] Tramer, 'Die Dreivölkerstadt Prag', 152.

[49] Pěkný, *Historie Židů v Čechách a na Moravě*, 538.

[50] For more on this otherwise forgotten periodical, see Ines Koeltsch, 'Gustav Flusser: Biographische Spuren eines deutschen Juden in Prag vor dem Zweiten Weltkrieg', *Flusser Studies* 5 (2007): 9-10; Koetzsch, 'Geteilte Kulturen', 245-62.

Figure 3.1. The editors of the *Prager Presse*. At the far right, its editor-in-chief, Arne Laurin.

Henlein party, and, in the decisive days before the Munich Agreement, the editors expressed their belief that they need not appeal to their readers to distance themselves from the Henlein membership drive, because they were 'adherents of Masaryk's ideas of *Humanität* and democracy'.[51]

It remains unclear whether *Die Wahrheit* was somehow connected to the eponymous periodical in Vienna. The Vienna *Wahrheit* was the official newspaper of the Austrian Jews who supported the idea of integration into the German (or Austrian) nation. Like the Czech periodical *Rozvoj*, the Vienna *Wahrheit* was full of articles in which the editors took issue with Zionist opinions. The periodical also carefully reported on events in the Jewish Community of Vienna. *Die Wahrheit* in Prague, by contrast, published no articles criticizing Zionist ideology. None the less, the journalists on the Prague *Wahrheit* were greatly interested in the Jews of Bohemia and also of the neighbouring countries. It reported in detail on the Jews of Germany and also on antisemitism at the German university in Prague, and it reported on lectures given in Bet Ha'Am (Hebrew for 'House of the People'), the Jewish centre in Dlouhá ulice (Langegasse). Many Jewish journalists contributed to *Die Wahrheit*, including – as was also the case with the *Prager Tagblatt* and *Bohemia* – many supporters of Zionism. Articles by Brod, Mannheimer and Pick appeared with particular frequency. The arts sections reflected an interest in bringing Czechs and

---

[51] *Die Wahrheit* no. 17 (1938): 3.

Germans closer together. *Die Wahrheit* was intended for a wider readership, not only Jewish, though it emphasized problems related mainly to the Jews. *Die Wahrheit* thus provides further evidence that German Jewish society, unlike the Jews of Vienna, did not need to distinguish itself clearly from the non-Jewish milieu, nor, indeed, from Zionism. It is even doubtful whether the German Jews were concerned about having a German national identity. Instead, their frequent sympathy for Jewish nationalism leads one to conclude that at least some of them were concerned about clinging consciously to Jewish identity. It is then reasonable to interpret their declaration of German nationality in the census as a sign of approval of the German culture with which they had grown together, but not of their agreement with the German national and political programme.[52]

The Special Nature of the German-Speaking Jewish Elite in the Bohemian Lands

The smooth integration of the German Jews into the Prague German community, however, makes research on them in the second half of the nineteenth century and in the early twentieth century difficult. Rather than attempting to discuss the national identity of the Jews of Bohemia comprehensively, I shall try here to explore the organised forms of the national movements of people of the Jewish faith. No organised movement of Jews of German nationality similar to the Czech-Jewish or Zionist movements existed, but even this negative fact is significant. Particularly during the First Republic it would have been unthinkable for German Jews to campaign in any way for Jews to adopt German culture. German Jews too were loyal citizens of Czechoslovakia, and were aware of the problems that the German minority was causing for the vision of a one-nation Czechoslovak state. For that reason, as well, many German Jews opted to declare Jewish nationality in both censuses during the First Republic (in 1921 and 1930), and even those who did not declare Jewish nationality still became great supporters of the German anti-Hitler parties, in particular the Social Democrats.[53]

Despite the absence of an organised movement, the German Jews can reasonably be portrayed, though with certain limitations, by considering B'nai B'rith, an élite Jewish organisation. Such a description is limited by the fact that many Zionists, as well as a small number of Czech speaking

---

[52] See Rozenblit, *Reconstructing a national identity*, 168. Rozenblit also claims that German identity of Jews in Bohemian Lands was cultural, rather than national.
[53] Hahn, 'Němečtí Židé a politické strany', 100–04.

Jews and even few members of Czech-Jewish movement, became members of B'nai B'rith during the First Republic. The B'nai B'rith leadership, however, comprised mainly German Jews, who were not part of the Zionist movement, though many sympathized with it. Even the B'nai B'rith monthly, published until the outbreak of World War II, was in German, though from the 1930s onwards it also ran articles in Czech. Another potential serious reservation is that B'nai B'rith cannot be considered a form of national society like the societies of Zionists or Czech-Jews. It was not intended to represent a wider group. Rather, it was an élite order, whose many activities remained concealed from the public. None the less, research reveals certain special features of the upper middle classes of German Jewish society in Bohemia.

The B'nai B'rith Order

The first B'nai B'rith lodge was founded in the United States in 1843 by German Jewish immigrants. The founders' aim was to assist German Jews to integrate into American society. B'nai B'rith (Hebrew for 'Sons of the Covenant') also endeavoured to encourage immigrants not to give up their Jewish identity and to remain true to Jewish traditions. The American B'nai B'rith gradually expanded to include Jewish immigrants from other countries as well.

The first B'nai B'rith lodge in Europe was established in Berlin almost forty years later, in 1882. By that time about 600 lodges existed throughout North America.[54] Soon lodges were established in other German towns, and in 1885 the American leadership set up a German District. Shortly afterwards, B'nai B'rith lodges were established in several towns in Romania. In 1889 a lodge was also established in the Polish town of Bielsko (Bielitz), in Teschener Schlesien (Cieszyn Silesia), and, three years later, in Cracow and Pilsen, then Prague, Carlsbad and Liberec (Reichenberg). The six lodges in Austria-Hungary (actually, only in Cisleithania) were enough to constitute an independent district, and thus the Austrian District (X) was established in November 1894. Prague became the District headquarters, because four of the six lodges were in Bohemia and, moreover, the Prague Lodge, called Bohemia, had the most members and property. The chairman of Bohemia, Moritz Hammerschlag, was made 'Großpräsident' of the Austrian District. Of the seven members of the district board, five came from Bohemian lodges.[55]

---

[54] AŽMP, shelf no. 51921, Verzeichniß der Institutionen und Logen des U.O.B.B.
[55] Bohumil Stein, 'Geschichte des X. Distriktes', B'nai B'rith: Monatsblätter der Grossloge für den Čechoslovakischen Staat X., I. O. B.B (henceforth B'nai B'rith: Monatsblätter) (1935): 263–66.

Figure 3.2. Presidents of the Grand Lodge of B'nai B'rith in central Europe, at the Carlsbad conference, 23 August 1924.
First row, from the left: David Yellin, Palestine; Berthold Timendorfer, Germany; Salomon Ehrmann, Austria; Josef Popper, Czechoslovakia; Chief Rabbi Jakob Isaak Niemirower, Romania; Leon Ader, Poland; second row, from the left: Osias Thon, a member of the B'nai B'rith Supreme Council, Poland; Edmund Kohn, vice-president of the Grand Lodge, Austria; Ignaz Ziegler, president of the Carlsbad Lodge; Emil Wiesmeyer, secretary general of the B'nai B'rith in Czechoslovakia.

The B'nai B'rith statutes of the newly constituted Austrian District of 1894 state that the task of the Austrian lodges consists in 'developing and elevating the intellectual and moral character of the people of our faith, particularly the members of the Association; inculcating the purest principles of philanthropy, honour and patriotism; mitigating by counsel or deeds the blows of fate, which might affect them; supporting the arts and sciences; alleviating the wants of the poor and needy; visiting and caring for the sick; protecting and assisting the widow and the orphan'.[56]

Hammerschlag went to Vienna in 1895 to campaign for B'nai B'rith. On 22 March 1895 he invited possible candidates for membership to the Grand Hall of the Kaufmännischer Verein (Business Association), and gave a speech about the aims of B'nai B'rith.[57] His fiery words hit the mark.

---

[56] AHMP, SK II/143.
[57] AŽMP, shelf no. 51919, 'Entwicklung, Ziele und Zwecke der Vereinigungen B'nai B'rith: Vortrag gehalten zu Wien am 22. März 1895 von JUDr. Moritz Hammerschlag (Prag), Präsident des Verbandes der israel. Humanitätsvereine B'nai B'rith für Oesterreich'.

As early as October of that year the Vienna Lodge was established. The core of this new lodge comprised ten members of different lodges from Bohemia, who, because of their professions, lived part-time in Vienna.

The second president of the Vienna Lodge and, after World War I, also president of the Austrian District was Salomon Ehrmann (1854-1926), professor of dermatology. Born in the village of Ostrovec (Ostrowitz) near Písek, south Bohemia, Ehrmann was one of the few eminent Jews with a rural background. While a student of medicine at Vienna, he became a close friend of Sigmund Freud.[58] Freud became a member of the Vienna Lodge in 1897 and even brought his friend and physician Oskar Rie (1863-1931) to the lodge.[59]

From 1911 to 1918 the headquarters of the Austrian District were moved to Vienna. When, however, shortly before the Great War, the Austrian District was divided up into Czechoslovak, Austrian and Polish districts, it was renamed the Czechoslovak District, because the Bohemian and Moravian lodges were clearly stronger, both in terms of numbers of members and amount of property. The new Austrian District (XII), with its centre in Vienna, and the Polish District (XIII), with headquarters in Cracow, were established.[60] Contacts between Prague and Vienna remained, however, very close even after the war; many members of the Vienna Lodge came from Bohemia and Moravia. B'nai B'rith in the Bohemian Lands soon began to work closely also with the German and Polish lodges.

The Most Prosperous Jewish Elite in Central Europe

In the 1920s and 1930s the Jewish German élite of the Bohemian Lands was the richest, most prosperous élite of any central European Jewish community. The German, Austrian and Czechoslovak districts were among the most influential B'nai B'rith districts in Europe. Whereas before World War I the German District, with almost a hundred lodges, was clearly the most important in Europe, after the war the balance changed greatly. Inflation, which in Germany began during the war and came to a peak in 1923, meant the severe loss of the savings of the German B'nai B'rith and all other Jewish foundations and charity organisations in Ger-

---

[58] Salomon Ehrmann, 'Meine persönlichen Beziehungen zu Sigmund Freud', *B'nai B'rith: Monatsblätter* (1926): 114-15.
[59] Edmund Kohn, 'Bruder Freud', *B'nai B'rith: Monatsblätter* (1926): 117.
[60] For similar essays concerning Poland, which list all documents related to the history of B'nai B'rith in Cracow, see Bogusława Czajecka, *Archiwum Związku Żydowskich Stowarzyszeń Humanitarnych 'B'nei B'rith' w Krakowie (1892-1938): Zarys dziejów związku, historia zespołu i inwentarz* (Cracow, 1994).

many.[61] In 1923 the lodges in Czechoslovakia announced a collection for their German brethren, and in one month collected 145,795 Czechoslovak crowns (more than US $1,800).[62] The situation was so grave that the lodges of Bohemia and Moravia had to provide financial support to some charities in Germany, which had previously been completely dependent on funding from the German B'nai B'rith. In addition, the Czechoslovak District sent direct funding to the Verein zur Gründung und Erhaltung einer Akademie für Wissenschaft des Judentums (Society for the Founding and Maintenance of an Academy of Jewish Studies) and supported individual lodges as well as the publishing of a periodical, *Der Jude*, whose editor-in-chief was Martin Buber (1878-1965).

In February 1924 a conference was held in Berlin in response to the Jüdische Welthilfskonferenz (Jewish World Relief Conference), to discuss questions of assistance for the suffering Jews of Germany. The conference was presided over by the Russian Zionist leader Leo Motzkin (1867-1933) from Paris. Emil Wiesmeyer, from the Bohemia Lodge, gave a report on behalf of Czechoslovakia. The aim of the conference was to coordinate aid from Switzerland, Czechoslovakia, the Netherlands, Sweden and Great Britain for the Jews of Germany. Czechoslovakia was the only country of central Europe willing and able to come to their aid. As early as 1925, more than 88,000 Czechoslovak crowns (roughly US $1,100), the largest part of the budget of the Czechoslovak District of B'nai B'rith, was donated to the Grand Lodge in Berlin.[63] Individual lodges also organised events for children from Germany, whom B'nai B'rith members took in to their families.

An even more serious blow to the German District was of course Hitler's coming to power. The Jews of Czechoslovakia offered a helping hand to their fellow-Jews in Germany also in this period of Nazi danger. In November 1935 the leadership of the Czechoslovak Grand Lodge decided that each Czechoslovak lodge that funded the sojourn of one of its 'brothers' from Germany and his wife in Czechoslovakia would have half its costs covered by the Grand Lodge.[64] The opportunity for German B'nai B'rith members, as a 'bonus', to send their children to families in Bohemia was offered again. In 1936 the Czechoslovak Grand Lodge even planned to pay for three-hundred children from Germany to spend a holiday in Bohemia. The Czech organisers had already chosen the holiday camps, inter-

---

[61] See Donald L. Niewyk, 'The Impact of Inflation and Depression on the German Jews', *Leo Baeck Institute Yearbook* 28 (1983): 19-36.
[62] 'Protokoll der 65. Tagung des Generalkomitees am 14. Oktober 1923 im Sitzungssaale der israelitischen Kultusgemeinde in Troppau', *B'nai B'rith: Monatsblätter* (1923): 207-08.
[63] 'Finanzbericht der Großloge für den čechoslovakischen Staat X.I.O.B.B. für das Jahr 1924', *B'nai B'rith: Monatsblätter* (1925): 38.
[64] 'Großloge', *B'nai B'rith: Monatsblätter* (1936): 396.

views were held for camp staff, and the exact day of the children's arrival and other details were planned. The project came to naught, however, because the children were refused permission to leave Germany.[65]

From 1933 onwards the number of members of the lodges in Germany rapidly decreased. Many members could no longer afford to pay so much for charity; others chose to emigrate. Similarly, in Austria, membership dwindled in the 1930s. Things were different in Czechoslovakia. From the founding of the first lodges in the 1890s, the number of members of the Bohemian and Moravian lodges increased continuously until the late 1930s.

The Arts and Sciences First and Foremost

Another special feature of the German Jewish élite was their highly positive attitude to the arts and sciences. In the Bohemian Lands this aspect of the German Jewish community particularly came to the fore, because many German Jews introduced the German public to Czech culture.

The attitude of the German-Jewish upper middle classes towards the arts and sciences has been considered by Dolores Augustine. In her research on the rich merchants of Wilhelmine Germany, comparing Roman Catholic businessmen in Westphalia with Jewish businessmen in Berlin, she concludes that the greatest difference between the two was their attitude to the arts and sciences. The Roman Catholic businessmen of Westphalia, together with the families of several Protestant businessmen, used to meet mainly with each other, and usually for business reasons. In Berlin, by contrast, business circles were linked with people in the arts and sciences. The Jewish élite was inextricably linked with the social and cultural life of Berlin. Jewish businessmen became generous patrons of talented Jewish artists and scholars, who were then frequent guests at private parties and debates. Even the biggest Jewish industrialists, and more often their wives, found time to read belles-lettres or play a musical instrument. Many rich Berlin Jews could boast art collections.[66]

A similar attitude of the Jewish élite to the arts and sciences emerges in an analysis of the work of the B'nai B'rith order. Some insight into the breadth of the interests of its members is provided by the lists of talks given at the individual lodges in the monthly bulletins of the Austrian, German or Czechoslovak districts. The talks were usually given by the lodge members themselves; sometimes a guest was invited to give a talk. The topics ranged from belles-lettres to history, philosophy, religion, sociology, economics and the natural sciences. B'nai B'rith members were

---

[65] 'Ordensleitung', *B'nai B'rith: Monatsblätter* (1936): 399.
[66] Dolores L. Augustine, 'Arriving in the Upper Class: The Wealthy Business Elite of Wilhelmine Germany', in *The German Bourgeoisie*, ed. David Blackbourn and Richard J. Evans (London and New York, 1991), 46–86.

interested not only in Judaism and the history of the Jews; they also spent a lot of time discussing the latest works of Jewish scholars on topics not directly related to the Jewish faith. Probably the best example is Sigmund Freud. In December 1897 he gave a talk at the Vienna Lodge on the interpretation of dreams. His book on the topic was not published until three years later. The then-president of the lodge, Edmund Kohn, a gynaecologist, wrote about Freud on his seventieth birthday: 'On 7 December he lectured on the interpretation of dreams, a topic he came back to talk about again. From beginning to end, everyone present listened to Freud's works with bated breath. He explained the latest results of his research superbly, in a way that everyone could understand.'[67]

B'nai B'rith members also regularly kept up to date on the latest belles-lettres. That is evident from the reviews published in the *B'nai B'rith* monthly bulletins of Czechoslovakia, Germany and Austria. The reviewers considered the works by writers from all over the world (for example, Upton Sinclair, James Joyce and Sigrid Undset). Among the most frequently discussed books, however, were works by Austrian and German Jews – Peter Altenberg (1859–1919), Richard Beer-Hofmann (1866–1945), Arthur Schnitzler (1859–1931), Paul Kornfeld (1889–1942; born in Prague, but moved to Germany in 1914), Rudolf Borchardt (1877–1945), Arnold Zweig (1887–1968) – and a whole range of authors from the Bohemian Lands writing in German, including Felix Weltsch, Max Brod, Willy Haas, Franz Kafka and Oskar Baum. The extent to which B'nai B'rith businessmen-members were interested in the arts and sciences, and how they endeavoured to understand new works of art and scientific discoveries and also to support artists and scholars, was indeed unique. In this sense the Jewish élite was most strikingly different from other élites in society.

Compared to its counterparts in Germany and Austria, B'nai B'rith in the Bohemian Lands was also in a unique position, for here two dominant cultural groups overlapped. It is admirable that although most B'nai B'rith members gravitated to German culture, the order did not fail to keep up to date and support Czech culture as well. The most frequent reporter on Jewish topics in Czech literature, or about literature written in Czech by Jews, was Oskar Donath (1882–1940). He later compiled his talks on Czech literature in *Židé a židovství v české literatuře 19. a 20. století* (Jews and Jewry in Czech Literature of the Nineteenth and Twentieth Centuries, in two volumes, 1923 and 1930), a work that remains unsurpassed to this day.[68] He was not alone, however, in acquainting B'nai B'rith members with new works of literature. Each issue of *B'nai B'rith* concluded with a number of short reviews by a variety of authors. One issue, from 1926,

---

[67] Edmund Kohn, 'Bruder Freud', *B'nai B'rith: Monatsblätter* (1926): 116–17.
[68] Oskar Donath, *Židé a židovství v české literatuře 19. století* (Brno, 1923); Oskar Donath, *Židé a židovství v české literatuře 19. a 20. století* (Prague, 1930).

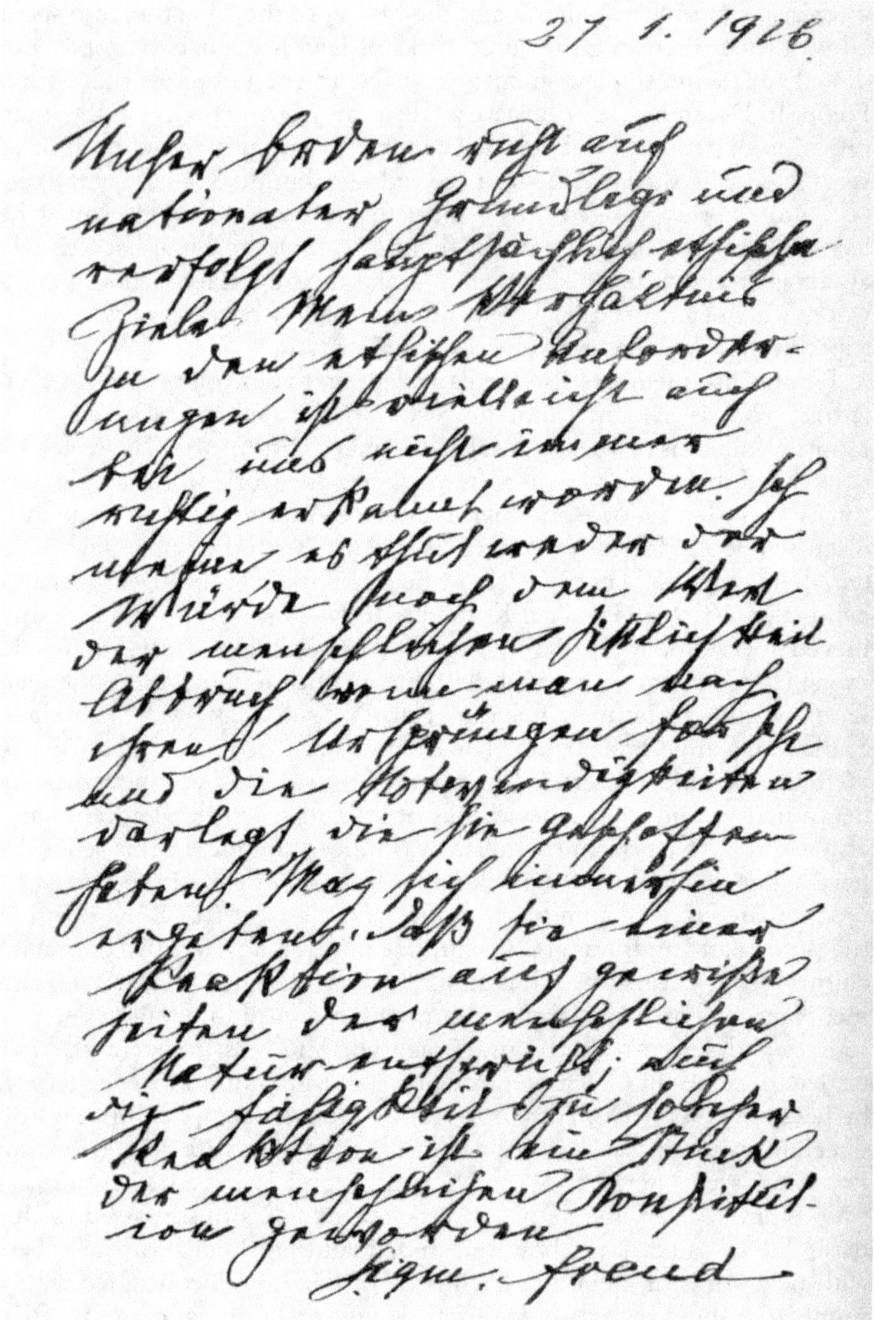

27 1. 1926

Unser Orden ruht auf nationaler Grundlage und verfolgt hauptsächlich ethische Ziele. Meine Wertschätzung zu den ethischen Bestrebungen ist vielleicht auch bei uns nicht immer richtig erkannt worden. Ich glaube es thut weder der Würde noch dem Wert der menschlichen Sittlichkeit Abbruch wenn man nach ihren Ursprüngen forscht und die Notwendigkeiten darlegt die sie geschaffen haben. Mag sich [illegible] ergeben, daß sie einer Reaktion auf gewisse Seiten der menschlichen Natur entspricht; auch die Fähigkeit zu solcher Reaktion ist ein Stück der menschlichen Konstitution geworden

Sigm. Freud

Figure 3.3. A short statement by Sigmund Freud on the importance of the B'nai B'rith Order.

for example, includes reviews of a Czech translation of Otto Weininger's (1880-1903) *Geschlecht und Charakter* (1903), Willy Haas's weekly *Die literarische Welt* (which was launched in 1925), Kafka's *Prozess* (1925) and *Periférie* by František Langer (1888-1965) translated into German in 1926 by Otto Pick.[69]

Figure 3.4. The programme of an evening organised by the B'nai B'rith lodges Bohemia and Praga on 28 April 1920. It included a ballet, a humorous talk, puppet theatre, an adaptation of Goethe's *Faust* and the reading of a film-script by Pavel Eisner, *Don Juan v městském parku* (Don Juan in the Municipal Park).[70]

---

[69] 'Bücher und Zeitschriften', *B'nai B'rith: Monatsblätter* (1926): 187-89.
[70] Eisner's script was never published; it was perhaps written solely for the purpose of the B'nai B'rith evening.

A number of Czechoslovak artists were B'nai B'rith members, including, in addition to Max Brod and his brother Otto, Oskar Baum, Felix Weltsch and Rudolf Fuchs, and two of the foremost translators of Czech and German literature, Otokar Fischer and Pavel Eisner. All of these people contributed a good deal to helping Germans and Czechs to become familiar with each other's literature. B'nai B'rith members were also the mediators through whom most German-speaking Europeans came to know the works of Jewish authors writing in Czech. Apart from Langer, one would mention Vojtěch Rakous (born Adalbert Österreicher, 1862–1935). The following is a letter Rakous wrote in 1925, in somewhat poor Czech, to Rudolf Fuchs:

> Dear Sir,
>
> Not until today did *Tribuna* send me your kind letter, which is why I am replying only now. Please forgive me also for replying in Czech, but I am afraid you would not understand my German very well. I know you as an outstanding translator, and would be delighted if you chose any of my untranslated stories to translate into German. I should only point out that most of my earlier works have already been translated into German by Emil Saudek, and were published by Obelisk (at No. 15 Karlovo náměstí, Prague) two years ago in two volumes entitled *Die Geschichten von Modche und Rezi*. Of my still untranslated later works, I would recommend for translation the short story 'Prodané hroby' [Sold Graves] from the 'Dědeček a babička' [Grandfather and Grandmother] series or, if you want something longer, 'Dny nedělní' [Days of Rest] from the same series, or the longer 'Modche před odvodem' [Modche before Call-up] from the 'Modche a Rezi' [Modche and Rezi] series. All three stories are in the last (fifth) edition of *Vojkovičti a Přespolní* [The People of Vojkovice and Nearby Villages]. . . . I should be delighted if any of those three stories would be found suitable for translation.
>
> Yours faithfully,
> Vojtěch Rakous[71]

Of the older generation of writers, Hugo Salus (1866–1929) also worked with B'nai B'rith. His name appears in a report by the police commissioner, Johann Chlum, who, because of increased surveillance during the war, went to a B'nai B'rith meeting in October 1916. He writes that Salus read some of his new verses at a meeting of the Praga Lodge.[72]

B'nai B'rith also funded the *Jahrbuch für die Geschichte der Juden in der Čechoslowakischen Republik*, edited by Steinherz. The articles in this journal

---

[71] PNP, Fond Rudolfa Fuchse, a letter from Vojtěch Rakous to Rudolf Fuchs, 4 February 1925.
[72] AHMP, SK II/202.

remain to this day a unique source for research into the history of the Jews of the Bohemian Lands. The first two volumes, from 1929 and 1930, are published in Czech and German versions, and the others, until 1937, are only in German.

A perhaps even greater B'nai B'rith contribution to Czech society was its support for original work by Jewish writers. It helped to finance the publishing of a number of books, including several from the Czech-Jewish Kapper Society, such as the internationally known *Nine Gates* by Jiří Langer (1894-1943)[73] and the important work by the thinker Jindřich Kohn (1874-1935), *Asimilace a věky* (Assimilation over the Centuries, in three volumes, 1936). B'nai B'rith made its name in the history of Czech and German literature, however, mainly by founding the Herderverein, a society of German students.

The Herderverein

Established in 1910 by the Praga and Bohemia lodges, the Herderverein was a society for promising young Jews. Most of its members were the sons and daughters of B'nai B'rith members, who were then supposed to recruit new members from it for B'nai B'rith. Thanks to generous financial support, the Herderverein could undertake far-reaching cultural activities.

From 1911 until the outbreak of World War I it published a periodical, the *Herder-Blätter*, whose main contributors were the journalist, film critic and screenwriter Willy Haas and the poet-translator Otto Pick. The periodical published the first works by what would later be the renowned writers of the Prager Kreis, in particular Werfel, Brod and Kafka, as well as works by writers from elsewhere in Bohemia, for example the young poet Franz Janowitz (1892-1917) of Poděbrady (Podiebrad), who was greatly appreciated by Brod, and the Austrian writer, Robert Musil (1880-1942).[74] Other active members of the Herderverein included the Prager Kreis members Weltsch, Baum and Fuchs. Apart from Haas, they all became members of B'nai B'rith. As in many other aspects of his life, Kafka remained aloof; though he was surely interested in the activities of his friends, he saw no need to join. In late November 1912, he was, nevertheless, invited by Haas on behalf of the Herderverein to an evening at which young Prague

---

[73] See František Langer, 'Můj bratr Jiří,' in František Langer, *Byli a bylo* (Prague, 1992), 148-64; Walter Koschmal, *Der Dichternomade: Jiří Mordechai Langer – ein tschechisch-jüdischer Autor* (Cologne, Weimar, and Vienna, 2010).

[74] See *Herder-Blätter: Faksimile-Ausgabe zum 70. Geburtstag von Willy Haas* (Hamburg, 1962). See also the review of this edition: Kurt Krolop, 'Herder-Blätter', *Philologica Pragensia* 6, no. 2 (1963): 211-22, and Kurt Krolop, 'Ein Manifest der "Prager Schule"', *Philologica Pragensia* 7, no. 4 (1964): 329-36.

authors would read from their works. Kafka replied to Haas that he was delighted to have been invited.[75] In early December in the Hotel Erzherzog Stephan (since 1948, the Hotel Evropa) on Wenceslas Square, he read his as yet unpublished story *Das Urteil* (The Judgement). A report on the evening, by Paul Wiegler (1878-1949), was published in *Bohemia*.[76] Kafka mentions the event in a letter to Felice Bauer:

> I enclose an invitation to a reading. I shall be reading your short story [*The Judgement*]. Believe me, you will be there, even if you stay in Berlin. To appear in public with your story, and thus as it were with you, will be a strange feeling. The story is sad and painful, and no one will be able to explain my happy face during the reading.[77]

For Fuchs, Kafka's reading was an unforgettable experience. In his 'Reminiscences of Franz Kafka', he writes:

> Willy Haas once talked him into appearing with Prague authors in a small hall in a hotel on Wenceslas Square. On this occasion he read his story *The Judgement*, later published by Wolff. He read with such a quiet magic of despair that, even after an interval of what has certainly been not less than twenty years, I see him before my eyes in that dark cramped hall. But I have forgotten all the rest.[78]

In March 1919, barely three months after the Armistice, Willy Haas, Ernst Popper (1890-1950) and Arthur Rosen[79] wrote a manifesto called *Die jüdische Aktion: Programmschrift des Herdervereines in Prag*.[80] It is an appeal to the Jewish public, which seeks to present a kind of manual to life in post-war Europe. The solution offered in the manifesto corresponds fully to the conception of Jewry in the B'nai B'rith order. First of all, the authors explain that three chief possibilities for Jewish self-realization already exist – assimilation, Orthodoxy and Zionism. And they explain the weaknesses

---

[75] Franz Kafka, *Briefe 1902-1924* (Frankfurt am Main, 1958), 112, 25 November 1912. This entry does not appear in Max Brod, ed., *Franz Kafka. The Diaries 1910-1923*, trans. Joseph Kresh and Martin Greenberg (New York, 1976).
[76] Paul Wiegler, 'Prager Autorenabend', *Bohemia* 6 December 1912, quoted in Jürgen Born, *Franz Kafka: Kritik und Rezeption zu seinen Lebzeiten 1912-1924* (Frankfurt am Main, 1979).
[77] Franz Kafka, letter of 30 November 1912, *Letters to Felice*. ed. Erich Heller and Jürgen Born, trans. James Stern and Elisabeth Duckworth (New York, 1973), 78.
[78] Rudolf Fuchs, 'Erinnerungen an Franz Kafka', in Max Brod, *Über Franz Kafka* (Frankfurt am Main, 1974), 368.
[79] Arthur Rosen, together with Willy Haas and Thea von Harbou (1888-1954), wrote the script for the film *Der brennende Acker* (The Field on Fire, 1922) directed by F. W. Murnau.
[80] *Die jüdische Aktion: Programmschrift des Herdervereines in Prag* (Prague, 1919).

of each. Assimilation was not the right solution, because it can lead even to the negation of Judaism. Orthodoxy, which was strong in eastern Europe, cannot be the solution, because it does not correspond to modern times. For modern Europe the old form of the Jewish religion was now too limited, narrow and, moreover, could turn into fanaticism. Zionism contradicted the Jewish spirit, particularly with its endeavour to establish an independent Jewish state, where the Jews would have all the outward signs of national and state sovereignty. What possibility, then, remained?

The authors present the reader with a compromise – namely, to declare oneself consciously for Judaism of a nature neither religious nor national, something more like the 'Jewish spirit' or 'Jewish reason':

> Caustic Jewish reason can be described as the spice of scepticism in methodological investigations, a lively impetus in the most rigorous formulations and also merciless in witty reflections. This element of spiritual difference appears in a similar way wherever Jews are involved in the development of ideas and activities. And each of them senses the vitality of that spirit, the special essence, which is mixed in with his blood like the blood with which the Lord anointed his chosen people.[81]

In the manifesto we then also find a carefully considered compromise between assimilation and Zionism: Let's remain in the Diaspora. Let's be good members of the nations in whose midst we live. Let's not forget, however, our Jewish identity. Let's develop the Jewish spirit, and let's look after the welfare of Jews all over the world.

Haas, Popper and Rosen believed that the manifesto would rouse the Jewish masses and unite them. The result, however, was negligible.[82] The initiative of Haas and his friends can reasonably be compared to the efforts of Siegmund Kaznelson (1893–1959) and others, who sought to organise a Congress of all Jews from Cisleithania in order to reach an agreement on how to form a Jewish identity during and after World War I. Like the *Jüdische Aktion*, the 'Kongressbewegung' broke up owing to splits and disagreements among the individual Jewish interest groups.[83]

---

[81] Ibid., 2.
[82] Brod reacted to the Herderverein manifesto chiefly by pointing out the similarities between it and the programme of Cultural Zionism, particularly the Ha-Po'el Ha-Tsa'ir organisation. He also pointed out the exaggerated criticism of the term 'nationalism' in the *Jüdische Aktion*. He understands 'nationalism' mainly as the endeavour to refine and develop the special spiritual/mental features of a certain ethnic community. See Max Brod, 'Der Herderverein', in Max Brod, *Im Kampf um das Judentum* (Vienna and Berlin, 1920), 65–70.
[83] David Rechter, *The Jews of Vienna and the First World War* (London and Portland, OR, 2001), 137–60.

Willy (Vilém in the police records) Haas, who was (according to the police register of clubs, societies and associations) elected chairman of Herderverein on 29 October 1919, organised three evenings of public talks that same year. Apart from Haas, talks were repeatedly given at those evenings by Rudolf Fuchs, Hans Lichtwitz, Liese Mittler and a number of actresses from the Deutsches Landestheater. The programme included works by renowned poets and other writers like Rimbaud, Verlaine, Dante, Heine and Hugo; works by contemporary German Jewish writers like Fuchs and Werfel; and also German translations of works by Czech authors like the poet and short-story writer Petr Bezruč (born Vladimír Vašek, 1867–1958), who is associated with Silesia; the poet, novelist, playwright Fráňa Šrámek (1877–1952); and the poet Karel Toman (1877–1946).[84]

The last big event of the society, which the organisers announced at police headquarters, was a talk, in late January 1920, by Egmont Münzer (1865–1924), professor of medicine, on educating people to be pacifists. The police files also note only the regular election meetings attended by representatives of the Bohemia and Praga lodges.

When Haas stepped down as Chairman and moved to Berlin in 1921, it was a milestone in the history of the society.[85] Scanty reports in the *B'nai B'rith* monthly show that the activities of the society continued throughout the 1920s and 1930s. Every week, the Herderverein organised a talk by one of its members. Sometimes the organisers asked B'nai B'rith members to help out by giving a talk. The work of the Herderverein, however, was no longer fundamentally different from that of other Jewish student societies. The days were gone when famous European writers presented their as yet unpublished works to each other at readings.

One of the numerous reasons the activities of the Herderverein diminished after the war was that many of the German-speaking writers left Prague. They felt that in the capital city of the new republic their audience was limited, and so they went to Germany or Vienna to seek their fortunes. As the writer Viktor Fischl (1912–2006) remarked, for a young Czech artist of Jewish origin the B'nai B'rith had a 'bourgeois tinge' and was too pro-German.[86]

---

[84] AHMP, SK II/305.
[85] The subsequent chairmen of the Herderverein were Paul Schleissner, Karel Grünbaum, Otta Fanta, for a longer period Hans (Hanuš) Schur, and then Jörn Moller. From 1933 onwards, the society was run by Leopold Kettner of Štětí (Wegstädtl), Egon Adler, Lev Schulz, and, the last person to be elected chairman, in May 1938, František Štědrý. See, AHMP, SK II/305.
[86] Part of the interview was published as 'Pak to ale dopadlo ještě jinak: Rozhovor s Viktorem Fischlem o českých sionistech, asimilantech a židovské politice', *Věstník židovských náboženských obcí v českých zemích a na Slovensku* (2001) no. 3, 6–7 and 15.

In 1933 the Herderverein sought to get rid of its German name and thereby express its distaste for Nazism. At the general meeting of 28 November 1933 it was decided to call the society Menorah Brith Hanoar (Menorah Young People's Association).[87]

Numerous literary critics and historians have sought to explain why from the end of the nineteenth century to World War I so many talented artists appeared in Prague, Vienna and Berlin, many of whom were Jews. One of the basic yet neglected reasons is, I believe, that this generation of Jewish intellectuals received moral and financial support from the previous generation. Some parents of Jewish artists had grown up in the ghettos, and became wealthy only by tremendous industry and tenacity. Most of them were shop-keepers or entrepreneurs, whose greatest wish was to have their offspring attend university. It is true that many of them wanted their sons to take over the family businesses and were disappointed if that did not happen. Nevertheless, the founding of the Herderverein and the reviews and articles full of praise in the *B'nai B'rith* periodical clearly demonstrate that the older generation ultimately appreciated their offspring's artistic activity and supported it generously. A fitting example is a review in the *Die literarische Welt* by Friedrich Thieberger (1888–1958), editor-in-chief of *B'nai B'rith*:

> I should like to bring this journal [*Die literarische Welt*, a weekly published by Ernst Rowohlt, Berlin] to the attention of everyone looking for a permanent link with modern European intellectual work. This superbly written weekly, which in various ways helps one to find one's way, also enables individuals from even the most remote place in the world to keep in step with the times. In a recent issue our brother Felix Weltsch has an article about our brother Max Brod, chronologically analyzing this writer's ethical problems. The journal is run by the son of our brother, ex-President Dr Haas, the outstanding essayist Willy Haas. During his sojourn in Prague Haas did a great deal for the activity of the Herderverein.[88]

This review, one of many, clearly shows the close link between B'nai B'rith and authors writing in German, and also that B'nai B'rith members did not lost sight of their artistically talented young generation even after they left Czechoslovakia.

Sympathy for Zionism

Compared to upper-middle-class Jews in other countries, particularly Germany and Austria, German Jews in Bohemia showed an almost surpris-

---
[87] AHMP, SK II/305.
[88] 'Bücher und Zeitschriften', *B'nai B'rith: Monatsblätter* (1926): 188.

ing interest in the ideology of Zionism. This was most likely because the integration of Jews into the German upper middle classes took place smoothly. Jews were able to become members of prestigious German liberal organisations in Prague and a number of other Bohemian towns as well without having to give up or suppress their Jewish identity. On the contrary, they often played important roles as representatives of Jewish communities and local charities, not only in Prague, but also, for instance, in Teplitz-Schönau (Teplice-Šanov), the second largest Jewish community in the Bohemian Lands.[89]

It was therefore typical, particularly of Prague, that the German-speaking Jewish élite quite naturally became linked with the nascent Zionist movement. In 1885, for instance, the Centralverein zur Pflege jüdischer Angelegenheiten (The Central Organisation for Jewish Affairs) was established. The aim of the society was 'to protect and to strengthen the Jewish community and all cultural and humanitarian interests of Jewry, to support and develop existing Jewish institutions, and to establish new ones'.[90]

The most important projects of the society were the founding of a legal-aid section as well as a home for Jewish apprentice craftsman and a home for nurses. I mention this society because the two original Zionist societies – the Jüdischer Volksverein Zion and the Jüdischer Frauenverein – stated in the last section of their statutes that in the event of dissolution the society's property would accrue to the Centralverein zur Pflege jüdischer Angelegenheiten.[91] Also among the Centralverein dignitaries there were often relatives of the first Zionists. One acting secretary of long standing, for example, was the lawyer Theodor Weltsch (d. 1922), the father of Robert Weltsch (1891–1982).[92]

The relatively close collaboration between the German Zionists and the Prague German élite is also evident from the interest of German-speaking Jews in the talks organised by Bar Kochba, a Zionist society. With these talks the society earned money for itself. The first in the series was one of the famous three talks given by Buber in 1909. To draw a larger Prague German audience, the chairman, Leo Herrmann, also invited Salus, a frequent guest at B'nai B'rith cultural events. The evening talk was consequently an unparalleled success, and Buber won over the Prague audience (and not only the Zionists) to such an extent that for the next talk one had only to mention his name and the Prague Jewish Community hall

---

[89] Meir Färber, *Dr. Emil Margulies: Ein Lebenskampf für Wahrheit und Recht* (Tel Aviv, 1949), 36.
[90] AHMP, SK XXII/35, Society Statutes of 1889.
[91] AHMP, SK XXII/119; SK XXII/216.
[92] Tramer, 'Die Dreivölkerstadt Prag', 158.

completely filled up. For Prague upper-middle-class German Jews Buber was acceptable also because he did not advocate a militantly political programme, preferring instead the cultural revival of the Jewish people.

The collaboration between Zionists and German-speaking Jews did not end there, however. One of the important joint projects was the establishment of a 'Toynbee Hall'. This charity project took up the ideas of Arnold Toynbee (1852–1883), Professor of Economic History at Oxford, who believed that material assistance to the poor, particularly the homeless, had to be provided together with spiritual assistance. He therefore proposed that lecture courses and other cultural events should be organised for the poor, both to edify and to entertain them. The events, for which no admission fee would be charged, were to include refreshments with tea. The project for the first Toynbee Hall was carried out by Toynbee's followers in London, one year after his premature death. Professor Leon Kellner of Vienna, who was in London at the time, took the idea to Vienna. The project was adopted by the Vienna Lodge of the B'nai B'rith, which founded the first Jewish Toynbee Hall in December 1900. Afterwards, similar institutions were built in Brno and Prague, Hamburg, and, later, Berlin.[93] The 'Jewish' character of these institutions consisted mainly in the lecture topics, which related to Jewish culture, history or religion. The organisers did not particularly care whether those attending were of Jewish origin.

The Toynbee Hall in Prague was built in collaboration with the Bar Kochba Society, the four Prague lodges of B'nai B'rith, and the Zionist Club of Jewish Girls. B'nai B'rith financed the project, members of Bar Kochba saw to the organisation of the lectures and other cultural events, and the girls prepared the refreshments. Every week (in the winter months, because in summer the homeless were not interested in the events) a large crowd of people interested in the arts used to meet in the Hotel Europa in Masná ulice (Fleischgasse), and were also, as is evident from reports in the B'nai B'rith bulletin, particularly interested in the refreshments afterwards. Even Kafka appeared once before an audience of homeless people, reading to them from a work by Heinrich Kleist.[94] During World War I B'nai B'rith worked with Bar Kochba in organizing aid for eastern European refugees.[95]

The German-speaking upper-middle-class Jews became even more markedly linked with the Zionists during the First Republic. Compared to the

---

[93] Maximilian Stein, 'Zur Begründung einer jüdischen Toynbee-Halle in Berlin 1904', in M. Stein, *Vorträge und Ansprachen von* (Frankfurt am Main, 1929), 142–49.
[94] CZA, Bar Kochba / Barissia Collection, A 317/c 8, Arthur Bergmann's history of Bar Kochba, manuscript, 13.
[95] Karl Schwager, 'Ein kleines Kapitel zur Geschichte Bar Kochba's', *Bar Kochba Zirkular*, January 1966, 7.

B'nai B'rith lodges in Germany, which often had a very reserved attitude towards Zionism even in the interwar period, many important Zionist functionaries became members of the Herderverein and B'nai B'rith in Czechoslovakia. In addition to Zionist artists, there were also, for example, Angelo Goldstein and Chaim Kugel, who were deputies to the National Assembly for the Jewish Party, and Josef Rufeisen, a long-standing chairman of the Central Committee of the Zionist Organisation in Czechoslovakia, whose head office was in Moravská Ostrava (Mährisch Ostrau). Looking back, Rudolf Popper, a pre-war member of B'nai B'rith, even claimed that a clear majority of Zionists of the first generation had later become members of B'nai B'rith.[96]

The sympathy was mutual, as was demonstrated in 1929, when the leadership of the Zionist Organisation decided to set up the Jewish Agency to coordinate the whole Palestine project. Jews who were not active in any Zionist organisation were also represented in the Jewish Agency. At a meeting, the Jewish Agency delegated two non-Zionists for Czechoslovakia, both of whom were German-speaking B'nai B'rith members. One of them, Josef Popper of Prague, was for many years the chairman of the Czechoslovak Grand Lodge of B'nai B'rith and a member of the board of the Prague Jewish Community. The other was Arnim Weiner of Brno, who at the time was also on the board of the Czechoslovak Grand Lodge of B'nai B'rith.[97] At a ceremonial gathering, the chief rabbi of the Bohemian Lands, Heinrich Brody (1868–1942), a leading member of Mizrahi, an Orthodox Zionist organisation, explained to the two delegates the aims of the Jewish Agency.[98]

The Thirties

In the 1930s co-operation between German Jews and Zionists expanded considerably. In the borderlands, local Zionist youth organisations sprang up in reaction to growing antisemitism. More and more German Jewish youths were becoming interested in *hakhshara* (agricultural training before departing for Palestine). The strength of the Zionist organisation in the German-speaking borderlands is also described in a letter from Franz Kahn to Leo Lauterbach of the Zionist Organisation, sent in October 1938, just after Hitler's Reich annexed the Sudetenland. In the letter

---

[96] CZA, Bar Kochba / Barissia Collection, A 317, letter from Rudolf Popper to Richard Pacovský, December 1972.
[97] AHMP, SK II/143.
[98] NA, PP, 1921–1930, 28/4, k. 907, Keren Hajessod society conference, Prague, 23 June 1929.

Kahn complains that the Zionists in Bohemia had lost twenty-four local groups comprising about 3,000 shekel-payers (the shekel being the membership dues of each Zionist), which left only nine groups here with about 2,600 shekel-payers.[99]

In the interior of the country, however, there was another possibility for German Jews threatened by German antisemitism. Since most Jews in the Bohemian Lands were bilingual, many were able from the mid-1930s onwards to declare themselves Czech. Rare documentation of this is provided by a report written by Ferdinand Marek, the Austrian envoy to Czechoslovakia, sent to Engelbert Dollfuss, the chancellor of Austria. In March 1933 Marek began to write detailed despatches about the impact that the Nazi victory in Germany was having on Czechoslovak politics, economics, and public opinion. In his report of 7 April 1933, he writes:

> The local Jews, particularly from Prague, who have so far, mainly together with their financially strong representatives, stood in the German camp, are beginning demonstratively to go over to the Czechs. This represents a great danger to the German minority in Prague, which is mostly weak in numbers, though hugely important culturally and economically. One already observes many German Jews' quitting local German clubs, for example the Deutsches Haus [Deutsches Casino] and Urania. Jewish physicians are systematically boycotting medicines from the Reich, and similar tendencies are increasingly appearing also in private life.[100]

In spring 1933 *Die Wahrheit* published an article entitled 'Deutsch? - Tschechisch? - Jüdisch?', most probably written by Franz Lederer, an editor of *Prager Tagblatt*. In the article he also comments on the 'Umgruppierung von Deutsch auf Tschechisch' (the change of group identity from German to Czech) among Bohemian Jews. Though he understands the reasons for it, he criticizes the change, since, he argues, Jews should strengthen democracy among the Germans as well as be loyal to the Czechoslovak state.[101]

It is fair to assume therefore that if a third census had been held before the end of the First Republic, the number of people of the Jewish faith in Bohemia who stated their nationality as German would have rapidly declined, increasing the number of persons of Jewish and Czechoslovak nationality.

---

[99] CZA, Organisation Department Collection, S5/435, Franz Kahn to Leo Lauterbach, letter of 14 October 1938.
[100] Österreichisches Staatsarchiv, NPA, 751, Bundeskanzleramt, Geschäftzahl 21 758, report by Ferdinand Marek, 7 April 1933.
[101] Koeltzsch, 'Geteilte Kulturen', 259.

Chapter 4

CZECH-JEWS

In 1918 Czechoslovakia was largely established as a nation-state in which the Czechs and Slovaks were each given priority in terms of rights.[1] Most Jews in the Bohemian Lands (with the exception of the Communists) were completely loyal to the Czechoslovak state. Still, it was only the Czech-Jewish movement which could at the same time emphasize its own membership of the ruling nation. Representatives of the Association of Czech-Jews (Svaz Čechů židů), the umbrella organisation of the Czech-Jewish movement, endeavoured, sometimes even anxiously, to guess the tactics of Czech politicians on a wide range of questions in order to adapt accordingly, and thus to demonstrate their Czech patriotism.

The Roots and Special Nature of the Czech-Jewish Movement

The Czech-Jews developed the activities of their various societies from the 1870s onwards. From the beginning of the twentieth century, Czech 'assimilationists' (as they called themselves) mainly turned against the con-

---

[1] For more on the discussion about whether the 'Czechoslovak nation' during the First Republic was a political concept including all loyal citizens of the Czechoslovak Republic or whether, by contrast, Czechoslovakia was a nation-state of Czechs and Slovaks, see Jaroslav Kučera, 'Politický či přirozený národ? K pojetí národa v československém právním řádu meziválečného období', *Český časopis historický* 99, no. 3 (2001): 548–68, and Robert Kvaček, 'The Birth of Czechoslovakia and Considerations Leading Up to It', *The Prague Yearbook of Contemporary History* (1998): 1–18.

ception of Jewry as a national community. Particularly in their attitude to the Zionists they resembled the Jews in the Austrian Lands and in Germany, who came together in the Österreichisch-Israelitische Union and the Centralverein deutscher Staatsbürger jüdischen Glaubens. Nevertheless, close collaboration between the Czech-Jews and the Austrian and German Jews from those organisations did not take place. Between the Czech-Jews and organisations in the German-speaking milieu there was, particularly at the beginning of the Czech-Jewish movement, a fundamental difference.

The unique character of the Czech-Jewish movement becomes evident when one compares the various times when these organisations came into being and their aims. The Austrian Union and the German Centralverein were established in a period of growing antisemitism (the Union in 1886 and the Centralverein as late as 1893) and in reaction to it. Both began as groups of people who felt that the responses of the leaders of the Jewish communities to the growing antisemitism were weak.[2] The main purpose of the Union and the Centralverein, which worked closely together, was therefore to fight against antisemitism. Their ideology included a strong emphasis on the fact that the Jews of Germany and Austria were German and Austrian patriots who differed from their fellow-citizens solely in terms of religion.[3] The officials of these organisations turned against the Zionists as well, who (essentially in accord with the antisemites) emphasized the differences between the Jews and the majority population.

The first Czech-Jewish organisation, the Czech-Jewish Students' Society (Spolek českých akademiků židů), was established in 1876, at a time when the Jews of Austria-Hungary were still feeling euphoric after having been granted the same rights as the majority population. For the Jews, the years when the German liberals were in power, 1867–1879, were the most hopeful of the nineteenth century. After centuries of discrimination they now enjoyed the same rights as others and enthusiastically joined in the modernization of society, for which they were, because of their historical experience, in some respects better prepared than others. In the period before emancipation, Jews were not, for example, permitted to own land or even to lease it, whereas the vast majority of the Christian population was engaged in agriculture in the mid-nineteenth century and only slowly

---

[2] Steven M. Lowenstein, 'Die Gemeinde', in *Deutsch-jüdische Geschichte in der Neuzeit*, vol. III, *Umstrittene Integration 1871–1918*, ed. Steven M. Lowenstein et al. (Munich, 1997), 138, and Mosche Zimmermann, *Die deutschen Juden 1914–1945* (Munich, 1997), 30–31.
[3] Avraham Barkai, *'Wehr dich!': Der Centralverein deutscher Staatsbürger jüdischen Glaubens (C.V.), 1893–1938* (Munich, 2002); Jacob Toury, 'Defense Activities of the Österreichisch-Israelitische Union before 1914', in *Living with Antisemitism: Modern Jewish Responses*, ed. Jehuda Reinharz (Hanover, 1987), 167–92.

re-oriented themselves to doing business in industry. Jews, on the other hand, participated to a great extent in the industrialization of the Bohemian Lands. Similarly, urbanization took place among the Jews much more quickly. Another factor favourable to modernization was the Jewish emphasis on education.[4]

In this period, too, Jews met with expressions of anti-Jewish prejudice. They interpreted them, however, as a 'childhood illness' of a nascent liberal society founded on civil rights. The impulse for the creation of the first Czech-Jewish organisation was therefore not antisemitism, but the Czech national sentiment of Czech Jews, who in the period of the emergence of the first Czech-Jewish organisations constituted only a minority in the midst of the German-speaking Jews of Bohemia.

The Jews of rural Bohemia (particularly of south and east Bohemia), who grew up in a natural symbiosis with the Czechs around them, predominated among the first Czech-Jews. The birth places of the first members of the Czech-Jewish Students' Society – Tábor, Chrudim, Hradec Králové (Königgrätz), Písek and Příbram (Pibrans)[5] – correspond to the places where the first Czech secondary schools, including grammar schools, were established.[6] After coming to Prague to attend university or a polytechnic these first Jewish Czech patriots encountered only societies of German-speaking Jewish students. The Czech-Jewish Students' Society thus aimed to form a counterweight to the societies of German speakers. The aim of the Czech-Jewish Students' Society was, according to its statutes, 'to awaken and cultivate Czech national consciousness among the Jews, that is, Jews born in Bohemia and living in a Czech milieu'.[7] The editors of the Kalendář česko-židovský (The Czech-Jewish Almanac), the first periodical of the Czech-Jews, even compared themselves to Václav Matěj Kramerius (1753–1808), the founder and editor-in-chief of the first nationalist periodical in Czech and the owner of the first Czech nationalist publishing house.[8] The task of the society was to address Jews from the Czech milieu, who, because of the complicated political and linguistic situation in the Bohemian Lands, were indifferent to nationality questions. The Czech-Jewish Students' Society was meant to persuade them to choose Czech

---

[4] Victor Karady, *Gewalterfahrung und Utopie: Juden in der europäischen Moderne* (Frankfurt am Main, 1999).
[5] Kieval, *The Making of Czech Jewry*, 26.
[6] Řezníčková, *Študáci a kantoři za starého Rakouska*, 199.
[7] August Stein, 'Ze začátků Spolku českých akademiků-židů,' in *Vzpomínky a úvahy 1876–1926. Vydáno k jubileu padesátiletého trvání Akademického spolku 'Kapper' v Praze*, ed. Otakar Guth (Prague, 1926), 5.
[8] Kieval, *The Making of Czech Jewry*, 29.

Figure 4.1. An invitation from the Czech-Jewish Students' Society in Prague.

nationality rather than German. No alternative to organised Jewish nationalism existed yet.[9] Members of the society were expected publicly to declare not only Czech nationality, but also their own Jewishness.

The Czech-Jewish students mainly aimed to achieve cultural and social integration. Gradually they began to work with the Students' Reading Circle (Akademický čtenářský spolek), the Arts Club (Umělecká beseda), the Bohemian Forest National Union (Národní jednota pošumavská) and other Czech patriotic organisations.[10] They gained adherents for the idea of Czech-Jewish cultural collaboration among Czech writers, who then several times contributed to the *Kalendář česko-židovský*. Among them were writers whose works are now part of the curriculum in Czech schools, for example, Jakub Arbes (1840-1914), Jaroslav Vrchlický (born Emil Frída, 1853-1912), Gabriela Preissová (1862-1946), Adolf Hejduk (1835-1923), Zikmund Winter (1846-1912) and Josef Svatopluk Machar (1864-1942).

In 1883 the Czech-Jews established Or Tomid (Eternal Light), a society whose purpose was to promote Czech as the language used in the synagogue.[11] Mořic Kraus, a teacher of religion and a member of the Czech-Jewish Students' Society, translated prayers used in the synagogue into Czech.[12] Josef Kraus, a rabbi in Městec Králové, central Bohemia, published *Příležitostné řeči pro česko-židovské kazatele* (Occasional Speeches for Czech-Jewish Preachers, 1895).[13] Or Tomid succeeded in introducing Czech prayer books and sermons in south, east and central Bohemia, but it faced resistance in Prague until World War I.[14] Since so many Jews had moved from Czech-speaking areas to Prague beginning in the last third of the nineteenth century, most Prague Jews were fluent in Czech. Nevertheless, no Prague synagogue or prayer hall wanted to introduce services in Hebrew and Czech. In order to make at least Prague weddings and funerals possible in Czech, Or Tomid first rented a room in the Hotel Stein and then established its own prayer hall in Jindřišská ulice, opposite the main post office. The rabbi was Filip Bondy (1830-1907), who used to preach in Czech while working in rural Bohemia, long before the society was established. He also wrote Czech textbooks on the Jewish religion. After October 1918, most Prague synagogues began to use Czech instead

---

[9] Stein, 'Ze začátků Spolku českých akademiků-židů', 6-7.
[10] Vlastimila Hamáčková, 'Débuts du mouvement assimilateur tchéco-juif', *Judaica Bohemiae* 14, no. 1 (1978): 20.
[11] For Or Tomid see also Kieval, *Languages of Community*, 163-65.
[12] Mořic Kraus, ed., *České modlitby při veřejné bohoslužbě v synagoze spolku 'Or-Tomid' v Praze*, 2nd ed. (Prague, 1899).
[13] Josef Kraus, ed., *Příležitostné řeči pro českožidovské kazatele* (Prague, 1895).
[14] For the Czech-Jewish movement's difficulties in gaining members and support in Prague, see also Cohen, *The Politics of Ethnic Survival*, 163-65.

of German in parts of the service and the Or Tomid association therefore closed down.¹⁵

There were two main differences between the Jews who favoured assimilation in the German-speaking countries and the first generation of Czech-Jews in Bohemia. In Germany and the Austrian Lands the former group began to organise because a new wave of antisemitism was forcing them to defend their Germanness publicly, which was something most Jews there no longer questioned. To demonstrate that they were just as German or Austrian as the rest of the population, they defined their Jewishness as a confession. Instead of calling themselves German Jews or Austrian Jews, they called themselves Germans or Austrians of the Jewish faith. The main task of the first generation of Czech-Jews was, by contrast, to begin to campaign for Czech nationality among Jews, to ensure synagogue services in Czech, and to gain the support of Czech politicians for the integration of Jews into Czech society.

The second difference was how the members of these organisations understood their Jewish identity. Simply the names of the organisations reveal a great deal. The Austrian and German integrationists emphasized that they considered Jewishness 'merely' a confession, and therefore called themselves Israelites rather than Jews, since the word 'Jew' could be associated with the idea of a specific ethnic group. The Czech-Jews began their work at a time when the situation of Jews in Czech society was relatively favourable. Their concept of integration into Czech society was therefore connected to their open declaration of Jewishness. That is expressed clearly by Viktor Teytz (1881-1943), a veteran journalist of the Czech-Jewish press, in 'Několik poznámek k otázce českožidovské' (Some Notes on the Czech-Jewish Question, 1913):

> What does Jewishness mean for us assimilationists? Today, there is surely no one in our country who would want to oversimplify the problem by claiming that Jewishness for us means membership of a religious community. And probably few people would argue that the point of assimilation was to make it impossible to recognize who is Jewish. In that sense our Czech-Jewish movement was always different. We never came out as Czechs of the Jewish faith – unlike Jews in Germany. We linked Czechness with Jewishness in the very name of our movement, and were able to ensure that the term 'Czech-Jew' sounded reputable.¹⁶

From the beginning of the twentieth century onwards the programme of the Czech-Jews visibly shifted. Though the fight against the Jewish ad-

---
¹⁵ AHMP, SK I/12.
¹⁶ Viktor Teytz, *Několik poznámek k otázce českožidovské* (Prague, 1913), 14.

herence to German culture in the Czech parts of the country continued, the Zionists became the adversaries of the Czech-Jews, just as they were adversaries for integrationists in other countries.

A radical change took place after the declaration of Czechoslovak independence. People promoting total assimilation became leaders of the Czech-Jewish movement at that time. They were promoting indifference or an outright negative attitude towards the Jewish religion. For many of them, as for a large part of Czech Gentile society, religion was a relic of another age. Whereas in Germany and Austria in the interwar years, integrationists, in their fight against the Zionists, used the argument that Jewish nationalists were not sufficiently pious (for example, that the Hakoakh sports club in Vienna was willing to play football on Saturday), in Bohemia it was usually the Zionists who were considered more sensitive about Jewish traditions and rituals.

The Break-up of the Czech-Jewish Movement

At the time of the founding of the first Czech-Jewish society, a dramatic polarization of the Czech political spectrum was taking place. Whereas for the Jews the year 1867 meant a watershed, owing to the December Patent, which enshrined equal rights for all, regardless of confession, for Gentile Czechs it was a year of great disappointment. The Ausgleich (Compromise) of 1867, which resulted in the Habsburg Monarchy sharing power with the Hungarian government in the Dual Monarchy, dealt a harsh blow to Czech politicians' hopes in the rebirth of the Monarchy as a federation in which the Bohemian Lands would have their own autonomy based on state rights. Among other things, the National Liberal Party (Národní strana svobodomyslná), known as the Young Czechs (Mladočeši), came into being in 1874 in reaction to the failures of the Czech politicians.

The Czech-Jewish Students' Society was founded only two years later, in times of great political change. The political orientation of most members of the society soon became clear. Amongst the founders was Adolf Stránský (1855-1931), the future leader of the People's Party in Moravia, which proclaimed itself the Moravian off-shoot of the Liberal Party.[17] In its early years the society gained the official support of the Young Czech politician Josef Barák (1833-1883) and Julius Grégr (1831-1896), who together published *Národní listy* (The National Newspaper), the most important Czech periodical until Czechoslovak independence. Later the society

---

[17] Otto Urban, *Česká společnost 1848-1918* (Prague, 1982), 434.

also gained the support of Emanuel Engel (1844–1907), the chairman of the Young Czech parliamentary party.[18]

Four honorary members, well known from the generation before the Czech-Jewish students, backed the society, though they were still politically active in the Old Czech Party. Bohumil Bondy (1832–1907), who was a Kaiserlicher Rat, a member of the Prague Chamber of Commerce, a Knight of the Order of Francis Joseph and a Prague industrialist, had been an Old Czech deputy to the Bohemian Diet from the Old Town, Prague, since 1883. That same year, the lawyer Josef Žalud (1850–1923) and the owner of one of the largest Prague breweries Julius Reitler (1834–1922), both members of the Old Czech Party, were deputies to the Bohemian Diet for Josefov/Josefstadt, the Jewish quarter of Prague. Alois Zucker (1842–1906), professor of law at the Czech University of Prague, was elected as an Old Czech deputy to the Reichsrat (Austrian Parliament) in 1885.[19]

In the early 1890s the Czech-Jewish movement began to branch out further. In 1893 the National Union of Czech-Jews (Národní jednota českožidovská) was founded, and began the next year to publish *Českožidovské listy* (The Czech-Jewish Newspaper), which aimed to help Jews to integrate into Czech society, to defend integration against antisemitic attacks, and to promote 'small-scale work for the nation' (*drobná národní práce*, a term of the famous Czech journalist and politician Karel Havlíček from the mid-nineteenth century, which was later revived by Masaryk).[20] In addition to the popular *Kalendář česko-židovský*, published by the Czech-Jewish Students' Society and focusing mostly on the arts and sciences, adherents of the Czech-Jewish movement thus finally got a fortnightly, which provided commentary on political events.

By its statutes, however, the National Union of Czech-Jews was non-political, and its members often came from the Czech-Jewish Students' Society. Some of its activities (for example, the establishment of mobile lending libraries with Czech literature) were carried out jointly by both societies. It became increasingly clear, however, that the Czech-Jews needed a political organisation. They found one in the Czech-Jewish Political Union (Politická jednota českožidovská), established in 1897, with about 1,100 members.[21] One of the main tasks that the Political Union set itself was the struggle against German-language Jewish (confessional) schools, which had survived in Bohemia and Moravia since the days of Joseph II.

---

[18] Kieval, *The Making of Czech Jewry*, 29.
[19] Ibid., 49.
[20] Iveta Vondrášková, 'The Czech-Jewish Assimilation Movement and Its Reflection of Czech National Traditions', *Judaica Bohemiae* 36 (2000): 145, 150.
[21] Helena Krejčová, 'Českožidovská asimilace', in *Židovská Praha*, ed. Ctibor Rybár (Prague, 1991), 121. This article does not appear in the English version of the book.

In the same period when the Czech-Jews were celebrating their first successes, the antisemitism that was sweeping all of Europe came to the fore in Czech society as well. For the Czech-Jews the greatest disappointment was the anti-Jewish behaviour of the Young Czechs, with whom they had previously enjoyed many friendships. The antisemitic rhetoric of the Young Czechs and a number of other Czech public figures culminated during the nationalist conflicts over the Badeni language ordinances of 1897 and during the Hilsner Affair.[22]

Many Czech-Jews, disappointed in the Young Czechs, sought new political allies. They found them mainly in Tomáš Masaryk's Czech People's Party (Česká strana lidová, called the Realists), the Radical Progressive Party (Strana radikálně pokroková) of Antonín Hajn, and the Czecho-Slav Workers' Social Democratic Party (Českoslovanská sociálně demokratická strana dělnická).[23]

The wave of antisemitism in Czech society led not only to the political reorientation of most Czech-Jews, but also to a further ideological split in the movement. The young generation, led by Viktor Vohryzek (1864–1918), Bohdan Klineberger (1859–1928), Jindřich Kohn (1874–1935), Max Pleschner (1870–1932), Stanislav Schulhof (1864–1919, a physician and poet who wrote in Esperanto), Viktor Teytz, Eduard Lederer (1859–1944) and Max Lederer (1875–1937), publicly condemned the attitude of some older Czech-Jews who were willing to continue to support the Young Czechs. What bothered them most was that in the 1897 elections to the Reichsrat some of those older Czech-Jews had voted for Václav Březnovský (1843–1918), a Young Czech candidate for the Fifth Curia, even though he was widely known for frequent antisemitic remarks. His candidacy (against Karel Dědic, a Social Democrat) was advocated mainly by Jakub Scharf (1857–1922), a Czech-Jew and Young Czech deputy to the Bohemian Diet.[24] The election of candidates to the Fifth Curia of the Reichsrat was new in 1897. For the first time in the history of the Habsburg Monarchy universal male suffrage made it possible, at least with regard to this part of the Reichsrat, to vote. Considering the marked expansion of suffrage to the lower classes in elections for the Fifth Curia, the style and method of election campaigning changed as well and led in all political parties (except the Social Democrats) to the use of populist, antisemitic slogans.[25]

---

[22] For a discussion of antisemitism in Czech society in the 1880s and 1890s, see Frankl, 'Emancipace od židů', and Jan Křen, Konfliktní společenství: Češi a Němci 1780–1918 (Prague, 1990), 257–79.
[23] Kieval, Languages of Community, 200.
[24] Michal Frankl, 'The Background of the Hilsner Case: Political Antisemitism and Allegations of Ritual Murder 1896–1900', Judaica Bohemiae 36 (2000): 52–53; Kieval, The Making of Czech Jewry, 67–68.
[25] Frankl, 'Emancipace od židů', 200–21.

The behaviour of some older Czech-Jews at the time of the Reichsrat elections, however, only served to underscore the existing conflicts in the movement. In 1905 an article by Max Lederer was published in *Českožidovské listy* (The Czech-Jewish Newspaper), which summed up the various positions. The founding generation as well as the young Czech-Jewish nationalists that belonged to it (which, in addition to Scharf, included Maxim Reiner, Ignát Arnstein and Luděk Dux), was reproached by Lederer mainly for their strictly nationalist, hyper-patriotic ideology. For members of the new generation, Czechness had become, according to him, an integral part of who they were. They saw it not as a nationalist or linguistic conception, but as a cultural and spiritual legacy.[26]

Figure 4.2. Jakub Scharf, a Young Czech deputy to the Bohemian Diet and advocate of the narrowly nationalist programme of the Czech-Jews.

A new factor in the Czech-Jewish movement was the courage that these rebellious Czech-Jews showed in criticizing the Czech public and individual politicians. 'We changed tactics, because we were previously acting without backbone and self-respect,' claimed Viktor Vohryzek. 'We had to work with people whom we knew could not have cared less about us, and yet many people are still with them to this day.'[27]

Not only did this group of Czech-Jews leave the Young Czech Party, but Vohryzek, Lederer and Klineberger, for example, were not afraid to come out publicly against the venerable Czech nationalist politician František Ladislav Rieger (1818–1903) after he described Jews as a 'disintegrative element' in a 1901 interview with Karel Dostál-Lutinov (1871–1923), a priest, antisemitic writer and leading figure of the Katolická Moderna literary movement.[28] The Czech-Jewish Students' Society also reacted to

---

[26] Lederer's article is quoted from, and also paraphrased, in Vondrášková, 'The Czech-Jewish Assimilation Movement', 151–52.
[27] Viktor Vohryzek, 'Organisujme se!', in Viktor Vohryzek, *K židovské otázce: Vybrané úvahy a články* (Prague, 1923), 245.
[28] 'Interview u barona Riegra', *Rozkvět* 1, no. 1 (October 1901): 33–34. Quoted and commented on in Frankl, '*Emancipace od židů*', 301 ('Because of its hatred for Roman Catholicism', Masaryk's party was allegedly 'introducing disintegration into the nation, which is

Rieger's words and organised a discussion evening in a Prague restaurant on the topic 'Are the Jews a Divisive Element?'. Masaryk also participated in the meeting, probably because, among other things, he had been attacked by Rieger in the same interview. His chief partner in the discussion was Jindřich Kohn, whom, according to the memoirs of Otakar Guth (1882-1943), Masaryk was much impressed by.[29] It was perhaps in this period that Kohn's long friendship with Masaryk began.

In Pardubice, on 1 January 1904, Vohryzek, began on his own to publish *Rozvoj* (Development), the periodical of this group of assertive Czech-Jews. He continued to publish it until June 1907, when it merged with *Českožidovské listy*. The editorial offices of the new *Rozvoj* were moved to Prague, and Teytz became the editor-in-chief. In 1907 the Association of Progressive Czech-Jews (Svaz českých pokrokových židů) was established. This organisation hoped to become the alternative to the National Union of Czech-Jews.[30] The courage of the members of the Association of Progressive Czech-Jews is evinced, for example, by its successful protest against the Beilis trial in Russia, in which Mendel Beilis, a Jew, stood accused in 1913 of the ritual murder of a Christian boy, Andrei Yushchinsky. The Association of Progressive Czech-Jews initiated the writing of an appeal, published as 'Jménem slovanské humanity' (In the Name of Slav *Humanität*) on 26 September 1913, condemning the absurd accusation. The appeal was signed by leading Czech politicians, scholars and artists.[31] Among them was Jan Podlipný, a Young Czech, who was the chairman of the Czech National Council. Podlipný's signature on the petition was criticized by members of the executive committee of the Czech National Council. That came as no surprise, since the deputy chairman of the Czech National Council at the time was Karel Baxa (1863-1938), who, during the Hilsner Affair, had been an active proponent of the erroneous belief that Jews committed ritual murder. A heated debate erupted between the executive committee of the Czech National Council and the Association of Progressive Czech-Jews. This again demonstrates the independence of members of the Association of Progressive Czech-Jews.[32] The appeal against the Russian trial found support throughout Europe, and the Association of Progressive Czech-Jews thus clearly demonstrated that it did not intend to concern itself with a narrowly nationalist programme.

---

a Jewish trait. History shows us that the Jews have always adapted by means of disintegration, never by means of unification.').
[29] Dr. G. [Otakar Guth], 'Úvodem', in Vohryzek, *K židovské otázce*, 13; Otakar Guth, 'T. G. Masaryk ve Spolku akademiků-židů', in *Vzpomínky a úvahy*, 60.
[30] Kieval, *The Making of Czech Jewry*, 84-85.
[31] *Dějiny českožidovského hnutí* (Prague, [1932]), 11.
[32] NA, NRČ inv. 295, k. 511, minutes of a meeting of the executive committee of the Czech National Council, 4 November 1913.

The Progressive Czech-Jews differed from the older generation also in their attitude to religion. They typically sought to rediscover and reinterpret the importance of Judaism for modern times. Vohryzek summarized the situation in about 1900: 'The most momentous aspect about the whole matter is that the Jews are suffering for their religion and yet actually no longer have a religion; they abandoned it, probably not because they thought it inferior or destructive, but because agnosticism, which enthralled the whole world, also captured their imagination in recent times. The Jews did not lose only their religion; they also lost their heads.'[33]

Like Klineberger, who wrote a whole book about the value of religion for modern man, called *Náboženský cit* (Religious Feeling),[34] Eduard Lederer (Leda) devoted a large part of his two-volume work, *Kapitoly o židovství a židovstvu* (Jewishness and Jewry), to the importance of Jewish traditions.[35] In this work, Lederer often refers to Masaryk, who considered religion the foundation of morality.[36] Like the other Progressive Jews, Lederer advocated faith not as a traditional religious conception, but as an ethical one. Guth, for example, also expressed himself clearly on this point: 'A Jew who rejects the Jewish religion is not a Jew. . . . It matters not whether he is registered at a Jewish religious institution; form is not the same as content . . . . To be a Jew means to acknowledge the moral core of the Jewish religion.'[37]

The Association of Progressive Czech-Jews did not win over many Czech-Jews, and therefore remained, even before World War I, weaker than the original Czech-Jewish Political Union. It was, however, the members of the Association of Progressive Czech-Jews who considerably influenced the new Czech-Jewish generation. In contrast to the nationalistically oriented members of the Czech-Jewish Political Union, who were mostly active at the political and organisational levels, the Progressive Jews wrote works of philosophy and belles-lettres, including examples of some of the best works that Czech-Jews contributed to Czech society. The whole interwar period is characterized well by the paradoxical contradiction that the main ideologues and thinkers of the Czech-Jews seemed to be outside the institutional structure of the Czech-Jewish movement.

During World War I, Vohryzek and Klineberger demonstrated their courageous stance by making clear their disagreement with the policies of the Monarchy. In general, the Czech-Jews took the side of the Czechs during the war, but feared an alliance with Russia, because they were well in-

---

[33] Vohryzek, 'Epištoly k českým židům", 21.
[34] Bohdan Klineberger, *Náboženský cit* (Prague, 1906).
[35] Eduard Lederer, *Kapitoly o židovství a židovstvu*, vol. I and II (Prague, 1925).
[36] Ibid., vol. I, 12.
[37] Otakar Guth, *Podstata židovství a jiné úvahy* (Prague, 1925), 17.

formed about the situation of the Jews there.[38] When *Rozvoj*, for financial reasons, ceased publishing in 1915, Vohryzek started up a periodical in Pardubice, called *České listy* (Bohemian Mail, alluding to the eponymous title of a collection of verse by Siegfried Kapper from 1846). This periodical, however, was also closed down because of an article by Klineberger, in which he wrote that other monarchies that had been intended to last forever also declined and fell.[39] Vohryzek and Klineberger were accused of treason and interned in the fortress prison at Theresienstadt (Terezín) for sixteen days in late September and early October 1916.[40]

The Czech-Jews at the Beginning of the Czechoslovak Republic

One would have expected the Czech-Jewish movement to get stronger after the Czechoslovak declaration of independence. The birth of the Czechoslovak Republic really did mean in a certain sense the culmination of the Czech-Jews' efforts. Czech naturally became the language of the service in most synagogues in Czech areas. The German-Jewish (denominational) schools in Bohemia were all gradually closed down. Masaryk, who personally knew a number of leading Czech-Jews, became the president of Czechoslovakia. Adolf Stránský (1855–1931), one of the founders of the Czech-Jewish Students' Society, became the Minister of Industry and Trade (and had in the meantime converted to Christianity). Lev Winter (1876–1935), a Social Democrat, who became Minister of Social Affairs, had also been a member of that society.[41]

Though they had originally hoped for a Czech state comprising only Bohemia, Moravia and Silesia, the Czech-Jews were the only Jews of Bohemia and Moravia who wanted an independent Czechoslovakia as early as World War I. Zionists and German-speaking Jews would have liked to see the Habsburg Monarchy preserved. For example, Max Brod, together with Franz Werfel and one of the founders of Gestalt psychology, Max Wertheimer (1880–1943), sought at the beginning of World War I, in the name of some of Brod's colleagues, to persuade Tomáš G. Masaryk of the

---

[38] Heiko Haumann, 'Das jüdische Prag (1850 bis 1914)', in *Die Juden als Minderheit in der Geschichte*, ed. Bernd Martin and Ernst Schulin (Munich, 1981), 227.
[39] Kieval, *The Making of Czech Jewry*, 160–61.
[40] 'Klinebergrův večer', *Rozhled*, no. 9 (1920): 5; 'MUDr. Viktor Vohryzek zemřel', *Rozhled*, no. 46 (1918): 1.
[41] Winter left the society when its committee signed a manifesto accusing Omladina, a movement of radical Czech students and young workers who supported the Young Czech Party, of high treason. See Lev Winter, 'Epizoda', in *Vzpomínky a úvahy*, 30–31.

necessity of preserving Austria-Hungary. Masaryk refused to talk to them at the time.⁴²

The Czech-Jews hoped that an independent Czech state would prove their movement right, gain them recognition for what the movement had achieved under the 'Austrian yoke', and make their organisation the government's main partner in questions related to Czechoslovak Jews. A certain model for the Czech-Jews was provided by Jews in France and Germany, who were strong enough to withstand European and American Zionist pressures at the Paris Peace Conference in 1919 for the recognition of Jewish nationality in their own countries.

The hopes of the Czech-Jews, however, came to naught. Compared to the Zionist movement, which entered the social and political life of the First Republic strengthened beyond recognition, the Czech-Jewish movement in the same period found itself in crisis. At meetings of Czech-Jewish societies up until the autumn of 1919 debates took place on the programme of the movement in the new conditions. It was clear to everyone that their programme had to be changed. Some people even proposed stopping Czech-Jewish activities.⁴³

Several causes of the uncertain beginning of the Czech-Jewish movement after World War I can be identified. One of them is that Czechoslovakia, by joining Slovakia and Subcarpathian Ruthenia to the Bohemian Lands, could not adopt the French and German model of Jewish integration. The Czechoslovak government could not ask Jews to embrace Czech or Slovak national identity, if the vast majority of Jews in Slovakia and Subcarpathian Ruthenia were speaking primarily Hungarian, German and/or Yiddish. Even though Jews were under certain pressure to speak Czech in Bohemian Lands and Slovak in Slovakia, it was obvious that this language change would not occur over night. The option of the Jewish nationality in the census should have covered this linguistic reality. The Zionists, in contrast to the Czech-Jews, profited from this, eventually becoming the main partners of the Czechoslovak government on questions related to the Jews. Another cause of the crisis of the Czech-Jews was the anti-Jewish riots in the early years of Czechoslovakia.

The Zionist Advance

At the end of World War I, the leadership of the Czech-Jewish movement was taken unawares by the energetic rise of the Jewish nationalists.

---

⁴² See Max Brod, *Streitbares Leben* (Munich, 1960), 136–43.

⁴³ For a first-hand account of proposals to stop Czech-Jewish activities, see Kamil Neumann, 'Po válce', in *Vzpomínky a úvahy*, 50.

Despite great efforts the Czech-Jews were unable to do anything against the establishment of the Jewish National Council (Národní rada židovská) or against the recognition of Jewish nationality later. A great change also took place when the Zionists became the preferred partners of the government in the discussion of Jewish affairs. It is easy to understand why some politicians reversed their positions on this. The state institutions continued of course to support the Czech-Jews' efforts to make the Jewish population Czech. The effectiveness of the Czech-Jewish campaign, however, was basically limited only to Bohemia. The Jewish nationalists were incomparably more important for the national questions of Czechoslovakia, since they won over for Jewish nationality thousands of German-, Hungarian- and Yiddish-speaking Jews in the borderlands, other parts of Moravia, Slovakia and Subcarpathian Ruthenia. It was as if the Czech-Jews did not want to understand this tactic. For the whole period of the First Republic they railed against the alleged Germanness of the Zionists, calling them Germans in disguise, as if they did not know that the state institutions were impressed by the fact the Zionists had been successfully persuading a number of German-speaking Jews to declare their nationality as Jewish. In the First Republic, moreover, the number of Czech-speaking Zionists continuously increased.

But there were also sporadic instances of Czech-Jews arguing the other way round. They did not accuse the Zionists of being linguistically German, but of taking votes away from the Czech nation. During the general elections of 1920, for example, the Czech-Jews pointed out to the leadership of the Czech National Council that the Zionist list of candidates of the Associated Jewish Parties (Sdružené strany židovské) would take votes away not only from the Germans, Hungarians and Poles, but also from the Czechs. Furthermore, they argued, it was uncertain whether the deputies elected for this party would be loyal to the Czech nation in the National Assembly: 'Considering the sympathies of most Zionists, that is, people with a German or Hungarian past and upbringing, we may be certain that Zionist deputies will in many important matters find themselves on a side other than the one the representatives of the Czech nation are on, thereby somewhat diminishing the hope of a clear majority for the Czech nation.'[44]

The leadership of the Czech-Jewish movement at the time therefore recommended that all Czech political parties and periodicals be given 'instructions in the sense that when criticizing the candidate lists of other parties they should also reject the candidate list of the Associated Jewish

---

[44] NA, NRČ, inv. č. 108, k. 173, P 194, 3 April 1920.

Parties as inappropriate separatism in Czech areas, which harms the Jews themselves'.[45] The Czech National Council then sent the Czech-Jews' report about the 'harmfulness' of the Association of Jewish Parties to the executive committees of all Czech political parties.[46] The attitude of Masaryk, Beneš and other public figures largely contributed, however, to the Czech parties' tending to act positively towards Jewish nationalists.

A Wave of Anti-Semitism in the Early Years of Czechoslovakia

The 'Betrayal' of the Realists

The crisis of the Czech-Jewish movement at the beginning of the Czechoslovak Republic was intensified also by some Czech politicians' dilatory attitude towards the Czech-Jews. In the course of 1917 tangled talks were held among the Czech political parties concerning the possibility of merging the individual political factions. The Young Czech Party, the Progressive Party of Constitutional Law, the Czech Progressive Party and the Moravian People's Progressive Party (led by the former Czech-Jew, Adolf Stránský) ultimately decided in February 1918 to found a new party, the Czech State-Rights Democrats (Česká státoprávní demokracie), better known as the Czechoslovak National Democratic Party. Karel Kramář was elected its leader. The merging was preceded by meetings of the individual political groupings behind closed doors.

Before World War I, most of the eminent Czech-Jews were active members of the Czech Progressive Party, which was influenced by Masaryk's Realism. The Jewish members were not, however, invited to the conference of party secretaries on 16 December 1917. Indeed, not even those who had been party secretaries or members of the executive committee before the war were invited. Although some eminent politicians of the Progressive Party expressed regret that the Jews had been excluded from the talks, the Realist leaders stood firm. The exclusion of the Jews from the talks was explained as an attempt 'only to prevent lengthy debate about the Jewish Question, and to avoid at this meeting a vote to decide on the Czechness of Jewish party members, which has never been in doubt. The proposal [to exclude them], it was said, was no reflection of antisemitic tendencies . . . '.[47] The explanation could hardly have satisfied the Czech-Jews. Being excluded from the Realist talks led Eduard Lederer, Viktor Vohryzek, Jindřich Kohn, Geduldiger, Rakous, Lev Vohryzek and a num-

---

[45] Ibid.
[46] NA, NRČ, inv. č. 108, k. 173, ad P 194, 10 April 1920.
[47] The editors of Rozhled summarized the events in the Progressive Party in 'Na vysvětlenou (K událostem v české straně pokrokové)', Rozhled, no. 7 (1918): 4.

ber of others to quit the Progressive Party in protest. Not even Machar, long a friend of theirs from the Realist party, stood up for the excluded Czech-Jews.[48]

A debate developed in the periodical *Rozhled* (The Review) both among former devoted Realists from the Czech-Jewish camp (Viktor Vohryzek, Lederer and Rakous) and non-Jewish Realists (František Fousek and Jan Herben). Vohryzek accused the Progressive Party of betraying its programme and abandoning its original Realist traditions. One of the reasons for this development, he said (somewhat self-critically), was that the Realists, with few exceptions, were unable to influence a wider circle of people, since they were too caught up in their own intellectual theories. The rebirth of the political group as a political party thus led to excessive radicalization, so was unacceptable.[49] Lederer expressed his opinion on the matter not only in *Rozhled*, but also in the *Živnostenské listy* (Business News) in an open letter to the leading Realists František Drtina (1861-1925), a professor of philosophy and an organiser of the Czech educational system, Přemysl Šámal (1867-1941), a leading member of the World War I resistance group called the 'Maffie' (Mafia), who later headed the Office of the Czechoslovak President, and Jan Herben (1857-1936). In his own articles Lederer stated how greatly disappointed he was in the Realists' approach and rebuked them for trying to exclude Czech-Jews from the Czech nation, though he also expressed the hope that the future Czechoslovak state would be fully democratic.[50] More than a month later, Rakous also reacted to the lax attitude of what was now the Czech State-Rights Democrats on the matter of accepting Jewish members: 'It gives the impression that the leadership did not want to see the Czech-Jews in its organisations, while not wanting to lose its Jewish millionaires and all the other rich Czech Jews, whose Czechness cannot be denied, just as the Czechness of hundreds, indeed thousands, of other, less wealthy or even poor Jews cannot be denied.' Rakous claims to have been called upon to join the local National Democrats' organisation but declined the offer.[51]

In his article 'Na obranu realismu' (In Defence of Realism), Fousek, a lawyer, expert on the Prague stock exchange,[52] and frequent contributor to *Národní listy*, writes that the Czech-Jewish Realists had gone too far in

---

[48] 'J. S. Macharovi, spisovateli v Praze', *Rozvoj*, no. 6 (1919): 3.
[49] Dr. V. [Viktor Vohryzek], 'Ukončená fáse realismu', *Rozhled*, no. 9 (1918): 1; Vohryzek, 'Na různé adresy', *Rozhled*, no. 12 (1918): 1-2; Vohryzek, 'Realismem k realismu', *Rozhled*, no. 13 (1918): 1-2.
[50] Leda [Viktor Lederer], 'Moje věřící skepse', *Rozhled*, no. 10 (1918): 1-2.
[51] Vojtěch Rakous, 'Je to Čech? Není to Čech?', *Rozhled*, no. 16 (1918): 3-4.
[52] See František Fousek, *Příručka ku čtení bursovních a obchodních zpráv v denním tisku* (Prague, 1922).

their criticism of the former Progressive Party and had overestimated the 'antisemitic group's' influence on the operation of the whole party. He ends the article by saying: 'It seems to me not only narrow-minded, but also a bit unfair if the only conclusion one can draw from the fact that a certain coterie in the former party does not admit Dr Lederer and Dr Vohryzek is that it spells the end of Realism or something like that.'[53]

Even Herben, a leading Realist and the founder and editor-in-chief of the Realist's renowned journal, *Čas* (Time), and, from 1917, the editor of *Národní listy*, spoke out on the National Democrats' attitude to their Jewish members. In his article, he defends himself against the Czech-Jews' reproaches that he had not come out publicly against the antisemitic wing of the Progressive Party. Surprisingly, the reason he gives is that he also considered antisemitism justified. The war had apparently demonstrated the cowardice and 'non-Czechness' of the vast majority of the Jews of Bohemia, and so Czech society (including Herben) was seized by a wave of 'antisemitism of disappointment' (*antisemitismus zklamání*). This kind of antisemitism, he argued, was not the repulsive phenomenon of the uneducated lower classes, but a general phenomenon acceptable even to intellectuals. The antisemitism of disappointment, he writes,

> must be classified differently from the old, sporadic antisemitism of the pub, of commercial competition, of religious hatred (among the clergy), or racial hatred (among the chauvinists). That too is the source of antisemitism in the Realist Party. The Jew suddenly became an evil element in our national society, and has nothing in common with us. That is also why the new antisemitism says: Jews are aliens amongst us. No one wants to harm them because of that; no one wants to persecute them, to limit their rights. No one has considered it necessary to defend Jews as a whole, because no wrong is being done to them. Such is the state of affairs today. [Antisemitism] can only be acknowledged; it cannot be weakened or argued away. It seems I am the first to state that fact to the Jews; no one had said it to them yet.[54]

From that point on, 'antisemitism of disappointment' became a standard term in the vocabulary of journalists. Herben's claim 'I wouldn't dare to deny that my acquaintances Edvard, Salomon, Viktor, Rudolf, Vojtěch, Otto, Gustav thought like Czechs or felt like Czechs,' did little to mitigate his otherwise condemnatory words. Though he ultimately came out against 'generalizing about Jews', the first and most serious part of his article is nothing but a demagogic generalization.

---

[53] František Fousek, 'Na obranu realismu', *Rozhled*, no. 10 (1918): 1.
[54] Jan Herben, 'K dnešní židovské otázce', *Rozhled*, no. 11 (1918): 5–6.

Anti-Jewish Unrest

Herben's statement, which struck the Progressive Czech-Jews like a bolt from the blue and led to a heated debate, leads us to another fact that shook the foundations of the Czech-Jewish movement. The radicalization of the political parties and their lax or outright negative attitude towards their Jewish fellow-citizens merely reflects the antisemitic passions of larger parts of the population in the first years after the war. Threatening the standing and ideology of the Czech-Jewish movement, antisemitism spread throughout the new republic like an avalanche. The pogrom in the town of Holešov, Moravia, on 3 and 4 December 1918, is particularly well known. In the course of two days the locals, in collaboration with the Holešov police, pillaged more than fifty houses, causing about five million crowns worth of damage. Twenty-six Jewish shops were robbed, and the Jewish council offices and prayer hall were damaged. Two Jews lost their lives in the unrest. Were it not for the intervention of the army from nearby Kroměříž, the ransacking and pillaging would have continued over the next days.[55]

The Holešov pogrom was not, however, the only instance. In December 1918 anti-Jewish attacks also took place, for example, in the south Bohemian town of Tábor. Four Jews were beaten up, and the mob of Tábor then managed to rob several Jewish shops and break a few windows of their Jewish fellow-citizens' property. Jewish-owned shops remained closed the next day because their owners were afraid that the attacks would continue. Fortunately, the mayor intervened, calling for help from the local Sokol organisation and the National Defence Force.[56] Nor did anti-Jewish riots end in 1918. The offices of Jewish periodicals continued to receive reports about physical attacks on local Jews, the pillaging of Jewish-owned shops, and acts of discrimination against Jews in Czech national societies (particularly Sokol, the leading national sports organisation) and also at celebrations to mark Czechoslovak independence. Attacks occurred mainly in small towns. According to reports in the Jewish press (including *Rozhled*, *Rozvoj*, *Židovské zprávy* and *Selbstwehr*) there were attacks or acts of discrimination also in 1919, for example, in Benešov near Prague, Bzenec, Čáslav, České Budějovice (Budweis), Heřmanův Městec, Hořovice, Jindřichův Hradec, Kamenice nad Lipou, Klatovy, Kolín, Kralupy nad Vltavou, Kutná Hora, Mělník, Náchod, Německý Brod, Nová Cerekev, Nymburk, Pečky, Písek, Poděbrady, Příbram, Rataje and Sadská.

The Jews of Prague were not spared either. Two days before the pogrom in Holešov the capital city witnessed anti-German riots, which in many

---

[55] Zdeněk Fišer, *Poslední pogrom: Události v Holešově ve dnech 3. a 4. prosince 1918 a jejich historické pozadí* (Kroměříž, 1996).
[56] 'Protižidovské výtržnosti bez konce', *Rozhled*, no. 1 (1919): 8.

cases turned into Jew baiting. This included the slogans 'Thrash the Jews!' 'Give them what they got in Lwów!',⁵⁷ referring to the Polish-organised pogrom there in November 1918, in which between 70 and 150 Jews lost their lives and hundreds were injured.⁵⁸ In November 1920 other anti-Jewish attacks occurred in Prague. In this case too the attacks were initially related to the Czech-German conflict. During anti-German demonstrations the crowd took over the Theatre of the Estates and the German Casino.⁵⁹ Demonstrators also damaged a number of Jewish-owned shops on Na Příkopě street, and forced their way into the Jewish Town Hall in Maislova ulice, where they destroyed part of the archives of the Community and several Torah scrolls. *Bohemia* reported that some Czechs had run through Maislova ulice shouting: 'Hang every German and Jew from the nearest lamp-post!'⁶⁰

The anti-Jewish attacks also included so-called 'forced sales', in which the crowd forced shopkeepers to sell groceries at hugely reduced prices. Though these forced sales resulted in the bankruptcy also of several non-Jewish shopkeepers, they frequently caused such chaos that Jewish shopkeepers (much more often than non-Jewish ones) were glad to escape with their lives while their goods were being carried off by the mob.

In the first few years after the war there were also many reported cases of Jews' being barred entry to public institutions or Jews' contributions to organisations with Czechoslovak 'national aims' being refused. Documented examples include Jews' being barred entry to the swimming pool in Černošice (near Prague), a sign 'No Jews or Dogs Allowed!', and Czech Jews' contributions to aid Slovaks in Kutná Hora being refused.⁶¹ The temper of the times is described in an April 1920 report to Berlin from the German Embassy in Prague:

> Nor can one pass over in silence the fact that indignation at the shortage of the basic necessities and rising prices is being manifested in such strong moral indignation against the Jews, who are considered the culprits, that

---

⁵⁷ 'K pražským událostem', *Rozhled*, no. 47 (1918): 1.
⁵⁸ See William W. Hagen, 'The Moral Economy of Ethnic Violence: The Pogrom in Lwów, November 1918', *Geschichte und Gesellschaft* 31, no. 2 (2005): 203–26; Przemysław Różański, 'Pogrom lwowski 22 listopada 1918 roku w świetle zeznań organizacji syjonistycznej złożonych przed komisją Morgenthaua', *Kwartalnik Historii Żydów*, no. 211 (2004): 347–58.
⁵⁹ Jan Havránek, 'Univerzita Karlova, rozmach a perzekuce 1918–1945', in Havránek and Pousta, *Dějiny Univerzity Karlovy*, vol. IV, *1918–1990*, 30.
⁶⁰ Nancy M. Wingfield, *Minority Politics in a Multinational State: The German Social Democrats in Czechoslovakia, 1918–1938* (New York, 1989), 26.
⁶¹ 'Nejsprostší formy antisemitismu', *Rozhled*, no. 26 (1919): 4; P-k., 'Se stanoviska psího', *Židovský socialista*, no. 4 (1919): 2.

I should not be surprised if a pogrom took place, which would, as corresponds to these coarse people, be very bloody, and involve not only the so-called German Jews, but also Polish Jews, of whom very few are visible. The Czech people are antisemitic to an extent that I have yet to see in any other nation.[62]

Members of the Czechoslovak Government and of course Masaryk himself strongly condemned the pogroms and anti-Jewish outbursts in their official statements. They did not miss a single opportunity to ensure representatives of Jewish organisations (whether of the Czech-Jews, the Zionists, or the representatives of the Jewish Community) that it was in the interest of the Czechoslovak state to suppress the anti-Jewish excesses. A deputation of Czech-Jewish organisations was, for example, received on 14 December 1918 by Prime Minister Karel Kramář, and a few days before that by František Soukup, the Minister of Justice.[63] Again and again, politicians expressed the idea that the maturity of Czechoslovak democracy would be judged by how the Czechoslovak state dealt with the antisemitic riots. In his inaugural address to the Czechoslovak National Assembly, Masaryk even said he wanted to make the fight against antisemitism one of the main points of post-war Czech politics. According to Peroutka, however, Masaryk had been forced by the government to remove the article about antisemitism from the programme. The government, Peroutka said, 'did not at the time believe such a warning to be necessary'.[64]

In Bohemia and Moravia from 1919 onwards, pillaging was rarely participated in by the police or town guard. Only further research on anti-Jewish outbursts in Czechoslovakia (particularly in Slovakia) will reveal whether the Czechoslovak government was able to turn words into deeds, whether it did as much as it could to defend its Jewish citizens.[65]

---

[62] Manfred Alexander, ed., *Deutsche Gesandtschaftsberichte aus Prag: Innenpolitik und Minderheitenprobleme in der Ersten Tschechoslowakischen Republik*, vol. I, *Von der Staatsgründung bis zum ersten Kabinett Beneš 1918–1921* (Munich and Vienna, 1983), 267–68. Quoted also in Frank Hadler, '"Erträglicher Antisemitismus"? – Jüdische Fragen und tschechoslowakische Antworten 1918/19', 195.

[63] 'Deputace čž. organisací', *Rozhled*, no. 49 (1918): 6.

[64] Ferdinand Peroutka, *Budování státu. Výbor 1918–1923* (Prague, 1998; 1st ed., 1933–1938), 94–95.

[65] The Czechoslovak armed forces apparently also participated in the anti-Jewish violence in Slovakia. See Ladislav Lipscher, 'Die soziale und politische Stellung der Juden in der Ersten Republik', 270; concerning anti-Jewish violence in general, see Jerzy Tomaszewski, 'Židovská otázka na Slovensku v roku 1919', in *Historik v čase a priestore: Laudatio Ľubomírovi Liptákovi*, ed. Ivan Kamenec, Elena Mannová and Eva Kowalská (Bratislava 2000), 173–86; Yeshayahu Andrej Jelínek, 'Prevrat v rokoch 1918-1919 a Židia (poznámky a úvahy)', in *'Spoznal som svetlo a už viac nechcem tmu...': Pocta Jozefovi Jablonickému* (Bratislava, 2005), 29–43. For clear evidence of the state administration's antisemitism in Slovakia,

Post-war antisemitism dealt a blow to the Czech-Jewish movement. The Czech-Jews themselves compared the events of the immediate post-war years to the wave of anti-Jewish passions which they had encountered in the debates over the Badeni language ordinances of 1897 and the Hilsner Affair of 1899–1900. The impact of the attacks and discrimination after the war was all the greater because the Czech-Jews had expected too much from Czechoslovak independence. They had hoped that the creation of a nation-state of Czechs and Slovaks would mean the implementation of a programme of Jewish integration into Czech society. But just after the declaration of independence, and in the years that followed, many Czechs allowed themselves be carried away with antisemitic passions. Czech society in general made no distinction between 'good Czech Jews' and Jews that were indifferent to the Czech cause or felt German. A report in *Rozhled*, for example, about the exclusion of Jews from Czech clubs and societies in the market-town of Nová Cerekev notes: 'There are, we are told, Jews here and not just German or indifferent Jews, but also *good Czech Jews*, who have been excluded from all the clubs and societies' (emphasis in original).[66] In this sense and others, one perceives fundamental differences in the conception of antisemitism among the Czech-Jews and the Zionists.

The Special Nature of the Czech-Jewish Understanding of Antisemitism

The Jewish nationalists in Bohemia did not really concern themselves with the essence of antisemitism, nor did they greatly distinguish among its racial, religious, national or economic varieties. They considered antisemitism an eternal problem of the Gentiles, which one should vehemently protest against in collaboration with state institutions. The Czech-Jews also tried to intervene in questions related to the rights of the Jews, though mainly the rights of Jews of Czechoslovak nationality. The Czech-Jews anxiously sought also to trace the causes of antisemitism, because they believed that if these causes were removed, antisemitism would disappear. Their attitude to antisemitism is well illustrated by part of an appeal to 'fellow-Czech graduates of the Jewish faith', which the Czech-Jewish Students' Society had sent to secondary schools in Czech areas as part of a membership drive just after Czechoslovak independence had been declared. It says, among other things:

> Do not be drawn in by the noisy slogans of Zionism, which has entered the arena with the bold idea of the existence of a Jewish nationality. This

---

see Rebekah Klein-Pejšová, 'Among the Nationalities', 101–06. See also Miloslav Szabó, '"Židovská otázka" na Slovensku v prvých rokoch Československej republiky'. *Střed*, no. 2 (2011): 59–81.
[66] 'Nová Cerekev', *Rozhled*, no. 4 (1919): 6.

idea, with no basis in reality, hurled into the masses, is, with its appeal to the emotions, meant to lure throngs of Jews who are dissatisfied with their social standing. Antisemitism, which is the source of the unfortunate status of the Jews, must be worked against by making the people politically conscious and removing the shortcomings amongst the Jews themselves. Consequently, the development of morality and the individual's growing responsibility for himself are the guarantee that antisemitism will die out.[67]

Antisemitism, according to the Czech-Jews, would therefore cease to exist when amends were made both by the Christians and by the Jews. Christians would henceforth act truly democratically, as educated, moral and true individuals. At a Czech-Jewish demonstration in 1919 Otto Bondy added that it was also important that Christians should take care not to become alcoholics. 'Alcoholism', he explained, 'particularly the mood induced by beer, spawns beer-hall politics, and that is usually antisemitic. The more sober, reasonable and honest politics, the more democratic it is.'[68]

To clarify its causes, which could, they argued, be attributed in part to the Jews themselves, the Czech-Jews divided antisemitism into a number of varieties. In their analysis they did not concern themselves with antisemitism as an international phenomenon, but instead analyzed its causes chiefly in the context of the Bohemian Lands and, later, Czechoslovakia. (An important exception to this narrow approach was the thinker Jindřich Kohn.[69]) Apart from racial antisemitism, they considered religious, economic, cultural, national (or linguistic) and social antisemitisms. The fundamental idea of the leading ideologists of the Czech-Jewish movement was that the Czech nation (in contrast to the German) was free from racial antisemitism.[70] This idea appeared in the Czech-Jewish press at the end of the nineteenth century, and appeared repeatedly until the German occupation in mid-March 1939. Czech-Jews nevertheless admitted that in

---

[67] AUK, Všestudentský archiv, A 129.
[68] Otto Bondy, 'O antisemitismu v Čechách: Referát z manifestační schůze českožidovské', *Rozhled*, no. 19 (1919): 4.
[69] Jindřich Kohn, 'Náboženství antisemitismu', *Rozhled*, no. 28 (1919): 4; idem, 'Úvodní črta sociologická k dějepisu židů v republice československé (Se zřetelem k problematice Masarykově k slavnostnímu roku jeho)', *Ročenka Společnosti pro dějiny židů v Československé republice*, vol. 2 (Prague, 1930), 1–14; Jindřich Kohn, *Asimilace a věky*, vols I–III (Prague, 1936). In his theoretical essays Kohn includes antisemitism amongst other examples of xenophobia in general (in his terminology, 'antigerism', where *ger* is Hebrew for stranger or alien). He also published a number of articles on the topic in *Rozvoj* in 1919.
[70] In 1900, Eduard Lederer claimed even that Czech antisemitism was imported from Germany. See Miloslav Szabó, 'National Conflict and Anti-Semitism at the Beginning of the Twentieth Century: The Case of the Czech Slovakophiles Karel Kálal and Eduard Lederer', *Judaica Bohemiae* 44 (2009): 61.

Czech society one did encounter certain anti-Jewish moods. But this, according to them, was mostly economic and national antisemitism, which had, in contrast to racial antisemitism, a rational core. The reason for economic antisemitism was, they explained, the unequal social structure of the Jewish population. National antisemitism was, they concluded, clearly rooted in the Jews' pro-German attitude (*němčení*) in the Czech parts of the country.

Concerning the question of the disproportionate representation of the Jews in some occupations, the Czech-Jews began the discussion in the Order of B'nai B'rith. A Czech-Jewish member of B'nai B'rith, Luděk Dux, in 1929, summarized the main conclusions of discussions and questionnaires among the members of the order. The questionnaires did not confirm the assumption (and the antisemitic prejudice) that the Jews were overly represented in commerce and finance. The number of Jews in these fields, even in comparison with the pre-war period, had rapidly declined. From the questionnaire, however, it is clear that the Jews were represented above average in the professions, that there was among them an 'excess' of lawyers, doctors with private practices, freelance scholars and journalists.[71]

One of the slogans of the Czech-Jews was 'restratification' of the Jewish population. The Zionists, too, promoted restratification, so that the Jews could create an independent infrastructure of a Jewish state, from farmers and tradesmen to teachers and scientists. The Czech-Jews, on the other hand, were pushing for a change in the social and occupational structures of the Jewish population, so that the Jews would proportionately integrate into all spheres of social life and not be conspicuous. Their model for the 'process of restratification' was, paradoxically, the Soviet Union, which could boast a relatively high proportion of Jewish workers and farmers. Palestine, according to them, was geographically too small to carry out this process.[72] At least that is what Otto Stross, the then-chairman of the Association of Czech-Jews, claimed in his talk at the YMCA (which was published as propaganda by the culture committee of the Association of Czech-Jews). Ervín Neumann (1905–1943), a novelist and playwright, gave his views on the topic in 1937:

> We shall endeavour to make sure that commerce and the professions are not the only forms of employment for Jews of future generations. We shall study the sociological basis of the western Jews, and endeavour to make

---

[71] Luděk Dux, 'Přeskupení v povolání: Výsledky dotazníkové akce', *B'nai B'rith: Monatsblätter*, no. 2 (1929): 45–53.
[72] In the USSR 14.8 per cent of the Jews were said to be workers and 9.1 per cent were allegedly farmers. Otta Stross, *Vývoj židovské otázky po světové válce* (Prague, 1937), 56.

sure that Jews return to industry, farming, and the primary sector. . . . We do not wish to force intellectuals to do work that they do not know how to do and is therefore of no use to human society. But we shall educate the new Jewish generation in the conviction that manual labour is the most blessed kind of work.[73]

Neumann's booklet says that the Czech-Jews have a 'practical plan' to influence the economic orientation of the Jews.[74] No detailed or concrete elaboration of their plan, however, appears in their newspapers or other documents. Mention is made of career-counselling offices but they were actually initiated by the B'nai B'rith, which also funded these offices, not by Czech-Jews.

In July 1938 Ota Richter, who was in charge of the youth committee of the board of the Association of Czech-Jews, admitted that the Czech-Jews had no concrete plan for restratification. Only individuals, not Jewish youth as a whole, could be influenced, he claimed.[75] And so, until the outbreak of war, current or future lawyers, journalists, intellectuals and physicians constituted the absolute majority of the members of the Czech-Jewish organisations.

Appeals for restratification in the Czech-Jewish press met with little response, yet Czech-Jewish attempts to do away with the causes of national antisemitism were all the more energetic. And the greater the antisemitic pressure the Czech-Jews had to face, of course, the more their anti-German rhetoric intensified. This occurred at the end of the nineteenth century, just after World War I, at the beginning of the Czechoslovak Republic, and, most of all, in the 1930s.

Apart from the uneven social structure of many Jews in the Bohemian Lands and their use of the German language, some Czech-Jews were also concerned with other 'Jewish vices' that could foster anti-Jewish moods. Otto Bondy, for example, claimed that Jewish men played cards too much and that Jewish women dressed ostentatiously. Pavel Gutfreund, another Czech-Jew, reacted to Bondy's article by saying that he did not think Jewish women should dress ostentatiously, but he agreed that Jews in Bohemia played cards far more than Gentiles. The reasons, he says, were that in pubs no non-Jews conversed with Jews and also the Jews were few in number ('just right for a game of cards').[76]

---

[73] Ervín Neumann, *Práce, program a cíl Svazu Čechů židů v ČSR* (Prague, 1937), 18–19.
[74] Ibid., 19.
[75] Ota H. Richter, 'Má židovská mládež budoucnost?', *Rozvoj*, nos. 31–32 (1938): 2–3.
[76] Otto Bondy, 'O antisemitismu v Čechách: Referát z manifestační schůze českožidovské', *Rozhled*, no. 19 (1919): 5; Pavel Gutfreund, 'O židovských nectnostech', *Rozhled*, no. 22 (1919): 3.

The Czech-Jewish view of antisemitism took root in Czech historiography.[77] Consequently, some Czech historians today even believe that racial antisemitism either never existed in the Bohemian Lands or was greatly subdued. They believe, on the other hand, that national, economic and religious antisemitism, which were apparently milder and to some extent even understandable, were pronounced here.[78] But other historians, including some Czechs, have clearly demonstrated that the phenomenon of anti-Jewish hatred cannot be mechanically divided up by kind, since all are closely interlinked in antisemitic propaganda.[79] Nor is it reasonable to assume that the core of antisemitism (or xenophobia in general) is rational. A pseudo-rational justification, such as the Jews' being linguistically pro-German in times when the absolute majority of Jews in the Bohemian Lands spoke Czech, or that Jews controlled Czech industry or finance, cannot be understood except as a cloak for the otherwise irrational hatred of Jews.

The tremendous strength of antisemitism consists in its being a flexible ideology, which reacts quickly to the needs of the times. It is therefore understandable that antisemites in the Czech milieu used the hostile image of the German nation, and attached it to the image of the Jew. This identification was supported by the fact that most Jews in the early nineteenth century initially adopted German culture. But if one considers, for example, the nationalist arguments of the Czech antisemites, it is relatively easy to show that they operated like the arguments of the German antisemites,

---

[77] For two recent views opposing this dominant idea, see especially Michal Frankl, '"Sonderweg" of Czech Antisemitism? Nationalism: National Conflict and Antisemitism in Czech Society in the Late 19th Century', *Bohemia* 46, no. 1 (2005): 120-34, and Robert Pynsent, 'The Literary Representation of the Czechoslovak "Legions" in Russia', in *Czechoslovakia in a Nationalist and Fascist Europe 1918-1948*, ed. Mark Cornwall and R. J. W. Evans (Oxford, 2007), 63-88.

[78] For example Jan Rataj, 'Český antisemitismus v proměnách let 1918-1945', in *Židé v české a polské občanské společnosti*, ed. Jerzy Tomaszewski and Jaroslav Valenta (Prague, 1999), 45-64; Helena Krejčová, 'Židovská komunita v moderní české společnosti', in *Židé v novodobých dějinách*, ed. Václav Veber (Prague, 1997), 22. Rybár even adopted the Czech-Jews' idea that their task was to free Czech society from antisemitism. Assessing the Czech-Jews' activities during the First Republic, he writes: 'Some of the movement's efforts of course came to naught. It did not manage to rid Czech society of antisemitism.' See Ctibor Rybár, 'První republika', in *Židovská Praha*, 141. This passage does not appear in the English version of the book.

[79] Shulamit Volkov, 'Antisemitismus als kultureller Code', in Shulamit Volkov, *Jüdisches Leben und Antisemitismus im 19. und 20. Jahrhundert* (Munich, 1990), 13-36; Yehuda Bauer, 'In Search of a Definition of Antisemitism', in *Approaches to Antisemitism: Context and Curriculum*, ed. Michael Brown (New York and Jerusalem, 1994), 10-23; Bedřich Loewenstein, 'Motivy antisemitismu', in *Antisemitismus v posttotalitní Evropě* (Prague, 1993), 19-25.

which were premised on notions of racial inferiority. In Germany in the late nineteenth century and early twentieth century, racial antisemitism (like 'national antisemitism' in Bohemia) helped Germans in the 'self-definition of their nascent national community'.[80] In Bohemia, on the other hand, there was no need to employ arguments about a 'different (inferior) race'. Instead, the argument was about the alleged 'national unreliability' (*národní nespolehlivost*) of the Jews and their affinity for the German nation. Evidence of this is that the antisemites in times of anti-Jewish unrest had no intention of distinguishing between Jews who spoke Czech and whose culture was Czech and those who spoke German and supported German culture, despite the protests of the organised Czech-Jews.

The idea that racial antisemitism did not exist in Bohemia and that national antisemitism predominated became an integral part of Czech-Jewish ideology. The reason was that only anti-Jewish hatred which was explained in this way gave Czech-Jews the hope that a synthesis of Jewishness and Czechness (or complete assimilation) stood a real chance of success. Though one may therefore sympathize with the Czech-Jews' faith in the Czechs' allegedly 'dove-like' nature and their belief in Czech democratic traditions (which the Zionists also depended on), the Czechs-Jews often paid for their profoundly ardent support for the Czech nation by their animosity towards Jews who were brought up in German culture. A good example is the introductory sentence from a 1918 article by Rakous, written after several years of silence:

> I never wrote kindly of the German-speaking Jews of Prague and other places in Bohemia, and never wrote unkindly of antisemites if they directed their attacks against pro-German Jews. For that reason the German Jews always included me among the antisemites, and they were right to the extent that I never hated anyone in my whole life as ardently as German-speaking Jews in Czech areas. I hated them ardently because it was always innocent people, poor Jews who perhaps did not even know German, who were the sacrificial lambs taking away the sins of these pro-German Jews. . . . War came and my hatred for the pro-German Jews increased, if that was possible. With clenched teeth, in helpless rage, with people who thought like me, I watched the mindless, disgraceful strutting about of the German Jews in Prague, which insulted the best sentiments of the Czech people. And we told ourselves in a premonition of things to come: The innocent will pay for this.[81]

---

[80] The central role of antisemitism in the 'self-definition of a nascent national community' is discussed, for instance, in Loewenstein, 'Motivy antisemitismu', 23; for the Czech case, see also Frankl, '*Emancipace od Židů*'.
[81] Vojtěch Rakous, 'Je to Čech? Není to Čech?', *Rozhled*, no. 16 (1918): 3.

The Czech-Jews' efforts to assimilate with the Czech nation were, however, also accompanied by their aversion to Jewish immigrants. They believed that the immigrants contributed to the rise in antisemitism. Xenophobic tendencies appeared in the Czech-Jewish movement even before the end of World War I. At that time it was Jews from the east, mainly Galicia and Bukovina, who were the object of their contempt. Just as later, in the 1930s, with the refugees from Nazi Germany, so too at this earlier time Czech-Jews tried to alleviate the inhumane conditions of some of these refugees with material aid, but never concealed their belief that the one real solution to the problem was the expulsion of these uninvited guests.

In September 1917, for example, the editors of *Rozhled* voiced their agreement with the views expressed in the Social Democrats' paper, *Právo lidu*, that the inhabitants of Prague and the countryside could hardly bear the Polish Jews' abuse of Czech hospitality and their 'outrageous wheeling and dealing'. Although, allegedly, only about half the Polish Jews were behaving in that way, it became necessary, according to *Právo lidu*, to solve the problem by 'removing them from the Bohemian Lands'. The editors of *Rozhled* quoted the article, and reiterated the last idea: 'Today, when Galicia and Bukovina are again free, there is no reason Polish Jews should remain here. On the contrary, it is in the general interest that they go back home again as quickly as possible.'[82] Most Galician refugees left the Bohemian Lands of their own accord even before the end of the war. Whereas, for example, in April 1915 they numbered 17,000 in Prague alone, there were only about 1,300 of them there at the end of the war.[83] Most of the remaining Galician refugees were then 'evacuated' from Czechoslovakia in November 1918 under a decree of the Czechoslovak National Committee, the main political representative body at that time. The expulsion was carried out despite the protests of Czech and foreign Zionists.[84]

Even the Czech-Jewish statements of 1919, however, contain rhetoric aimed against the Galician Jews. At a demonstration in April 1919, Otakar Guth, for example, mentions that the wartime antisemitism had 'increased even more with the arrival of the Polish Jews, who soon began

---

[82] 'Židovská hlídka', *Rozhled*, no. 3 (1917): 3.
[83] Jiří Kuděla, 'Galician and East European Refugees in the Historic Lands: 1914-16', *Review of the Society for the History of Czechoslovak Jews*, vol. 4 (1991-1992), 23, 29. In the article Kuděla summarizes the Czech-Jews' attacks against Polish Jews in the Czech-Jewish press.
[84] The Swiss Zionist Association, for example, came out sharply against the evacuation of Galician refugees in an open letter to the National Committee, 25 November 1918. See 'Neutrale Bemuehungen zugunsten der Galizianer in Boehmen', *Juedisches Pressebureau Wien*, no. 1 (26 November 1918): 1.

their dodgy business'.[85] The leaders of the Czech-Jewish movement came out against any foreign Jews, in order to show that the national interests of the Czechs were their main concern.

A Clash of Two Conceptions of Czech-Jewish Ideology

In the early years of the Czechoslovak Republic the Czech-Jewish movement underwent dramatic changes. In reaction to different political and social circumstances a conflict arose among proponents of radical assimilation, for whom the nationalist programme and the suppression of Jewish elements were paramount, and among some former Progressive Czech-Jews who were seeking a synthesis of Jewishness and Czechness ('Czechness with a Jewish tinge'[86]). A new factor in the history of the Czech-Jewish movement was the endeavour to establish Czech-Jewishness on a broader base. This entailed publishing a democratic Czech daily newspaper free from antisemitism and also developing a country-wide organisation that would work in conjunction with Jewish and non-Jewish members to solve the problems of society as a whole, particularly in the area of law and the economy. Both ambitious projects came to naught, however, in the early 1920s, and the leadership of both the Association of Czech-Jews and the Kapper Society, the two principal Czech-Jewish organisations, was largely taken over by proponents of radical assimilation.

'Czechness with a Jewish Tinge'

In addition to external obstacles to Czech-Jewish assimilation in the early years of the Republic, there was also internal ideological dissension. The core of the problem was how to determine the chief aim of Czech-Jewish activities. Was it to be complete assimilation with the Czech nation? Adherents of this view considered Czech-Jewish organisations to be but a temporary phenomenon, which would exist until antisemitism disappeared and assimilation was completed.

All the opponents of radical assimilation had come from the former Association of Progressive Czech-Jews. Their credo was the synthesis of Czechness and Jewishness, which was supposed to lead to the spiritual enrichment of both the Jews and Czech society. In reaction to Herben's claim that during the war the Czechs had realized that the Jews were an 'alien element' in their midst, Eduard Lederer remarked: 'Even we admit

---
[85] 'Manifestační schůze českožidovská', *Rozvoj*, no. 18 (1919): 1.
[86] Dr. V. [Viktor Vohryzek], 'Na obranu pravdy', 5.

that we bring to Czech life something different from the Czech Christian outlook, something that developed in us by way of our different origin, different tradition, different church. It is only a question of whether our difference harms the Czech cause or whether it fertilizes it, increases its value.'[87] Viktor Vohryzek immediately came out in support of Lederer's view. 'I fully agree with my friend Leda,' he said, 'that our Czechness has to have a Jewish tinge and that only that kind is desirable for the [Czech] nation as a whole and beneficial to it.'[88] Otakar Guth wrote an article in the same spirit, reacting to the reproaches of the Czech public that Czech-Jews, unlike the Zionists, conceal their Jewish roots and try to get rid of them. The greatest promoter of a Czech-Jewish synthesis, however, was Kohn. His key work, *Asimilace a věky*,[89] a three-volume collection of articles published posthumously, is clear evidence of this.

The sporadic voices of members of the Association of Progressive Czech-Jews were lost, however, among the claims of the Czech-Jews, who promoted a narrowly nationalist programme. The view was often stated that it was necessary to merge unconditionally with the Czech milieu. An extreme view was expressed in an article by an occasional contributor to *Rozhled*, Oldřich Weiner (1895-?; survived the Shoah in Theresienstadt), opposing Vohryzek and Lederer. 'I think we have to realize that we are completely assimilated,' he wrote, 'and that consequently our Czechness cannot differ at all from the Czechness of the rest of the nation. I reject the view that something of a Jewish nature must remain in us. On the contrary: nothing of the Jewish nature should remain, that is, no signal mental characteristic.'[90] He even claimed that Herben was correct to say that Czech society was justifiably antisemitic. As a fully assimilated Czech-Jew, Weiner believed the problem was that most Jews were 'uncultured, amoral and parasitic'.[91] His article, a prime example of Jewish antisemitism, helped to deepen the crisis between the editors of *Rozhled* and the Progressive Czech-Jews led by Viktor Vohryzek.[92] The Progressive Czech-Jews then tended to contribute to *Rozvoj*, which began to publish again in 1918.[93]

---

[87] Leda [Eduard Lederer], 'Čechové křtění a nekřtění', *Rozhled*, no. 13 (1918): 5.
[88] Dr. V. [Viktor Vohryzek], 'Na obranu pravdy', 5.
[89] Kohn, *Asimilace a věky*.
[90] Oldřich Weiner, 'K našemu češství', *Rozhled*, no. 15 (1918): 5.
[91] Ibid. In his negative view of the Jews, Weiner quotes Antonín Uhlíř, 'Židovství a národ', *Rozhled*, no. 12 (1918): 4.
[92] The disputes between Vohryzek and the editors of *Rozhled* are described in Vohryzek's obituary, 'MUDr. Viktor Vohryzek zemřel', *Rozhled*, no. 46 (1918): 1.
[93] *Rozhled* was first published in 1917. *Rozhled* and *Rozvoj* were both published in 1918-1920.

The ideological disputes in the Czech-Jewish camp elicited reactions even from non-Jewish observers. In his article 'České židovství' (Czech Judaism) the prominent Czech philosopher Emanuel Rádl, for example, expresses his sympathy for Zionism, religious and national consciousness and *Humanität*. He comes out in favour of assimilation, though only the sort that does not lead to levelling. Rádl is thus reacting to the predominant tone in the Czech-Jewish press, which was promoting radical assimilation. 'The assimilationists', he states,

> let themselves be confused by unacceptable, despicable theories about the Jews' dissolving into Czechness. From the point of view of freedom of individual conviction one cannot protest strongly enough against these automatic, bullying tendencies. Allowing themselves to be seduced, the assimilationists succumb to levelling tendencies, denying free will, substituting cosmopolitanism for individualism, denying religion its creative power, wiping away racial characteristics and glossing over tradition, and in general confusing equal rights with the suppression of physical and mental distinctiveness.[94]

In an attempt to demonstrate the contradictory nature of assimilationist ideology Rádl presents the reader with many quotations from Czech-Jewish periodicals and booklets. He agrees with Eduard Lederer's article 'Čechové křtění a nekřtění' (Czechs, Baptized and Not Baptized), quoted above, and with the conception of Czech-Jewishness in Teytz's 1913 pamphlet on the Czech-Jewish Question.[95] He is critical, however, of an article by Lederer, where it is argued that Jewishness has already fulfilled its mission and 'is not even necessary in the interest of the future culture of mankind'.[96] He also takes issue with Klineberger, who, in his article 'Naše budoucnost' (Our Future), writes that assimilation was a result of the fact that the Jews, as weaker individuals, must give in to the pressure of the stronger society in the state. Rádl then deals with Schulhof, Karel Scheinpflug (1869–1948), and, last but not least, Rakous who, in one of his articles argues that he was a Czech because of the pressure of the Czech milieu.[97]

In his article, Rádl manages to pinpoint the main contradiction in Czech-Jewish ideology at the end of World War I. The article is important for us because Rádl does not consider the conflict between the Political

---

[94] Emanuel Rádl, 'České židovství', *Rozhled*, no. 23 (1918): 4.
[95] Teytz, *Několik poznámek k otázce českožidovské*.
[96] Quoted in Eduard Lederer, *Českožidovská otázka* (Prague, 1899). For an analysis of other writing by Eduard Lederer with an antisemitic tinge, see Miloslav Szabó, 'National Conflict and Anti-Semitism at the Beginning of the Twentieth Century', 64–65.
[97] Rádl, 'České židovství', 4–5.

Union and the Association of Progressive Czech-Jews. He quotes only from the works of the Progressive Czech-Jews. His article therefore provides evidence that under the pressure of the nationalistic narrative of the Czechs even figures like Klineberger and Lederer ceased to be consistent in their progressive views.

Ferdinand Peroutka's critical assessment of the Czech-Jews is equally interesting. In a series of four articles in *Rozhled*, in 1917, Peroutka, the leading Czech journalist of the interwar period, and close to President Masaryk, comments on the aims of Czech-Jewish assimilation and the obstacles it faced.[98] In the fourth article, he makes his main point – namely, that equal rights for the Jews (meaning not only legal equality, but also social equality) could be achieved only by the democratization of all Czech life. The task of the Czech-Jews is, he argues, to overcome the 'narrow confines of the Czech-Jewish movement'. He reproaches them, for example, for not publishing in book-form the articles of Vohryzek, whom he describes as a 'man with a gift and a penchant for philosophy the likes of which are currently absent amongst Czech university philosophers'.[99]

New Projects

The Czech-Jews at the very beginning of the First Republic truly did try to win broad-based support for their movement. Two of their ambitious projects are particularly noteworthy. One was the plan to start up a Czech-Jewish daily newspaper. The second was to establish a Business and Arts League (Jednota pro péči hospodářskou a kulturní). It was Vohryzek who, as early as 1910, came up with the idea of Czech-Jews' publishing a Czech newspaper. In a detailed article in *Rozvoj* he proposed publishing a Czech daily that could compete with the *Prager Tagblatt* in mainly Jewish Czech families. His article was republished in January 1919.[100] After the war, he was joined by other members of the Association of Progressive Czech-Jews. The proposal met with resistance, however, among supporters of radical assimilation, that is, among members of the Czech-Jewish Political Union and the editors of *Rozhled*. In their May 1918 statement, the committee members of the Czech-Jewish Political Union provide a detailed

---

[98] Ferdinand Peroutka, 'Českožidovské otázky I', *Rozhled*, no. 13 (1917): 4-5; idem, 'Českožidovské otázky II', *Rozhled*, no. 14 (1917): 5; idem, 'Českožidovské otázky III', *Rozhled*, no. 15 (1917): 4-5; idem, 'Českožidovské otázky IV', *Rozhled*, no. 16 (1917): 5-6.
[99] Peroutka, 'Českožidovské otázky IV', 5-6. Peroutka became interested in Czech-Jewish movement thanks to an accidental meeting with editor Fischer from *Rozvoj* (and *Rozhled*) when visiting Stanislav Minařík in 1917. Fischer asked him to write an article about the situation in post-revolutionary Russia for one of his journals. See Ferdinand Peroutka, *Deníky...dopisy...vzpomínky*, ed. Slávka Peroutková (Prague, 1995), 88.
[100] Viktor Vohryzek, 'Česká žurnalistika', *Rozvoj*, no. 3 (1919): 1-2.

explanation of their negative position. They point out that the proposal to publish a Czech-Jewish daily had first been made back in the 1890s and then, much later, at the private meeting of Czech-Jews in February 1918, where the majority had reacted negatively to it, 'not only for financial reasons, but also for fundamental reasons and reasons related to the programme'. The Czech-Jewish Political Union leadership was 'definitely against the publishing of dailies by Czech-Jewish circles', because the Czech-Jews sought total assimilation with the Czechs. If they had their own newspaper the Czech-Jews would 'cut themselves off' from the rest of the nation. The newspaper would also lack a clear political line since the Czech-Jews were highly diverse politically. It would, they claimed, also be an extremely expensive undertaking.[101]

At its 16 May 1918 meeting, the Association of Progressive Czech-Jews, on the other hand, came to the conclusion that it was truly necessary to start up a new daily newspaper. The chairman of the association, Mořic Hirsch (1871–1942), explained the 'need for a new progressive, democratic daily that would not only fill a gap in the Czech daily press, but also squeeze German periodicals out of Jewish homes and away from non-Jewish businessmen. In the new periodical special attention would be paid to economics'.[102] A daily newspaper financed largely by Czech-Jews was supposed to guarantee that the Czech public would be kept truthfully informed about Czech-Jewish efforts and that the newspaper would be free from antisemitic remarks. Moreover, the daily was to provide objective information on politics and devote itself in particular to questions of the economy, which the Czech press mostly ignored.

Members of the Association of Progressive Czech-Jews eventually managed to found a daily.[103] Called *Tribuna*, the first issue was published on 1 February 1919, and, not surprisingly, Peroutka was made an editor. Its first editorial says:

> [W]e wish to serve our nation and new state, we wish to work with all our strength to ensure that the new circumstances in which we have found ourselves in every aspect of our lives develop only to the benefit of our people, so that today, when all our long-standing hopes and dreams have come true, when we have become masters of our own fate, we Czechs can fully achieve our mission and tasks. . . . We want to make a good Czech daily

---

[101] The statement is signed by Maxim Reiner, Otakar Guth, Vítězslav Markus and Hugo Benda. 'K projektu nového denníku', *Rozhled*, no. 21 (1918): 4.
[102] Ibid., 5.
[103] For a more detailed analysis of this project, see Kateřina Čapková, 'Mit *Tribuna* gegen das *Prager Tagblatt*: Der deutsch-tschechische Pressekampf um die jüdischen Leser in Prag', in *Grenzdiskurse: Zeitungen deutschsprachiger Minderheiten und ihr Feuilleton in Mitteleuropa bis 1939*, ed. Sibylle Schönborn (Essen, 2009), 127–40.

newspaper, and that means of course keeping a close watch on all Czech political, cultural, and economic life. We need no other programmes or slogans – this is our simple programme.[104]

Its editor-in-chief was Bedřich Hlaváč (1868–1936), a close friend of Masaryk's and an author of articles for the periodicals *Čas* and *Naše doba*. Hlaváč came from a Czech-Jewish family and decided in his twenties to convert to Roman Catholicism. He was completely bilingual, and so worked not only for the Czech press, but also sometimes for the German.[105] In 1921 he and Arne Laurin (born Arnošt Lustig, 1889–1945), another *Tribuna* editor, applied for the job of editor-in-chief of the daily *Prager Presse*. Laurin was hired for that job, and Hlaváč applied again for the job of editor-in-chief of *Tribuna*. Three members of the board, Max Pleschner, Lev Vohryzek and Teytz, opposed him because they did not want an editor-in-chief who was willing to work for a German paper. Eduard Lederer, a member of the board of trustees, tried to persuade Alois Hajn to take the job of editor-in-chief of *Tribuna*, but Hajn declined the offer. Eventually Hlaváč was rehired for his old job.[106]

Tribuna provided Peroutka with his first big opportunity to demonstrate his ability as a journalist. Twenty-four years old at the time, he accepted the position enthusiastically, and thus helped the Czech-Jews to surmount the 'narrow confines of the Czech-Jewish movement'. His main colleagues were Arne Laurin, the dramatist and journalist Josef Kodíček (1892–1954) and Alfred Fuchs (1892–1941), a writer, translator and expert on the literature of Roman Catholic mysticism.

The newspaper gradually grew, publishing morning and evening editions as well as the *Pondělní sportovní věstník* (Monday Sports News), *Tribuna filatelistů*, *Technická Tribuna*, with information related to industry, and the *Módní revue* (Fashion Magazine), run by Milena Jesenská (1896–1944), who is known today primarily for her passionate correspondence with Franz Kafka, but who was also an important Czech journalist.[107] She also translated contributions from German for *Tribuna*, including several stories by Franz Kafka. In the beginning, Michal Mareš (1893–1971), an anarchist, and Josef Reiner (1897–1920), a left-wing poet, worked on the paper. The well-known fiction writer Karel Poláček (1892–1944) also began to publish his commentaries there, and his first work of fiction, *Povídky*

---

[104] *Tribuna*, no. 1 (1919): 1.
[105] Pavel Kosatík, *Ferdinand Peroutka, život v novinách (1895–1938)* (Prague and Litomyšl, 2003), 60.
[106] Eduard Lederer, *Epištola k Čechům-židům o tom, jak se dosud tajnosnubná panna 'Tribuna' šťastně provdala a co všechno tomu předcházelo* (Prague, 1927), 6–7.
[107] Kosatík, *Ferdinand Peroutka*, 61.

pana Kočkodana (The Tales of Mr Kočkodan), was first published there in instalments. Other contributors included the writer-philosopher Ladislav Klíma (1878-1928), the historian Vilém Julius Hauner (1877-1941), the fiction writers František Langer (1888-1965) and Jaroslav Hašek (1883-1923; known especially as the author of *The Good Soldier Švejk*), the diplomat Hubert Masařík (1896-1982) and the literary critic and columnist F. X. Šalda (1867-1937).[108] Under the pseudonym J. K. Pravda, Jindřich Kohn also wrote for *Tribuna*.[109]

Tribuna became a popular daily not only among Czech Jews.[110] Jewish topics appeared in the daily only sporadically, and the Czech-Jewish publishers gave the editors a good deal of freedom. Only occasionally did Klineberger, Rakous and Eduard Lederer publish in *Tribuna*.[111]

Tribuna published until 1928, but from the mid-1920s part of the daily was in the hands the Agrarian Party, which managed to persuade the paper to hire some of its own journalists. It is truly an irony that what was at first largely a Czech-Jewish daily ended up being controlled by the Agrarians, whose newspaper, *Venkov* (The Countryside), was long known for its anti-Jewish commentary. The way *Tribuna* gradually came under Agrarian control is described in expressive detail by Eduard Lederer in his 'Epištola k Čecho-židům o tom, jak se dosud tajnosnubná panna "Tribuna" šťastně provdala a co všechno tomu předcházelo' (Epistle to the Czech-Jews about How the Cryptogamous Virgin, *Tribuna*, Was Happily Married Off, and about Everything That Led Up to That). Lederer was on the board of the newspaper until 1921. He and the other people running the daily - Pleschner, Lev Vohryzek, Teytz and Rakous - later parted on bad terms.[112] In 1922 *Tribuna* began to find itself in serious financial difficulties, so the board began searching for sponsors also among German companies or companies owned by members of the Agrarian Party. In May 1924 *Národní osvobození* (National Liberation) ran an article by Lederer titled 'Komu patří dnes Tribuna?' (Who Owns *Tribuna* Today?) in which he explains that *Tribuna* was no longer linked with the Czech-Jewish movement.[113]

In the summer of 1926 Laurin turned to President Masaryk to ask for help for *Tribuna*, bringing his attention to the right-wing, antisemitic

---

[108] Ibid., 64-66. See also Egon Hostovský, 'The Czech-Jewish Movement', in *The Jews of Czechoslovakia*, vol. II, 151.
[109] Many of the articles Kohn published in *Tribuna* were later compiled in *Asimilace a věky*.
[110] 'Na různé adresy', *Rozvoj*, no. 3 (1919): 6.
[111] Kosatík, *Ferdinand Peroutka*, 68.
[112] At the end of his 'epistles' Lederer writes that he and the people on the management board had such differences that he eventually broke off all contact with them. Lederer, *Epištola k Čechům-židům*, 14.
[113] Ibid., 10.

tendencies among the editors. Masaryk appears to have taken some steps in the matter, because Laurin, in another letter, thanks him for having taken on the 'unpleasant task of saving *Tribuna*' despite his busy schedule. Laurin also reminds Masaryk that two years earlier Masaryk had, through the good offices of Prime Minister Švehla, helped to salvage *Tribuna*.[114] In 1926, however, the operation to save the paper failed. At the end of the year, a group of Agrarians mediated transactions for companies to become its majority shareholders.[115] The men allegedly behind the deal were Josef Vraný, an Agrarian senator, and Josef Šimonek, the director of the Škoda Works. Particularly in the economics columns the editors now had to subordinate their wishes to those of the Agrarians.[116] When, in 1932, the student and future writer Egon Hostovský (1908-1973) reproached the older generation of Czech-Jews for having lost the Czech-Jewish daily,[117] he provoked Lev Vohryzek to a written reply:

> I must, out of respect for my brother's dream, immodestly say that several friends and I started up the daily almost alone, based on what was then the Association [of Progressive Czech-Jews], and I was, together with a number of its formers members, part of the management until it was taken over by the Agrarians. And because in those years I was critical of the content and the business dealings of the paper, I have, I believe, a right to say that those who ran the business did not squander it. The causes of the demise of *Tribuna*, a serious, plain-speaking daily, a paper that today is missed not only by us but by all Czechs, were mostly beyond the management's control.[118]

The second, ambitious project that went far beyond what was at first the narrowly Czech-Jewish programme was the Business and Arts League. Established in November 1918 after many meetings, the League[119] was intended to provide the framework for the entire Czech-Jewish movement on the basis of collaboration between Progressive Jewish and non-Jewish

---

[114] Kosatík, *Ferdinand Peroutka*, 62–63.
[115] For more about the negotiations to save *Tribuna*, see Andrea Orzoff, '"The Literary Organ of Politics": Tomáš Masaryk and Political Journalism, 1925–1929', *Slavic Review* 63, no. 2 (2004): 293–97. Koeltzsch has recently drawn attention to the German-language supplement of *Tribuna*, called *Der neue Weg*, which was published in 1925 to inform German readers about articles in Czech. The editor-in-chief of this supplement was a Czech-Jew, Max Pleschner. See Koeltzsch, 'Geteilte Kulturen', 241–43.
[116] Lederer, *Epištola k Čechům-židům*, 13.
[117] Egon Hostovský, 'Co jsme a co chceme', *Věstník akademického spolku Kapper*, no. 2 (November 1932): 9.
[118] Lev Vohryzek, 'Kvas v našem studentstvu', *Věstník akademického spolku Kapper*, no. 6 (February, 1933): 41.
[119] In some leaflets the board used the name Jednota pro péči hospodářskou a kulturní but it was officially registered simply as Jednota.

citizens. 'Its purpose,' as stated in *Rozhled*, 'is not merely to intensify the existing work of Czech-Jewish organisations, but also to expand it here in terms of quality and quantity beyond the framework of these organisations. The establishment of the League is intended as a step towards winning over, if possible, all suitable people for economic, cultural and national work in the Czech nation.'[120] The words 'Jew' and 'Jewish' consequently do not appear at all in the League statutes. On behalf of the steering committee Leon Bondy, Otakar Guth, Jindřich Waldes, August Stein, Luděk Dux and Otto Taussik state: 'According to the principle that confession is not, nor can be, a dividing line in the Czech nation, it is the aim of the society to work towards the harmonious collaboration of all members of the Czech nation for its cultural and economic development.'[121]

To achieve this aim the League developed a range of activities. They included cultivating social contacts, supporting the Czech school system and Czech libraries, the publishing of periodicals, setting up an office that would help people find employment free of charge, and developing collaboration in agriculture, small business, industry, commerce and finance. The constituent general meeting was held in the Chamber of Trade and Commerce in Prague on 3 November 1918.

The place of the meeting and the fact that Leon Bondy (1860-1923), the president of the Chamber in Prague, was unanimously elected the head of the League suggest that he probably initiated the whole project. Though in the statutes it states that the members wanted to work together for the national, economic, cultural and social development of the Czechoslovak nation, it was work on economics that clearly predominated. Apart from Bondy, other leading figures in Czech economics and law gave talks at the League on the economic and financial conditions in the new political environment, the situation in agriculture and transport and financial law. Among the people giving the talks were Antonín Basch, from the Ministry of Trade and a university teacher of economics at the Faculty of Law; Richard Morawetz, a factory-owner and businessman from Světlá nad Sázavou; Václav Schuster, the secretary of state at the Ministry of Trade; and Bohdan Živanský, a secretary of the Chamber of Trade and Commerce in Prague. They were all members of the League as well. Among the guest speakers at the League were Karel Veith, a department head at the Ministry of Agriculture; Václav Verunáč, a university teacher of social and industrial policy at the Czech polytechnic in Prague; Josef Drachovský, a university teacher of financial law; Jaroslav Kříženecký, a university teacher at the agricultural college in Brno; and even Karel Engliš, the minister of

---

[120] 'Jednota', *Rozhled*, no. 21 (1918): 6.
[121] AHMP, SK XXII/680, statutes of 9 April 1918.

finance.[122] Apart from talks on economics there were sometimes equally excellent ones on philosophy. Among the members of the League were the philosophers Emanuel Rádl, Ferdinand Pelikán (1885-1952) and Jindřich Kohn and the journalist Josef Penížek (1858-1932).

Though the League was created at the impetus of Czech-Jewish societies and members of the Czech-Jewish élite sat on its committee,[123] the work of the society in law and economics went far beyond the usual Czech-Jewish activities. Many Jews who were affected by antisemitic outbursts, for example, turned to the League's legal section.[124] Apart from that, the board was involved in questions affecting the whole country, like the shortage of housing and commercial space, Czechoslovak exports and imports, the dismal state of insurance and bad legislation in agrarian reform. A small savings and loan company, called the Jednota (League), was also established. Advertisements for the purchase of shares in the company appeared regularly in Czech-Jewish leaflets and periodicals. Arts events (particularly the funding of works by Czech-Jewish authors)[125] and social activities (fund-raising for charities) tended to be less central to its interests.[126]

Thanks in particular to its chairman, Bondy, a broad base for collaboration between Jewish and non-Jewish Czechs was established in the sphere of economics. The emergence of the League was also welcomed by representatives of the Czech National Council.[127] The importance of the League consisted mainly in the fact that here Czech-Jews were con-

---

[122] AHMP, SK XXII/680.

[123] Apart from Leon Bondy, Morawetz, Basch, Schuster, Živanský, Rádl and Kohn, the Committee in 1918-1924 included Ignát Arnstein (a lawyer), Luděk Dux (the owner of the Maurice Halphen company), Leopold Eisner (a lawyer in Kralupy nad Vltavou), Otto Fischer (an editor), Jindřich Freiwald (an architect in Karlín), Viktor Graf (a businessman), Otto Gratum (the director of Lloyd's Insurance in Prague II), Otakar Guth (a lawyer), Milena Illová (a clerk), Hynek Kettner (a factory owner in Vinohrady), Bohdan Klineberger (a lawyer and writer), Josef Lederer (a partner in the Lederer & Popper company), Otto Lederer (a partner in the K. Brummel company), Josef Lion (the owner of a banking operation in Prague II), Evžen Loewy (a lawyer in Klatovy), Vojtěch Österreicher (Vojtěch Rakous, a factory owner and writer), Zdeněk Pštross (an architect and university teacher at the Czech Polytechnic), Maxim Reiner (a lawyer), Zikmund Robitschek (the owner of a large estate in Veltruby near Kolín), Josef Růžička (a lawyer), Heřman Růžička (a lawyer), Leon Saxl (a leaseholder of a large estate in Drásty near Klecany), Jakub Scharf (a lawyer), August Stein (a Prague town councillor), Jindřich Stross (a wholesaler), Otto Taussik (a self-employed clerk), Jindřich Waldes (a factory owner in Vršovice), Alfred Winternitz (a businessman), and Gustav Wittler (an authorized representative of the Otto publishing house). See AHMP, SK XXII/680.

[124] 'Následky nepokojů v československém státě', *Rozhled*, no. 3 (1919): 5.

[125] The Union published, for example, the booklet by Jan Krejčí, *Siegfried Kapper* (1919).

[126] *Zpráva z Jednoty pro péči hospodářskou a kulturní* (Prague, 1920).

[127] 'Jednota: Ustavující valná hromada', *Rozhled*, no. 43 (1918): 6.

structively involved in the search for solutions to problems that were felt throughout the country. The League began with great promise but wound up its work in 1924, less than a year after the death of Bondy, in October 1923. That again suggests that Bondy played a central role in the organisation. In July 1924 a new board was elected. The chairman was Václav Schuster (1871–1944), who was at the time the chairman of the General Union of Czech Banks (Všeobecná česká bankovní jednota), and amongst its members were Tomáš Baťa (1876–1932), the well-known shoe-factory owner from Zlín; and Václav Klement (1868–1938), the general director of the Laurin & Klement motorcar factory in Mladá Boleslav.[128] Even with the election of such a distinguished board, however, the era of the League came to an end. As Dux noted in his report for the chief of police in Prague, the society had not been involved in any activity since 1924, and had experienced a rapid decline in membership.[129]

In the mid-1920s the Czech-Jews failed in their two serious attempts to move Czech-Jewishness onto an ideologically and economically broader level than narrowly defined Jewish problems. One attempt, the establishment of the League, met with great enthusiasm amongst all adherents of Czech-Jewish movement, leaders and rank-and-file alike. But only Bondy, by the strength of his personality and social standing, could maintain the programme and activities of the League at such a high level. The fate of the other attempt, *Tribuna*, was different. From the beginning it had been rejected by adherents of radical assimilation. The position of some Progressive Czech-Jews, who supported this daily, was also seriously weakened by the untimely death of Viktor Vohryzek. What to some extent sealed the fate of the Czech-Jewish movement, however, was the fact that people who tended to promote total assimilation into the Czech nation became dominant in the leadership of the movement.

Total Assimilation

The new political conditions of the First Republic, as well as ideological crystallization within the movement, led to a considerable simplification in the structures of the various societies. Many pre-war Czech-Jewish societies wound up their activities when Czechoslovak independence was declared, or they simply faded out of existence. A decline in the number of members was experienced, for example, by the National Union of Czech-Jews, which, in the First Republic, was almost inactive. The

---

[128] AHMP, SK XXII/680.
[129] Ibid.

police in Prague even asked several times whether the society had not already ceased to exist.[130] In the course of twenty years, the individual Prague chapters of the society closed down.[131] The Star (Hvězda) Society (founded in 1912), a charity organisation in the Association of Progressive Czech-Jews, continued its activities in the interwar period, even though the Association of Progressive Czech-Jews had folded in 1919 and the Association of Czech-Jews was established. In the interwar years it was led by Hirsch and Teytz. In reply to continuous questions from the police about where the Star Society was continuing its work, Teytz wrote: 'With the change in the economic and social circumstances after the war, the society lost its purpose, particularly when, during the war, most of the members left. We attempted to put the society on a new basis and to maintain it. These attempts came to naught, and we therefore intend to hold a general meeting in the near future, which would pass a resolution on the dissolution of the society.'[132] The society was not voluntarily dissolved, but when it was forced to close in July 1939, four months after the German occupation began, it had only thirty-seven members in all of Bohemia and Moravia.[133]

The Or Tomid Society was inactive during the First Republic because, as its deputy chairman Maxim Reiner admitted, 'the activities of the society were pointless' after the declaration of Czechoslovak independence.[134]

The Association of Czech-Jews

Gradually the individual societies united in order to prevent the complete atomization of their weakened forces. In January 1918, representatives of the pre-war Association of Progressive Czech-Jews and the Political Union of Czech-Jews decided to band together under the name Political Union of Czech-Jews. *Rozhled* was meant to be its official daily.[135] Because of disputes between some of the Progressive Czech-Jews and the others (which were intensified particularly by the controversy over the Czech-Jewish daily), the pre-war Association of Progressive Czech-Jews was revived in April 1918.[136] The Progressive Jews again began to publish *Rozvoj*. The next attempt to unite, a year and half later, was successful.[137] The new society, the Association of Czech-Jews (Svaz Čechů-židů), was an official

---

[130] AHMP, SK XXII/81.
[131] AHMP, SK XXII/173 and SK XXII/127.
[132] AHMP, Zpráva o likvidaci a návrh na rozdělení jmění, 19 July 1939.
[133] Ibid.
[134] AHMP, SK I/12.
[135] 'Českožidovské veřejnosti!', *Rozhled*, no. 3 (1918): 6.
[136] AHMP, SK XXI/108.
[137] AHMP, SK XXI/149.

representative body of the Czech-Jews until World War II, both in public and in political negotiations behind closed doors.

It was former functionaries of the Political Union of Czech-Jews who tended to have the main say in the leadership of the Association of Czech-Jews. Seven of its members were elected to the executive committee of the Association of Czech-Jews.[138] By contrast, the Association of Progressive Czech-Jews had only three representatives on the committee.[139] It is striking that not one of the important figures of the Progressive Czech-Jews, such as Lev Vohryzek (his brother Viktor had died in November 1918), Eduard Lederer, Max Lederer, Klineberger or Kohn, was appointed to the first committee of the Association of Czech-Jews. The dominant position of the leaders of the Political Union influenced the political programme of the Association of Czech-Jews. The association henceforth limited itself mainly to national campaigning and sought the total assimilation of the Jews with the Czech nation, which they called *asimilace usque ad finem*.

Not all former members of the Association of Progressive Czech-Jews agreed that their society should merge with the Political Union of Czech-Jews. Pleschner and Vohryzek in particularly were opposed to the idea. At the meeting of 12 October 1919, where the decision to merge had been voted on, Pleschner expressed his 'fear that the merger would mean a timid compromise, and recalled some old disputes among proponents of the former Realist Party and the Young Czech Party'.[140] Similarly, Vohryzek was reluctant to reconcile himself to the fact that he would have to bow to the ideology of the Association of Czech-Jews. In 1921 he tried to re-establish the Association of Progressive Czech-Jews. When he resubmitted the society statutes for approval (which were identical to the prewar programme), the Bohemian governmental authorities in Prague, in a decision on 23 March 1922, approved the establishment of the society. Vohryzek failed, however, to find enough people for a constituent general meeting. In May 1925 the society was therefore once again removed from the register of clubs and societies.[141]

Even after the establishment of the Association of Czech-Jews the tendency to limit the number of Czech-Jewish societies continued, in order to guarantee the unity of the movement. The secretary of the new association, Kamil Kleiner (1892–1954), a member of the management board of the Škoda Works, expressed this clearly in his article 'Několik poznámek

---

[138] One of them, Max Bondy, became deputy chairman of the Association.
[139] Heřman Růžička, however, became chairman of the Association of Czech-Jews; Milan Kodíček, an official; and Karel Brod was elected a full member of the committee. See AHMP, SK XXI/51, SK XXI/149, SK XXI/108.
[140] 'Reorganisace', *Rozvoj*, no. 41 (1919): 1.
[141] AHMP, SK XXI/108, SK XXI/161.

o organisaci' (Some Remarks on the Organization). Concerning relations between the Czech-Jewish societies and the politically orientated Association of Czech-Jews, he recommended, on behalf of the executive committee of the Association, that 'such societies, if they do not pursue some altogether special aim that they could not achieve as an organisation, should dissolve. . . . They would thus strengthen the unity of the movement and limit the atomization of our work.'[142]

After the merger of the Political Union of Czech-Jews and the Association of Progressive Czech-Jews, the problem arose of whether the official periodical of the Association of Czech-Jews should be *Rozvoj* or *Rozhled*. After long debates it was decided that *Rozhled* would continue to be sent information on the activity of the Association of Czech-Jews, but only as a 'periodical independent of the Association', whereas *Rozvoj* (owing to its pre-war tradition) would become the official newspaper of the association. The editor-in-chief of *Rozhled*, Otto Fischer, took over the editing of *Rozvoj*,[143] and in 1920 *Rozhled* ceased to publish. Thus, from 28 May 1920 until the outbreak of World War II, *Rozvoj* was the only official Czech-Jewish periodical.[144]

The Kapper Students' Society

Like the Association of Czech-Jews, the Czech-Jewish Students' Society, the second most important Czech-Jewish society in the interwar years, aimed for total assimilation after World War I. Its statutes and name were changed. At its meeting on 16 November 1919, the committee for the new statutes chose the name the Kapper Students' Society (Akademický spolek Kapper),[145] after the writer, translator and graduate of the University of Vienna Siegfried Kapper (1821–1879), whom the movement called the first Czech-Jew.[146] The declaration of the society says, among other things: 'Seeing the solution to the Czech-Jewish question as a national task (rather than a particularly 'Jewish' task), and endeavouring to popularize the movement so that it is nation-wide, let us make it our duty to gain as much sympathy as possible and the collaboration of progressive

---

[142] Kamil Kleiner, 'Několik poznámek o organisaci', *Rozvoj*, no. 47 (1919): 1.
[143] 'K otázce časopisecké', *Rozvoj*, nos. 49–50 (1919): 7.
[144] 'Stoupencům a přátelům českožidovského hnutí', *Rozhled*, no. 21 (1920): 1.
[145] 'Akademický spolek "Kapper"', *Rozhled*, no. 48 (1919): 4. By a decree of 11 June 1920, the Bohemian political authorities (*zemská správa politická*) in Prague did not forbid a change of name of the statutes. AHMP, SK X/15.
[146] In addition to many articles about Kapper in *Kalendář česko-židovský*, see also Demetz, 'Tschechen und Juden: Der Fall Siegfried Kapper (1821–1871)', in Peter Demetz, *Böhmen böhmisch: Essays* (Vienna, 2006), 157–71; Oskar Donath, 'Siegfried Kapper', *Jahrbuch der Gesellschaft für Geschichte der Juden in der Čechoslovakischen Republik* 6 (1934): 323–442; Kieval, *Languages of Community*, 65–94.

Czechs regardless of confession!'[147] Article 7, which stipulated that a member must be of the Mosaic confession, was removed from the statutes. In his memoirs, Kamil Neumann, an active member of the society, says, however: 'the influx of non-Jewish colleagues was insignificant. . . . I often recall how our colleague, Ervín Hirsch, . . . ironically used to welcome the absent non-Jewish colleagues to the meeting soon after the change of name of the society.'[148]

For the new leadership, working for assimilation meant more than only the defence of Jewish interests; it also became 'the most sacred Czech interest'. 'Assimilationist principles' should, according to it, become part of the programme of the individual Czech cultural and political groups. 'Our society has ceased to be the "left wing" of the Czech-Jewish movement, because we are substituting the term Czechness [češství] for the term Czech-Jewishness [českožidovství]. The society is becoming a Czech cultural society. Our aim is to work for the moral revival of the nation, which we want to free from antisemitism, the cult of hatred and evil, which always harms the ones who preach it.'[149]

The programme of the revamped students' society of Czech-Jews achieved more in the ideology of total assimilation than the Association of Czech-Jews. The reason is obvious. One of the striking differences between the Association of Czech-Jews and the Kapper Society was that almost everyone of the young generation of Czech-Jews was already fully integrated into Czech society. Its members had grown up in the Czech-speaking milieu, they went to Czech schools, and they actively participated in Czech cultural life. Most of them, moreover, had no close connection to the Jewish religion. The Kapper Society members thus had to face the reproaches of the older generation of Czech-Jews, who said that they were already 'over-assimilated'.[150] The efforts of the Czech-Jewish Students' Society to obliterate their Jewishness and to demonstrate their total Czechness quite naturally led to mocking commentaries from the Zionists.

In 1918, when a change in the name of the students' society was first considered, a writer for *Židovské zprávy* (Jewish News), Ben Jomtov (the pseudonym of Felix Kornfeld), announced a competition for a new name for the society, whose old name 'is now out-dated and does not at all correspond to the Slav ideals of society. How unsuitable, un-Czech and un-Slav the noun "Jew" is! Czech-Jews, who are more Czech than even Gebauer's grammar,[151] write "Žid" [Jew] with a lower-case "ž", because the Jewish na-

---

[147] 'Akademický spolek "Kapper"', *Rozhled*, no. 48 (1919): 4.
[148] Kamil Neumann, 'Po válce', in *Vzpomínky a úvahy*, 50.
[149] 'Akademický spolek "Kapper"'.
[150] Ibid.
[151] Jan Gebauer (1838–1907) was an important Czech linguist whose grammar of the Czech language was used in Czech schools during the interwar period.

tion, as far as they are concerned, vanished long ago. And the thought that the Czech-Jewish Students' Society might have some religious tendencies is dreadful to a progressive person, yet this is what may be judged from this damned unsuitable name.'[152] The editors of *Židovské zprávy* then proposed names for a Czech-Jewish student society like 'the Forefather Čech Society of Real Czechoslav Students (Praotec Čech, spolek pravých českoslovanských akademiků) and 'the Jan Žižka Society of Czechoslovak Hussite Students' (Jan Žižka z Trocnova, spolek husitských akademiků českoslovanských). Regardless of their derogatory tone, Kornfeld's satirical remarks had a grain of truth.

The Czech-Jewish Society

Apart from the Association of Czech-Jews and the Kapper Society, the third most important organisation of the Czech-Jewish movement in the interwar years was the Czech-Jewish Society (Českožidovské společenské sdružení).[153] The association statutes were also changed to enable non-Jews to become members. According to the 1921 statutes, the aim of the association was 'to work for the reconciled co-existence of the citizens of the Czechoslovak Republic regardless of confession, to combat any kind of prejudice, in particular religious and social, to support the raising of the standard of living in national, spiritual, social and economic respects, to educate in an all-round way its members, and to cultivate reciprocity among them'.[154] The organisers of the association aimed in particular to hold cultural and social events. It was famous for the performances of its drama club. The association theatre company was so good that it occasionally gave guest performances at the Švanda Theatre in the Prague district of Smíchov.[155] The high standard of its arts programme was thanks mainly to the dramatist Vítězslav Markus (1877–1942), who led the theatre company until 1922. He organised regular evening talks on literature, rehearsed plays with association members, particularly by Czech-Jewish authors (including Viktor Lederer, Vojtěch Rakous and himself), and occasionally invited special guests. It was not unusual for an actor, a musician, or even the ballet company of the National Theatre to give a guest performance there.[156]

---

[152] Ben Jomtov, 'Soutěž', *Židovské zprávy*, no. 9 (1918): 3–4.
[153] When it was founded in 1896, it was called the Circle of Czech-Jewish Youth (Kroužek českožidovského dorostu), from 1907 to 1921 the Czech-Jewish Circle (Českožidovský kroužek), and from 1921 onwards the Czech-Jewish Society (Českožidovské společenské sdružení).
[154] AHMP, SK XI/134.
[155] It was later called the Realistické divadlo, then the Labyrint, and, most recently, the Švandovo divadlo again.
[156] 'Českožidovský kroužek v Praze', *Rozhled*, no. 9 (1920): 5.

The Czech-Jewish Society, unlike the Kapper Society or the Association of Czech-Jews, was not concerned with theoretical or political discussions about assimilation. Its main interest was cultural activity, largely continuing those of the pre-war Czech-Jewish movement. Compared to the Kapper Society, which consisted of university students, the Czech-Jewish Society was intended for 'young people in business'.[157] During the First Republic the group of interested people expanded to include all Czech-Jewish youth.

An Attempt to Expand Czech-Jewishness beyond Bohemia

In the second half of the 1920s Czechoslovakia was in its heyday. Compared to Germany, which was recovering from the serious economic crisis that began in 1923, Czechoslovakia was enjoying an economic boom. Stabilizing the economy went hand in hand with stabilizing politics. The security of the state was supposed to be guaranteed by a system of international treaties. Particularly important was Czechoslovakia's being anchored in the Versailles system and the diplomatic rapprochement with Romania and Yugoslavia as part of the Little Entente.[158] Although relying on one's partners in this treaty turned out to be illusory, the Little Entente, when it first came into being, contributed significantly to the sense of security. The stable political and economic framework of Czechoslovakia in this period thus also had a beneficial effect on the position of the Jews. Anti-Jewish riots and accusations of corruption during the war ceased.

The calming of antisemitic passions and the stabilization of the Czechoslovak state contributed to the quicker integration of the Jews into Czech-speaking society. In consequence this meant less interest in an organised Czech-Jewish movement. Many Jews in Czech areas already felt so rooted in Czech society that the activities of the Czech-Jews seemed superfluous to them. The integration of the Jews into the Czech nation was, as far as they were concerned, already a fact.

Like the political situation of the country, the situation within the Jewish community also calmed down. Czech-Jews had already reconciled themselves to the existence of both the Jewish National Council and the Jewish Party. It was now a matter of winning over as many indifferent Jews as possible to the Czech-Jewish movement. The chief handicap of the Czech-Jews compared to the Zionists was that the latter campaigned with

---

[157] 'Dvě Jubilea', *Kalendář česko-židovský* (1926–27), 5.
[158] Oldřich Tůma and Jiří Jindra, eds., *Czechoslovakia and Romania in the Versailles System* (Prague, 2006); Jindřich Dejmek and František Kolář, eds., *Československá zahraniční politika a vznik Malé dohody 1920–1921*, vols I–II (Prague, 2004–2005).

great success for their movement throughout Czechoslovakia, whereas the influence of the Czech-Jews was mostly limited to Bohemia, not including the German-speaking borderlands. Consequently, Moravia and later also Slovakia were placed on the agenda. Because of the different historical development of the individual parts of Czechoslovakia, however, the idea of Czech-Jewish assimilation did not really take hold in Slovakia or Moravia.

Moravia

The Prague organisers had been trying to expand Czech-Jewish activity to Moravia and Silesia since the beginning of the twentieth century. In 1911 they managed to set up the National Union of Czech-Jews in Silesian Ostrava, and in 1913 the Union of Czech-Jews in Brno was founded.[159] Before World War I individual Czech-Jews from Moravia also tried to put together a National Union of Czech-Jews in Moravia. Josef Musil, a businessman in Olomouc, became the leading organiser at the time. The campaign was nevertheless thwarted, according to Musil, by 'outright antisemitism and personal insults'.[160] He did not reiterate his appeal to the Moravian Czech-Jews till 1919, after Czechoslovak independence, when the committee of the future National Union of Czech-Jews was set up in Moravia.[161]

In addition to Olomouc, Czech-Jews in Brno began to get involved after the war, and had, shortly before the outbreak of war, even managed to establish a Czech-Jewish National Union for Moravia and Silesia (Národní jednota českožidovská pro Moravu a Slezsko). All members of the committee, however, were soon called up for military service, and three of them were killed. At the beginning of 1919 the Brno society resumed its work under the leadership of Richard Bäumel (1881-1944), a lawyer. In the course of the year, talks took place between the Brno and Olomouc organisers about beginning to work together.[162]

In May 1919 the Society of Progressive Czech-Jews for the Bohemian-Moravian Uplands (Spolek českých pokrokových židů pro Českomoravskou vysočinu) was also established. The society had been initiated by Jews from German-speaking Jihlava (Iglau) because, its organisers explained, compared to Bohemian towns the Czech minority in Jihlava did not take

---

[159] Gustav Roubíček, 'Pracovní anketa předsjezdová pořádaná Svazem Čechů židů v ČSR', *Rozvoj*, no. 43 (1919): 2.
[160] 'Stoupencům českých pokrokových židů na Moravě!', *Rozhled*, no. 6 (1919): 6. The same statement was also published in *Rozvoj*, no. 3 (1919): 5
[161] 'Stoupencům českých pokrokových židů na Moravě!', *Rozhled*, no. 6 (1919): 6.
[162] 'Česko-židovské hnutí na Moravě', *Rozhled*, no. 6 (1919): 6.

Jews into its ranks. 'Since the leaders of the Czech minority in Jihlava either publicly expressed their racial, social and economic antisemitism or, by contrast, those who needed the Jews flirted outwardly with Zionists, there was no choice but to establish our own milieu, which would enable us Czech Jews to carry out assimilation with the Czech people in the national, social and economic respects.'[163] The example of Jihlava demonstrates the paradox that the Czech-Jewish organisations tended to come into being during the First Republic in places where Jews had not managed to integrate into the Czech nation.

The Society of Progressive Czech-Jews for the Bohemian-Moravian Uplands soon established a network of activists in all the larger towns there. Many members were soon elected to municipal councils – for example, in Batelov, Pacov, Pelhřimov, Německý Brod, Světlá nad Sázavou, and a number of villages as well. Bohemian-Moravian Jews then used to meet in Jihlava to listen to talks by leading figures such as Eduard Lederer, Richard Morawetz (from Business and Arts League), Max Lederer and Alfred Fuchs. After the establishment of the Association of Czech-Jews, the Society of Progressive Czech-Jews for the Bohemian-Moravian Uplands became a branch of it.[164]

Four Czech-Jewish organisations existed in Moravia in November 1919. The number of members in each, however, was very different. The society in Jihlava had about 300 members, Olomouc 104, Moravská Ostrava 100 and Brno had only 40. In his report, Roubíček expresses his astonishment at the difference in numbers. He conceded that the admission procedures of new members in Jihlava had probably been too loose, and they had failed to verify the 'national reliability' of candidates.[165]

The setting up of new Czech-Jewish centres in Moravia and the maintenance of the existing ones throughout the interwar period could not have happened without the assistance of the Prague leadership. After World War I, it was the Kapper Students' Society that first tried to establish contacts in Moravia. In 1920 a Brno chapter of the Kapper Society was established. The founding members (for a long time the only members) of the chapter were students from Bohemia who studied at the school of veterinary medicine in Brno (the only school of its kind in Czechoslovakia at the time). In the first half of the 1920s they failed to win over the local Moravian Jews to the idea of integration. Moreover, the Czech-Jewish students of veterinary medicine came into conflict with their teachers, which severely weakened the already moribund activity of the society.[166]

---

[163] 'Z Českomoravské vysočiny', *Rozhled*, no. 3 (1920): 4.
[164] Ibid.
[165] 'Pracovní anketa předsjezdová pořádaná Svazem Čechů-židů v ČSR'.
[166] 'Zprávy spolkové', *Kalendář česko-židovský* (1927–28), 236.

The year 1926 marks a milestone, for it was then that the Czech-Jews made it their priority to win over as many Moravian supporters as possible to the idea of integration into the Czech nation. In Prostějov, in May 1926, the Association of Czech-Jews held a congress of Czech-Jewish activists from Moravia, and in November a congress of the association took place in Brno. The 'guidelines for future work in Moravia and Silesia' were drafted, the Moravian-Silesian secretariat of the Association of Czech-Jews, led by the journalist Vilém Prager (1901–1944, pseudonym Vilém Pražský), embarked on a far-reaching campaign. He managed to establish groups in Prostějov and Olomouc and also to revive the Brno group.[167] A turnaround came in the Brno chapter of the Kapper Society as well. Moravians now entered the new committee and initiated a thorough reorganisation of the society. The result was an increase in the number of members and an expansion of the lecture activity.[168] The Brno students also took part in the revival of the Brno branch of the Association of Czech-Jews.[169]

The Czech-Jews put the emphasis mainly on instruction in school. Their campaigning was aimed at registering Jewish children from Moravia and Silesia in Czech schools. In this they did not differ from the Czech nationalists.[170] Also the instruction of the Jewish religion in German was a thorn in the side of the Czech-Jews. In its 'schools operation' in Moravia and Silesia the Association of Czech-Jews was supported by the Matice osvěty lidové (a Czech nationalist institution for popular enlightenment) and the National Union of Czech-Jews.[171]

The Prague leadership of the Czech-Jewish movement was now enjoying its hard-won successes. Many of the newly established centres in Moravia, however, soon folded. One example is the Brno chapter of the Kapper Society, the only chapter of this organisation outside Prague. From 1929 onwards the Brno students were not involved in any activity, and in 1933 this chapter of the Kapper Society was removed from the register of societies at police headquarters in Prague.[172] Campaigning in Brno had to begin again from scratch. At a conference of the Association of Czech-Jews in 1935 the importance of renewing the Brno branch of the Kapper Society was again debated: 'The operation is to be carried out by a colleague from Prague who will go to Brno for one or two semesters to do the initial organisational work.' Special funds were also set aside for the operation.[173] The Brno branch, however, was not revived.

---

[167] 'Zprávy spolkové', *Kalendář česko-židovský* (1926–27), 201.
[168] 'Zprávy spolkové', *Kalendář česko-židovský* (1927–28), 236.
[169] 'Zprávy spolkové', *Kalendář česko-židovský* (1926–27), 204.
[170] Zahra, *Kidnapped Souls*, esp. 106–41.
[171] Ibid.; 'Zprávy spolkové', *Kalendář česko-židovský* (1926–27), 201.
[172] AHMP, SK X/15.
[173] 'Spolkové zprávy', *Kapper*, nos. 5–6 (February 1935): 57.

The situation in Moravia was complicated for Czech-Jews particularly by the strong Zionist movement, which was based on the support of whole Jewish congregations. In an Ostrava synagogue, for example, the Zionist anthem 'Hatikvah' (today, the Israeli national anthem) was usually played, and teachers of Judaism in Moravia often also taught it at Czech schools.[174] Many former German-language Jewish religious schools were merely changed into Jewish schools with secular instruction, but the emphasis was on Jewish history, religion and the arts. The headquarters of the Zionist Organisation for Czechoslovakia were in Moravská Ostrava, where the Zionist leaders could count on the strong structure of the Zionist Organisation in the region of Moravian Silesia.

Another factor that hindered the expansion of Czech-Jewishness to Moravia was the fact that most Moravian Jews during the First Republic used German in everyday communication. The Moravian Jews had traditionally preferred Vienna to Prague, and many Christians there also spoke German, particularly in the larger towns. The attitude to the German language was also influenced by German sermons and religious instruction. Unlike in Bohemia, no movement for Jewish religious services in Czech took hold in Moravia. A large role in this was played by the fact that when Czechoslovak independence was declared dozens of Moravian towns still had Jewish quarters with Jewish self-government, where the language of daily life was often German or Judendeutsch.

Not even in the late 1930s did any striking expansion of the Czech-Jewish movement take place. Only the rise of Nazism motivated Czech-Jews in Moravia to demonstrate their Czech national feeling publicly. That is why, in 1936, all chapters of the Association of Czech-Jews in Moravia – in Brno, Olomouc, Přerov and Moravská Ostrava – intensified their activity.[175] Zionism, however, which previously German or Czech nationalist Jews had already begun to support, now, in the 1930s, experienced a real boom.

Slovakia

The programme of the Czech-Jewish movement in the First Republic was given a new dimension by Czech-Jews seeking to expand, following the model of government policy enlarging the concept of the Czech nation into Czechoslovakism,[176] and they campaigned among the Slovaks as well.

---

[174] 'Valný sjezd Svazu Čechů-židů v ČSR', *Rozvoj*, no. 6 (1937): 2.
[175] Little groups of supporters began to campaign in Vizovice, Napajedla, Vyškov and Moravské Budějovice as well. See ibid., 3.
[176] See Elizabeth Bakke, 'The Making of Czechoslovakism in the First Czechoslovak Republic', in *Loyalitäten in der Tschechoslowakischen Republik 1918–1938: Politische, nationale und kulturelle Zugehörigkeiten*, ed. Martin Schulze Wessel (Munich, 2004), 23–44.

The situation of the Slovak Jews, however, was strikingly different from that of the Bohemian Jews. Moreover, Czech-Jews from the beginning made no secret of their prejudice towards the Jews of Slovakia and Subcarpathian Ruthenia. 'By attaching Slovakia and Subcarpathian Ruthenia [to the Bohemian Lands], we got a piece of the Jewish Orient. That, in our circumstances, is something completely new,' wrote the Czech-Jewish writer Kamil Neumann about the situation after World War I.[177]

As in Moravia, in Slovakia the Kapper Students' Society first tried to establish contact. It sought to win over to its ranks Slovak students at Prague universities. Written in Slovak, a campaign leaflet from the early years of the Czechoslovak Republic says:

> The aim of our society is to support the assimilation of Jews in the Czechoslovak Republic with the Czechoslovak nation. . . . Our library and our debates give you the scientific certainty that assimilation is not only a natural fact, but also a universal one, which cannot be taken away by the efforts of the antisemites or Zionists. Once finally informed, you will be able to teach those who remained behind, at the halfway point, and you will thus be carrying out your mission as intellectuals.[178]

The situation of the Slovak Jews was so different from that of the Bohemian Jews, however, that important work between the Jewish students of Bohemia and those of Slovakia did not begin till the mid-1930s. Evidence that the Slovak assimilationist movement was late to emerge is provided by the report by Otakar Levý (1896–1946) delivered at the general meeting of the Association of Czech-Jews in early 1937. Levý was an important Czech literary historian, a scholar of Romance languages and literatures and a translator, who taught at grammar schools in Košice and Bratislava in the 1920s and 1930s.[179] He began his address with the words 'We in Slovakia are at the beginning of the work that you in Bohemia completed forty or even fifty years ago.'[180] From Levý's analysis it is clear that the fundamental difference between the beginning of the Slovak and the Czech assimilationist movements was that the Slovaks had to face an already highly organised Zionist movement.[181] Another key problem of the Slovak Jews was the fight against antisemitism.[182]

---

[177] Neumann, 'Po válce'.
[178] AUK, k. A 129.
[179] See in particular Otakar Levý, *Baudelaire, jeho estetika a technika* (Brno, 1947).
[180] 'Valný sjezd Svazu Čechů židů v ČSR', *Rozvoj*, no. 6 (1937): 3.
[181] See also Katarina Hradská, 'Židovská komunita počas prvej ČSR: Vzťah slovenskej majoritnej spoločnosti voči židovskej menšine', *Česko-Slovenská historická ročenka* (2001): 49–58, esp. 53–54.
[182] 'Valný sjezd Svazu Čechů židů v ČSR', 3.

Most Jews in Slovakia who declared Czechoslovak nationality, however, did so because of the growing national identification of the surrounding population with Slovak nationality, not the campaigning of the Slovak-Jewish or Czechoslovak-Jewish movement. The integration of Jews into the Slovak nation did not begin until the 1930s, largely because that was also when the first generation of Slovaks who had graduated from Slovak schools had come of age. In his report Levý admits that the organisational activity of the local Slovak assimilationists had no real influence on strengthening Slovak nationality among Slovak Jews. 'It is surely remarkable,' he notes,

> that although organised assimilation in Slovakia is actually still in its early stages, only 65,385 out of 136,737 Slovak Jews declared themselves to be Zionists in 1930, and 71,351 declared themselves to be of another nationality. Of those, 44,000 Jews declared themselves to be of Czechoslovak nationality, about 10,000 declared themselves to be of Hungarian. It is also worth noting that the more Slovak a district is, the more assimilation there is, to the detriment of Zionism. In purely Slovak districts already today, without any organisational work, two thirds of the people declare themselves to be of Slovak nationality. In purely Magyar and nationally mixed districts Jews declare themselves to be of Jewish nationality.[183]

It was at the beginning of the 1930s that the first periodical of the 'Slovak-Jews', *Slovenský domov* (Slovak Home), was started up as the mouthpiece of the Development (Rozvoj) society in Košice and Bratislava. Members of Development in Košice also held important positions in Slovak national and cultural institutions.[184] The Association of Slovak-Jews (Zväz slovenských židov) was also established, appealing mainly to Jewish intellectuals and students, though with little actual influence on Jews or Slovaks.[185] A leading figure of that association was Hugo Roth (1890-1937), a renowned gynaecologist and cancer specialist. He also financed the Slovak-Jewish journal *Svornosť* with his own money.[186]

A milestone in the collaboration between Czech and Slovak Jewish students was the arrangement between the Kapper Society and the As-

---

[183] Ibid.
[184] 'Valná hromada spolku Slováků židů "Rozvoj" v Košicích', *Rozvoj*, no. 10 (1937): 5.
[185] Ivan Kamenec, *Po stopách tragédie* (Bratislava, 1991), 13-14.
[186] Karol Makovíni, *Svedectvo o Židoch na Slovensku* (Prague, 1936), 6-7. Makovíni also describes how he began to publish the periodical *Slovenská tribúna* (The Slovak Tribune) in Turčiansky Svätý Martin, in 1933. Intended to contribute to understanding between the Christians and Jews of Slovakia, the project eventually failed because neither the proponents of integration into the Slovak nation nor the Zionists could bear the idea that the Christian publishers wanted to foster good relations with both Jewish movements.

sociation of Jewish Slovak Students of Bratislava (Sdruženie slovenských akademikov židov v Bratislave), which was made at the congress of the Association of Czech-Jews in January 1935.[187] Apart from collaborating on the periodical *Kapper*, the Association of Jewish Slovak Students also decided to publish the periodical *Úsvit* (Dawn).[188]

On the whole it is therefore fair to say that the expansion of Czech-Jewish activities to Moravia and Slovakia met with little response, certainly not commensurate to the energy expended by the leaders in Prague. It is also reasonable to assume, however, that were it not for the unfortunate developments in the late 1930s, the movement of Jewish Slovaks, largely independent of the Czech model, would have gradually grown.

On the other hand, the scanty success of Czech-Jews in Moravia, Slovakia and the German-speaking borderlands of Bohemia was somewhat compensated for by the strong position of Czech-Jews in Czech areas. south and east Bohemia, where a number of leading Czech-Jews came from, became the strongest bastions of the Czech-Jews even back in the late nineteenth century. The vast majority of the Jews of Bohemia nevertheless grew up conscious of belonging to the Czech nation without organizing in the Czech-Jewish movement. So, looking back, the leaders of the Czech-Jewish movement admitted that in the First Republic the number of active Czech-Jews had declined compared to the period before World War I.[189]

The Revolt of the Young

In the early years of the First Republic, as we have seen, far-reaching changes took place in the organisation of the Czech-Jewish movement. A regroup-

---

[187] 'Zo Sdruženia židovských akademikov Slovákov v Bratislave,' *Kapper*, no. 7 (March, 1935): 69. The agreement reads: '(1) The SŽAS [the Association of the Jewish Slovak Students of Pressburg] will have a special Bratislava branch of the editorial board of *Kapper* for articles from Slovakia; articles accepted by it will be subject only to a limited check by the chairman and the editor responsible in Prague. (2) The SŽAS and *Kapper* will, if possible, exchange speakers with each other and inform each other about the various debates. (3) At the initiative of either of the executive committees, both societies will consider a joint approach, position, and resolutions on events. (4) Both societies will endeavour to organise a summer camp in Slovakia. (5) The approach taken in all points of this agreement and in our collaboration in general will be as friendly as possible and with the unbending will to achieve our aims.' 'Spolkové zprávy', *Kapper*, nos. 5–6 (February, 1935): 57.
[188] 'Spolkové zprávy', *Kapper*, nos. 5–6, 58.
[189] NA, ZÚ pres. 207-1402-24, 8/5/53/64, from a speech by the secretary of the Association of Czech-Jews (Svaz Čechů židů), Viktor Müller, to journalists, 3 November 1938.

ing and reduction in the number of societies were undertaken, and important changes were made in their statutes and programmes. All the societies opened up to non-Jewish members too. In the ideology of the Association of Czech-Jews and the Kapper Students' Society the emphasis was put on Czechness in the nationalist sense. In this, the Kapper Society went farthest; it now considered itself a Czech organisation, no longer a Czech-Jewish one. Not surprisingly, some members later left the Kapper Society, because they no longer felt the need to organise in this way. For several years the remaining members sought to solve the intellectual crisis of the movement.[190]

An important change took place in the early 1930s. The young generation clarified its position and came out boldly against the official leadership of the Czech-Jews. The Kapper Society, in October 1932, began to publish in typescript the *Věstník akademického spolku Kapper* (Bulletin of the Kapper Students' Society), whose editor was Ervín Freund (1907–1943). In January 1933 the monthly *Kapper: List Českožidovských akademiků* (Kapper: The Newspaper of the Czech-Jewish Students), run by Arnošt Pick (1911–1942), began to come out. In his article 'Do práce' (To Work!) Pick describes how the new programme of Czech-Jewish youth gradually crystallized. According to him the youth had first voiced their disagreement with the political line of the leadership of the Czech-Jews at the Pardubice congress of the Association of Czech-Jews in 1931. The youth, however, were still unclear about what the positive core of their programme should be. The programme therefore states: 'We are Czechs of Jewish origin, whose duties to Czechness have been expanded by responsibility stemming from Diaspora experiences. Our main task is to protect humaneness and freedom of thought, to fight against antisemitism and for understanding among the nations. At a time of growing chauvinism that is truly no easy task.'[191]

In his speech to new members at the beginning of the academic year 1932–1933, Egon Hostovský explained in sharp words the conflict between the programme of the students and the official Czech-Jewish leadership. He condemned the older Czech-Jewish generation as 'bankrupt' and finished his speech with the words 'You, and you alone, have to find a way out, and together with you also those who are still young despite their grey hair.'[192]

---

[190] *Výroční zpráva Akademického spolku 'Kapper' v Praze za rok 1921–1922* (Prague, 1922), 1; Josef Beck, 'K jubileu', in *Vzpomínky a úvahy*, 48–49; František Fischer, 'Hrst vzpomínek' in ibid., 54.
[191] Arnošt Pick, 'Do práce', *Věstník akademického spolku Kapper*, no. 1 (October 1932): 1.
[192] Hostovský, 'Co jsme a co chceme', 9.

The young Czech-Jews vigorously protested against the view that Czech-Jewish organisations might be merely a temporary phenomenon until total radical assimilation was successful, which was how representatives of the Association of Czech-Jews often formulated it. The young Czech-Jews argued, for example:

> It is painful to hear that the whole Czech-Jewish movement is only temporary. We want after all to build lasting values. We want to contribute. And if we cannot yet move ahead, we want at least to keep in step with the times. The ideal of humanitarianism is the most glowing aim of human endeavour. We Czech-Jewish youth want to achieve it our way. And this, the highest aim, pursued by means of religion, politics, the arts and science, has become a necessity for us if we want our organisation to continue to make sense ideologically.[193]

The difference in programme becomes clear when we compare the activities of the students with those of the Association of Czech-Jews. The latter at that time was fighting for the status of the Czech-Jews in the Jewish religious communities, campaigning for the admission of Jewish children to Czech schools in the Bohemian borderlands and in Moravia, and was accusing the Zionists of being merely Germans in disguise or of introducing a new ghetto.[194]

In addition to the pugnacious Association of Czech-Jews oriented to a national programme, the young generation of Czech-Jews decided to elaborate something more like a cultural and ethical mission of the Czech-Jews. As Zdeněk Thon said:

> The question of our Czechness is no longer of concern to us. That has been solved. We are Czechs. We cannot be anything else. The question of the consciousness of our Jewishness is, however, of concern to us. Our relationship to it, to Jews, is of concern to us. We want to be sure whether Jewishness still has value today and is a measure of values, whether it shows us ways, offers answers to our questions and solutions to the problems of the times, whether it is something objective and lasting, whether it guides us in our relationship to national and supranational questions, to problems of all human beings. . . . By assimilating to Czechness we do not want to lose a valuable part of ourselves, our Jewishness. By that, however, we mean pure Jewishness: we are not concerned with dogma; we want to give the old ideas new expression; the spirit must remain; the formulation can be adapted to the times. It is a matter of principle, not of names. . . .

---

[193] Karel Bondy, 'Za novým cílem: Glosy k programovým debatám,' *Věstník akademického spolku Kapper*, no. 3 (December, 1932), 17.
[194] See, for example, Viktor Müller, 'Můžeme si rozumět?', *Věstník akademického spolku Kapper*, no. 6 (February, 1933), 37–38.

What we want in the Czech-Jewish movement.

We want our movement to emphasize the ethical and cultural side more than the political. We want the movement, conscious of its Czech mission, not to forget its Jewish mission; we want the movement to understand its Czech task as well as its Jewish task, that is, to unite its Czech life with Jewish values. For that reason we call for everyone to collaborate with each other. Harmonious co-existence, not strife, is our aim.[195]

The revolt of the young students manifests several elements of the programme of the pre-war Progressive Czech-Jews. The same criticism of the narrowly nationalistic conception of Czech-Jewishness appears here, as does the rediscovery of the Jewish religion freed from dogma. Lev Vohryzek, a pre-World War I leader of the Progressive Jews, sincerely welcomed the initiative of the Czech-Jewish Students. He was delighted to note:

[T]he young people are following on from where the former Association of Progressive Czech-Jews left off, considering their Czechness to be something obvious, anchored firmly in their Jewishness. . . . Today's youth now know very little of the defunct movement of Progressive Jewry, which, like today, sought to rouse, and did rouse, the movement out of the lethargy that had set in after years of unfortunate elections in the Fifth Curia, where our Czech-Jewish hyper-patriots urged Jews to vote for the antisemitic Václav Březnovský rather than the decent Social Democrat candidate [Karel] Dědic.[196]

Compared to their grandparents, the Czech-Jewish youth of the Kapper Society no longer needed to discover Czech culture. They were already firmly anchored in it. What they lacked, however, was knowledge of Judaism. They sought to fill in the gap by means of discussions with leading experts on the Jewish religion, literature and folklore. For their periodical, they asked August Stein (1854–1937), one of the few Czech-Jewish figures knowledgeable about traditional Jewish scripture, to write something. They debated with Jiří Langer about Hasidism, and the society published the first edition of his *Devět bran* (Nine Gates, 1937), which was eventually translated into several languages and achieved world renown. The society also published a large work by the Czech cultural historian, ethnographer and bibliographer Čeněk Zíbrt (born Vincenc Jan Zíbrt, 1864–1932) about the Haggadah at Passover,[197] as well as an anthology of Jewish authors

---

[195] Zdeněk Tohn, 'Co je asimilace', *Věstník akademického spolku Kapper*, nos. 3–4 (January, 1933): 27.
[196] Vohryzek, 'Kvas v našem studentstvu', 40.
[197] Čeněk Zíbrt, *Ohlas obřadních písní velikonočních (Haggadah) v lidovém podání* (Prague, 1928).

writing in Yiddish.[198] Rather than suppress their Jewishness, members of the Kapper Society sought to learn about it.[199]

The leaders of the Kapper Society soon began to implement the idea of collaboration, in the sphere of religion and in the national sphere. The Kapper Society developed relations with the Czech Students' YMCA (Akademická YMCA). In 1932 the Students' YMCA organised a talk by its secretary, Jaroslav Šimsa (1900–1945), which was called 'YMCA a židovská otázka' (The YMCA and the Jewish Question), and hosted an evening of debate with the Jerome Society of Protestant Students.[200]

The Kapper Society also began to work with the principal adversaries of the Czech-Jewish movement, the Zionists. In 1931 they organised a debate with the Theodor Herzl Zionist Society of Czech Students. The topic of the debate was a talk by Eugen Tochten (born in 1909, died during World War II),[201] a

Figure 4.3. August Stein, one of the few Czech-Jewish experts on Jewish Scripture, a long-serving chairman of the Jewish Community in Prague

---

[198] Šolom Alejchem, Isaac Leib Peretz and Abraham Reisen, *Povídky z Ghetta: Výbor ze žargonové prózy*, trans. Vincenc Červinka (Prague, 1932). For a list of works published by the Society of Czech-Jewish Students or, later, the Kapper Students' Society (Akademický spolek Kapper), see Helena Krejčová, 'Publikační činnost akademického spolku Kapper', *Documenta Pragensia* 2, no. 2 (1990): 513–19.

[199] Erich Kulka, 'The Jews in Czechoslovakia between 1918 and 1968', in *Czechoslovakia: Crossroads and Crises, 1918–1988*, ed. Norman Stone and Eduard Strouhal (London, 1989), 272.

[200] 'Spolkové zprávy', *Kalendář česko-židovský* (1933–34), 179.

[201] According to his sister's testimony in the Yad Vashem Museum, Eugen Tochten died in Hnúšťa, a town in the border area between Slovakia and Hungary, during the war. Tochten, who, after studying medicine at Prague, returned to his birth place in Považská Bystrica and was among the very few Jews who officially protested against the deportation of Slovak Jews to occupied Poland. In his complaint, Tochten states that the 4 November 1938 decree of Jozef Tiso, the Premier of the Slovak Autonomous Region of the Czecho-Slovak state, on the deportation of the Jews, is invalid because it violates the Constitution of the Czecho-Slovak Republic. See Eduard Nižňanský, 'Majorita a židovská minorita v ob-

young Zionist, titled 'Why I Am Not an Assimilationist'. The young Czech-Jews decided to continue the debates with the Czech Zionists in future, in order to find out what the two societies had in common and so that their members could combine forces in the fight against antisemitism.[202]

The students of the Kapper Society chose Jindřich Kohn as their intellectual leader. This is not surprising to those who know Kohn's works. It was, after all, Kohn, in his many articles, who reflected upon the advantages of a synthesis of Czech, Jewish and Christian (particularly Protestant) traditions, and never failed to remind his readers that Zionism and assimilation were two equal solutions to the situation of the Jews in modern times.[203] At a public meeting convened by the Jewish National Council in November 1918, Kohn defended the right of every Jew freely to choose his or her own national identity: 'Whoever experiences his Czechness in a Jewish way, let him call himself a Jew. Whoever experiences his Jewishness in a Czech way is a Czech. Let's preserve both ways and the purity of our ultimate intentions.'[204] Just after Kohn, Jakub Scharf took the floor and gave a fiery speech, concluding with a discussion of the differences between Zionism and assimilation, and saying: 'Between our views there can be no agreement: there can be only struggle.'[205]

This is also a good example of the conflicts within the Czech-Jewish movement on fundamental questions. Unlike Scharf and other leading Czech-Jews, Kohn considered assimilation and Zionism to be a 'unified, mutually forming complex'. This tension between assimilation and Zionism, he argued, guaranteed that assimilation would not become mere historical imitation, but a conscious, creative process.[206]

The journal *Kapper* was full of Kohn's articles and responses to them, as well as his lectures and seminar papers for Czech-Jewish students. It was also the Kapper Society which sought hardest to get Kohn's *Asimilace a věky* published, eventually achieving this aim in 1936. What Buber meant to the first generation of Jewish nationalists in Prague, Kohn meant to the last generation of assimilationists.[207] It is fair to make this parallel also in

---

dobí holokaustu: Poznámky k problematike sociálneho prostredia holokaustu', in *Národ a národnosti na Slovensku v transformujúcej sa spoločnosti – vzťahy a konfliky*, ed. Štefan Šutaj (Prešov, 2005), 191.

[202] 'Spolkové zprávy', *Kalendář česko-židovský* (1932–33), 183.

[203] In the 1920s, Kohn also took part in many discussions organised by the Theodor Herzl Society. See, for example, 'Spolek Theodor Herzl', *Židovské zprávy*, no. 14 (1924): 4.

[204] 'My a sionisté', *Rozhled*, no. 44 (1918): 3.

[205] Ibid., 4; 'Velká hromadná schůze židovská v Praze', *Židovské zprávy*, nos. 16–17 (1918): 7–8.

[206] Jindřich Kohn, 'Tresť mých studií česko-židovských', in *Vzpomínky a úvahy*, 32.

[207] Buber is compared with Kohn, for example, in Viktor Müller, 'Martina Bubera smysl židovství', *Rozvoj*, no. 4 (1937): 3.

the sense that, just as Buber's teaching had been comprehensible to only a small group of Zionist intellectuals, Kohn's ideas required more profound knowledge not only of Judaism, but also, indeed mainly, of contemporary philosophy. A good example of this is Kohn's statement of what Czechness and Jewishness meant to him:

> In short, the thing that I experience as Czechness – by its active nature and ubiquity – establishes the feeling of 'I am'. Jewishness, on the other hand, because I experience it fragmentarily and not as something integral, as a reaction and not as a source of something active in my life, I experience more as a vital part of myself, rather than as animation itself, in other words as the active core of the power of my life, which I am. . . . Biologically this inherited mass of Jewishness would be something fundamental, and my sense of myself as Czech would be something added on. But Czechness, biosophically, as I experience it, is the original internal form that gravitates to a related external expression, so that the sentence 'I am a Czech – of Jewish origin' cannot be interpreted as a petition to my fellow-citizens. It is mainly a confession, which expresses my deepest sense of myself.[208]

This article manifests the clear influence of Henri Bergson, particularly his distinction between the profound self and superficial self and the emphasis on internal experience.[209]

The new ideological orientation contributed to the increase in the number of Kapper Society members. 'The earlier complaints that our youth are outside the sphere of the Czech-Jewish organisations are long a thing of the past. The youth effectively add to our ranks, thus becoming a sturdy support of our movement,'[210] says the bulletin of the Association of Czech-Jews, summarizing the situation for 1931.

Work between the Kapper Society and the Association of Czech-Jews, however, came to a standstill. Ervín Freund, a leading member of the Kapper Society, stated: 'For the third year now, the Kapper Society has been publishing its own periodical. During that time many theoretical and other serious articles about assimilation have been published by the Kapper Society. Young people are the representatives of the new times and new ideas. *Rozvoj*, however, never reacts with even a line to the ideological statements of the young, just as the Kapper Society is unconcerned about what is written in *Rozvoj*. This state of affairs is unhealthy.'[211] That

---
[208] Kohn, 'Tresť mých studií česko-židovských', 32.
[209] See, in particular, Henri Bergson, 'Essai sur les données immédiates de la conscience' (1889), in H. Bergson, *Œuvres* (Paris, 1970), 83–92. I thank my husband, Jakub Čapek, for finding this quotation for me.
[210] 'Spolkové zprávy', *Kalendář česko-židovský* (1931–1932), 145.
[211] E. F. [Ervín Freund], 'Několik slov o kolektivisaci hnutí a jeho podmínkách', *Kapper*, nos. 5–6 (February 1935): 52.

is how Freund assessed the situation in 1935. In subsequent years articles by Kapper Society members occasionally appeared in *Rozvoj*. Neither the appeal of the young for closer collaboration with the Zionists, nor their endeavour to surmount the narrowly nationalist programme met, however, with much response from the leaders of the Czech-Jewish movement. The differences between the idealistic youth and the pragmatic leadership came to the surface with unexpected urgency in 1937-1938 in discussions on current political affairs.

In the Shadow of Nazism

The Nazis' coming to power in Germany, with Hitler's being sworn in as Chancellor of Germany on 30 January 1933, came as a great blow to the Czech-Jewish movement. The Czech-Jews, like the rest of the population of Czechoslovakia, Jews and non-Jews alike, were shocked by the end of democracy in Germany and by the distress of the Jews there. Moreover, the wave of antisemitism that had, with the help of Nazi propaganda, engulfed the Reich with unexpected speed undermined the very foundations of the Czech-Jewish ideology. The leaders of the Czech-Jewish movement had been made uneasy by the wave of antisemitism in Czechoslovakia in the early years of the First Republic. As they had done many times before, even back then, however, the Czech-Jews hoped that it was only a passing phenomenon. And their expectations had in fact been met; the second half of the 1920s in the Bohemian Lands was a period of relative calm, free from significant antisemitic excesses.[212]

The idyll of the 1920s, however, ended drastically with Hitler's coming to power. The first nationwide anti-Jewish boycott in Germany, organised by the Nazis on 1 April 1933, made it clear that the process of Jewish emancipation was not irreversible, that a militant regime could, without much difficulty, take away from the Jews the rights that they had won.[213] For many Jews in Europe the ideas of progress, humanity and human rights, which they had harboured throughout their lives, were now shattered. It took the main ideologues of the Czech-Jewish movement a while to figure out what to do next. Should they admit that Jewish integration into majority societies was impossible in central Europe? Should they ac-

---

[212] For a detailed analysis of antisemitic stereotypes in interwar Czech society, see Koeltzsch, 'Geteilte Stadt', 167-95.
[213] For a German Zionist's cogent description of the Jews' shock after the pogrom of 1 April 1933, see Georg Landauer, 'Über das Erbe des deutschen Judentums', in *Georg Landauer: Der Zionismus im Wandel dreier Jahrzehnte*, ed. Max Kreutzberger (Tel Aviv, 1957), 117-18.

cept as valid the argument of some Zionists, who claimed that Nazi Germany was evidence that a high degree of Jewish integration only led to even more drastic forms of antisemitism?

Not surprisingly, the Association of Czech-Jews resolved to be consistent in its ideology. True, some members left the organisation, and, as had happened in the late nineteenth century, many of those who left joined the Zionists, now convinced that integration was ultimately only a chimera.[214] Most members of the Association of Czech-Jews, even in the 1930s, were, however, unflagging in their promotion of integration into the Czech nation, recognizing that not only Jews but all Czech society was threatened by Nazi Germany. To a certain extent the external threat to the Czechoslovak republic could, they believed, help the Jews to integrate into the Czech nation. In this sense the situation in the 1930s was fundamentally different from the situation at the time of the Hilsner Affair or at the beginning of World War I, when Czechs themselves took part in anti-Jewish outbursts.

From 1933 onwards the Czech-Jews endeavoured in every possible way to demonstrate that the German tragedy was no threat to the position of the Czech-Jewish movement and that Czech 'assimilation' was still possible and necessary. A booklet by Ervín Neumann, *Práce, program a cíl Svazu Čechů židů v ČSR* (The Work, Programme and Aims of the Association of Czech-Jews in the Czechoslovak Republic), published in April 1937, is a prime example of the new interpretation of the differences between 'assimilation' in Germany and in the Bohemian Lands. In this long essay Neumann appears to adopt a number of myths or creates his own. The part about Czech and German assimilation merits quotation in full:

> The Czech assimilationist movement shows the way.
> The organised assimilationist movement in Czechoslovakia stems from the revolutionary anti-Austrian tradition. Its origin is very different from that of similar movements in other countries, for example in Germany. Jewish assimilation into the Czech nation came about in the days when all things Czech were facing hard times. It was not born in the palaces of princes as assimilation dictated from above by the aristocracy, but as a movement born in the rural cottages of smallholders and shopkeepers. It is a tree that has grown from the fertile soil of the Czech idea of humaneness. At the beginning of the last century, Jews clearly recognized that they were linked to the Czech nation by fate in an indivisible community of spirit and blood. Those of them who realized that fact are now following the idea uncompromisingly. The first generation fought on the barricades against Windischgrätz in 1848, the second with [František] Palacký and [František

---

[214] 'Valný sjezd Svazu Čechů židů v ČSR', *Rozvoj*, no. 6 (1937): 2, quoting the speech by the chairman, Viktor Lederer.

Ladislav] Rieger to create a Czech Prague, and the third eventually fulfilled the long-standing dream of previous generations: an independent Czechoslovakia. The third generation helped to create a national army, and has stood unflinchingly in the service of the young state at its worst moment.

In Germany assimilation took another route.

Its prophet was the renowned writer [Moses] Mendelssohn, who visited all the courts of Germany, and persuaded kings and princes of the necessity of Jews' working together with the German people. Unfortunately, he turned more to princes and noblemen than to the common people, for the latter did not understand the Jews, and were still susceptible to countless mysterious superstitions and myths. German assimilation is therefore a movement that did not grow out of the people for the people. Jews in Germany, with all the same civil rights as their fellow-citizens, never stopped creating a spiritual ghetto. The psyche of the Jewish people remained unknown to the masses of the German people because the German assimilationist movement never had a broad popular base. 1933 is the progeny of this policy.[215]

These two paragraphs alone, which are but a fraction of the whole booklet, contain a number of inaccuracies and half-truths. Neumann wanted to distinguish clearly and radically the ideology of the Jews in Germany and in Bohemia. Certain differences did indeed exist. An especially important one was that the Czech-Jewish movement comprised Czech Jews (particularly from rural south and east Bohemia) who aimed to awaken Czech national feeling in the Jews of the Czech areas, and thus to free them from the influence of German politics and culture. Also during the First Republic it remained one of the main goals of the Czech-Jews to persuade the greatest possible number of Jews from the German-speaking areas (by now a minority) to join the Czech side. Jews in Germany did not have to awaken German national consciousness in the Jews of Germany. That consciousness was already there; it just needed to be defended against the antisemites.

In his booklet, however, Neumann alters this difference beyond recognition. In particular the opposition of the 'mass popular nature' of Czech-Jewish assimilation and German-Jewish 'assimilation from above' is glaring. True, the Czech-Jewish movement had its roots in rural Czech areas and, true, the Czech national movement spread upwards, eventually reaching the top level of the state administration. That this was not the case in Germany has no connection to Mendelssohn, but to the fact that in Germany there was nothing like the Czech-German conflict in the Bohemian Lands. Germany was a nationally uniform state, so the integration of the Jews into German culture proceeded extremely quickly in all

---

[215] Neumann, *Práce, program a cíl Svazu Čechů židů v ČSR*, 16–17.

social strata. It would, however, be an exaggeration to say that the Czech Jews 'clearly saw', even at the beginning of the nineteenth century, that they were, in Neumann's words, 'linked with the Czech nation by fate in an indivisible community of spirit and blood'. The larger number of Bohemian Jews did not declare their nationality as Czech till the 1870s. The antisemitic riots of 1848, on the other hand, got in the way of understanding between the Jews and the Czechs.

The questionable claim that Czech society, unlike German, knew no racial antisemitism, and that Jews could therefore feel safe, also came to the fore again. So, for example, Max Lederer, at a talk organised by the Association of Czech-Jews at the Corn Exchange on 18 May 1933, with the title 'Německý antisemitismus a židé v Československu' (German Antisemitism and the Jews of Czechoslovakia), could say: 'No representative of the Czech nation ever promoted antisemitism. It was only promoted by reactionaries who could not stand criticism. But even then, it was never a matter of racial antisemitism. That kind would always be considered shameful.'[216] Maxim Reiner, in a speech at the same meeting, went even further. He claimed to the audience of about 450 people that the Czechs were not antisemites and never had been. He also uncritically viewed the beginning of the Czechoslovak state, which was accompanied by a number of anti-Jewish excesses. 'In the Czech nation', he said, 'there was never any antisemitism. Here, love and freedom of conscience were always propagated. Antisemitism in the Czech nation was always caused by the Jews themselves because of their unnecessary Germanization. Here, no one ever came out against the Jews because they were Jews. The wonderful Czechoslovak revolution hurt no one, and gave everyone equal rights.'[217]

In reaction to German nationalism the Czech-Jews, like many Czechs, began to emphasize their nationalist programme to a much greater extent. Earlier, too, they promoted the use of the Czech language in synagogues, in the Jewish communities, and in the education of Jewish children. Now, however, they began to fight vigorously, strengthened by the sense of the threat to the Czech nation.[218] At meetings of representatives of the Jewish community in Prague, the Czech-Jews made repeated appeals for the consistent use of Czech in public,[219] and there were also numerous appeals in the Jewish press.

---

[216] NA, ministerstvo vnitra presidium, Report of the Chief Police Commissioner, 225-979-13, X/Ž/6/2.
[217] Ibid.
[218] 'Spolkové zprávy', Kalendář česko-židovský (1933–34), 181.
[219] See, for example, the minutes of the meeting of the representation of the Jewish Community in Prague, 11 July 1934, AŽMP, protokoly schůzí reprezentace ŽNO v Praze.

A remarkable manifesto was written in June 1933 by the important Czech-Jewish rabbi Richard Feder (1875-1970), one of the few Czech-Jewish activists who did not eschew dialogue with Zionists. For example, he published his 'Rady a pokyny' (Advice and Instructions) in the Zionist journal *Židovské zprávy* after the Nazis took power in Germany. In thirteen points he summarizes how a real Czech or German Jew should behave in the Bohemian Lands. In the first point, he urges his co-religionists in Bohemia and Moravia: '[I]f you live in Czech towns and villages and in areas with a predominantly Czech majority, speak Czech! If you don't yet speak Czech well, make it perfect.'[220] He also urges Jews in the Communist movement to quit. The best thing to do, he recommends, is not to be a member of any party. In other points he calls upon Jews who had been baptized to return to the Jewish Community and urges Jews in mixed marriages to bring up their children Jewish. He strongly advises young people not to marry non-Jews, and tells Jews to have Jewish funerals. Jewish parents, he says, should educate their children to be modest. Jews should not have servants and should teach children to help. A Jew should take the cheaper seats in the cinema. Jews, he said, should not stay at spas owned by Nazis and should support their fellow-Jews. They should go to fewer German films, read less German literature by Nazi writers and should instead get Holy Scripture and study it. They should also learn Hebrew. And Feder asks German-speaking Jews to go on holiday to German-speaking areas rather than Czech ones. He finishes his list of advice with the appeal that they all buy government bonds to support the Czech economy.[221]

In a number of ways Feder's stance was influenced by Czech-Jewish ideology. Not only were Jews supposed to speak Czech, but Jews who did not know the language were advised not to travel to Czech areas. Typical of Czech-Jews was the attempt not to stand out in other ways, not to provoke anyone by their behaviour, their property, or their political convictions. Nevertheless, Feder differed from the Czech-Jewish leadership with his emphasis on the Jewish religion, which he believed would not be harmed by integrating into the surrounding society. He was one of the few rabbis in the interwar period to declare himself part of the Czech-Jewish movement, and he was respected as the author of Czech primary-school textbooks on Jewish religion and Hebrew.

The leaders of the Czech-Jewish movement, however, took another route. Feder's emphasis on faith, Jewish tradition and custom, and the study of Scripture and Hebrew seemed to them exaggerated, even unnecessary, and his advice for German-speaking Jews seemed weak – if Nazism

---

[220] Richard Feder, 'Český rabín mluví k Židům: Rady a pokyny', *Židovské zprávy*, no. 23 (1933): 23. Feder was the Chief Rabbi of the Bohemian Lands in 1960-1970.
[221] Ibid.

threatened the whole republic from outside, German-speaking Jews in the Bohemian Lands constituted, in the eyes of the Czech-Jews, a fifth column of the Reich in Czechoslovakia. In an article titled 'Ideologie českožidovství' (The Ideology of Czech-Jewishness), the anonymous author reminds his readers of the original aims of the movement – namely, the fight against the 'unnatural' Germanness of the Jews of Bohemia. 'All of that remains just as true today,' he writes. 'And the Czech-Jewish programme has acquired greater meaning after the events of recent years, when it has become clear that Jewry has no greater or more fanatical enemies in the world than the Germans, wherever they are and in whatever social class.'[222]

The Association of Czech-Jews was, however, also under pressure from forces within the country. In particular, the Czechoslovak National Council forced the Association of Czech-Jews into the position of defenders of the Czech cause among the Jews. A good example is Arthur Rosenzweig (1883–1936), who in 1934 was invited to be the rabbi of the Spanish Synagogue in Dušní ulice, Prague. Rosenzweig was born in Teplice (Teplitz) in the German-speaking borderlands, the son of the local rabbi, but his father had been granted German citizenship and in 1887 was invited to serve as a rabbi in Berlin. Rosenzweig studied in Heidelberg and at the rabbinical seminary in Breslau, and except for the years of World War I, when he served as a rabbi in Cheb (Eger), west Bohemia, he worked in various Jewish communities in Germany until 1934.[223] In a letter of 22 October 1934 to the board of the Association of Czech-Jews, Bohumil Němec (1873–1966), a former senator of the National Assembly who was the chairman of the Czechoslovak National Council and a professor of botany and plant physiology, wrote: 'The Czechoslovak National Council has learnt, as is also clear from the daily press, that a preacher from the Reich who does not know a word of Czech was hired for the Jewish [sic] synagogue in Dušní ulice without the job opening first being advertised. Although we have received news that he has promised to learn the Czechoslovak state language within two years, the approach of the synagogue administration is incomprehensible to us.'[224] Němec called upon the board of the Association of Czech-Jews to take notice of the matter and to send a report to the Czechoslovak National Council concerning their next steps.

In his reply to Němec, the chairman of the Association of Czech-Jews, Otto Stross (1900–1942), states the prosaic reason for the choice of Rosen-

---

[222] Dr. O. R., 'Ideologie českožidovství', *Rozvoj*, no. 4 (1937): 1.
[223] Peter Simonstein Cullman, *History of the Jews of Schneidemühl: 1641 to the Holocaust* (Bergenfield, 2006), 129.
[224] NA, Národní rada československá, inv. č. 118, k. 234/1, P 2612/13.262/3/4/5, 22 October 1934.

zweig: 'We learnt . . . that several rabbis had preached in Czech for a trial period, . . . but that a German citizen, Rosenzweig, though he does not speak the state language, was chosen because he was satisfied with the annual salary of 36,000 Czechoslovak crowns, whereas the other rabbis, and mainly those who are Czechoslovak citizens and speak Czech, had rather higher demands regarding salary.' In the letter Stross also says, '[K]nowing the situation in the private synagogue in Dušní ulice, whose congregation comprises some of the richest Prague Jews, we can assure you that the situation is financially such that the salary for the preacher and the rabbi can be satisfactorily adjusted.'[225]

For the German-speaking Jewish élite in Dušní ulice it was certainly no problem that Rosenzweig was a German citizen. On the contrary, they may have believed it was desirable to take in a refugee from Germany. Moreover, why should they spend more money on a Czech candidate, they may well have asked, if they preferred to have the service conducted in German anyway? But their pragmatic approach ran up against state policy and the nationalist programme of the Czech-Jews. The representatives of the Association of Czech-Jews managed to make sure that Rosenzweig was not hired by the Prague Jewish Community. They sent a report to the Bohemian authorities, describing the situation and demanding that the candidate not be approved, and they sent a copy of the report to the Ministry of Social Affairs.[226] Nor was Němec remiss in the matter. He wrote to the head of the Bohemian authorities, Josef Sobotka, asking him not to approve a candidate who was a German citizen.[227] Only a few months later Němec ran (unsuccessfully) as the Agrarian candidate against Beneš for the office of president of Czechoslovakia. Rabbi Rosenzweig died suddenly in 1936 after a brief illness.

Another feature of Czech-Jewish ideology in the 1930s was the tactic of the 'localization of danger'. It was formulated clearly by the Czech-Jews' main thinker, Jindřich Kohn, at a special meeting of the Association of Czech-Jews on 6 April 1933, which had been called in reaction to the political events in Germany: 'Our by-word today is not to protest, not to demonstrate, but to localize and protect our borders so that the threat remains beyond them.'[228] Kohn's words were often quoted by leading Czech-Jewish officials even in the late 1930s.

With the greatest urgency this idea appears in an article by the student Zdeněk Tohn, a frequent contributor to the *Kalendář česko-židovský*:

---

[225] Ibid., P 2612/11.376, 27 October 1934.
[226] Ibid.
[227] Ibid., P 2612/13.409/13.410, 31 October 1934.
[228] NA, ministerstvo vnitra presidium, 225-979-13, 7 April 1933.

The German nation is breaking the thread of civilization, a thread linking it with the rest of the world, and in this situation it is imperative that everyone for whom the term humanity is not meaningless also to break the last threads that have not yet been broken. From these threads ropes and nets must be woven to link together those who still live by the principles of humanity, and thus completely to isolate those who are trampling humanity under foot.... The individual must be sacrificed if the whole is to be saved. A raging disease must be localized, a raging fire must be localized, and that can only be done by isolation.[229]

Links with Germany, political, economic and cultural, must, according to the Czech-Jews, therefore be severed. By contrast, work with Jews in the countries of the Little Entente came to the fore. The leaders of the Association of Czech-Jews truly did consider working with assimilated Jews of Yugoslavia and Romania. In his *Práce, program a cíl Svazu Čechů židů v ČSR*, Neumann writes that forming friendly alliances among the Jews of all three states would certainly be a 'powerful boost to the economic policy of the Little Entente.... The Association of Czech-Jews is trying to achieve such collaboration, in the firm belief that its work will meet with understanding among the authorities abroad.'[230] Neumann's booklet was published in April 1937, and it is highly unlikely that this collaboration ever began, particularly since right-wing and largely Fascist parties came to power in Romania after the December 1937 elections. But, according to Neumann, Czech-Jews successfully began work with Bulgarians.[231]

The Attempt to Revise the Czech-Jewish National Programme

For the subsequent political and ideological orientation of the Association of Czech-Jews the year 1937 was decisive. In the Czech-Jewish movement a debate was underway about the extent to which its policy should henceforth be nationalistic and anti-German, and also about the extent to which work with the Zionists was admissible. The young Czech-Jewish students at the time managed to publish several articles in *Rozvoj*, in which they tried to revise the narrowly nationalist programme of the Association. A good example is the contribution by Arnošt Gerad (1916-1942), a student of philosophy. In his article 'O syntetické asimilaci' (Concerning Synthetic Assimilation), he clearly distinguishes between two kinds of assimilation – negative and positive (also called synthetic). Negative as-

---

[229] Zdeněk Tohn, 'Německo z perspektivy česko-židovské', *Kalendář česko-židovský* (1933-34), 105.
[230] Neumann, *Práce, program a cíl Svazu Čechů židů v ČSR*, 23.
[231] Ibid., 23-24.

similation means denying one's original identity either voluntarily or under pressure. Synthetic assimilation, by contrast, means an 'endeavour to achieve the harmonization and meshing of two cultural strata, a synthesis of two views of life, two perspectives, two ethics'. Since Gerad (following the example of Kohn) did not see assimilation as the Jews' only way out of their situation in modern society, he considered work with the Zionists to be acceptable.[232]

The fight between the members of the nationalistically minded older generation and young students came to a head at the congress of the Association of Czech-Jews in late January 1937. The opening address at the congress was given by the chairman of the association, Viktor Lederer, who assumed the role of defender of the nationalist programme. In his speech he emphasized that 1936 clearly demonstrated the strength of Czechoslovak democracy. Even the right-wing parties 'flirting with Fascism were unable to do away with democracy in their own ranks'. Lederer spoke out in favour of working with these parties. It was, according to him, necessary even with right-wing parties 'to reach agreement by conciliation' on the Jewish Question, so that the Czech public did not think that the whole right-wing camp was antisemitic.[233] Nor did he avoid the problems of Zionism. For the Jews in the Diaspora, Palestine could not be a solution, he argued, because it was 'threatened with force and barbarity that was often more primitive than what was in Europe in 1933'. The Zionists in Czechoslovakia could not, he continued, be partners for the Czech-Jews, because 'they did not cease to claim that assimilation was failing'. From the many reactions of the Zionists, according to Lederer, it follows that they were not responsible democrats, and it was necessary to deal with them accordingly.[234] He also spoke out directly against the oppositionist point of view of the young generation, claiming that Czech nationalism, unlike the nationalisms of other nations, was not so destructive that it was essentially synthetic. 'We are convinced that much of the recent human suffering was caused by nationalism, but Czech nationalism was always synthetic and gravitated to universalism. Czech history provides the best evidence of that,' he said.[235] Lederer told the young people criticizing the nationalist programme of the association that although he did not wish to deny them the right to be sceptical, he most definitely rejected 'pointless opposition and unconstructive, aimless passivity'. The youth, he argued, should also realize that the policy of the association had to be full of compromises, because its members came from various political camps.

---

[232] Arnošt Gerad, 'O syntetické asimilaci', *Rozvoj*, no. 11 (1937): 2.
[233] 'Valný sjezd Svazu Čechů židů v ČSR', *Rozvoj*, no. 6 (1937): 1.
[234] Ibid., 2.
[235] Ibid., 1.

The nationalist programme, moreover, could not be dismissed simply because of the history of the Czech-Jewish movement: 'If we wish to create a new ideology, we cannot forego vital contact with tradition. Sixty years of Czech-Jewish work must be a covenant for us, something which binds us.'[236] His words were met with applause.

Herbert Langer (1914-1943), a law student, was the only speaker there on behalf of the young generation. His short but clear speech demonstrates the way in which the Czech-Jewish youth sought to revise the programme of the older generation. The editor of *Rozvoj* summarized Langer's speech:

> He turns to the congress, aware that the movement's past weighs on the young as much as the future does. One must realize, however, that the declaration of Czechoslovak independence on 28 October 1918 is an important milestone in the Czech-Jewish movement. The fight against Germanization cannot be our only programme. We became equal members of the larger nation, and from that follow our new duties. Today, we must understand the assimilation programme as a process of rapprochement. The foremost aim of the Czech-Jews in the newly independent state must be the struggle to strengthen democracy based on humanitarian principles. Here, however, we must clearly see on whose side the antisemites are assembling. We see that it is where reaction is. Reactionary tendencies are sinking their roots into the right-wing parties. The whole public must clearly see that the Czechoslovak democracy and the Czech-Jewish movement are fighting on a shared platform. Following this programme we must extend the fight against antisemitism more broadly and more thoroughly. The time is coming when it will be our duty to take in assimilationists of other nations as well. The youth have already established their own attitude to the Zionists. They are our political adversaries, not our political enemies. We fully understand, however, that Political Zionism is an anti-democratic, reactionary movement. But in day-to-day, small-scale politics we and the Zionists have one common enemy, and that is antisemitism.[237]

Langer's speech led to a heated debate, which demonstrated, however, that among the Czech-Jews the youth were completely isolated. All the leading functionaries (Otto Stross, the past and future chairman; Josef Beck, the deputy chairman; František Fischer, a member of the executive committee; Karel Stross, the official delegate for north Bohemia; and Josef Bondy, the official delegate for Moravia) agreed that the young generation was wrong on all points of its programme. In no case was it possible to retreat from the national programme, closer collaboration with

---

[236] Ibid., 2.
[237] Ibid.

the Zionists was impossible, and the choice of party was a private matter of each Czech-Jew. The association congress in 1937 confirmed the decision of the 1935 congress that it would determine whether expressions of antisemitism among the political parties 'were sporadic or whether antisemitism was their programme and principle'.[238] The association would consider only the parties from the latter group to be its enemies. Concerning the question of antisemitism the speakers agreed that there already existed an independent organisation to fight it – namely, the League against Antisemitism (Liga proti antisemitismu) – and that the task of the association was to defend the rights of Czech-Jews and to win over to its side Jews who were nationally indifferent. At the end of the debate, the chairman, Lederer, did not mince words in his condemnation of the youth. The Czech-Jewish movement, according to him, 'cannot and must not conform to the views of the Prague street, and we must not share the fear of the Jewish panic-mongers of the Prague cafés'.[239]

The position of the youth was greatly weakened by the death of their long-standing adviser and teacher, Jindřich Kohn, in 1935. It remains a question what their situation would have been in 1938 if the opposition of the young generation could still have based itself on Kohn's authority. It is certain that without Kohn their views would not have won acceptance. At the congress in 1937, only Ota Richter was elected to represent the youth on the ten-member executive committee. At the January 1938 congress, the chief 'rebel', Herbert Langer, was also elected to the executive committee.[240] They were nevertheless unable to change the nationalist policy of the association or its negative attitude to all immigrants other than those of Czech nationality.

In 1938 nothing more was heard of the dispute between the young students and the old nationalists.[241] The youth probably understood that they were not strong enough to achieve a revision of association policy, so they focused their future activity on the arts. Their improved periodical, *Směry* (Trends), sought above all to keep in step with Czech life in the arts.[242] They left political matters, for example the refugee question, to the association leadership.

---

[238] Ibid., 1.
[239] Ibid., 2.
[240] AHMP, SK X/15.
[241] At the January 1938 conference of the Association of Czech-Jews, the senior members (Viktor Lederer and Otto Stross) and the junior members (Kurt Heller, editor of *Směry*, on behalf of the Kapper Society) approvingly spoke about there allegedly no longer being fundamental points of dispute between the university students and the association. 'Valný sjezd Svazu Čechů židů v ČSR', *Rozvoj*, no. 5 (1938): 1–2.
[242] Ibid., 2, from the speech of Kurt Heller.

Figures 4.4. and 4.5. Rare photographs from the congress of the Association of Czech-Jews, 29 January 1938: the board, chaired by Otto Stross (first from the right), and the floor.

Send Them Elsewhere!

Right up until the end of 1937 it was generally assumed that aid to refugees would be limited to the now basically stable number from Germany and Austria. The Czech-Jews did not become particularly involved in assisting them. Maxim Reiner, who had become the chairman of the Prague Jewish Community in July 1934, was, even in 1935, against supporting German refugees. When the Jewish Centre for Social Welfare (Židovská ústředna pro sociální péči) appealed to the individual Jewish congregations to make greater self-sacrifice to help the refugees, a list of whom was attached to the appeal, Reiner responded: '[O]ne understands from the list that between 60 and 70 per cent of the refugees are political refugees, and it is up to their political parties to look after them.'[243]

Rozvoj, however, sporadically ran appeals for material assistance. Jan Hart, an unknown Czech-Jewish author, for example, wrote in October 1937: 'The tradition of Czech émigrés runs from Comenius to Masaryk. . . . The few hundred German émigrés whom we enable to live are our repayment of a debt that we owe to the world, mankind and our history.'[244]

After the annexation of Austria to the Reich in March 1938, the Czechs felt even more threatened. The question of Sudeten autonomy was also raised with increasing urgency. Czech-Jews tried to imagine what Sudeten autonomy might mean for the Czech-Jewish movement. Otto Stross, the newly elected chairman of the Association of Czech-Jews, spoke on this point in connection with the Carlsbad congress of the Henlein Party, where demands for the separation of the Sudetenland from Czechoslovakia had been clearly voiced. At the 28 April 1938 meeting of the association, he stated that the possible expansion of autonomy to the German minority would pose a 'great threat to the Jewish Question, because the Jews will be forced to move to Czech areas, and that will necessarily lead to resistance also from the Christian Czechs'.[245]

These words contain echoes of Stross's opinion that a radical solution would have to be found to the question of Jewish and German refugees from the Sudetenland. In the same report, he mentions that the threat to the Jewish population of the Sudetenland must not, on the other hand, scare Czech Jews of the interior into thinking about emigrating. Czech-Jews should by no means give up their hard-won positions in the economy and politics. 'The Czech-Jewish movement,' he writes, 'requires more than loyalty to the state. It is aware of its life-and-death bond to the Czechoslo-

---

[243] AŽMP, Protokoly schůzí reprezentace ŽNOP 1935, 16 January 1935.
[244] Jan Hart, 'Emigrujeme německé emigranty', *Rozvoj*, no. 43 (1937): 1.
[245] NA, ZÚ pres. 207-1402-24, 8/5/53/64.

vak nation. Its representatives must adjust their financial dealings accordingly. They must not convert their assets into cash, keep their savings at home, or stop doing business.'[246] Nor should they be absent, he writes, from any place 'where the Czechoslovak nation and democracy are at stake.' In this sense Stross most appreciated the fact that four association members had been elected to advisory committees of the Czechoslovak National Council.[247]

As early as 30 September 1937, the association asked the Ministry of the Interior to provide it with 'financial support for its political tasks which follow the non-partisan line of work in the interest of building the state'.[248] The ministry passed on the request to the cabinet in January 1938, which turned to the Ministry of Education, asking it to grant the association's request if possible, since 'the Cabinet in its preliminary budget did not have monies earmarked from which it could provide the requested support'.[249] The Ministry of Education, however, on 8 February, also expressed that its budget lacked the requested amounts and that, moreover, it was a matter of supporting a political task 'outside the sphere of religion'.[250] Thanks to a Ministry of the Interior investigation into the source of the demand for financial support, we know that the association, in all its chapters in Bohemia and Moravia, had 2,023 members in April 1938.[251]

In the leadership of the Association of Czech-Jews the view began to be accepted that it would be necessary to distinguish between refugees whose social integration in the remaining Czech regions was desirable (in other words, citizens of Czechoslovak nationality) and those who should be helped when currently in need, but who must then be relocated as soon as possible somewhere outside Czechoslovakia. Before the occupation of the Sudetenland and the intensification of the question of the German-speaking refugees, the association's negative attitude towards immigrants from outside the country was revealed in connection with Romanian Jews who, in the course of 1938, were escaping the dictatorship in Romania. In December 1937, after the Romanian general elections, right-wing parties took charge, in particular the fascist Iron Guard. The new premier, Octavian Goga, began immediately to introduce antisemitic legislation modelled on that of Nazi Germany, and it was expected that thousands

---

[246] 'Členská schůze pražské komise Svazu Čechů židů', *Rozvoj*, no. 18 (1938): 4, based on a report by chairman Otta Stross.
[247] Ibid.
[248] NA, ministerstvo vnitra presidium, 225-1324-3, X/Ž/6/2.
[249] Ibid., čj. 5529/38, 1 March 1938.
[250] Ibid.
[251] NA, ministerstvo vnitra presidium, 207-1402-24, 8/5/53/64, 20 April 1938.

of Romanian Jews would try to save their lives by fleeing to what were still democratic countries.[252] In a long article, Josef Bondy, an association official who was in charge of association matters in Moravia, commented on the Romanian émigrés: 'It was right to say that we cannot save humanity all over the world and we must first and foremost defend what can be defended in our own state. To accept the immigration of Romanian Jews is not in the interest of our state. Indeed, the opposite could be said, and that is what is decisive for us.'[253]

For Bondy, however, it was not only the Romanian Jews who were a thorn in the side. It was also those who, in consequence of economic problems, were coming from Subcarpathian Ruthenia. 'Economic hardship,' he said, 'is forcing those Jews to move, and so we are witness to what is for the time being a small influx of Jews from Subcarpathian Ruthenia into the historic lands [of the Bohemian crown]. To be honest, we must admit that this migration is not something we like. The same thing is true of the Romanian Jews. It has to do with another culture, another understanding of morality and religion.'[254]

Czechoslovakia, according to Bondy, should learn from the Soviet Union, which, he said, let the Jews decide whether to assimilate or live according to their own national and cultural way of life in a territory reserved specially for them. Bondy was referring to the Jewish Autonomous Oblast, whose capital was Birobidzhan.[255] He could perhaps be forgiven for holding this opinion only if he was grossly ignorant of the situation of the Jews in the Stalinist Soviet Union (including the disastrous situation of the Jews in the Jewish Autonomous Oblast). Unfortunately, Bondy was not the only Czech-Jew who believed Soviet propaganda.

The Soviet project played a relatively important role in Czech-Jewish ideology in the second half of the 1930s. The Czech-Jews also understood that integration was not a solution for all the Jews of the world. The Jewish Autonomous Oblast, at the Soviet frontier with China, represented a more acceptable alternative for Czech-Jews than Jewish settlement in Palestine. The Association of Czech-Jews even began to work with the Society of Friends of Birobidzhan (Společnost přátel Birobidžanu), which was founded in September 1935.[256] The society was not, however, particularly active. From its founding to its dissolution in 1939, it organised only

---

[252] Michal Frankl, '"Židovstvo ztrácí své základy": Československo a rumunská uprchlická krize (1937–1938)', *Terezínské studie a dokumenty* 2005, 297–309.
[253] Josef Bondy, 'Několik poznámek k židovským problémům', *Rozvoj*, no. 7 (1938): 2.
[254] Ibid.
[255] For the Soviet project in Birobidzhan, see Antje Kuchenbecker, *Zionismus ohne Zion: Birobidžan. Idee und Geschichte eines jüdischen Staates in Sowjet-Fernost* (Berlin, 2000).
[256] Neumann, *Práce, program a cíl Svazu Čechů židů v ČSR*, 24.

six officially announced talks. One of them was by Eduard Lederer, who, together with Bohumír Šmeral, a Communist senator, gave a talk titled 'Current Problems of Jewry, Palestine and Birobidzhan'.[257] No manuscript of the lecture has survived, but it is fair to assume that the main idea was criticism of Zionist activities in Palestine, praise for the Soviets, and the depiction of the Jewish Autonomous Oblast as a model 'solution to the Jewish Question' in the Diaspora.

The members of the Society of Friends of Birobidzhan, however, never at all considered that they themselves would ever move there. That is clear from a police report of July 1936, which states: 'Support for emigration to Birobidzhan was not discussed. On the contrary, at the general meeting it was pointed out that organizing emigration to Birobidzhan was not a task of the society, not to mention the fact that neither the members of the society nor the broader Jewish public is interested in emigrating to the USSR.'[258]

The Birobidzhan project, however, inspired the association leaders so much that they considered creating a kind of Soviet autonomous oblast in Subcarpathian Ruthenia. Bondy proposed establishing a special Jewish administrative area there. All Jews who were dissatisfied in the Bohemian Lands would thus have a place to go. There would surely be money for the project: 'Rich Jews would make donations simply to limit the immigration of Jews to the Bohemian Lands.' The project would certainly find sympathizers abroad. According to Bondy:

> The fundamental guidelines for the solution of the Jewish Question in Czechoslovakia would therefore be as follows: the closing of the frontiers to various Jewish immigrants, the thorough assimilation in the Bohemian Lands and Slovakia, and the establishment of a special homeland in Subcarpathian Ruthenia for Jewish nationalists from Czechoslovakia. . . . Our state would demonstrate that it was possible to solve the Jewish Question and how to solve it, how it was possible to use the hidden strengths of the Jews to everyone's benefit, and to show the whole world that our state knows how to solve any problem in a truly progressive, masterful way.[259]

After the Munich Agreement the situation became even more acute. Previously, it had been only a matter of words. Now, it was a matter of deeds. In late October 1938 the leaders of the Association of Czech-Jews came out with an official statement on 'moving out the German-Jewish émigrés', which it sent also to the Czechoslovak National Council. It says:

---

[257] AHMP, SK XXII/2233.
[258] Ibid.
[259] Bondy, 'Několik poznámek k židovským problémům'.

> The Association of Czech-Jews in the Czechoslovak Republic, as the centre of all citizens of Czech nationality of Jewish origin, fully agrees with the position and actions of the Czech towns and Czech press, that the Government, in agreement with the Great Powers, should see to the [German and Jewish refugees'] moving out, by suitably locating them outside the Czechoslovak Republic. It is inadmissible that the emigrants settle in our towns and threaten not only the national character of those towns but even the existence of Czechs regardless of confession. It is a matter of the existence of our republic, and Czech-Jews are willing to work with all their might together with the governments of the towns and the whole Czech public for the well-being and security of the state and nation.[260]

The statement was also published in *Rozvoj*. The same issue contains an article 'of explanation' by Kurt Heller (1914–1944). The article is an appeal for self-sacrificing assistance to the people of the Sudetenland. Heller soon admits, however, that the refugees from the Sudetenland would have to be categorized: 'On the one side there are the Czech border people [Czechs who lived in the otherwise German borderlands and, according to nationalist propaganda, kept watch on the borders of the Czechoslovak state]; on the other there are the rest [that is, everyone who was not of Czechoslovak nationality].' A 'decent living' would of course have to be made possible for the Czech border people in the interior. The others would have to be sent elsewhere, and Heller proposes some British colony – Australia, Canada or South Africa.[261]

The statement of the Association of Czech-Jews naturally led to a heated debate, mainly in the Zionist press. The chairman, Stross, therefore felt obliged to defend the position of the Czech-Jews. He explained that dividing Jewish refugees from the borderlands into Czech refugees and the others was based on information provided by the 'competent authorities'. From them the leaders of the Association of Czech-Jews had learnt that 'the right of opting in favour of the current Czechoslovak Republic would probably be granted only to those of our former [sic] fellow citizens domiciled on the annexed territory who are of Czechoslovak nationality'. The Association of Czech-Jews, according to Stross, accepted this idea and did not think it would be possible to make an exception for the Jews. The right of option would be granted according to the nationality one had declared in the 1930 census.[262]

The Association of Czech-Jews then organised an 'informal evening with Prague journalists' in the clubroom of the Národní kavárna, on

---

[260] NA, NRČ, inv. č. 107/171, P 3548/26.516, 25 October 1938.
[261] Kurt Heller, 'Problém ze všech nejtíživější', *Rozvoj*, no. 43 (1938): 2.
[262] Otta Stross, 'Spravedlnost pro všechny!', *Rozvoj*, no. 44 (1938): 1.

Národní třída, on 3 November 1938. Among the participants were the editors of *Národní listy, Národní Střed, Právo lidu* and *Telegraf*, as well as Josef Beck, the director of the Bank of the Czechoslovak Legions (one of the most successful Czech banks at the time). The programme included a 'discussion of the Jewish Question today'.[263] The chairman and the secretary of the association addressed about fifty guests on behalf of the Association of Czech-Jews.[264] Both men emphasized their negative attitude towards the German refugees, and appealed to the journalists to make a clear distinction between Czech Jews and the rest. At the end of the meeting the journalists and the association representatives agreed that in 'solving the Jewish Question' it was necessary to use the national, not the racial, criterion.

Czech-Jews therefore sought to help their adherents to the detriment of Jews of German or Jewish nationality. Stross openly admitted in his article 'Válka židovská' (The Jewish War): 'The Czech-Jews will not abandon their position and mission in the Czech nation, and therefore cannot allow themselves to get distracted by any all-Jewish political causes, unless they are compelled to do so by force.'[265] He probably already suspected, however, that the Czech-Jews would ultimately be forced to work with the Zionists, for the article continues:

> If, after all, things came to the worst – which would, however, only be temporary – and Czech-Jews were by some external force perhaps pushed into a political all-Jewish community, . . . they would not go there hanging their heads in shame, looking down at the ground. Instead, they would go, heads held high, in the knowledge that during the decades of their involvement in politics they had done nothing to create a rift between the Jews and the non-Jewish milieu, but had, on the contrary, expended all their energy to ensure that this rift was bridged only by a just solution of the Jewish Question – namely, by merging the local Jews and the Czechs as one nation.[266]

Stross did not suspect, however, that in only a few months the Czech-Jews, under the leadership of the Zionist leaders, would be concerned not with their rights, but with the physical survival of every Jew.

The end of the organised Czech-Jewish movement in Bohemia is all the sadder because thousands of the Jewish citizens of Czechoslovakia,

---

[263] NA, ZÚ pres., 207-1402-24, 8/5/53/64, 4 November 1938.
[264] The senior police officer Antonín Jakubec identified Müller as the secretary of the Association of Czech-Jews, but according to the police register of clubs and associations no one of that name was in the executive committee of the Association of Czech-Jews at that time. See AHMP, SK XXI/149.
[265] Otta Stross, 'Válka židovská', *Rozvoj*, no. 47 (1938): 2.
[266] Ibid.

though not organised in any Czech-Jewish society, had experienced the symbiosis of Czechs and Jews every day, as it was proclaimed by Jindřich Kohn and the students of the Kapper Society, and they had contributed to it. Since most of the Jews in the Czech areas had no problem co-existing with the Czechs, these Jews had no need to organise in special societies. The Czech-Jewish organisations were therefore dominated by extreme Czech nationalists and people who felt threatened by antisemitism. This considerably helps to explain how the Association of Czech-Jews, which actually represented only an insignificant fraction of the Jews who declared 'Czechoslovak' as their nationality, let itself be carried away by the Czech nationalist ideas of its board.

Chapter 5

ZIONISTS

Some historians make a clear distinction between Jewish nationalism and Zionism in Czechoslovakia.¹ The former may be understood as a superior category that includes all the movements whose exponents declared Jewish as a nationality. The Zionists endeavoured, in addition, to achieve the foundation of a Jewish state. Other times the concept Jewish nationalism is understood as being in opposition to Zionism; unlike Zionists, Jewish nationalists never intended to leave the countries of their birth. Their chief aim was to ensure, and guard, the rights of the Jewish national minority in the country in which they lived.

A strict distinction between Zionism and Jewish nationalism, I would argue, is not useful when describing the situation in Bohemia. There were groups there whose members called themselves only Jewish nationalists, but the interests and aims of the Jewish nationalists and Zionists in Bohemia overlapped to such an extent that it is difficult to tell who fit where.² Zionists too, after all, tried to get Jewish nationality recognized and to develop Jewish culture in the Diaspora. They even had a special name for it – *Gegenwartsarbeit* (avodat ha-hoveh, work in the present). This term sug-

---

[1] See, for example, Meir Färber, 'Die jüdisch-nationale Bewegung in der Tschechoslowakei', *Zeitschrift für die Geschichte der Juden in der Tschechoslowakei*, nos. 3–4 (1965): 150; Fred Hahn, 'The Dilemma of the Jews in the Historic Lands of Czechoslovakia, 1918–38', *East Central Europe*, no. 10 (1983): parts 1–2, 26.

[2] See also Tatjana Lichtenstein, 'Making Jews at Home: Jewish Nationalism in the Bohemian Lands, 1918-1938', PhD thesis, University of Toronto 2009; Martin J. Wein, 'Zionism in Interwar Czechoslovakia: Palestino-Centrism and Landespolitik', *Judaica Bohemiae* 44, no. 2 (2009): 5–47.

gests that Zionists understood work in the Diaspora as a necessary stage in the mobilization of the Jewish population, at least before some of them decided to emigrate to Palestine. In Bohemia the work of the Jewish nationalists and the work of the Zionists were closely linked also because their common opponents were the Czech and the German 'assimilationists'. If one compares Zionism in Poland or Subcarpathian Ruthenia with Zionism in the Bohemian Lands, Germany or the countries of western Europe, the fundamental difference becomes clear. It was evident to almost all the Jews in the former countries that a Jew differed from the rest of the population not only by religion but also often by way of life or language spoken at home. This notion was fostered by the opinion of the majority society, which mostly saw Jews as a distinct national group. The Zionists thus differed from other Jews only in that they promoted the establishment of a secular Jewish state in Palestine. In Poland, for example, Jews from the Bund (founded in Wilno, in October 1897, the full name of which is the Algemeyner Yidisher Arbeter Bund in Lite, Poyln un Rusland, or the General Union of Jewish Workers in Lithuania, Poland and Russia), constituted the strongest group in opposition to the Zionists. Bund members, at the same time, promoted Jewish nationalism. Their chief aim was to defend the rights of the Jews in Poland and to develop their cultural traditions in Yiddish.[3]

Zionists or Jewish nationalists in western Europe, on the other hand, differed from the other local Jews by pointing out the national character of Jewry. Zionism in western Europe can reasonably be described as 'post-assimilationist'. That is what the German Zionist leader Kurt Blumenfeld (1884–1963) called Jews who turned to Zionism only after they failed to integrate into the surrounding nations.[4] Similarly, in Bohemia the first generation of Zionists comprised Jews who had previously been fully integrated into Czech or German culture (or both).

The difference between western and eastern Zionism was clear also in Czechoslovakia. The fact that in Slovakia and in Subcarpathian Ruthenia many people of the Jewish faith declared their nationality to be Jewish does not mean that Zionism was particularly successful in those areas.[5]

---

[3] Ezra Mendelsohn, 'Zionist Success and Zionist Failure: The Case of East Central Europe between the Wars', in *Essential Papers on Zionism*, ed. Jehuda Reinharz and Anita Shapira (New York, 1996), 171–90; Zvi Gitelman, ed., *The Emergence of Modern Jewish Politics: Bundism and Zionism in Eastern Europe* (Pittsburgh, 2003). For the inter-war history of the Bund, see Gertrud Pickhan, *'Gegen den Strom': Der allgemeine jüdische Arbeiterbund 'Bund' in Polen, 1918–1939* (Stuttgart, 2001).

[4] Shaul Esh, 'Kurt Blumenfeld on the Modern Jew and Zionism', *Jewish Journal of Sociology* 4, no. 2 (1964): 236.

[5] No real Zionist movement was in evidence in Subcarpathian Ruthenia by the time of World War I. See Yeshayahu A. Jelinek, *The Carpathian Diaspora: The Jews of Subcarpathian Rus' and Mukachevo, 1848–1948* (New York, 2007), 202.

Many of those who declared their nationality Jewish were Orthodox Jews who vigorously rejected the secular programme of Jewish nationalism and the project of the Jewish State of Palestine. In the 1920 elections to the Czechoslovak National Assembly two parties were formed in Slovakia in opposition to the Zionist-run Jewish Party – namely, the Jewish Conservative Party (Židovská konzervativní strana) and the Jewish Party of Business (Židovská hospodárská strana).

For the leaders of Czechoslovak Zionism it was therefore difficult to harmonize the demands of the Jews from Subcarpathian Ruthenia and east Slovakia with those of the Zionists of the Bohemian Lands. Walter Kohner considers this in a 1929 article published in *Selbstwehr*: 'As things appear now, it is no longer possible to formulate a programme that would satisfy the cultural, economic and linguistic requirements of the Jews in both the east and the west.'[6]

An example of the different conditions is Jewish schools. In their endeavour to establish Jewish schools in the Bohemian Lands, in which instruction would be in both German and Czech, the Zionists ran up against the resistance of the Czech-Jews. The Czech-Jews reproached the Zionists for establishing special Jewish schools and thereby again separating Jews from the rest of society. Other arguments were heard in the east of the republic. In Subcarpathian Ruthenia the Zionists managed to establish a Hebrew grammar school (*gymnásium*) in Mukachevo (Munkács), with Hebrew as the language of instruction. The Rebbe, the leader of the Hasidic Jews of Mukachevo, Chaim Elazar Spira (1871–1937), however, called the school a hot-bed of evil. Together with other Orthodox Jews he criticized Zionists for their lukewarm attitude to religion and for using Hebrew, the sacred language, for everyday communication instead of Yiddish.[7]

The Beginning of Zionism in the Bohemian Lands

The most important leaders of the Zionist movement in interwar Czechoslovakia came, with few exceptions,[8] from Bohemia and Moravia, the provinces with the lowest number of Jews. Thanks to their secular education and special social standing, the leading Jewish figures from Bohemia and

---

[6] Walter Kohner, 'Zur Diskussion über Landespolitik', *Selbstwehr*, no. 7 (1929): 3.
[7] For the negative attitude of the Mukachevo Hasidim to the Hebrew grammar school, see, for example, Aryeh Sole, 'Modern Hebrew Education in Subcarpathian Ruthenia', in *The Jews of Czechoslovakia*, vol. II, 411.
[8] The main exceptions were Chaim Kugel and Julius Reisz, who became Jewish Party deputies to the Czechoslovak National Assembly and Gisi Fleischmann of Bratislava, the head of the Women's International Zionist Organisation in Slovakia. Two other important Zionists, Jakob Edelstein and Emil Margulies, came from Galicia and Polish Russia.

Moravia gained authority not only in part of the Jewish population, but also in relations with the leaders of the state. The position of the Zionists in Slovakia and Subcarpathian Ruthenia was made more complicated by the strong opposition of most of the Orthodox Jews.

A different argument is offered by Martin Wein. He explains that the Jews of Slovakia and Subcarpathian Ruthenia had only a limited influence on the Zionist movement in Czechoslovakia because the Zionists from the Bohemian Lands looked down on the Jews in the east of the state and prevented them from getting into leading positions.[9] Bohemian Zionists could speak truly disparagingly of their colleagues from Slovakia and Subcarpathian Ruthenia. Still, without being in touch with the Czechoslovak political leaders, and lacking a well-organised movement like the one in the Bohemian Lands, Zionism would never have achieved such a prominent position in Czechoslovak society.

The character of the Zionist movement in Bohemia was in many respects different also from that in Moravia. Owing to Moravian Jewish students' contacts with Vienna (a negligible number of Moravian Jews studied in Prague, as most preferred Vienna), the ideas of Theodor Herzl spread to Moravia within a few years of his proposing them, much more quickly and effectively than in Bohemia. The special character of the Zionist movement in Moravia consisted mainly in the fact that in some cases whole Jewish communities became involved in Jewish nationalist activities.[10] After the formation of the Jewish National Council in October 1918, it was the Moravian Association of Jewish Communities (Moravský zemský svaz židovských náboženských obcí), which recognized the council, right after it was established, as the representative of its interests.

The pioneers of the Zionist movement in Moravia were Otto Abeles (1879-1945), Robert Stricker (1879-1944) and Berthold Feiwel (1875-1937), who founded the Veritas society in Brno (Brünn) in 1897. While a student at Vienna, Feiwel became a close friend of Herzl, and helped him to organise the First Zionist Congress. He also became a member of the editorial board of *Die Welt*. Regardless of his friendship with Herzl, Feiwel co-founded a democratic faction at the Fifth Zionist Congress, in 1901. Critical of Herzl's conception of Political Zionism, the faction was led by Chaim Weizmann (1874-1952), later chairman of the Zionist Organisation and then the first president of the State of Israel. Feiwel also gained renown for establishing the Jüdischer Verlag in Berlin together with Buber.[11]

---

[9] Martin Wein, 'Czechoslovakia's First Republic, Zionism and the State of Israel', MA thesis, Emory University, 2001, 57, 61-64, 70.
[10] For example, Uherské Hradiště. See my interview with Fischl, 'Pak to ale dopadlo ještě jinak', 6.
[11] Gideon Shimoni, *The Zionist Ideology* (Hanover and London, 1995), 282.

The impulse to create the first student Zionist society in Bohemia originated with students from Russia, not Bohemia.[12] The Maccabäa society was established in 1893 in reaction to the anti-Jewish *Burschenschaften* at the German University of Prague. Students from Russia gave the Zionist society a character that corresponded to trends of the young generation of Jews in their Tsarist homeland more than in Bohemia. The Zionist society was against liberalism, against the religious identity of Jewry, and also strictly against integration, whether into the Czech nation or the German.[13]

In Prague, however, there were few Jewish students interested in this sort of society. After three years of dwindling activity the society transformed itself into the Verein der jüdischen Hochschüler in Prag (the Jewish University Students Union in Prague), which retreated from the original Jewish-nationalist programme. The original Maccabäa aimed 'to awaken and ennoble the national sense of belonging of all Jewish students and to care for national history and literature'.[14] The Verein outright excluded all political and nationalist tendencies within it, and set itself the aim of 'defending and supporting the ethical and material interests of Jewish students and care for Jewish history and literature'.[15]

Not till 1899 did the leadership decide to rename the society Bar Kochba with the bilingual additional name of Verein der jüdischen Hochschüler in Prag/Spolek židovských akademiků v Praze.[16] The new name was connected with a change in programme. Bar Kochba again openly came out in support of Jewish nationalism. In Article 28 of its statutes and by-laws it even says that if a plenary session of the society has to decide to change the aim of the society to anything other than nationally Jewish, it would then be dissolved.[17]

An interesting aspect of the history of Bohemian Zionism is that some former Czech-Jews strengthened the first Zionist society.[18] Important figures like Alfréd Löwy, Arthur Klein and Josef Kohn were originally mem-

---

[12] Hugo Bergmann, 'Zum dreissigsemestrigen Stiftungsfest des Vereines Bar Kochba', *Selbstwehr*, no. 2 (1908): 1.
[13] Kieval, *The Making of Czech Jewry*, 94.
[14] AUK, Statuten des Vereines 'Studentenverein Maccabäa', AS NU, U, Maccabäa.
[15] AUK, Statuten des Vereines 'Verein der jüdischen Hochschüler in Prag', AS NU, U, Maccabäa.
[16] AHMP, SK X/56. The change in the statutes was not confirmed by police headquarters until 1900.
[17] AUK, Statuten des Vereines 'Bar Kochba, Verein jüd. Hochschüler in Prag', AS NU, U, Bar Kochba, 8.
[18] This fact was first pointed out in Ruth Kestenberg-Gladstein, 'Atḥalot Bar Kochba', in *Prag vi-Yerushalayim*, ed. Felix Weltsch (Jerusalem, 1954), 89. See also Kieval, *The Making of Czech Jewry*, 94–95.

bers of the Czech-Jewish Students Society (Spolek českých akademiků židů). The wave of antisemitism in the 1890s was evidence for them that integration into the Czech nation was impossible. Löwy, who was from Domažlice, south Bohemia, was elected the first chairman of Bar Kochba. Among the 'defectors' from the Czech-Jews was Ludvík Singer, who holds an exceptional place in the history of Czech Zionism. In 1910 he became chairman of the Zionist Organisation in Bohemia, and after World War I was made chairman of the Jewish National Council as well. Together with Max Brod he became the principal mediator between the Zionist Organisation and the representatives of the Czechoslovak state. In 1929, two years before his death, Singer was one of two Jewish Party deputies elected to the Czechoslovak National Assembly. In his unpublished history of the Bar Kochba Society, Arthur Bergmann, the elder brother of Hugo Bergmann (1883-1975) and the chairman of the Czechoslovak Keren Hayesod (the Foundation Fund), recalls that it was the former members of the Czech-Jewish Students Society who, after joining the Verein der jüdischen Hochschüler in Prag, led the change into the 'utraquist' (that is, bilingual) Bar Kochba Society with a clearly Zionist programme.[19]

Two other important figures of Czech Zionism entered the ranks of the Zionists from Czech-Jewish organisations, but only shortly before World War I or just after it. Emil Waldstein (1889-1942), the founder and long-serving editor of *Židovské zprávy* (Jewish News), and František Friedmann (1897-1945), an official of the Jewish Party and an important promoter of Zionist ideas in Czech areas.

Even without the former Czech-Jews, Jews from linguistically Czech areas, mostly students of Czech universities and polytechnics in Prague, constituted a large part of the Bar Kochba membership. They predominated in the leadership till 1903, when a distinctive generation of mostly German-speaking students, led by Hugo Bergmann, began to get involved in the society.

Czech-speaking Zionists endeavoured to promote Zionism among Czechs of the Christian, as well as the Jewish faith. In 1901, for example, Löwy organised an evening of discussion on Zionism at the Slavia Society, Prague, which at that time was regarded by Czech students as the central Czech student society.[20] Czech Zionists from Bar Kochba initiated the translation into Czech of works by Max Nordau (born Simon Maximilian Südfeld, 1849-1923), and also acquainted German-Jewish families

---

[19] CZA, Bar Kochba / Barissia Collection, A 317/c 8, Arthur Bergmann's history of Bar Kochba, manuscript, 2.
[20] CZA, Bar Kochba / Barissia Collection, Hugo Bergmann to Viktor Freud, A 317/10, letter of 4 January 1934. See also Kieval, *The Making of Czech Jewry*, 109.

with Czech political events. At the recommendation of the young Czech-speaking Jewish student Emil Oplatka of Praskolesy, southwest of Prague, German-speaking Zionists, including Hugo Bergmann and Julian Herrnheiser, attended Masaryk's series of talks for workers, which shows that Bergmann and others who published in German only were able to understand Czech without difficulty.[21] Many of the otherwise German-speaking members of Bar Kochba had at least a passive mastery of Czech usually because their parents came from Czech-speaking villages.[22]

The number of Czech-speaking Zionists in Bar Kochba kept growing, and after World War I became the majority. All the Czech-speaking students were also fluent in German, but not all German-speaking members had an active knowledge of Czech. Consequently, a Czech section of Bar Kochba was formed, which was oriented to Zionist publications in Czech and to campaigning among Czech-speaking Jews. In 1909, the independent Theodor Herzl Society of Jewish Students (Spolek židovských akademiků Theodor Herzl) was established.[23] At the constituent meeting, on 9 December, Angelo Goldstein, the first chairman of the society, stated that Bar Kochba would at first be predominantly in the hands of Czech-speaking Zionists and only later would German-speaking students or 'Utraquists' make their way into the leadership. Among the Utraquists who helped to surmount the language barrier were the brothers Arthur and Hugo Bergmann. After reaching agreement with the German-speaking leadership of Bar Kochba, the Czech-speaking Zionists decided to establish their own society.[24]

The Theodor Herzl Society was, in the early years, financially dependent on Bar Kochba.[25] The two societies worked closely together, both in the period before World War I and in the interwar period. Only the bal-

---

[21] 'Zur Geschichte des Bar-Kochba. 3. Fortsetzung', *Bar Kochba Zirkular* (April 1967), 9. See also Kieval, *The Making of Czech Jewry*, 108-09.

[22] See especially Dimitry Shumsky, 'Czechs, Germans, Arabs, Jews: Franz Kafka's "Jackals and Arabs" between Bohemia and Palestine', *Association for Jewish Studies Review* 33, no. 1 (2009): 83. Shumsky vehemently objects to what by far most historians have so far written about the leading members of Bar Kochba - namely that they were people who had merged with the Prague German élite. From his analysis of their social relations, education and family origin, Shumsky demonstrates that most of them did not at all see their identity as being strictly German. See 78-90. See Shumsky, *Beyn prag li-yerushalayim: tsiyonut prag ve-ra'yon ha-medinah ha-du-le'umit be-erets-yisrael* (Jerusalem, 2010); Shumsky, 'On Ethno-Centrism and Its Limits: Czecho-German Jewry in Fin-de-Siècle Prague and the Origins of Zionist Bi-Nationalism', *Jahrbuch des Simon-Dubnow-Instituts* 5 (2006): 173-88.

[23] AHMP, SK X/173.

[24] According to the report of the police commissioner Bohdan Škvora, 24 December 1909. AHMP, SK X/173.

[25] Hugo Herrmann, Bericht über die Tätigkeit des Vereins der jüd. Hochschüler Bar Kochba in Prag während des 34. Vereinssemesters (Winter 1909-1910) (Prague, 1910), 20.

ance of forces changed. Whereas before Czechoslovak independence Bar Kochba had dominated the student Zionist movement, after the war and with the establishment of the Czechoslovak Republic the Theodor Herzl Society took the lead.

Although other Zionist societies existed before the war, it was Bar Kochba that set the tone for the whole Zionist movement in Bohemia. That was owing to the generation of Zionists who gained renown for Bar Kochba not only in the Bohemian Lands, but also far beyond its frontiers. The ranks of Bar Kochba were strengthened by many outstanding people: Hugo Bergmann and his brother Arthur, Felix Weltsch and his cousin Robert Weltsch, Hugo Herrmann and his cousin Leo Herrmann, Siegmund Kaznelson, Oskar Epstein, Hans Kohn, Viktor Freud and Victor Kellner. In 1903 Hugo Bergmann was elected chairman of the society, thus opening a new chapter in the history of Zionism in Bohemia.

The fundamental problem of the Prague Zionists was that they were not sure what their Jewish national identity consisted of.[26] Only some individuals could boast that their parents sympathized with Jewish nationalism. Most Bar Kochba members had grown up in families where only a shadow of Jewish religion and traditions remained, and their education had been no different from that of the rest of the people in their social class. Depending on the milieu they had come out of, they were brought up on the works of the German classics, Schiller and Goethe, or, if Czech-speaking, the nationalist historical novelist Alois Jirásek (1851-1930) or the poet, short-story writer, and virulent antisemitic journalist Jan Neruda (1834-1891). They were no different from their non-Jewish milieu either in language or way of life.

A foundation stone of the Jewish revival of the Bar Kochba members was therefore supposed to be, according to Bergmann, knowledge of Hebrew. Even before that, Israel Aronowitsch (Aharoni, 1882-1946), a student from Russia, established a group within the Bar Kochba Society, called Hebräische Propaganda, where only Hebrew was spoken. Few people were interested in the society, however. Just after having been elected chairman, Bergmann in his inaugural address mentioned that every Zionist should of course consider learning Hebrew. 'A Zionist student who doesn't know Hebrew,' he said, 'is a contradiction in terms.'[27] In 1910

---

[26] For an analysis of the problems the Prague Zionists faced in defining their Jewish nationality, using the example of the periodical *Selbstwehr*, see Scott Spector, 'Die Konstruktion einer jüdischen Nationalität - die Prager Wochenschrift Selbstwehr', *brücken. Neue Folge* (1991-1992), 37-44.

[27] 'Zur Geschichte des Bar-Kochba', *Bar Kochba Zirkular* (April 1967): 3. See also Kieval, *The Making of Czech Jewry*, 94, 101. Concerning the importance of Hebrew for Hugo Bergmann, see Spector, *Prague Territories*, 82-83.

Hugo Herrmann, the then Bar Kochba chairman, stated with satisfaction that wherever Hebrew was spoken in Prague at the time, Bar Kochba members helped out as interpreters for Czechs and Germans.[28] Apart from courses in Hebrew, Bar Kochba also began organising courses in Jewish literature and history.

Prague Zionists considered 'eastern Jews' (in German, 'Ostjuden')[29] a great inspiration. Before World War I Prague had not been a destination for eastern European refugees. Zionists in Prague, unlike those in Berlin or Vienna, thus learnt about Hasidim, *shtetlekh*, and Yiddish literature only indirectly. Bergmann, longing to see 'real' Jews, set out for Galicia in 1903.[30] Upon his return he organised courses in Yiddish. For Prague Zionists, *Ostjuden* became a model of 'authenticity'. Bergmann and the other Prague Zionists were fascinated by how directly and naturally the Jews in eastern Europe were conscious of their religion and identity.

Before World War I this interest tended to be in the form of intellectual enthusiasm for Yiddish literature and folklore. That is evident in the meeting of Bar Kochba members and actors of the Yiddish theatre company in Prague in 1910-1911. The members of Bar Kochba tended to be contemptuous of the poor itinerant actors and lacked sympathy for their poverty. Kafka, whom Brod had invited to a performance, befriended the actors and was willing to help them on their difficult tour of Bohemia, during which they met with the indifference of the locals.[31] On the other hand, it was Bar Kochba members who led the way in assisting Galician refugees during World War I.

Bar Kochba and Barissia: A Clash of Ideologies

The spiritual and to a large degree intellectual character of the Bar Kochba Society did not, however, suit all its members. Some students advocated customs that were usual among the Burschenschaften and other *Verbin-*

---

[28] Bericht über die Tätigkeit des Vereins der jüd. Hochschüler Bar Kochba in Prag während des 34. Vereinssemesters, 11.
[29] For the limits of this term, which was first used by Nathan Birnbaum in 1902 and mirrored positive and negative stereotypes that German Jews had about Eastern European Jewish refugees, see Anne-Christin Saß, 'Berlin - Ir VaEm BeIsrael: Osteuropäisch-jüdische Migranten in der Hauptstadt der Weimarer Republik', PhD thesis, Freie Universität Berlin, 2011, 34-35.
[30] Bericht über die Tätigkeit des Vereins der jüd. Hochschüler Bar Kochba in Prag während des 34. Vereinssemesters, 4. Later, other Bohemian intellectuals sought inspiration among the Hasidim. The most famous was Jiří Langer, who became a Belzer Hasid; two others were Egon Hostovský and Ivan Olbracht.
[31] Bruce, *Kafka and Cultural Zionism*, 34-56; Spector, *Prague Territories*, 86-92; Čapková, 'Kafka un der yidisher teater', 362-71.

dungen (student societies) – wearing badges and society colours, creating couples of one 'Bursche' (full member) and one 'Fuchs' (would-be member) or singing student songs. In Bar Kochba these customs did not catch on, and many members also feared that the Czech public might perceive the wearing of colours and national badges to be a provocation.[32] The group around Robert Neubauer, Jakob Fraenkl, Julius Löwy and Ernst Gütig therefore decided, in 1904, to found their own society, which they called Barissia.[33] Its leaders believed that placing emphasis on symbols of Jewish nationalism, organising duels with German nationalists, and consciously cultivating friendly relations amongst its members would be more convincing to Czech-speaking and German-speaking 'assimilationists' than the academic theorizing of Bar Kochba.[34]

The different conception of Jewish nationalism in Bar Kochba and Barissia led to great disputes, and, as mentioned in post-war memoirs, an ideological barrier existed among former members of each of these societies throughout the interwar years.[35] The differences between the two societies also had relatively deep roots. To a certain extent the dispute between Barissia and Bar Kochba ran parallel to the dispute between the Political Zionism of Herzl and the Cultural Zionism of Aḥad Ha'Am and Buber.[36] Political Zionism differed from Cultural Zionism both in the principal questions it raised and in its views on how to make Zionist ideas a reality. The Zionist movement was of course far more complicated than merely consisting of these two conceptions. The tension between Political Zionism and Cultural Zionism became, however, a kind framework for the debates within Zionism in central Europe.

---

[32] CZA, Bar Kochba / Barissia Collection, A 317/c 8, Arthur Bergmann's history of Bar Kochba, manuscript, 15. For the dichotomy of Bar Kochba and Barissia, see also Kieval, *The Making of Czech Jewry*, 115-23; Spector, *Prague Territories*, 139-40.
[33] AHMP, SK X/116.
[34] Walter Kohner, 'Barissia. Portrait einer Studentenverbindung', *Zeitschrift für die Geschichte der Juden in der Tschechoslowakei*, nos. 2-3 (1966): 125-32. A detailed history of Barissia is given in the twenty-fifth anniversary publication *Fünfzig Semester 'Barissia': Festschrift* (Prague, 1928).
[35] In Israel after World War II, however, former members of both societies reconciled. See CZA, Bar Kochba / Barissia Collection, A 317/c 8, Arthur Bergmann's history of Bar Kochba, manuscript, 15-16.
[36] 'Zur Geschichte des Bar Kochba, 3. Fortsetzung', *Bar Kochba Zirkular* (April 1967), 5, 11; Kohner, 'Barissia. Portrait einer Studentenverbindung', 131-32. Kohner writes: 'Their [Barissia's] Zionism was the Zionism of Herzl's and Nordau's, clear and thoroughly pragmatic. Its aim was not so much the intensification of Zionist thinking as it was its dissemination and activation, the struggle against assimilation, the winning over of the youth and Jewish society.' For the Cultural Zionism of Bar Kochba, see also Kieval, *The Making of Czech Jewry*, 93-153, and Spector, *Prague Territories*, 135-59.

In general, Political Zionism and Cultural Zionism were considered equal alternatives. In Bohemia the Bar Kochba Society emerged victorious from the competition, though not in terms of membership: both Barissia and Bar Kochba had only a few dozen active members before World War I.[37] It was, however, mainly Bar Kochba members who contributed to the revival of Jewish national identity in Bohemia and to informing the Czech public about Zionism. The Bar Kochba programme, orientated particularly to the cultural regeneration of the Jewish nation, was greatly respected by non-Jewish Czechs, foremost among them being Masaryk.

From 1910 onwards Bar Kochba members set the tenor of the first official Zionist periodical in Bohemia. It was founded by Barissia members in 1907,[38] and they also chose its name, *Selbstwehr* (Self-defence), which reflected their ideology based both on a sense of being threatened by antisemitism and on the need to defend Jews against it. In 1910 Leo Herrmann of Bar Kochba took over the editing of *Selbstwehr*, and until the end of the First Republic *Selbstwehr* remained under the ideological influence of past and present Bar Kochba members. In the early years of editing the journal, Herrmann found great support in Hugo Bergmann, Hans Kohn, Robert Weltsch and Siegmund Kaznelson.[39] Throughout the First Republic Felix Weltsch was editor-in-chief.

The importance of Bar Kochba, however, was also due to the fact that its members initiated Zionist events and organisations and supported many others. They offered great support to two societies of the older generation of Zionists – the Jüdischer Volksverein Zion (Jewish People's Society)[40] and the Jüdischer Frauenverein (Jewish Women's Society).[41] Among the members of these two societies there were mothers and fathers of Bar Kochba members – for example, Siegmund and Johanna Bergmann (the parents of Arthur and Hugo) and Karl Resek (the wine merchant father of Felix Resek). Another founding member of the Volksverein was Philipp Lebenhart, who in 1900 founded *Jung Juda*, a magazine for young people, which continued to publish in the First Republic. In the mid-1920s it had about 1,500 subscribers.[42] The magazine offered, among other things, a

---

[37] In 1910 the Bar Kochba Society had, for example, 52 active members and 41 members of the Alte Herren club for older members who had already graduated. See *Bericht über die Tätigkeit des Vereins der jüd. Hochschüler Bar Kochba in Prag während des 34. Vereinssemesters*, 4.
[38] Kieval, *The Making of Czech Jewry*, 117.
[39] 'Zur Geschichte des Bar-Kochba. 6. Fortsetzung', *Bar Kochba Zirkular* (March 1968), 4. For *Selbstwehr*, see also Kieval, *The Making of Czech Jewry*, 119–23; Spector, *Prague Territories*, 161–65.
[40] AHMP, SK XXII/119.
[41] AHMP, SK XXII/216.
[42] *Židovské zprávy*, no. 1 (1924): 4.

basic course in Hebrew, which was prepared by Aronowitsch and then Hugo Bergmann and Viktor Kellner, both of Bar Kochba.

Arthur Bergmann writes in his memoirs that all founders and members of the Zion Society and of the Women's Society came from 'good' Jewish families, that is to say, from the middle or upper-middle classes. The activities of women Zionists in the society consisted essentially only of organising celebrations for children at Purim and Hanukkah. The Zion men's society held evenings of debates, which were dominated by Bar Kochba members.[43]

Things were different with the first Zionist Women's and Girls' Club (Sionistický klub paní a dívek/Klub jüdischer Frauen und Mädchen), which was called the Mädchenklub for short. This society was established on the initiative of Bar Kochba in 1912. Among the founding women, the sisters or young wives of the Bar Kochba members predominated, including the wives of Hugo Bergmann and Max Brod, the sister of Robert Weltsch, and also Marta Schick, Růža Löwy, Grete Obernik and the sisters Mirjam and Fritzi Scheuer. (Fritzi later became the wife of Emil Margulies.) Members of Bar Kochba helped also with the cultural and education programme of the society, with the lecture series on Jewish history and on Zionist ideology and with the Hebrew courses run by Hugo Bergmann.[44]

The fact that the members of the individual Zionist societies before World War I were for the most part close relations points clearly to the family nature of the Zionist movement in Bohemia in this period. One sees this, for example, in the obituary of Frieda Weltsch (née Böhm). She was the mother of Robert Weltsch, the aunt of Felix, the cousin of Adolf Böhm, and the mother-in-law of Siegmund Kaznelson. The obituary, from October 1938, calls her '[a] respectable and modest lady, in whose hospitable home a considerable part of Prague Zionist life took place in the years of Bar Kochba', and continues: 'She was greatly respected in Prague Zionist circles.'[45]

The first known Bohemian Jew to settle in Palestine was Marta Schick of the Mädchenklub. This revolutionary act, dating from 1913, outraged not only her family but also many others in the Prague Jewish commu-

---

[43] CZA, Bar Kochba / Barissia Collection, A 317/c 8, Arthur Bergmann's history of Bar Kochba, manuscript, 8.
[44] CZA, Irma Pollak Collection, A 459/3, 'Geschichte der zionistischen Frauenbewegung in der CSR', manuscript, 2.
[45] 'Paní Frída Weltschová mrtva', *Židovské zprávy*, no. 41 (1938): 9. In the late 1920s and early 1930s Frieda Weltsch moved to Berlin, where her son-in-law, Kaznelson, the owner of the Jüdischer Verlag, lived, and in 1935 moved to Palestine, where she stayed till the end of her life.

nity.⁴⁶ Her story provides evidence that the Zionists in Bohemia before World War I tended only to theorize about settlement in Palestine.

The Bar Kochba Society also tried to attract the young generation. For that reason Hashachar (Hebrew for 'the dawn'), a society for secondary school students, was founded.⁴⁷ Members of Bar Kochba also founded the Jewish Society for Song and Music in Prague (Židovský spolek pro zpěv a hudbu v Praze/Jüdischer Gesangs- und Musikverein in Prag).⁴⁸ Under the leadership of Richard Taussig of the German Theatre in Prague, the society focused on Jewish choral music.⁴⁹ And, as we have seen, Bar Kochba also founded the Toynbee Hall.

Buber and Bar Kochba: Mutual Sympathy

Under the leadership first of Hugo Bergmann, then of Viktor Freud and Leo Herrmann, the members of Bar Kochba tried to discover the roots of Jewishness according to Cultural Zionism.⁵⁰ They carefully read the works of Aḥad Ha'Am, and Viktor Kellner translated some of his articles from Hebrew into German.⁵¹ It should come as no surprise therefore that Martin Buber became popular among the Prague Zionists of Bar Kochba. The sympathy was mutual.

1909 is generally considered the year that Buber and members of Bar Kochba first met. That year Buber came from Berlin at the invitation of Leo Herrmann to give the first of his renowned *Drei Reden über das Judentum* (Three Addresses on Judaism⁵²). The collaboration between Buber and the Prague Bar Kochba had, however, begun earlier. Back in 1899, when Buber began to publish in Herzl's *Die Welt*, the Prague Zionists were reading his articles with great sympathy. In 1903 Bar Kochba, together with the 'democratic faction' of the Zionists (Buber, Feiwel and Weizmann), came out firmly against the project to settle Jews in Uganda.⁵³ The British had offered the Zionists Uganda for the establishment of a Jewish colony,

---

⁴⁶ Irma Polak, 'The Zionist Women's Movement', in *The Jews of Czechoslovakia*, vol. II, 140-41.
⁴⁷ Hugo Bergmann, 'Pacovsky - 70 Jahre', *Bar Kochba Zirkular* (February 1958), 2.
⁴⁸ AHMP, SK XII/78.
⁴⁹ CZA, Bar Kochba / Barissia Collection, A 317/c 8, Arthur Bergmann's history of Bar Kochba, manuscript, 13.
⁵⁰ See also Scott Spector, 'Another Zionism: Hugo Bergmann's Circumscription of Spiritual Territory', *Journal of Contemporary History*, 34, no. 1 (January 1999): 85-106.
⁵¹ Hans Kohn, *Martin Buber: Sein Werk und seine Zeit: Ein Beitrag zur Geistesgeschichte Mitteleuropas 1880-1930*, 3rd ed. (Cologne, [1930] 1961), 315.
⁵² For an English version, see Martin Buber, *At the Turning: Three Addresses on Judaism* (New York, 1952).
⁵³ Kieval, *The Making of Czech Jewry*, 102.

and Herzl eagerly accepted the offer. He felt responsible for the Russian Jews, who at that time faced a new wave of pogroms. Ernst Gütig and Hugo Bergmann at the time published the society's negative statement on the Uganda project in the *Jüdische Volksstimme*. Also in 1903, the Bar Kochba leadership invited Buber and Feiwel to a celebration marking the tenth anniversary of the society. Buber gave a talk, typically called 'Die Jüdische Renaissance'.[54] Buber would later visit Prague frequently. His relations with the Prague Zionists remained strong throughout the interwar period.

Though collaboration between Buber and the Prague Zionists was of an earlier date, that changes nothing about the fact that the *Three Addresses on Judaism* had a far-reaching influence on the future of Zionism in Bohemia. Buber's first talk also initiated a new tradition in the activities of Bar Kochba. Until 1909, when Leo Herrmann became chairman, the society organised, on the model of Czech and German student societies, the Bar Kochba-Kränzchen. Dances or balls were an important source of income for the student societies. Unlike German-speaking Jews, but like Czech-speaking Jews, the Zionists could not count on financial support from rich German student organisations for people of the Jewish faith. The Verein Israelitischer Techniker and the Verein Israelitischer Universitätshörer provided financial support only to Jewish students who were considered 'faithful in spirit to the German nation' (*treudeutscher Gesinnung*).[55] Herrmann decided not to organise dances and balls anymore, and chose instead to obtain funding by organising lectures.

At the first gala evening, in January 1909, Herrmann invited Felix Salten and Martin Buber to give talks. The music programme was in the hands of two artists from the German Theatre (today the Theatre of the Estates) – Philipp Manning and Lia Rosen. Salten, a writer popular in Prague German high society, was supposed to draw an audience, whereas Buber was meant to teach them about Judaism and Zionism. The plan succeeded superbly. The hall in the Hotel Central, one of the grandest lecture halls in Prague at the time, was full to capacity.[56] The Prague Jews, mostly middle class, listened intently to how every Jew was supposed to develop his or her ties to Jewish culture and the community and not to be

---

[54] 'Zur Geschichte des Bar Kochba. 5. Fortsetzung', *Bar Kochba Zirkular* (December 1967), 5. To mark its anniversary, the Bar Kochba Society published *Neue Wege: Festschrift* (Prague, 1903); see also Kieval, *The Making of Czech Jewry*, 103–05; Spector, *Prague Territories*, 147.
[55] CZA, Bar Kochba / Barissia Collection, A 317/c 8, Arthur Bergmann's history of Bar Kochba, manuscript, 4–6; 'Zur Geschichte des Bar-Kochba, 3. Fortsetzung', *Bar Kochba Zirkular* (April 1967), 8.
[56] Viktor Freud, manuscript of a history of Bar Kochba, untitled, *Bar Kochba Zirkular*, Hanukkah 1954, 11–12.

ashamed of his or her Jewish roots. The ideas of Political Zionism would probably have aroused the indignation of this audience. Buber's teaching about Zionism as a spiritual process of revival, however, fascinated many. The essence of Zionism was, for Buber, the return to Jewish traditions and a consciousness of belonging to the Jewish community.

For the next two special addresses by Buber, held at the town hall of the Prague Jewish community in Maiselova ulice, the organisers no longer required any popular advance speaker. Buber's name was by then guarantee enough that there would be no shortage of listeners. The three Buber talks from 1909-1910, titled 'Judaism and the Jews', 'Judaism and Humanity' and 'The Renaissance of Judaism', were first published in periodicals in Germany.[57] In 1912, they were published in Czech,[58] translated by Arnošt Kolman (1892-1979), at the time a member of the Theodor Herzl Society and later an extremely *engagé* Communist.[59] The cultural orientation of the Bar Kochba Society is clear also in *Vom Judentum* (1913),[60] a collection of essays by leading Bohemian Zionists. In Europe generally it is considered a gem of intellectual Zionism aimed at the revival of Jewish culture.[61]

To other, practically oriented Zionists in other countries, Bar Kochba seemed to be a society of dreamers. During his Prague sojourn in January 1913, Kurt Blumenfeld, the leader of the Zionist movement in Germany, wrote in a letter to his friend Martin Rosenblüth: 'The Prague Bar Kochba is less and less usable. Buber, who educates theosophically, is their rebbe and leads people away from ... Zionism proper.'[62]

The truth remains, however, that because of the meeting of Bar Kochba and Buber both sides increased their influence in the Zionist organisation. Thanks to his public speaking in Prague Buber gained not only supporters among Bar Kochba members, but also a wider audience receptive to his spiritual conception of Zionism.[63] A peak in this collaboration was Buber's talk at a Prague gathering of Jewish youth (*Jugendmeeting*) in

---

[57] For an analysis of Buber's talks, see Kieval, *The Making of Czech Jewry*, 127-36.
[58] Martin Buber, *Drei Reden über das Judentum* (Frankfurt am Main, 1911), translated by Arnošt Kolman into Czech as *Tři řeči o židovství* (Prague, 1912).
[59] 'Zur Geschichte des Bar Kochba. 5. Fortsetzung', *Bar Kochba Zirkular* (December 1967), 4.
[60] *Vom Judentum: Ein Sammelbuch* (Leipzig, 1913).
[61] For more on this collection, see Kieval, *The Making of Czech Jewry*, 148-53, and Andreas Herzog, 'Vom Judentum: Anmerkungen zum Sammelband des Vereins Bar Kochba', in *Kafka und Prag*, ed. Kurt Krolop and Hans Dieter Zimmermann (Berlin and New York, 1994), 45-58.
[62] Kurt Blumenfeld, *Im Kampf um den Zionismus: Briefe aus fünf Jahrzehnten*, ed. Miriam Sambursky and Jochanan Ginat (Stuttgart, 1976), 42-43.
[63] Kohn, *Martin Buber: Sein Werk und seine Zeit*, 91.

March 1920.⁶⁴ Bar Kochba members were indebted to Buber to a certain extent for establishing closer ties with the leadership of the world Zionist Organisation, which, until the end of World War I, had its head office in Berlin.

After 1921 Buber did not get involved in organizing the Zionist movement. His personal friendship and work with former members of Bar Kochba, however, did not suffer from that. He continued to be invited to Prague from time to time to give public lectures, and people who had settled abroad in the interwar years kept in touch with him. It is to Hugo Bergmann's great credit that, as a professor of philosophy at the Hebrew University of Jerusalem, he arranged a professorship for Buber in 1938. Buber worked at the Hebrew University throughout World War II and afterwards, and his philosophy influenced several generations of intellectuals in Israel.⁶⁵

Buber also joined Bergmann and other former members of Bar Kochba in Prague in their efforts to achieve a rapprochement between Jews and Arabs in Palestine. Together with Arthur Ruppin (1876-1943) and others, Hugo Bergmann, Hans Kohn and Robert Weltsch established the Brit Shalom (Covenant of Peace), an organisation that, in Jerusalem, in 1925, advocated a bi-national solution for the future state in Palestine.⁶⁶ Like Gershom Sholem, Buber joined Brit Shalom later on. Buber and Bergmann also became key ideologues of the subsequent organisation, Ikhud.⁶⁷

The Zionists and the Galician Refugees

Until World War I, Zionists from Bohemia considered their Jewish roots predominantly in theoretical terms. They endeavoured to learn Hebrew,

---

⁶⁴ For the beginnings of the Jewish youth movement during the war, see Rechter, *The Jews of Vienna and the First World War,* 101-28.
⁶⁵ Buber's importance in shaping Israeli public opinion has been stressed by the right-wing Israel historian Yoram Hazoni in his controversial *The Jewish State: The Struggle for Israel's Soul* (New York, 2000). Buber, who was always a proponent of Jewish-Arab dialogue, had, according to Hazoni, a negative influence on generations of Israeli intellectuals. Thanks to him, a willingness to negotiate with Arabs won out in Israeli politics and intellectual circles, even at the cost of Israeli territorial concessions. Though in his book Hazoni overestimates Buber's importance to the left-wing orientation of Israeli society, it is clear that Buber played a very important role in the movement for Jewish-Arab dialogue.
⁶⁶ Shumsky, *Beyn prag li-yerushalayim;* Yfaat Weiss, 'Central European Ethnonationalism and Zionist Binationalism', *Jewish Social Studies* 1 (2004): 93-117; Shalom Ratzabi, *Between Zionism and Judaism: The Radical Circle in Brith Shalom, 1925-1933* (Leiden, 2002); Dietmar Wiechmann, *Traum vom Frieden: Das bi-nationale Konzept des Brith-Schalom zur Lösung des jüdisch-arabischen Konfliktes in der Zeit von 1925-1933* (Schwalbach/Ts, 1998).
⁶⁷ Paul R. Mendes-Flohr, ed., *A Land of Two Peoples: Martin Buber on Jews and Arabs* (New York, 1983).

attended courses in Jewish history and debated about a possible homeland in Palestine. Aid for Jewish refugees from Galicia during World War I was for them a new dimension of Zionist work.

The first little groups of refugees from Galicia arrived in Bohemia in autumn 1914. The Zionists established a Hilfskomittee (Jewish Aid Committee), which raised funds and distributed them. Karl Schwager, a Bar Kochba member, later recalled how he used to walk through Prague streets with a wheelbarrow, collecting clothing for refugees. The secondary-school teacher Alfred Engel and some colleagues quickly set up make-shift classrooms for Galician children, in which about two thousand pupils were taught during the war. It was the first time a school of a strictly national Jewish character had been established in Prague.[68] Teachers were, however, in short supply, and so the work was taken on by Bar Kochba members who had not yet enlisted for military service. Among them was not only Schwager, but also, for example, Max Brod.[69] Work with the children of refugees would become for Brod the impulse to his greater interest in politics.[70] Brod's relations were also intensively involved in helping Galician refugees. His wife, Elsa, taught with him at the school, and it was thanks to his sister that a kindergarten for refugees was set up.[71]

Some Prague Zionists were also present at the creation of the Jüdischer Volksheim, Berlin in May 1916. In addition to the chief organiser, Siegfried Lehmann, other leading figures in the project were Martin Buber, Gustav Landauer, Chaim Arlosoroff and Max Brod. The Jüdischer Volksheim was meant to serve not only as a place for the care and education of refugees and their children, but also as a meeting place of 'eastern' and 'western' Jews, which would deepen the experiences of local Jews by putting them in touch with eastern European Jewish refugees. Franz Kafka was enthusiastic about the project and repeatedly urged Felice Bauer to take part in its work.[72]

The fate of the Galician Jews at the end of World War I and afterwards was also a matter of concern to the Jewish National Council. Its representatives repeatedly turned to the Czechoslovak government, requesting the postponement of the repatriation of these refugees, and also to make the criteria for the forced return less strict for those who found employment

---

[68] Tramer, 'Die Dreivölkerstadt Prag', 172-73.
[69] Karl Schwager, 'Ein kleines Kapitel zur Geschichte Bar Kochba's', *Bar Kochba Zirkular* (January 1966), 7.
[70] JNUL, Hugo Bergmann Archives, Arc. 4°1502/812, Hugo Bergmann, 'Max Brod. Zu seinem 80. Geburtstage', 27 May 1964.
[71] Tramer, 'Die Dreivölkerstadt Prag', 172.
[72] Mirjam Triendel-Zadoff, *Nächstes Jahr in Marienbad: Gegenwelten jüdischer Kulturen der Moderne* (Göttingen, 2007), 125-26; Bruce, *Kafka and Cultural Zionism*, 119-24.

Figure 5.1. Inscription of the Bar Kochba Society, commemorating members who died in World War I.

or an opportunity to study in Czechoslovakia. In Bohemia, according to *Židovské zprávy*, there remained about 7,000 Galician refugees in November 1918. With one of its first post-war decrees the Ministry of the Interior ended the advantages for refugees, which had included financial support provided to them by the Austrian government. The return of the Galician

Jews had been planned by the government for a time when 'rail transport and the situation in Galicia permits'.[73] Despite widely known information about extensive pogroms in Poland, the revolutionary National Committee decided to set the date for the transfer of the Galician Jews (about 15,000 people throughout Czechoslovakia) for the end of November. Thanks to its repeated interventions, the Jewish National Council managed to get the departure date postponed until 15 December. Support payments were also prolonged until that date.[74]

New Prospects in the New State

World War I was a watershed in the history of Zionism. Whereas before the war opponents of Zionism could consider the movement a utopian ideology, after the war even they had to admit that the Jewish national movement was gaining political influence and the settlement of Palestine was becoming a realistic political concept.

The Balfour Declaration of 1917, expressing British support for the Jews' right to establish a national homeland in Palestine, was a milestone in the history of Zionism. At the San Remo Conference in 1920 it was decided that Palestine would be placed under British mandate. The promise of the British Government shifted the plans for the creation of a Jewish state in the Near East from the realm of speculation to the agenda of international diplomacy.

Another important step, which facilitated the political talks with the Jewish nationalists, was United States President Woodrow Wilson's address of January 1918 with its Fourteen Points. Jewish nationalists, like Czechs and many other nationalities, henceforth referred to the tenth point, which concerned the right to national self-determination. As in other European countries, a Jewish National Council was established in Prague on 22 October 1918 (six days before Czechoslovak independence was declared),[75] which proclaimed itself the chief representative of nationally minded Jews in the Bohemian Lands and, later, Slovakia. This Jewish

---

[73] 'Intervence Národní Rady Židovské v záležitosti uprchlíků', *Židovské zprávy*, nos. 16–17 (1918): 9.

[74] 'Národní rada židovská', *Židovské zprávy*, no. 18 (1918): 11.

[75] The council was established as the National Jewish Council (Národní židovská rada). Since its abbreviation, NRŽ, and that of the National Czechoslovak Council (Národní rada československá), NRČ, are so similar, the one organisation's mail was sometimes sent to the other's address. In May 1919 therefore, the Jewish nationalists renamed the institution the Jewish National Council (Židovská národní rada). NA, NRČ, inv. no. 118, box 230, letter of 26 May 1919.

National Council statement naturally met with disagreement from Czech-Jews and some Jews of German nationality. The Zionists expected the disagreement of the political parties in which Czech-Jews were involved – the Czech Constitutional Democracy Party (Česká státoprávní demokracie), the Agrarian Party, the Social Democratic Party, the Czech Socialist Party, and, in particular, the Czech Liberal Party (Strana pokroková). None of the leaders of any party, however, came out against the setting up of the Jewish National Council.[76]

The representatives of the Jewish National Council then repeatedly stressed that they represented only people who considered themselves to be of Jewish nationality. In fact, however, the Jewish National Council became, for Czechoslovak politicians, the main partner in the search for solutions to problems related to the Jewish population in general. Particularly in the first months after the war, the Jewish National Council in Prague, like the Jewish National Council in Vienna, was basically the only Jewish organisation able to react to the changed political circumstances.[77] Only on questions exclusively concerning the Jewish Communities did state officials negotiate directly with representatives of the five Jewish associations in Czechoslovakia: the Silesian, the Moravian, the Greater Prague Associations (joined by Pilsen and Budweis), the Association of Czech Jewish Communities and the Association of German-speaking Jewish Communities in Bohemia.[78]

With the establishment of the Czechoslovak Republic, the Jewish national movement found itself in a completely new situation, because, among other things, the main actors in Zionist politics in Bohemia and Moravia assumed responsibility also for the nationally minded Jews of Slovakia and Subcarpathian Ruthenia. As we have seen, the needs of the Jews in the eastern parts of the republic were radically different from the needs of the Jews in the Bohemian Lands. One of the chief tasks of the Jewish National Council was first to convince the Slovak and Subcarpathian Ruthenian Jews to declare Jewish nationality in the census and to recognize

---

[76] 'Zbytečné protesty', Židovské zprávy, nos. 16–17 (1918): 12.
[77] Rechter, The Jews of Vienna and the First World War, 12.
[78] In the Bohemian Lands between the wars there were five associations of Jewish Communities (in chronological order): the Silesian Provincial Association (Slezský zemský svaz), the Moravian Provincial Association (Moravský zemský svaz), and the Association for the Jewish Communities of Greater Prague (Svaz pro náboženské obce Velké Prahy) which was joined by the Communities of Pilsen and Budweis, the Association of Czech Jewish Communities (Svaz českých náboženských obcí), and the Association of German-speaking Jewish Communities in Bohemia (Verband der Kultusgemeinden mit deutscher Umgangssprache in Böhmen). In 1927 the last two named bodies merged as the Supreme Council of Jewish Communities in Bohemia (Nejvyšší rada židovských náboženských obcí v Čechách).

the Jewish National Council as the representative of their interests. To that end, they obtained the support of President Masaryk. In September 1919 Max Brod was granted several months' leave from his position at the State Postal Service to campaign in Slovakia. In December of that year the Jewish National Council also sent Markus Ungar to Slovakia, to win supporters for Jewish nationalism.[79] His advantage was that he could speak to the Slovak Jews as an Orthodox Jew.

It is truly surprising how positively Zionism was accepted among the Czech intellectuals and also some leading politicians. A great role was of course played here by the authority of the president, though one should not overestimate Masaryk's influence. There were other leading figures who also observed the Jewish national movement with great sympathy, for example Rádl and Krejčí. As a deputy of the National Assembly, Krejčí also worked to achieve recognition of Jewish nationality among his fellow legislators. Another supporter was the literary historian and critic Professor Arne Novák. In a 1926 article titled 'Český národ a sionismus' (The Czech Nation and Zionism) he repeated the main idea of the Czech National Revival and quoted the verse of Jan Kollár (1793–1852) about the essence of nationality: 'but only ethics, language, and shared ideas are the inviolable boundaries of one's homeland'. 'None of the modern theorists of nationality,' he added, 'comported so much with our conception as the Zionist thinkers, who like us did not come out of Renaissance rationalism, but out of Romantic mysticism, and politically intensified Herzl's creative tendency; they too awakened and organised the nation, in order to prepare it for a nation-state.'[80]

Similarly, Přemysl Pitter, pastor, writer and pacifist, made no secret of his sympathy for Zionism. He too pointed out the similarities between the 'growing self-awareness of the Jews' and the early nineteenth-century 'awakening of the Czech nation'. He admired the efforts to establish a Jewish state in Palestine and also the Communist character of some *kibbutzim*. One sees, however, a certain naivety in the statement at the end of his 1930 talk to the League for Workers of Eretz Yisrael. A policeman who was present at the meeting summarized Pitter's view: 'The task of the Jews for the near future lies in revising their attitude to Jesus and thereby drawing considerably closer to Christians.'[81]

The broad-based Czech support for Jewish nationalists became clear at the first 'national Jewish congress in the state of Czechoslovakia', which

---

[79] Rozenblit, *Reconstructing a National Identity*, 145–46.
[80] Arne Novák, 'Český národ a sionismus', in *Sionismus: Idea a skutečnost* (Prague, 1926), 123.
[81] NA, policejní prezídium, 1921–1930, 28/4, k. 907, a lecture organised by the League for Workers of Erets Israel, 11 February 1930.

took place in early January 1919. The congress was attended, for example, by Jaroslav Kvapil, a representative of the Association of Czech Writers; František Sekanina, a writer; and František Kadeřávek, Professor of Descriptive Geometry at the Czech Polytechnic. Other supporters included representatives of political parties – Josef Kouša, a Social Democrat deputy; Josef Kopecký, a Socialist Party deputy; and Václav Němec, a deputy of the Czech Realist Party. The venerable Czech nationalist novelist, Alois Jirásek, full of respect for the efforts of the Jewish nationalists, sent his greetings to the delegates of the congress.[82]

This sort of appreciation for the efforts of the Jewish nationalists was extremely rare in Europe at that time. One reason was that in nation-states like France and Germany, Jews who favoured integration into the majority nation were in a strong position, not only in their Jewish communities but also in their relations with the politicians of those countries. The most important representative of the Jews there were the Centralverein deutscher Staatsbürger jüdischen Glaubens and the Alliance Israélite Universelle, which were against pushing for the recognition of Jewish nationality in those countries. In Poland and Romania, though most non-Jews did not deny that the Jews constituted a special nation, most of them linked negative prejudices with the claim. Nor was there in these two countries the unique cultural link between the Jewish nationalists and the artists and intellectuals of majority society which there was in the Bohemian Lands. In the Soviet Union any Zionist organisation was strongly suppressed. The only exception was the Marxist Po'ale Tsiyon and He-Ḥaluts, which organised *hakhsharah* courses (kibbutz training) in the Crimea. Both these organisations, however, were permitted to exist only until 1928.[83]

One important reason why the Zionists were favourably received in Bohemia was that the Zionists in the Bohemian Lands had a moderate national programme. That should come as no surprise, because they did not face any militant antisemitism, nor did they have to defend an Orthodox way of life (for example, observing the Sabbath), being for the most part secularized. They were concerned mainly to be able to declare their nationality as Jewish and to have, as a national minority, a right to state financial support for Jewish cultural and educational institutions.

Other factors in the overall positive acceptance of Jewish nationalist strivings in the Bohemian Lands was that in an environment of nationalist frictions between the Czechs and the Germans, the Czechs were sympathetic to the nationalist demands of the Jews, and the Jews in this

---

[82] 'První národní sjezd židovský ve státě československém', *Židovské zprávy*, nos. 22–23 (1919): 3.
[83] Peter Brod, *Die Antizionismus- und Israelpolitik der UdSSR: Voraussetzungen und Entwicklung bis 1956* (Baden-Baden, 1980), 38.

nationally tense atmosphere could more easily decide in favour of Jewish nationality. In his memoirs Kurt Blumenfeld, a leading German Zionist, admitted, for example: 'The political culture of Vienna and Prague was more instructive to me than anything I could ever have studied. In that tangle of nationalities Jews were forced to consider their position if they did not want to find themselves culturally and politically indistinct.'[84]

As early as 1897, during the stormy debates about the Badeni language ordinances, Herzl had stated that in the national conflict between the Czechs and the Germans, the Jewish national movement was the most acceptable solution for the Jews in the Bohemian Lands.[85] In the Czech milieu, moreover, Zionists could make use of the comparison between the Jewish national movement and the Czech National Revival. Similar comparisons were made by leading non-Jewish Czechs.[86] One ought to recall, however, that for Czech intellectuals, including Masaryk, the Zionist movement in Bohemia was acceptable owing to its specially cultural nature. The effort to revive Hebrew, as well as Jewish traditions and education, was dominant in the programme of the Zionists up to that point.

Among Czech intellectuals Jewish nationalism was largely accepted because a number of Zionists were in close touch with Czech and German writers and artists. Owing to the high degree of secularization and cultural integration the works of Jewish writers, including many Jewish nationalists, became an integral part of both Czech and German literature in the Bohemian Lands. In the renowned Prager Kreis, for example, all the leading figures, apart from Werfel and Kafka (who sympathized with Zionism), were active Zionists. After the war, Brod in particular, as a member of the Jewish National Council, could use to advantage his pre-war contacts with Czech writers and artists. That was also true of Emil Waldstein (1889–1942), the founder and long-serving editor-in-chief of *Židovské zprávy*. He too was well known among Czech writers and publishers. He was a frequent guest at meetings of writers at the home of Gabriela Preissová (1862–1946) and was a regular among the writers frequenting the Café

---

[84] Kurt Blumenfeld, *Erlebte Judenfrage: Ein Vierteljahrhundert deutscher Zionismus* (Stuttgart, 1962), 85–86.
[85] Benjamin Seff [Theodor Herzl], 'Die Jagd in Böhmen', *Die Welt* 1, no. 23 (1897): 1–2.
[86] For similarities between Czech and Jewish history, including a comparison of the Czechoslovak Republic and the State of Israel, see Martin J. Wein, 'Jüdisch-tschechischer Gedächtnistransfer im Schatten Deutschlands und Polens', in *Die Destruktion des Dialogs: Zur innenpolitischen Instrumentalisierung negativer Fremdbilder und Feindbilder: Polen, Tschechien, Deutschland und die Niederlande im Vergleich, 1900 bis heute*, ed. Dieter Bingen, Peter Oliver Loew and Kazimierz Wóycicki (Darmstadt and Wiesbaden, 2007), 103–13; cf. also the uncritical text of Livia Rothkirchen, 'Prologue: Prague and Jerusalem. Spiritual Ties between Czechs and Jews', in Rothkirchen, *The Jews of Bohemia and Moravia: Facing the Holocaust* (Lincoln, NE, 2005), 1–7.

Union (for instance, Milena Jesenská, Josef and Karel Čapek, Josef Lada, Jaroslav Hašek and František Langer). After he left *Židovské zprávy*, Waldstein began to work for *Lidové noviny*, the leading Czech liberal newspaper, in Užhorod.[87] Another example is Viktor Fischl,[88] an editor of *Židovské zprávy* in the late 1930s, and a poet whose first published verse before World War II was acclaimed by leading Czech critics. Karel Fleischmann (1897–1944) also worked closely with Czech artists, as is well described by his biographer, Hana Housková. She also mentions his being a member of the Makkabi, a Zionist sports organisation, and, at the same time, of Budivoj, 'a society of university students in south Bohemia (established in 1877), which was strongly Czech patriotic, and against the expansion of German culture'.[89] She does not mention, however, that Fleischmann was also a member of the Theodor Herzl Society.[90] In the Bohemian Lands, active participation in the Jewish national movement did not preclude close connections with Czech or German patriots.

The Jewish national movement here, however, also had a political, statewide dimension. Bohemian Zionists assumed responsibility also for Jews in Slovakia and Subcarpathian Ruthenia. For them the concept of Czech-Jewish integration or – as the Association of Czech-Jews often declared – 'assimilation' was unacceptable. For the Zionists in the leadership of the Jewish National Council or, later, the Jewish Party, the inclusion of Slovakia and Subcarpathian Ruthenia in a single Czechoslovak state was a great advantage. To be sure, the Orthodox Jews of Slovakia and Subcarpathian Ruthenia may have used every opportunity in the interwar years to thwart the activities of the Jewish Party, since they considered Zionism a secular movement that wrongfully interfered with the plans of God (not until the coming of the Messiah would Jews be called to the Promised Land). The resistance of the Orthodox Jews, however, did not change the fact that it was thanks particularly to Slovakia and Subcarpathian Ruthenia that representatives of the Jewish Party could claim to be representatives of most Jews in Czechoslovakia, who in the census declared Jewish as their nationality. Two other factors contributed importantly to the relative success of Zionism in the Bohemian Lands – the support of a large part of Moravian Jewry and the unusually positive attitude of the Orthodox Jews of the Bohemian Lands.[91]

---

[87] Otta Kraus, 'Emil Waldstein zum Gedenken', *Bar Kochba Zirkular* (January 1960), 3.
[88] Viktor Fischl took the name Avigdor Dagan after his emigration into Israel.
[89] Housková, *Česlicí času*, 31.
[90] CZA, Bar Kochba / Barissia Collection, A 137/5, 'Mein Lied wird gehört werden'.
[91] See also Hillel J. Kieval, 'Negotiating Czechoslovakia: The Challenges of Jewish Citizenship in a Multiethnic Nation-State', in *Insiders and Outsiders: Dilemmas of East European Jewry*, ed. Richard I. Cohen, Jonathan Frankel, and Stefani Hoffman (Oxford and Portland, Oregon, 2010), 103–19, esp. 116.

Moravia

The priority of the Jewish National Council was to get as much support as possible from the Jewish communities and various Jewish societies, in order to increase its own authority. In Moravia the council managed to do so surprisingly quickly, in no time establishing the Association of Jewish Communities in Moravia (Svaz židovských náboženských obcí na Moravě) and the Zionist District Association in Moravia (Sionistický svaz obvodový na Moravě).[92] In a letter from Moravia, printed in *Židovské zprávy*, it says that even synagogues 'in which hitherto only prayers were heard' were now opening up to Zionism. The writer then analyses in detail the situation favourable to Zionism in Kroměříž (Kremsier), Přerov (Prerau), Olomouc (Olmütz), Holešov (Holeschau) and Uherský Brod (Ungarisch Brod).[93]

What was decisive for organizing Zionism in Moravia after World War I was, however, the congress in Brno, on 22 and 23 March 1919. There, the Moravian National Jewish Council, which was completely subordinate to the Jewish National Council in Prague, was set up. Karl Sonnenfeld (1873–1942) became its chairman. One of the demands of the Moravian Zionists was the transformation of Jewish congregations into national communities. This demand then appeared in the programme of the Jewish National Council in Prague, but in Bohemia it did not stand a chance of success. In Moravia, by contrast, many Jewish Communities, even some of the larger ones like Prostějov and Uherské Hradiště, declared Jewish as their nationality.

The reports from the Moravian governor's office (*moravské místodržitelství*, several months later renamed the Moravian Political Administration in Brno) to the Ministry of the Interior in Prague about the Jewish national movement in Moravia note:

> The Jewish national movement in Moravia is rapidly spreading, because Jews, who before Czechoslovak independence, but for an inconspicuous fraction, all declared German as their nationality, see in it the surest path to improving their relationship with the Czechoslovak nation. The Jews of Prostějov are all coming out in support of the Jewish national movement and the same is true in Uherské Hradiště, and 80 per cent in Jihlava and Olomouc. In Brno, in the recent census, 5,470 of 8,400 Jews declared Jewish as their nationality; and 1,012 of 1,800 Jews in Olomouc declared Jewish as their nationality. The leaders of the Jewish national movement in Moravia are convinced that all the Jews are concentrated in their camp, with the exception of a small fraction, which is assimilating. Less favourable conditions for the Jewish national movement are in Bohemia, where

---

[92] 'Národní rada židovská', *Židovské zprávy*, no. 18 (1918): 11.
[93] 'Dopis z Moravy', *Židovské zprávy*, nos 16–17 (1918): 8–9.

the adherents of this movement hope to organise fifty per cent of the Jews. This is because the Czech-Jewish assimilationist movement has been promoted in Bohemia for a number of years.[94]

These estimates turned out to be considerably exaggerated. In the census in Moravia about half the people of Jewish faith declared their nationality as Jewish,[95] and in Bohemia 15 per cent did so in 1921 and 20 per cent in 1930.

The reasons Moravian Jews sympathized with Jewish nationalism more than the Jews of Bohemia did must be sought in the different demographic and also cultural and religious context of Moravia. Moravian Jews lived mostly in small towns and were united by a much stronger sense of belonging than the Jews of Bohemia, who lived either in the large towns, where they constituted a small proportion of the population, or in villages, where they were in close contact with the Christian population. The consciousness of Jewish national identity was strengthened also by the political status of a number of the Moravian Jewish communities. Last, but not least, a role was also played by the lower degree of secularization of the Jewish and Christian inhabitants of Moravia as opposed to Bohemia.

The Orthodox Are on Your Side!

A special feature of the Jewish community in Bohemia was the link between Orthodox Judaism and the Jewish national movement. Orthodox Judaism in Prague was bolstered after World War I by the arrival of the Jews from Subcarpathian Ruthenia. They did not, however, constitute an important part of the Prague Jewish population. Because of the high degree of secularization, religiously lukewarm Jews managed to get into the leadership of Jewish religious communities in Bohemia (unlike in Moravia). Most of them campaigned for integration into the Czech or German nation.

Not even in the Prague Jewish community, which was in charge of all the traditionally orthodox synagogues in the centre of town, were Orthodox Jews significantly represented. In the usually thirty-two-member board, between only two and four representatives were Orthodox in the interwar wars.[96] And they regularly had to listen to reproaches from the liberal Jews concerning expenses for kosher food and salaries for the *shokhtim*.

The main organisation, and apart from the charities the only one, in which Orthodox Jews in Bohemia gathered, was the Sinai Society for the

---

[94] NA, ministerstvo vnitra presidium, 225-164-18, IV/P/149.
[95] 48.74 per cent in 1921 and 51.67 per cent in 1930.
[96] Salomon Lieben and Berthold Jeiteles were the permanent representatives of the Orthodox Jews.

Support of Conservative Judaism in Prague (Sinai – Spolek k podpoře konservativního židovství v Praze). The word 'conservative' in the name of the society does not mean its members were proponents of Conservative Judaism in the sense of the teaching of Zacharias Frankel. Its board comprised Chief Rabbi Heinrich (Jindřich) Brody, Professor Eugen Lieben, Rudolf Stránský, Professor Salomon Ehrenfeld, Markus Ungar and, as its long-serving chairman, Isidor Jeiteles.[97]

What is striking is that the Sinai Society was one of the first to recognize the members of the Jewish National Council as the representatives of its interests.[98] This attitude of the Orthodox Jews towards Zionism in Bohemia (and also in Moravia, where, however, the whole religious community declared itself in support of Zionism) was unique compared to the situation in Slovakia and Subcarpathian Ruthenia, where the Orthodox Jews became the main opponents of Zionism. Also in Germany, the Orthodox were against Jewish nationalism. This special situation is also illustrated by the fact that in the Bohemian Lands, compared to the rest of Czechoslovakia and all the neighbouring states, no Agudat Yisra'el (Union of Israel) organisation of non-Zionist Orthodox Jews was established. In Poland this organisation was supported by a large part of the Jewish population and even held separate political talks with the Polish government.[99]

The situation in Bohemia was different mainly because the small number of Orthodox Jews here could not afford to develop an independent policy. When one compares the Czech-Jews' and Zionists' attitudes to religion, it becomes clear that the Zionists were a more acceptable option for the Orthodox Jews. Although most Zionists were not active members of a Jewish community, they did not renounce their Jewish faith, and they did seek to preserve Jewish traditions that could also be considered national. Many Czech-Jews, on the other hand, often called the Jewish religion, like religion in general, an anachronism, or they recognized it only as a source of ethics. Sympathy for the Zionist movement was, for example, expressed by Salomon Lieben, on behalf of the Orthodox Jews, at the national congress in Prague in early January 1919. He stressed, however, that joining the national Jews in political union did not mean that they had abandoned their view that 'only Orthodox Judaism embodies the true Jewish spirit'.[100]

The Orthodox Jews' positive attitude towards Zionism definitely also stemmed in part from the fact that the chief rabbi in the Bohemian Lands,

---

[97] AHMP, SK I/48.
[98] 'Národní rada židovská', *Židovské zprávy*, no. 18 (1918): 11.
[99] Mendelsohn, *The Jews of East Central Europe between the World Wars*, 55.
[100] 'První národní sjezd židovský ve státě československém', *Židovské zprávy*, nos. 22–23 (1919): 4.

Heinrich Brody (1868-1942), was an ardent Zionist. Brody was born in Užhorod and studied at yeshivot and universities in Pressburg (today's Bratislava), Berlin and Oxford. His scholarship was not, however, limited to religion. He also became a respected specialist on medieval Hebrew verse. After several years as a rabbi in Náchod, he accepted an offer to run the Talmud-Thora-Schule in Prague. There, he also married the daughter of the chief rabbi of Bohemia, Nathan Ehrenfeld (1843-1912), and took his place in 1912. Brody retired in 1930 and henceforth devoted himself to work in publishing at Schocken, Berlin, and, later, in Jerusalem.[101]

In 1899 and again in 1909 Brody published the pamphlet *Widerspricht der Zionismus unserer Religion?* (Does Zionism Contradict Our Religion?). In it he aims to convince Orthodox Jews that it is necessary to support the Zionist movement. Zionism, according to him, helps to revive Jewish traditions and seeks suitable, effective solutions for Jews in need all over the world. The impulse for a second edition was the conference of Orthodox Jews from Germany, held in Marburg. At the conference the delegates decided to condemn Zionism as a movement that contradicted the Jewish faith. Quoting abundantly from the Prophets and rabbinical literature, Brody seeks to convince the reader that Zionism definitely merits support from the Orthodox Jews.[102] Brody also became an important member of Mizraḥi, an organisation founded in Wilno (Vilnius) in 1902, which brought together Orthodox Zionists. In 1927 he was at the head of their ballot in the elections to the Fifteenth Zionist Congress.[103]

Another important rabbi who fought on all possible fronts for Zionism was Gustav Sicher (1880-1960). Like Brody, Sicher began his career as a rabbi of the important Jewish community in Náchod, before going to the Prague district of Královské Vinohrady in 1928. Sicher was not only a popular preacher; he also managed to establish close contacts with many important non-Jews. In Vinohrady, for example, he developed close ties also with the Archdeacon of St Ludmila's Church, Antonín Hoffmann.[104] Sicher was also invited to make radio broadcasts as a representative of the Jewish community in Bohemia, because the chief rabbi, Brody, had not mastered Czech. Like Brody, Sicher was also a member of Mizraḥi, and was also on the ballot of the Associated Jewish Parties (Sdružené strany židovské)[105] in the 1920 general elections. He was on the board of the

---

[101] Tobiáš Jakobovits, 'Vrchní rabín Dr. Jindřich Brody', *Věstník židovských náboženských obcí v českých zemích a na Slovensku*, no. 7 (1938): 72-74.
[102] Heinrich Brody, *Widerspricht der Zionismus unserer Religion?* (Leipzig, 1909).
[103] CZA, The Zionist Organisation – Central Office, London, Z4/3564, Hauptwahlkommission für den XV. Zionistenkongress.
[104] CAHJP, Papers of Gustav Sicher, P 209/5.
[105] That was the temporary name of the Jewish Party for these elections alone.

Association of Rabbis in Bohemia (Svaz rabínů v Čechách) and the Afike Jehuda society. In 1939 he managed to move to Palestine. After the war he was asked by the Jewish community in Prague to become Chief Rabbi. After much hesitation Sicher finally accepted the offer, and served in this office from 1947 till his death in 1960.

The Bohemian Orthodox Jews' sympathy for the Zionist movement, however, still did not mean that the representatives of the individual Jewish communities in Bohemia would stand behind the Zionists. At the beginning of the First Republic the Zionists, particularly in Moravia, repeatedly demanded that the Jewish communities be turned into institutions that were not only religious but also national and cultural. Another one of their demands was for the unification of the individual associations of Jewish religious communities under a single umbrella organisation. Throughout the interwar period, the Zionists endeavoured to win over as many adherents as possible in the individual boards. Unlike in Moravia, where the Jewish nationalists managed to win over the majority in several communities, in Bohemia German-speaking Jews or Czech-Jews dominated the representative bodies of the Jewish communities. That led the Zionists in Bohemia to change their tactics towards the Jewish communities.

This change was clarified by Emil Margulies at a meeting of the Zionist Central Committee in Moravská Ostrava in the 1920s. In talks that were described as 'strictly confidential', Margulies explained the situation. In Austria-Hungary, he said, the Austrian Zionists sought to create a unified association of Jewish communities. The Zionist movement was at the time still too weak to be able to represent all the Jews. An association of religious communities would, however, be able to make its authority felt. In the second step, the Zionists would be concerned to achieve the decisive influence in that body. The situation, however, radically changed after the declaration of Czechoslovak independence in 1918. With the successful rise of the Jewish National Council, which soon achieved general recognition despite the protests of the German and Czech 'assimilationists', the Zionists took the leading positions in talks with Czechoslovak political representatives. In Slovakia, too, Jewish nationalists went to the head of the Volksverband der Juden für die Slowakei which was established on 25 March 1919. It worked closely with the Jewish National Council in Prague,[106] which then often spoke on behalf of the Jewish nationalists in the east of the country. For that reason, the Zionists, from that time on, no longer sought to unify the religious communities, since they could undermine their leading position. The individual associations of Jewish

---

[106] Lipscher, 'Die soziale und politische Stellung der Juden in der Ersten Republik', 270.

communities each had different attitudes to Zionism. Since the Prague Community would have probably presided over an eventual Association of Czechoslovak Communities, the Zionists would then have hardly managed to play the leading role.[107] Officially, therefore, the Zionists were in favour of uniting the individual associations of religious communities. It was, however, supposed to be a merely formal unification, not limiting the autonomy of the Bohemian, Moravian-Silesian and other regional associations.[108]

The position of the Zionists in the Bohemian Lands thus radically improved after World War I. This success was not only in terms of their numerical dominance. Particularly in Bohemia, active Zionists constituted only a fraction of the total number of Jews. Nevertheless, the Zionist movement was positively received by a number of eminent Czechs, including politicians, and to a large extent pushed aside the Czech-Jewish movement. Members of the Jewish National Council and representatives of the Jewish Party, who from 1929 onwards had also won seats in the National Assembly, were often seen as representatives of the whole Jewish population or at the very least of those Jews to whom Jewish identity still mattered.

The Basic Currents of Zionism in Bohemia and Moravia

However, the growing number of Zionists and new political tasks after World War I also had a negative impact on the work of the Jewish nationalists. In considering the concrete aims of Zionist work, a gradual breaking up of the Zionist movement into factions took place. At first the situation was rather clear cut. The Jewish National Council, led by the Zionists, which was later reborn as the secretariat of the Jewish Party, represented all nationally minded Jews in the Bohemian Lands.

In addition, there was the independent structure of the Zionist Organisation itself. The Zionists in Czechoslovakia were to be represented in the world Zionist Organisation by the Zionist Territorial Federation, which was also meant to have the main say in the co-ordination of Zionist

---

[107] A clear example of the weak position of Zionists on the Council of the Prague Jewish community in the 1920s is the dispute about the stadium for the Hagibor sports organisation, which is described and analysed in Tatjana Lichtenstein, '"Heja, Heja Hagibor!" – Jewish Sports, Politics, and Nationalism in Czechoslovakia, 1923–1930', in *Leipziger Beiträge zur jüdischen Geschichte und Kultur*, vol. II, ed. Dan Diner (Munich, 2004), 191–208.
[108] CZA, The Zionist Organisation – Central Office, London, Z4/2338, Protokol der II. Plenarsitzung des Zionistischen Zentralkomitees für ČSR, 7 November 1926, 5.

activities in the Czechoslovak Republic. From the very beginning of the interwar period the Mizraḥi faction stood outside the federation. Other groups that wanted to organise their own programmes in their own way also gradually broke off from the Zionist Territorial Federation. As early as 1920, representatives of Po'ale Tsiyon left the board of the Jewish National Council as well as the Zionist Territorial Federation, followed by the Radical Zionists and Revisionist Zionists. Although the Federation formally existed throughout the interwar period, its influence on the activities of the individual factions was negligible. The most important body of the Zionist movement in Czechoslovakia was the Central Zionist Association of Czechoslovakia (Ústřední svaz sionistický pro ČSR). The officials of the Zionist Territorial Federation and the Central Association, however, to a large extent worked in both bodies. Both institutions were led by Josef Rufeisen (1887–1949) from 1921 to 1938. Both also had their headquarters in Moravská Ostrava (Mährisch Ostrau). The Central Zionist Association organised, among other things elections to the Zionist Congress, the supreme institution of the world Zionist Organisation.

Originally the centre of all Zionist activity in Czechoslovakia was Prague. The headquarters moved to Moravská Ostrava in 1921. It was argued that it had to be closer to the Jewish nationalists of Slovakia and Subcarpathian Ruthenia. Nevertheless, during the First Republic the view was heard several times, particularly from the headquarters of the world Zionist Organisation, that Prague was the natural centre of Czechoslovakia and that was where the headquarters of Zionists in Czechoslovakia should be.[109] The reasons given to justify why the headquarters would not be in Prague were relatively prosaic. In Prague there loomed a clash of jurisdictions with the representatives of the Jewish National Council, later with representatives of the Jewish Party and the board of the Jewish National Fund (in Hebrew, Keren Kayemet LeYisra'el). In Moravská Ostrava members of the Zionist leadership felt largely independent and the individual Prague commissions and boards of the Jewish nationalists took into consideration their statements without giving the matter much further thought. In a letter to Robert Weltsch, Rufeisen wrote:

> I do not now consider it necessary to move to Prague. It has turned out, on the contrary, owing to the unpropitious situation in Prague, that moving the Central Association to Ostrava has ... one big advantage – namely, that our authority is recognized without reservation by all the Prague commis-

---

[109] See, for example, CZA, The Zionist Organisation – Central Office, London, Z4/3564, a report on a trip through Central and Eastern Europe, by Adolf Pollak for Felix Rosenblüth of the Zionist Organisation in London, of 9 December 1927.

sions and our leading colleagues, which would probably not have happened to the same extent if we had our headquarters in Prague.[110]

Rufeisen here is alluding to something that was typical of Zionism in the Bohemian Lands (and elsewhere), that is, that some leading Zionists feuded and held grudges. This was also reflected in the large number of Zionist societies and organisations. In his confidential report on Zionism in Czechoslovakia in 1926, Weltsch told the world Zionist Organisation headquarters:

> Everyone has given up, and blames their lack of success partly on the lack of money, partly on the lack of people. They erroneously stress that all the better forces of Czechoslovak Zionism have moved away – partly to Palestine, partly to Berlin, London, and elsewhere. It seems to me that the main reason for the failure of Czechoslovak Zionism is the regrettable fact that the whole atmosphere is full of personal contradictions amongst the leaders. Amongst the few people who are available, most claim that they cannot work together. The individual leading figures also make a truly pathologically nervous impression, and their intolerance is sometimes of pathological dimensions.[111]

Viktor Fischl also describes the great differences of opinion and personal quarrels. In the 1930s he was a leading member of the Theodor Herzl Society; he edited *Židovské zprávy* and the last number of *Židovský kalendář*; and for a time he worked as a lawyer for Goldstein, a Jewish Party deputy to the National Assembly. In an interview Fischl said: 'You first have to realize that Jews are individualistic. That meant that each of them had their own agenda. Ultimately, it somehow came together, despite the differences of opinion among people. Even Felix Weltsch and Max Brod, who used to go to school together and had been friends ever since they were little, did not always get along.'[112]

Despite the lack of organisational unity of the Zionist movement in the Bohemian Lands, one can observe its basic currents, which can also be understood as its special feature in central Europe. In Bohemia there was a fundamental difference between Zionism in the linguistically German borderlands and in the Czech interior. In the former it took some time before significant numbers of Jews began to join Zionist organisations. That was because in the predominantly German milieu many middle-class

---

[110] CZA, The Zionist Organisation – Central Office, London, Z4/1659, a letter from Josef Rufeisen to Robert Weltsch, of 9 October 1924, 5. For disputes, particularly among Zionists in Prague, see also Fritz Tauber, 'Prag oder Ostrau?', *Selbstwehr*, no. 8 (1938): 5.
[111] CZA, The Zionist Organisation – Central Office, London, Z4/1659, Robert Weltsch, Bericht über den tschechoslowakischen Parteitag in Olmütz.
[112] Viktor Fischl, interviewed by the author, 'Pak to ale dopadle ještě jinak', 6.

Jews considered it inappropriate to separate themselves from their German neighbours and thus to draw attention to their different origin. In the Czech interior Jews from the Czech or 'utraquist' milieu very soon began to come out in favour of Zionism. The Czech-German nationalist disputes often acted as a catalyst for those Jews who had until recently not been concerned with national consciousness or were convinced of the possibility of integration into the Czech or German nation. Jews from the Czech milieu predominated at the creation of Bar Kochba, and only later were they joined also by Jews from the German milieu.

That was the beginning, but during the First Republic the tables were to a certain extent turned. An increasing greater number of Jews from the German-speaking borderlands began to declare Jewish as their nationality and to organise themselves in Zionist societies. They did so in reaction to the growing *völkisch* movement and antisemitism. In the interior of the country the children of former Zionists, by contrast, often no longer felt the need to organise in Zionist societies and naturally integrated into the Czech nation. That did not mean, however, that in the Czech interior the number of Zionists decreased. It just did not increase as quickly as in the border regions.

The difference between the interior and the borderlands somewhat reflects the ideological difference between the 'Synthetic', moderately left-wing Zionism of the main Zionist figures from the Czech interior and Moravia and, on the other hand, the strictly Political Zionism of Emil Margulies in the German-speaking borderlands. The first group from the interior comprised mainly the pre-war and also post-war members of the Bar Kochba and the Theodor Herzl societies. Even during the First Republic they largely influenced the nature of Zionism in Bohemia, in particular by running the main Zionist periodicals. In addition to *Selbstwehr*, there was, as we have seen, *Židovské zprávy*, a Czech Zionist periodical, which was run alternately by Emil Waldstein, František Friedmann and Zdeněk Landes, all members of the Theodor Herzl Society. The Herzl Society also began to publish the popular *Židovský kalendář*, the editors of which were again Waldstein and Landes together with two of the best-known Czech Zionist writers, František Gottlieb (1903–1974) and Viktor Fischl. The Jewish National Fund published a German version called the *Jüdischer Almanach*, edited by Friedrich Thieberger and Felix Weltsch.

What was also important, however, was that a number of them became important functionaries of the Zionist Organisation or the Jewish Party. Arthur Bergmann became the chairman of the Keren Hayesod in Czechoslovakia[113] and Leo Herrmann was the secretary general of this founda-

---

[113] 'Nekrolog Arthura Bergmanna', *Bar Kochba Zirkular* (November 1958), 4.

tion internationally. The head offices of the Keren Hayesod were first in London and then, from 1926, in Jerusalem.[114] Ludvík Singer of the Theodor Herzl Society became chairman of the Jewish National Council and later a Jewish Party deputy to the Czechoslovak National Assembly. After Singer's death, the next Jewish Party deputy for the Bohemian Lands was Goldstein, another member of the Herzl Society. Throughout the 1920s and 1930s the organisation of world Zionist Congresses in Czechoslovakia was repeatedly entrusted to either Hugo Herrmann or Franz Kahn. Kahn was at the same time a member of the Central Committee of the Zionist Organisation in Czechoslovakia.[115]

Another important factor was that, thanks to Leo Herrmann and Hugo Bergmann (who first became the head librarian of the Hebrew University of Jerusalem and later a professor of philosophy there), the Zionists of the Bohemian Lands had close links both with the leadership of the world Zionist Organisation in London and with the Jewish élite in Palestine. Moreover, in December 1919, Robert Weltsch became the editor-in-chief of *Jüdische Rundschau* in Berlin. After the folding of the *Die Welt*, a newspaper founded by Herzl, *Jüdische Rundschau* held first place among German-language Zionist periodicals.[116]

A certain counterweight to the moderately left-wing Zionists of *Selbstwehr*, *Židovské zprávy* and the Central Committee of the Zionist Organisation in Czechoslovakia was Emil Margulies. It was mostly owing to him too that the network of Zionist societies was developed in the borderlands, particularly in the north and west of the republic. At the beginning of the First Republic Margulies's position was very strong with regard to the growing number of Zionists from the towns in the borderlands, in which, because of migration in the second half of the nineteenth century, a large part of the Jewish population of Bohemia was concentrated. In the course of the 1920s, however, Margulies was increasingly in opposition to Weizmann's policies, and the ideological gulf between him and the rest of the Zionist leadership in the Bohemian Lands grew. Although Margulies was chairman of the Jewish Party in 1931–1935, his resignation, because of the Jewish Party's collaboration with the Social Democrats, meant his ultimate isolation in north Bohemia.

---

[114] Leo Herrmann then also published *The First Five Years* (Johannesburg, n.d.), an overview of the early work of the foundation.
[115] For the key role played by Kahn after the German occupation of the Bohemian Lands and in Theresienstadt, see Ruth Bondy, *'Elder of the Jews': Jakob Edelstein of Theresienstadt* (New York, 1989).
[116] Robert Weltsch, 'Looking Back Over Sixty Years', *Leo Baeck Yearbook* 26 (1982): 382.

Moderate Socialists

Let us first consider the changes in the activities of the Zionists in Bohemia after World War I who had been previously members of the Bar Kochba and Theodor Herzl societies. Whereas before they had tended to concentrate on the ideological or philosophical foundations of Zionism, after World War I they were involved in carrying out the Zionist programme.[117] The Zionist press in 1918 ran a number of critical articles about pre-war Zionism, which the authors condemned as abstract and disconnected from life. This view was most aptly expressed by Hugo Bergmann. Self-critically, he wrote:

> We did not manage to turn our ideas into forces that would have affected life, and so our whole movement, unrelated life, dissolved into lifelessness. Is it a coincidence that Zionism was a student movement and also largely remained one? Only a student, without real-life interests and workaday worries, in a stage of transition, free as a bird, can, like a merry guest sipping from all the goblets, completely merge with a movement that remains completely removed from everyday life. But no sooner does this student become an 'old man', a physician, a lawyer, or a clerk than he forgets his Zionism, and his life is no longer any different, even in its details, from the lives of other Jews.[118]

Bergmann was also critical of the pre-war praise of eastern European Jewish culture. 'For a while,' he writes,

> we assumed that Jewishness was the Jewishness of the *Ostjuden*; the *Ostjuden* poets were translated, 'New Jewish evenings' were organised. The work was very useful, but was not enough to give us more Jewishness. Life can only penetrate from the inside out; it cannot be evoked on the outside and transplanted inside. The western Jew, living in completely different conditions, cannot feel the life of the *Ostjuden* is his own.[119]

What, however, was the new programme of the post-war Zionists meant to be like? Bergmann puts it in very general terms: '"More Jewishness" can, for a national Jew, mean only a "higher form of humanity".'[120]

---

[117] In his history of Bar Kochba, Freud distinguishes between a romantic phase (from Buber's lectures to the outbreak of World War I) and a realist phase (from the end of World War I). See Viktor Freud's history of Bar Kochba, MS, *Bar Kochba Zirkular* (Hanukkah, 1954), 1–17.
[118] Hugo Bergmann, 'Židovský nacionalism po válce', *Židovské zprávy*, no. 12 (1918): 6–7.
[119] Ibid., 4.
[120] Ibid.

From other articles by Bergmann or the writings and activities of Felix Weltsch, Max Brod, Oskar Baum and their mentor Martin Buber, it is fairly easy to deduce what a 'higher form of humanity' meant for the former members of Bar Kochba. All these leading Zionist intellectuals were drawn to socialism after World War I, and were seriously concerned with fundamental social problems. In November 1918 Bergmann formulated the new programme. 'We must,' he argues, 'even with the greatest personal sacrifice, work together to ensure the just demands of the toiling masses are met.' In the Jewish context, that meant the introduction of democratic voting rights in the Jewish Communities and the organisation of the Jewish working class. In this sense Bergmann particularly appreciated the role of the Jewish socialist associations in the Po'ale Tsiyon organisation. He also called on the Jewish capitalists not to lay off workers or lower their wages in the critical months right after the war. 'The Jewish capitalist must always be part of the left wing of capitalism, which is ready to negotiate with the workers.'[121]

As early as 1917, Brod's *Die dritte Phase des Zionismus* was published. Typical of this new phase of Zionism, which began, according to Brod, just before the end of World War I, was the especially effective social and cultural work for the common people in the Diaspora. This work would include education, the youth movement, the choice of occupation, and, for example, popular education concerning health and sexual matters.[122]

The problem of marriage and the status of woman in society after World War I were considered seriously also by Oskar Baum, who was known best as a writer. In a letter to Bergmann of June 1919, he writes that women should be enabled to work at their occupations even after getting married. Children should therefore be brought up in smaller communities and the organisation of housework should not be left only to the women. The solution to this problem was, according to Baum, a 'point, thanks to which our sick social system could get back on its feet'.[123]

In his *Sozialismus im Zionismus* (1920) Brod commented on the actual movement that he and many of his Bar Kochba friends supported. He highlights the ideology of the Ha-Po'el Ha-Tsa'ir (Young Worker) organisation. An important aspect of Brod's book is the emphasis on the national character of socialist movements. Only the labour movement, which corresponds to the particular demands of its own nation and is anchored in

---

[121] Hugo Bergmann, 'Židé a sociální převrat v novém státě', *Židovské zprávy*, nos. 16–17 (1918): 1–2.
[122] Max Brod, *Die dritte Phase des Zionismus* (Berlin, 1917).
[123] JNUL, Hugo Bergmann Archives, Arc. 4° 1502/592, a letter from Oskar Baum to Hugo Bergmann, of 31 June 1919.

Figure 5.2. Like most Zionists of the Bar Kochba Society, Max Brod (first from right) also began to sympathize with left-wing thinking during World War I. In the photograph from 1935, he is visiting Moscow as a journalist.

a particular national culture, is able to join the international labour movement as an equal member.[124]

Po'ale Tsiyon and Ha-Po'el Ha-Tsa'ir

It is fair to assume that it is Brod who deserves the credit for persuading representatives of the Jewish socialists of Po'ale Tsiyon to become part of the leadership of the Jewish National Council at the end of World War I. Five members of the eleven-member board of the Jewish National Council, including its chairman, Rudolf Kohn, were members of Po'ale Tsiyon. Relatively soon, however, the ideological disagreements between the Po'ale Tsiyon members and the official Zionist leadership became clear. For Jewish socialists, who were also members of the Socialist International, the programme of the class struggle was, after all, more important than the ideology of Zionism. Work with 'bourgeois Zionists' in the Jewish National Council thus, according to them, cast doubt on the sincerity of their class convictions in the eyes of Czech and German socialists.[125]

---

[124] Max Brod, *Sozialismus im Zionismus* (Vienna and Berlin, 1920), 73.
[125] Karel Fischl, 'Židovská Národní Rada', *Židovský socialista*, no. 4 (1919): 1.

In the course of 1919 the Jewish socialist movement experienced a great influx of adherents. This is attested to by reports in *Židovský socialista* (Jewish Socialist), the official periodical of Po'ale Tsiyon, and by the results of the 1919 local elections, in which Po'ale Tsiyon members received, with their own ballot, 1,326 votes in Greater Prague. In the context of the Bohemian Lands, this was indeed a success.[126]

In 1920, however, Po'ale Tsiyon in Czechoslovakia was a complete failure. The reason was the dispute over whether to accept the conditions of the Comintern (the Communist International or Third International). At the Po'ale Tsiyon world congress in Vienna in July 1920 exactly half the delegates voted to accept membership in the Comintern, while the other half abstained.[127] In Bohemia, most members of the Po'ale Tsiyon leadership decided in favour of the Communist wing, and in May 1921 even Rudolf Kohn and Arthur Polak of the Prague leadership, together with Felix Loria from Brno, decided to abandon the Zionist platform completely, and became active Communists.[128] Kohn's joining the Communist Party also meant the end of the periodical *Židovský socialista*, of which he had been editor-in-chief. The editor-in-chief of the Brno periodical *Der jüdische Sozialist*, Arnošt Frischer, had earlier reproached Kohn for his lax approach to Zionist questions.[129] Frischer, however, was unable to prevent the decline of Po'ale Tsiyon in the Bohemian Lands.

In subsequent years, therefore, Po'ale Tsiyon in Czechoslovakia ceased to exist. Not until the meeting in Olomouc in January 1928, which was attended by delegates from Brno, Olomouc and Prostějov (in other words only from Moravia) was there a restoration of the Po'ale Tsiyon organisation. It was not, however, won over for work with the Central Committee of the Zionist Organisation until 1937. Among the Po'ale Tsiyon members it was Jakub Reiss and Jacob Edelstein (later the leader of the Jewish 'self-government' in Theresienstadt) who tried hardest to organise the Jewish socialists and workers.[130]

The reason the Po'ale Tsiyon movement was so weak was the particularly small number of Jewish workers in the Bohemian Lands. Another factor was that the Jewish workers' demands, because of the high level of cultural integration of the Bohemian and Moravian Jews, were no dif-

---

[126] P-K., 'Kapitola povolební', *Židovský socialista*, no. 3 (1919): 1.
[127] Only one delegate voted against. Rabinowicz, 'Czechoslovak Zionism', 80.
[128] Kohn even got elected to a senior position in the Czechoslovak Communist Party leadership, and Loria was among Dimitrov's advocates at the Leipzig trial of those who had allegedly set fire to the Reichstag in February 1933. Ibid., 81 and 121.
[129] Rudolf Kohn, 'Kdo ohrožuje jednotnost palestýnské práce?', *Židovský socialista*, no. 11 (1919): 1.
[130] Bondy, *'Elder of the Jews'*, 46.

ferent from the demands of the other workers. In one of his talks, Reiss summarized the situation in Czechoslovakia: 'Concerning our state, there is little point in the Jewish workers having a separate forum. No need for such a forum is felt in Bohemia or Moravia. Only perhaps in Slovakia and chiefly in Subcarpathian Ruthenia is the question of the Jewish worker more relevant, because in those lands there are many more Jews than in the historic lands [of the Bohemian crown].'[131]

Another socialist movement, Ha-Po'el Ha-Tsa'ir (the Young Worker), was much more successful in Czechoslovakia. It was supported by most of the leading Bar Kochba members and other leading Zionists of pre-war Bohemia. Ha-Po'el Ha-Tsa'ir was founded in Palestine in 1905. Its branches in the Diaspora either had the same name as in Czechoslovakia or, as in most of eastern Europe, were called Tse'ire Tsiyon (Youth of Zion). The adherents of this movement put the emphasis on the personal transformation of the individual, who would then decide to become a worker in Palestine. Hugo Bergmann, Max Brod, Oskar Epstein and Alex Feig were present at the creation of the Prague branch of the Ha-Po'el Ha-Tsa'ir movement in 1920. Brod then helped to establish the Brno branch.[132]

Ha-Po'el Ha-Tsa'ir was influenced by the ideas of Aharon David Gordon (1856-1922), whom the Bohemian Zionists were interested in even before World War I. An intellectual from Russia, Gordon fascinated the Zionists mainly by his readiness to settle at the age of 48 in Palestine and become a worker together with young men from the second aliyah. In some respects Gordon's teaching comported with the teaching of Aḥad Ha'Am, who had a number of adherents in Prague. Aḥad Ha'Am opposed Herzl's conception of Zionism as negativistic and he substituted for it the positive programme of the cultural regeneration of the nation. Even Gordon was against Herzl's purely political solution and against Marxists of the Ber Borochov ilk. A key leader of the Po'ale Tsiyon, Ber Borochov (1881-1917) believed that only with revolution and the tearing down of the old social order was it possible to establish justice and social reconciliation. Like Aḥad Ha'Am's programme, Gordon's programme was positive. He saw every individual as a social being, as a unit of society, who could, with the help of his or her family, contribute to the regeneration of the whole national community.[133] Gordon's attitude to assimilation is also noteworthy. Unlike Herzl, who considered assimilation impossible

---

[131] NA, policejní prezídium, 1921-30, 28/4, box 907, a talk given by Jakub Reiss at the Association of Jewish Craftsmen in Czechoslovakia (Svaz židovských řemeslníků v ČSR), 4 February 1930.
[132] Rabinowicz, 'Czechoslovak Zionism', 55.
[133] Shimoni, *The Zionist Ideology*, 208-09.

because of ubiquitous antisemitism, Gordon did not see assimilation as a process determined by external conditions and could imagine the assimilation of the Jews into the surrounding nations.[134] Assimilation was, according to him, a matter of personal choice. But he preferred Zionism, which expected the individual to take an active approach to his or her own traditions, as opposed to the passive acceptance of the traditions of other nations.

One of the important differences between Ha-Po'el Ha-Tsa'ir and Po'ale Tsiyon was in what each organisation emphasized about Jewish settlement in Palestine. Ha-Po'el Ha-Tsa'ir was a 'Palestine-centric' movement connected closely with life in the Yishuv (Jewish settlement in Palestine). Corresponding to that was close collaboration between the members of Ha-Po'el Ha-Tsa'ir and the other Zionist organisations. Po'ale Tsiyon, on the other hand, worked also with the socialist, non-Zionist organisation, the Bund, in Poland, and with non-Jewish Marxist-oriented political parties of individual countries. Also connected with that was, ultimately, the different approach to language. The Po'ale Tsiyon members were willing to acknowledge the equality of Yiddish and Hebrew, whereas adherents of Ha-Po'el Ha-Tsa'ir were from the start in favour of Hebrew, and most of the teachers and tutors at Hebrew schools came from their ranks.[135]

Another founding father of the Ha-Po'el Ha-Tsa'ir movement, though indirectly, was Buber. The three talks, which he gave in Prague in 1909–1911, can reasonably be considered a basis for opening young Zionists' minds to the ideas of Gordon. Buber too called for personal involvement and an active approach to Jewish traditions. Moreover, Gordon's *Letters from Eretz Israel* were first published in German in Buber's periodical, *Der Jude*, in 1917.[136] Buber also became the main actor in a great meeting of Jewish youth (Jugendmeeting), which was convened in Prague in March 1920. The purpose of the meeting was to win over as many new supporters of Ha-Po'el Ha-Tsa'ir as possible. This meeting is historic, because it was here that the main part of Tse'ire Tsiyon joined with the Ha-Po'el Ha-Tsa'ir organisation, and they created a common political party in the Zionist movement with a new name, Hit'aḥadut (Association).[137] Together with Eliezer Kaplan (1891–1952) and Joseph Sprinzak (1885–1959), Hugo Bergmann presided over this international meeting.

---

[134] Ibid., 211.
[135] Salomon Goldelman, *Das arbeitende Palästina. Zionistischer Sozialismus* (Prague, n.d.), 15–16.
[136] A. D. Gordon, 'Briefe aus Palästina', *Der Jude* 1, no. 10 (January 1917): 643–49; Gordon, no. 11 (February 1917): 728–36; Gordon, no. 12 (March 1917): 794–801.
[137] The full name was Hit'aḥadut ha-Po'el ha-Tsa'ir – Tse'ire Tsiyon.

Other Czechoslovak delegates were Max Brod, Oskar Epstein and Hans Kohn.[138]

In his long talk at the meeting Buber emphasized the importance of socialism. 'Real Socialism', according to him, did not consist in class struggle, but in one's voluntary decision to become a worker. Volunteer Jewish workers thus would, he argued, become a model solution to the labour question the world over. Although Ha-Po'el Ha-Tsa'ir, according to Buber, was not a religious movement, it could, because of its valuable ideology, become the germ of a new religious revival of the Jewish people.[139]

The conference was also attended by internationally known Zionists like Chaim Arlosoroff (1899-1933), Robert Weltsch (at the time the editor-in-chief of the *Jüdische Rundschau* in Berlin) and Gordon himself, and it made a great impression in Czechoslovakia. Throughout the interwar period the ideology of Hit'aḥadut had numerous adherents in the Bohemian Lands and considerably influenced the character of Zionism there. Hit'aḥadut, however, was not well organised, so could not make itself felt. In the elections of the delegates at the Thirteenth Zionist Congress, in Carlsbad in 1923, the Czechoslovak adherents of Hit'aḥadut did not dare even to put forward their own candidate, and instead joined the Hit'aḥadut ballot in Argentina and Belgium. One finds no document from after 1924 related to an organised Hit'aḥadut movement in Czechoslovakia.[140]

There were several reasons for such a failure. In the early 1920s the movement lost its two main leaders. Buber retired from political life in 1921, and Gordon died in 1922. The main propagator of Hit'aḥadut in Czechoslovakia, Hugo Bergmann, again in keeping with the ideology of the movement, moved to Palestine in 1920, where a number of other young ḥalutsim had also moved. Hans Kohn left Czechoslovakia as well.

The organisational failure, however, did not mean that the ideas of Gordon and Buber were any less influential. Adherents of the movement remained an informal group of like-minded people. Although the Hit'aḥadut organisation in Czechoslovakia had practically ceased to exist from the mid-1920s, the chairman of the Zionist Territorial Federation, Rufeisen, continued to insist that Hit'aḥadut still existed theoretically, because only this branch of the Zionist movement in Czechoslovakia was willing to become an integral member of the Federation. Three places were reserved for adherents of the former Hit'aḥadut in the Central Committee of the

---

[138] At the same time as the world conference, the first conference of the Czechoslovak Ha-Po'el Ha-Tsa'ir took place. It was there that Oskar Epstein was elected to head the Prague branch. Rabinowicz, 'Czechoslovak Zionism', 58.
[139] JNUL, Martin Buber Archives, Ms. Var. 350/56a vav, Rede Dr. Martin Bubers gehalten am Jugendmeeting am 25. 3. 1920 in Prag.
[140] Rabinowicz, 'Czechoslovak Zionism', 61.

Zionist Organisation in Czechoslovakia. In this way they acquired considerable influence over the organisation of Zionism in Czechoslovakia.[141]

Furthermore, some former Hit'ahadut members became strong supporters of Weizmann's policies, and in the elections to the Fifteenth Zionist Congress in 1927 voted as the 'Centre Left'. The Centre Left movement won 4,167 of the total 6,514 votes, and therefore had six of the nine delegates to congress.[142] At the top of the ballot of the Centre Left was Weizmann, together with Ludvík Singer, Hugo Herrmann, Erwin Vogl, Angelo Goldstein and Friedrich Eckstein of Děčín (Tetschen). All of them could take part as delegates to the Zionist Congress.[143]

Zionist Realists

Another group of former Hit'ahadut members, on the other hand, identified with the programme of 'Zionist Realism', which was, in the international context, absolutely unique. The Zionist Realists in many respects appealed to Masaryk's ideal of realistic and humane politics. Their programme was formed slowly, and culminated in 1925 and 1926 in statements published as separate booklets or in the periodical *Selbstwehr*.[144] At the head of the Zionist Realists stood Oskar Epstein. In 1925 he became a teacher at the Jüdisches Reform-Real-Gymnasium in Brno, and with the support of former Brno members of Hit'a adut he took on the tasks of organising the revival movement in Czechoslovak Zionism. In many respects he based himself on Gordon's ideas, particularly his concept of personal involvement and that each individual must take personal responsibility. In the ideas of the Zionist Realists, however, he strikingly reflected the influence of Masaryk's philosophy. All Zionist work should, according to the Zionist Realists, be in the arts and sciences. The Jewish national homeland in Palestine should, they argued, be founded on the humanitarian principles of social justice. This aspect of their programme was projected also in the burning question of relations between Jews and Arabs. Although the Arabs in Palestine were expected to accept the Jews' right to a fully developed national programme in their own state, the great powers should provide assistance to the Palestinian Arabs in choosing their leaders, who would, like the Jews, be able to lead their own people to national independence, including the building of national cultural institutions.[145]

---

[141] Ibid., 61–62.
[142] Ibid., 70.
[143] CZA, The Zionist Organisation – Central Office, London, Z4/3564, Hauptwahlkommission für den XV. Zionistenkongress, 19 July 1927.
[144] Oskar Epstein, *Proklamations- oder Tatsachen-Zionismus?* (Prague, 1925); 'Die Thesen des zionistischen Realismus', *Selbstwehr*, no. 19 (1926): 2–4.
[145] 'Die Thesen des zionistischen Realismus', 2–4.

At the conference of the Zionist Territorial Federation in July 1926, the Zionist Realists tried to convince the other delegates of the need to accept the individual points of their programme.[146] They managed to provoke a highly interesting debate, which continued in the Zionist press after the conference, but that was all they managed to do. From late 1927 this group ceased to develop, which Oskar Rabinowicz, an historian and contemporary active Zionist, ascribes particularly to the organisational incompetence of Oskar Epstein.[147]

Despite their brief existence, the Zionist Realists' programme is further evidence of the Jewish Czechoslovaks' admiration for President Masaryk. Just as the Czech-Jewish thinker Jindřich Kohn incorporated Masaryk's ideas into his own philosophical works, the Zionist Realists endeavoured to incorporate Masaryk's ideas into their concrete demands for the building of a Jewish homeland in Palestine and also organising Zionist work in the Diaspora.

Weizmann and His Adherents

Typical of the moderate socialists of the Hit'aḥadut, and also of subsequent groupings, was the support for Chaim Weizmann, the then-president of the world Zionist Organisation. Devotion to him grew after Joseph Sprinzak, one of the main promoters of Hit'aḥadut, was elected to the board of the world Zionist Organisation and was thus one of Weizmann's closest collaborators.

In interwar Czechoslovakia, Weizmann was supported not only by Hit'aḥadut adherents, but also by the so-called 'General Zionists' (*allgemeine Zionisten*), that is, those Zionists who did not belong to any particular group like Hit'aḥadut, Po'ale Tsiyon or Mizraḥi. Among those Zionists in the Bohemian Lands were important figures like Rufeisen, Goldstein, Oskar Neumann (later more active in Slovakia) and Hanna Steiner.

Felix Weltsch became the most important representative of the General Zionists. He promoted the ideology of the General Zionists, who were often considered colourless Zionists without a particular programme, on a higher, philosophical plane. Following on from Hegel's dialectics, Weltsch developed the theory that only by the creative search for compromises amongst extreme views could one achieve productive results that stood a chance of success. He set out his views in *Das Wagnis der Mitte* (Daring to Be in the Middle, 1937)[148] which was well received by members of the

---

[146] On behalf of the Zionist Realists the conference was attended by Robert Anders of Prague, Oskar Bachrach of Bratislava, Eduard Drachman, Oskar Epstein, Ernest Lamberger, Alois Zaitschek, Leopold Schnitzler, Samuel Zeisl of Brno and Hans Zweig of Prostějov.
[147] Rabinowicz, 'Czechoslovak Zionism', 68.
[148] Felix Weltsch, *Das Wagnis der Mitte* (Moravská Ostrava, 1937).

Prague Jewish élite. Weltsch also applied his ideas directly to the ideology of Zionism. In his *Allgemeiner Zionismus: Eine ideologische Skizze* (General Zionism: An Ideological Sketch, 1936)[149] he explained why he considered General Zionism neither colourless nor lax. Its adherents, he argued, did not elaborate any new programme that would lead to further factions in the Zionist movement, but instead creatively endeavoured to unite different opinions, which was far more difficult. The political, social and economic extremes, he claimed, were a threat to the very foundations of Zionism.

In 1931, however, even General Zionism split into two factions all across Europe. At the Seventeenth Zionist Congress, Weizmann failed to convince the delegates to re-elect him chairman of the world Zionist Organisation. In his programme-related speech he admitted that he himself did not believe that Jews ever constituted the majority population of Palestine and that it was therefore unrealistic for the primary aim of the Zionist Organisation to be the establishment of a Jewish state. It is not surprising, then, that his opponents disagreed with this view. Even within the camp of General Zionists Weizmann at this time lost most of his support. Of the total of 84 General Zionists, 58 were against him; only General Zionists from Great Britain, Germany, and Czechoslovakia stood behind him.[150] The 1931 elections are therefore further evidence of the Bohemian Zionists' devotion to Weizmann's policies.

In January 1924 Weizmann visited Czechoslovakia. The official meeting with the president of the world Zionist Organisation took place in the Lucerna building in Prague and was attended by more than three thousand people.[151] On other occasions, too, Singer, Goldstein and Rufeisen made it clear that they stood behind Weizmann.[152]

If one traces the development of Weizmann's conception of Zionism from the beginning of the twentieth century onwards, many similarities with the attitudes of the Zionists in the Bohemian Lands become clear. At the Zionist Congress in 1901 he helped to found the so-called 'democratic faction', which stood in opposition to Herzl's political conception of Zionism. He and his colleagues, in particular Feiwel (from Moravia) and Buber, considered it short-sighted that Herzl primarily emphasized diplomacy, which Herzl considered the most important means to achieve a Jewish state. They claimed that Zionism could not rest on the personal

---

[149] Felix Weltsch, *Allgemeiner Zionismus: Eine ideologische Skizze* (Prague, 1936).
[150] Rabinowicz, 'Czechoslovak Zionism', 49.
[151] NA, ministerstvo vnitra presidium, 225-556-5, X/Praha/N/27.
[152] For example, at the public meeting of the Jewish National Fund on 27 September 1930, Singer told an audience of about six hundred that he strongly supported Weizmann but was critical of the radical Zionists. NA, ZÚ pres., 207-422-20, 8/5/52/7.

involvement of several politically important figures. They considered, by contrast, the development of cultural and educational institutions in Palestine to be decisive for the future Jewish state. Weizmann went so far as to claim that even if the Jews obtained the internationally recognised right to settle in Palestine, it would be pointless if there was not yet a Jewish society in Palestine that had become a physical part of Palestine. Though Weizmann himself was not a socialist, he greatly appreciated the work of the first settlers (ḥalutsim).

The members of the democratic faction were present at the creation of the Jüdischer Verlag in Berlin in 1902, the first Zionist-oriented publishing house in western Europe. The aim of the Jüdischer Verlag was to publish treasures of Jewish art and religion and thereby to help the cultural renascence of the Jewish nation. In addition to Weizmann, Buber and Feiwel, Prague Zionists from Bar Kochba also took part in the project – namely, Hugo Bergmann and, above all, Siegmund Kaznelson, who ran the publishing house from 1920 till the Gestapo closed it down in 1938. While Kaznelson was in charge, the Jüdischer Verlag became the most important Zionist publishing house in the world.[153]

A milestone in the history of the Zionist movement was reached in 1907, when Weizmann managed to persuade most delegates to the Eighth Zionist Congress to accept the programme of 'Synthetic Zionism', a blend of Political Zionism and Practical Zionism. Weizmann was promoting the continuation of diplomatic efforts, but also supported the practical, concrete work of the first settlers. He emphasised, moreover, the importance of Zionist work in the Diaspora, chiefly in education and in fund-raising for the Jewish National Fund.

In 1920 Weizmann was elected president of the world Zionist Organisation. For almost two years his closest adviser was Robert Weltsch, who moved from Berlin to London for that period.[154] From 1929 onwards, Weizmann also led the Jewish Agency, which represented the Yishuv in talks with the British Mandate authorities. Except for a period between part of 1931 and 1935, he remained president till 1946, when David Ben-Gurion took his place.

Weizmann also played an important part in establishing the Hebrew University of Jerusalem. The idea to found a university in Jerusalem first appears in the book that Buber, Feiwel and he had co-authored, *Eine jüdische Hochschule*, which was published in 1902.[155] As president of the

---

[153] See Anatol Schenker, *Der Jüdische Verlag 1902–1938: Zwischen Aufbruch, Blüte und Vernichtung* (Tübingen, 2003).
[154] Hans Kohn, 'Rückblick auf eine gemeinsame Jugend', in Hans Tramer, Kurt Loewenstein (eds), *Robert Weltsch zum 70. Geburtstag von seinen Freunden* (Tel Aviv, 1961), 117.
[155] This was the second book published by the Jüdischer Verlag.

world Zionist Organisation, Weizmann took part in the ceremonial laying of the foundation stone of the university in 1920 and the opening ceremony in 1925.

From the political standpoint it was typical of Weizmann that he sought a conciliatory solution to the conflict with the Arabs. (Immediately after World War I he began talks with the leader of the Arab nationalists, the Emir Faisal, 1869–1937.) Only a few years later Hugo Bergmann, Hans Kohn and Robert Weltsch helped to found Brit Shalom. Similarly, in his relations with the British Mandate authorities Weizmann preferred diplomatic compromise to the radical solutions proposed by the 'Zionist Revisionists'. Weizmann's career culminated in his becoming the first president of the State of Israel.

The Opposite Pole: Emil Margulies

A pro-Weizmann, moderately left-wing approach to Zionism, emphasising the regeneration of Jewish culture, including of course Hebrew, was typical of the vast majority of Zionists from the Bohemian interior. That, however, was not the case with Margulies of north Bohemia. Originally from Sosnowiec (Sosnowitz), a town in part of Poland annexed by Russia, Margulies grew up in an Orthodox Jewish family. His religious and political milieu was thus different from that of most Bohemian Zionists. He joined the Zionists while a student of law at Vienna, under the influence of his elder brother, Isidor. In Vienna he also became personally acquainted with Herzl. In 1903 he settled in Teplitz-Schönau, north Bohemia, as a trainee in a law firm, and immediately began to organise the local Zionist movement. From Vienna he brought his experience of founding local Zionist societies.

At that time there was still little Zionism in north Bohemia. Most people living there were linguistically German. Many Czechs (particularly workers) had not come to the area until the second half of the nineteenth century. Similarly, most Jews arrived from linguistically Czech or German villages and small towns only after the lifting of the ban on Jewish migration in 1849. After Prague it was here, in territory later called the Sudetenland, that many Bohemian Jews were concentrated because of industrial development.

Margulies's and his friends' Zionist campaigning in north Bohemia met with the strong opposition of the Jewish middle classes, which were linked with German liberals. Unlike Prague, where non-Jewish Germans were willing to respect the different religious and also national identity of the German-speaking Jews, in the borderlands the Jews often feared Zionism as a movement that could lead to their isolation from dominant

German society. Thus, for example, the editors of the *Teplitzer Zeitung* refused to publish Margulies's invitation to the Zionist general assembly, arguing that eminent Jews of the town had come out against publishing it. Similarly, the leadership of the liberal Deutsche Fortschrittspartei (German Progress Party) spoke negatively about Zionism, after consulting with 'leading members of the Mosaic faith'.[156] Arthur Bergmann, who became a tutor to the children of a middle-class family in Teplitz-Schönau in 1904, also struggled with the opposition of the Jewish Germans.[157]

Margulies decided to overcome the lack of interest of German-speaking Jews. His first step was to publish the booklet *Zionismus und Deutsche Fortschrittspartei: Offener Brief an Herrn Dr. Karl Eppinger von Prag*. In it, Margulies expresses his sympathies as a Zionist with the liberal programme of the party yet demands that its leaders fully respect the right of the Jews to their own nationality. At the political level the Jews would, he argues, therefore support this party, but the leaders of the Fortschrittspartei, in return, must not interfere in Zionist affairs.[158] Margulies's public appeal led to a rift in the Jewish community in Teplitz-Schönau. The younger generation, particularly students, came out in favour of Zionism, but only exceptionally did an older, better-off member of the community become enthusiastic about Jewish nationalism.

Margulies did not, however, abandon his attempts, despite the difficulties that his campaigning caused him in his legal practice. His enthusiasm for the Zionist cause is evinced also by the many offices he held in a wide variety of Zionist organisations, committees and sections. From 1905, for example, he participated in all the Zionist Congresses and also the local Bohemian Zionist meetings, and before the war he was even deputy chairman of the Zionist Central Committee for Cisleithania. From 1910 to 1935 he was deputy chairman of the Zionist Central Committee of the Bohemian Lands (later of Czechoslovakia), and in 1921 he was a member of the committees of two Zionist funds – the Jewish National Fund and the Keren Hayesod.[159]

Margulies tirelessly campaigned, town by town, through north and west Bohemia. This is evinced by the voluminous correspondence with Zionist societies in Trutnov (Trautenau), Žatec (Saaz), Ústí nad Labem (Aus-

---

[156] Meir Färber, *Dr. Emil Margulies: Ein Lebenskampf für Wahrheit und Recht* (Tel Aviv, 1949), 36.
[157] 'Dr. Arthur Bergmann', *Bar Kochba Zirkular*, no. 1 (November 1958): 3.
[158] Emil Margulies, *Zionismus und Deutsche Fortschrittspartei: Offener Brief an Herrn Dr. Karl Eppinger von Prag* (Teplitz-Schönau, 1904). Eppinger (1853–1911) was the leader of this party from 1901 onwards.
[159] For all the positions he held, see Emil Margulies, 'Kurze Selbstbiographie' in Färber, *Dr. Emil Margulies*, 163–68.

sig), Děčín-Podmokly (Tetschen-Bodenbach), Postoloprty (Postelberg), Podbořany (Podersam), Chomutov (Komotau), Most (Brüx), Mariánské Lázně (Marienbad) and Carlsbad. He often wrote to the local organisers well ahead of time, telling them what they should publish in the local liberal press and in what words they should praise him before he arrived.[160] He eventually created a network of Zionist societies in the towns of north and west Bohemia.

Margulies's conviction was greatly influenced by Herzl's ideas of Political Zionism. Before the war he became a member of the Bar Kochba Society, even though his conception of Zionism was closer to that of Barissia, which promoted a self-confident Jewish-nationalist policy. He probably became a member of Bar Kochba because most of the leading figures of the Zionist élite of Bohemia were members of this society at the time. Nonetheless, in Bar Kochba Margulies remained in opposition. That is evident also from the report on the activity to the society in the 1910-1911 academic year. Margulies made no secret of the fact that the ideas of Aḥad Ha'Am were to a large extent incompatible with his own. He defended Herzl's Political Zionism against the majority, and claimed that without Herzl the organisation of world Zionism would never have got off the ground.[161]

Perhaps because of the disagreements between the Prague cultural Zionists and the political-nationalist conception, which tended to correspond to the conditions in the border regions, Margulies decided at the end of World War I to take a quite surprising step. He submitted to the atmosphere of the times, and endeavoured to form an independent Sudeten Zionist organisation.[162] He based himself on the quickly established 'provincial government', which had been created in the autumn of 1918 by the pro-Austrian Germans in four predominantly German areas called Deutschböhmen (of which Liberec/Reichenberg was the centre), the Sudetenland (an area, at the time, only of north-west Bohemia), Deutschsüdmähren (south Moravia) and the Böhmerwaldgau (Šumava and south Bohemia). He most certainly made his decision partly because of the statement by the leader of the Sudeten Germans, Rudolf Lodgman von Auen (1877-1962), who supported the national autonomy of the Germans and came out in support of recognising Jewish nationality and Jewish minority rights.[163] Thanks only to the diplomatic efforts of Viktor Freud, at the time

---

[160] For example during his lecture tour to Žatec, Postoloprty and Podbořany, NA, fond Emila Marguliese, box 2, inv. no. 7.
[161] Bericht über die Tätigkeit des Vereins der jüd. Hochschüler Bar Kochba in Prag während des 34. Vereinssemesters, 10-11.
[162] Letter from Ota Kraus to Richard Pacovský, *Bar Kochba Zirkular* (April 1958), 3.
[163] Aharon Moshe K. Rabinowicz, 'The Jewish Party', in *The Jews of Czechoslovakia*, vol. II, 255.

the Chairman of the Zionist district for the Bohemian Lands, a breakup of the Zionist organisation in Bohemia and Moravia was averted.

Great differences remained, however, between Margulies's conception of Zionism and that of most Bohemian and Moravian Zionists. At the Thirteenth Zionist Congress, in 1923, Margulies joined a group later known as the Radical Zionists. Among its well-known figures were Nahum Goldmann, Max Soloweitschik (1883-1957) and Robert Stricker, a native of Brno (Brünn) who became the leader of the Vienna Zionists. The Radical Zionists were united mainly by their criticism of Weizmann's leadership of the world Zionist Organisation. They reproached Weizmann for his moderate stance towards Great Britain. They would have preferred putting considerable political pressure on the British Government and to push for the creation of a Jewish state, rather than merely a 'Jewish homeland'. Another reason for disagreement with Weizmann's leadership was his decision to expand the organisation of the Jewish Agency by bringing in prominent Jewish philanthropists and patrons, who, though not themselves Zionists, would be willing to support the Yishuv financially. The Radical Zionists were worried that this expansion would weaken the position of the Zionists and hamper their diplomatic talks.

For Margulies therefore an independent, self-confident Jewish minority policy constituted the basis of Zionism. Unlike the General Zionists of the central Zionist Organisation or the Jewish National Council in Prague, Margulies had no intention of making compromises. That was most clearly manifested in his resistance to the coalition of the Jewish Party and the Social Democrat Party in 1935, when in protest he resigned the chairmanship of the Jewish Party. There are other examples as well. Margulies took it badly when Karel Baxa, the infamous lawyer for the plaintiff in the Hilsner trial, became mayor of Prague, owing to the vote of, among other people, Singer, a member of the city council and also chairman of the Jewish National Council.[164] In a separate article Margulies spoke out on this, admitting 'sometimes one can vote for an antisemite, because sometimes one can make political pacts even with one's enemies, but [that candidate] cannot be a bully who spreads the notion of ritual murder, particularly when he has not expressly disowned his past.'[165]

The editors of *Selbstwehr* were so loyal to the chairman of the Jewish National Council that they decided not to publish the article. Even when, at a meeting of the Czechoslovak Zionist District, Margulies complained about what he called this 'scandalous case', he found no one there sympa-

---

[164] For more about the controversy around Baxa's election, see Koeltzsch, 'Geteilte Stadt', 110-25.
[165] NA, fond Emila Marguliese, box 2, inv. no. 7, letter to Yitshak Grünbaum, a member of the action committee in London, 23 October 1923.

thetic to his position. Baxa's election to the mayorship of Prague further confirmed Margulies in his opposition. In a letter to Yitsḥak Grünbaum (1879-1970) of the world Zionist Organisation in London, he wrote: 'Since that meeting I am even more conscious of my opposition than before. I differ from those who are not with me, not just in the tactics and principals of Zionism, but in my whole outlook.'[166]

Even earlier, in the election of delegates at the Twelfth Zionist congress, in 1921, Margulies campaigned on an independent ballot. At the top of the other ballots of the Central Committee of the Zionist Organisation in Czechoslovakia were Josef Rufeisen, Hugo Bergmann and Norbert Adler. An analysis of the voting in the individual towns of the Bohemian Lands clearly reveals that Zionists in the predominantly Czech towns of Bohemia and in Moravian towns voted for the ballot of Rufeisen and Bergmann, both of whom were moderately leftwing and pro-Weizmann. By contrast, the predominantly German towns of west and north Bohemia often stood unanimously behind Margulies and his pugnaciously Jewish-minority policy of a more right-wing orientation.[167]

A milestone in the relationship between Margulies as a representative of Zionists from the borderlands and the headquarters of the Zionist Organisation in Moravská Ostrava was the year 1925, when he appeared on the electoral list of the Radical Zionists, who constituted the Konferenzgemeinschaft radikaler Zionisten (Radical Zionists Conference).[168] Margulies's membership in this opposition organisation aroused the great indignation of the Zionist leadership in the Bohemian Lands – particularly of the chairman of the Zionist Territorial Federation, Rufeisen, and the chairman of the Jewish National Council, Singer. In the debate at the Third Plenary Session of the Central Zionist Committee, in July 1925, one of the main points was whether to make it possible for Margulies to stand as he had done hitherto, that is, on his own ballot for the Czechoslovak Zionists at the world Zionist Congress. The fact that he was against Weizmann's policy and also the fact that he associated more with his colleagues from Germany, Austria and Poland than with those from Czechoslovakia were a thorn in the side of the members of the Central Committee of the Zionist Organisation in Czechoslovakia.[169] The political differences therefore became clear, and despite further collaboration

---

[166] Ibid.
[167] 'Offizieller Wahlbericht über die Wahlen Zum XII. Zionisten-Kongreß in der Tschechoslowakei', *Selbstwehr*, no. 34 (1921): 4.
[168] For the manifesto of the Konferenzgemeinschaft, see NA, fond Emila Marguliese, box 2, inv. no. 8.
[169] NA, fond Emila Marguliese, box 2, inv. no. 8, Zionist Central Committee in Czechoslovakia, Proceedings of the Third Plenary Session, 19 July 1925.

the rift in the Jewish Party between Margulies and the rest of the Zionist leadership grew.

One of the manifestations of the conflict was the fact that both *Selbstwehr* and *Židovské zprávy* refused to publish Margulies's articles. Margulies then began to accept offers from a Brno periodical, *Jüdische Volksstimme*, the editors of which had been favourably inclined to him in previous years. He even challenged the other Radical Zionists, who were led by Nahum Goldmann, to contribute regularly to the *Jüdische Volksstimme* and to turn it into the main competition of *Selbstwehr*.[170]

Among the few Zionist figures who stood behind Margulies were Alfred Engel of Brno, who, during World War I and at the beginning of the First Republic, selflessly looked after Galician refugees, as well as Margulies's sister-in-law, Miriam Scheuer and Paul März (1894-1981), who, in 1938, took Rufeisen's place as chairman of the Central Committee of the Zionist Organisation in Czechoslovakia. März had expressed his sympathy for Margulies as early as 1925, the critical year when Margulies decided actively to support the Radical Zionists. In the same letter as the one in which he expresses his sympathies, März speculates about who Margulies's other allies in the Bohemian Lands might be – the Jüdische Lese- und Redehalle (The Jewish Reading Room and Lecture Hall) in Brno and Barissia, led at that time by Hugo Kohner in Prague.[171] In the letter März also complains that in Moravská Ostrava he was completely isolated in his opinions.[172]

Revisionists

In some respects the attitude of Margulies and the Radical Zionists accorded with the programme of the Zionist Revisionists. Whereas the Radical Zionists won over to the programme only a group of intellectuals, the Revisionists succeeded in building up a mass organisation.[173] At the head of the movement of Zionist Revisionism was Vladimir Jabotinsky (1880-1940), who also spoke very critically of Weizmann and in 1935 even aspired to the chairmanship of the world Zionist Organisation. Moreover, Jabotin-

---

[170] NA, fond Emila Marguliese, box 2, inv. no. 8, letter from Margulies to Goldmann, 9 September 1925.

[171] The Barissia Society's positive attitude to the ideology of the Radical Zionists is evident in the talk given by Nahum Goldmann of Berlin. Organized by Barissia in November 1927, the talk consisted mainly in criticism of Weizmann's policies. See NA, policejní prezídium, 1921-30, 28/4, box 907, report from the police commissioner, 22 November 1927.

[172] NA, fond Emila Marguliese, box 2, inv. no. 8, letter from März to Margulies, 14 September 1925. In subsequent years, März kept Margulies closely informed of what was happening in the Central Zionist organisation in Moravská Ostrava.

[173] Donald L. Niewyk, *The Jews in Weimar Germany* (Manchester, 1980), 158.

sky, like the Radical Zionists, was against Weizmann's moderate policy towards Great Britain and against the expansion of the Jewish Agency by admitting non-Zionist members. A similarity is evident in their view that a Jewish majority had to be formed in Palestine as soon as possible.

Margulies was very interested in the activities of the Zionist Revisionists.[174] And the Czechoslovak Zionist Revisionists made no secret of their admiration for Margulies. For his sixtieth birthday, in 1937, their periodical, *Medina Iwrit*, published an article celebrating him as the leader of the Jewish nationalists and of the movement of minorities, which had the lion's share in the development of Zionism in the borderlands.[175]

In pushing for their aims, however, the Revisionists used means that the Radical Zionists were hardly willing to employ to their own benefit. Jabotinsky even went so far as to negotiate with the Polish government about help in the evacuation of the Jewish population of Poland. His intention to move about 750,000 Polish Jews in the course of several years met with interest, of course, from many Polish politicians who did not conceal their antisemitic prejudice.[176]

The fundamental difference between the Radical Zionists and the Zionist Revisionists appears also in military questions. Jabotinsky promoted the creation of a strong Jewish army (sometimes called a 'legion' after the experience of the Jewish legions in World War I), which would protect Jewish settlement from Arab attack. The Arabs would, according to Jabotinsky, have to understand the historically justified claim of the Jews to a Jewish state in Palestine on both banks of the River Jordan. In the Jewish state the Arabs would then have the rights of a national minority. Connected with this militant view was the endeavour of Jabotinsky and particularly his Polish colleagues to prepare as many people as possible in the Diaspora to be members of the future Jewish army or police. The camps of the Brit Trumpeldor youth organisation in Poland were often organised as military boot camps, and even with the support of the Polish Ministry of Defence in 1938-1939.

In Czechoslovakia the Zionist Revisionist movement did not have as militant a character as in Poland. Particularly in the Bohemian Lands the Brit Trumpeldor camps were not unlike the camps of Scouting organisations, except perhaps for their greater emphasis on physical education. Whereas in the Bohemian Lands the Brit Trumpeldor youth movement

---

[174] This is evident from the numerous Revisionist leaflets among his papers. See the fond Emila Marguliese at the National Archives, Prague.
[175] 'Dr. Emil Margulies sechzig Jahre', *Medina Iwrit*, no. 30 (1937): 7.
[176] See Laurence Weinbaum, *A Marriage of Convenience: The New Zionist Organisation and the Polish Government 1936-1939* (New York, 1993).

caught on only to a very limited degree, in east Slovakia and Subcarpathian Ruthenia the opposite was true.[177]

The Jewish Party

Against the background of disputes between Margulies and the Central Committee of the Zionist Organisation in Czechoslovakia it is now time to consider briefly the political activities of the Zionists in the Jewish Party. This was a liberal national minority party, entirely loyal to the Czechoslovak state. A long-standing functionary of the party, Friedmann, saw the reason for the emergence of the independent Jewish Party in the national character of the political parties of Czechoslovakia. Apart from the Communists the national parties, for example the Czechoslovak Social Democratic Party and the German Social Democratic Party, as well as the Agrarian Party, always existed separately from one another, based on nationality. It was not possible for a person of another nationality to stand for office on the ballot of a party thus constituted. By contrast, in Great Britain, parties were not formed on the basis of national (ethnic) criteria, and for Jewish nationalists it was therefore not a problem, according to Friedmann, to be on the ballot of, say, a liberal party in general elections.[178] This also explains why in the interwar history of the Jewish Party so many disagreements and new attempts at unification appear. For a small number of Jewish nationalists in Czechoslovakia their success in gaining seats in the National Assembly was determined by their unity. Functionaries and adherents of the Jewish Party, however, were not divided only by their political views, which corresponded to the political spectrum of the other nationalities. Their views on such fundamental Jewish topics like Zionism and Orthodox Jewry were also different.

The Jewish Party was founded in January 1919, and ran candidates at all levels – in municipal, district, provincial and general elections. Considering the electoral system of the First Republic, in which gaining a seat in the National Assembly required at least 20,000 votes in one region and 120,000 votes throughout the Republic, a great deal depended on electoral results in Subcarpathian Ruthenia. The year 1925 was a great disappointment for the Jewish Party. Even non-Jewish analysts predicted that the Jewish Party would win at least one seat.[179] Because of the astute policy

---

[177] Kateřina Čapková, 'Piłsudski or Masaryk? Zionist Revisionism in Czechoslovakia 1925–1940', *Judaica Bohemiae* 35 (1999): 210–39.
[178] František Friedmann, *Strana židovská* (Prague, 1931), 10–11.
[179] Jaromír Nečas, *Politická situace na Podkarpatské Rusi (rok 1921)* (Prague, 1997).

of the Agrarians, however, this did not happen. They took advantage of internal disagreements in the Jewish Party in Slovakia and Subcarpathian Ruthenia and contributed to the formation of an independent Jewish Party of Business (Židovská hospodárská strana), which took potential votes away from the Jewish nationalists.

In subsequent years, Margulies managed to win a court case in which he demonstrated that the Agrarian Party had helped to fund the establishment of the Jewish Party of Business and its election campaign. Before the elections, Antonín Rozsypal, the vice-governor of Subcarpathian Ruthenia and an Agrarian Party member, had donated 100,000 crowns (about US $1,250) to Ungar, who was a Slovak Zionist, and to two rabbis, Koloman Weber of Piešťany and Simon Hirschler of Bratislava. Ungar, however, eventually returned to the Jewish Party, sent the unspent 80,000 crowns to the vice-governor, and had Rozsypal confirm this sum in writing.[180] Margulies thus had evidence of corruption. Despite the efforts of Weber and Hirschler, the Orthodox leaders of the Jewish Party of Business, to postpone and thwart the trial, a judgement was delivered in March 1928. It was absolutely typical that Margulies was not afraid to be involved in a lawsuit against members of one of the government parties. In addition, he successfully demonstrated that Weber had been involved in defrauding an American charity, taking money which had been intended for alleviating poverty in Subcarpathian Ruthenia.[181]

In 1928 further splintering took place in the Jewish Party. Julius Reisz, a well-known figure among the Slovak Jews, decided to unite the Slovak and Subcarpathian Ruthenian Jewish nationalists under one umbrella party and thus to succeed in the provincial elections. For this purpose, however, he removed Zionist slogans from the programme. Only in this way could he win over even hardcore opponents of the Zionists from the ranks of the Orthodox Agudat Yisra'el. Reisz's actions of course met with great resistance from the Bohemian Zionists. They could not stand the 'betrayal' of the Zionist programme or the fact that the Jewish Party in Slovakia, led by Reisz, had slipped out from under their influence.[182]

---

[180] Regarding the sum of 100,000 crowns, see Färber, *Dr. Emil Margulies*, 99. Rabinowicz puts the figure at 300,000 crowns, referring to the statement by Paul Meretz in Rabinowicz, 'The Jewish Party', 272. The sum stated by Färber, however, is correct. See 'Interpelace senátora A. Fahrnera na veškerou vládu o tom, že viceguvernér Rozsypal vyplatil hospodářské straně peníze na volby a prominul složení částky 28 000 Kč za rozmnožení kandidátních listin', Společná česko-slovenská digitální parlamentní knihovna, http://www.senat.cz/ISO-8859-2.cgi/zajimavosti/tisky/2vo/tisky/T0631_04.htm (accessed 25 January 2010).

[181] Färber, *Dr. Emil Margulies*, 98–100.

[182] Reisz's speech in 1928 is described in detail in Marie Crhová, 'Sionistická volební politika na konci 20. let', *Paginae Historiae* (1999): 166–88.

For the general elections of 1929, the Zionists in the Bohemian Lands decided no longer to count on Subcarpathian Ruthenia, and they entered into a coalition with three Polish parties.[183] The concentration of Polish voters in the Těšín region of Silesia was the guarantee that a shared ballot would win enough votes in a single province. The Jewish voters on the other hand, who were spread throughout the country, added to the Polish vote. Before the elections the Jewish Party leadership managed to begin working again with the Jewish Party in Slovakia. Thanks to the advantageous coalition and the re-establishment of collaboration with the Slovak Jewish nationalists, two Jewish Party candidates – Reisz for Slovakia and Singer for the Bohemian Lands – won seats in the National Assembly. After Singer's sudden death in 1931, Goldstein took his place.

The results of the general election helped somewhat to consolidate the Jewish Party. In early January 1931 the party was officially united throughout Czechoslovakia. Margulies became its chairman. His election to the position is entirely understandable, since he had pushed for a pragmatic minorities policy that was like that of other Czechoslovak national minorities. It seems odd, however, that he did not become a deputy to the National Assembly. Probably it was because he lacked sufficient support from the Bohemian Zionists, but an even more important reason was that he did not speak Czech. Though an excellent lawyer, organiser and orator, Margulies spoke no language but German. That shortcoming kept him from entering the Czech political scene. Even though German and languages of the other national minorities could be used in the Czechoslovak parliament, the Zionists were aware of the crucial role that language played in the national conflicts in the state. In order to demonstrate their loyalty to the Czechoslovak state and probably also in order to fight against Czech nationalist prejudices against 'Germanizing' Jews, all the Jewish Party candidates for election to the National Assembly spoke a Slavic language (Singer and Rufeisen Czech, Reisz Slovak and Kugel Russian).

Margulies did not remain the leader of the Jewish Party for long. In 1935 the majority of the Central Committee of the party decided (by 35 votes out of 48) not to have independent candidates, and instead to take up the offer of the Czechoslovak Social Democratic Party for a joint ballot. It was not, however, to be a coalition (as it had been with the Polish parties). The Social Democrats offered the Jewish Party only some winnable places on their ballots. Margulies, together with eight of his supporters, was against the idea.[184] For him, an alliance with the Social Democrats

---

[183] The Jewish Party campaigned together with Związek Śląskich Katolików, Polskie Stronnictwo Ludowe and Polska Socjalistyczna Partia Robotnicza w Czechosłowacji.
[184] CZA, Collections of Documents on the History of Zionism in Czechoslovakia, F 15/2, Circular of the Socialist Zionists in Czechoslovakia, No. 9, 18 April 1935, 3.

was unacceptable: not only did collaboration with a left-wing party not suit him, but also, indeed mainly, he considered a solution in which the name of the party was absent from the ballot to be a betrayal of self-confident Jewish minority policy. He resigned the chairmanship, and right to the end of the First Republic limited his work mainly to north and west Bohemia. Arnošt Frischer became chairman of the Jewish Party, and kept the position until 1938. He later became a member of the State Council of the Czechoslovak government-in-exile in London.[185]

In 1935, in addition to Goldstein, Chaim Kugel (1897–1966), a left-wing Jewish Party member from Subcarpathian Ruthenia, won a seat in the National Assembly. Kugel, unlike Reisz, was a convinced Zionist, who in his interpellations was concerned mainly with the problem of Hebrew schooling and Ruthenian-Jewish relations in Subcarpathian Ruthenia.

A closer examination of the speeches of the Jewish Party deputies to the National Assembly from 1929 to 1938 reveals several characteristic features. The first is the Jewish nationalists' loyalty to the Czechoslovak Republic. That was a chief aspect that distinguished the Jewish Party from the parties of other national minorities. The Germans and Hungarians, because of their numbers, could afford to allow themselves more national-minority parties, including both 'activist' parties, which supported the Czechoslovak government, and 'negativist', which stood in opposition to it.

Concerning the particular demands related to the Jewish minority, Reisz, Singer, Goldstein and Kugel unanimously demanded funding for Hebrew schools in Slovakia and Subcarpathian Ruthenia. This puts the frequently praised attitude of Czechoslovak governments towards the Jewish minority in a less favourable light. Although support for Hebrew schooling (limited to only several primary and secondary schools and a grammar school in Mukachevo) constituted in essence the principal demand of the Jewish nationalists, little additional government funding was provided.[186] The grammar school in Mukachevo received no government

---

[185] See more in Jan Láníček, *The Czechoslovak Government-in-Exile and the Jews during the World War 2 (1938–1948)*, PhD thesis, University of Southampton, 2010.

[186] See also the memorandum of the Central Committee of the Zionists for Czechoslovakia, in Moravská Ostrava, of 25 June 1924, which Rufeisen handed to President Masaryk during the president's visit to Moravia. The memorandum includes a complaint that nine minority Hebrew schools in Subcarpathian Ruthenia had not been granted any state subsidies in 1924 and that the 'Zionist public has a very hard time accepting the fact that the Jewish agenda in the Church department of the Ministry of Education and National Enlightenment has been entrusted to a high-profile assimilationist [Eduard Lederer], the chairman of the Association of Czech-Jews, whose public statements about mixed marriages, Hebrew schooling, and so forth had have the effect that we cannot see him as an objective civil servant but rather as a political opponent, who tends to be guided by a programme that is antithetical to us'. AKPR, D 3487/1924.

funding in the early years, but President Masaryk made a large private donation. Despite the repeated requests of Jewish Party deputies, in particular Kugel, who was the founder of the Mukachevo grammar school and its long-standing headmaster, the Czechoslovak government tended to look at Hebrew schooling as a charity project rather than a true requirement of Jewish minority policy.[187] Hebrew schooling was therefore the concern mainly of Tarbut, a Zionist charitable society.[188] Not until March 1937 did the Jewish nationalists manage to get a promise from Prime Minister Milan Hodža that Hebrew schooling would receive state funding. Two primary schools with instruction in Hebrew then passed into state administration, others were funded at least in part, and the Mukachevo grammar school received an important one-off grant from the state.[189]

The Jewish Party deputies also repeatedly demanded a more liberal assessment of the requirements that had to be met before one was granted Czechoslovak citizenship, and they called for a more just approach to the potential deportation of people without Czechoslovak citizenship. These requirements related to a relatively large number of the Jews of Subcarpathian Ruthenia.[190] The Jewish Party deputies were also concerned with general matters. Goldstein, for example, drafted legislation on the protection of the Czechoslovak currency and the circulation of legal tender.

The Young Generation

As elsewhere in the world, the moving force of the Zionist movement in Czechoslovakia was its young proponents. Whereas before World War I, Zionist activities had been concentrated in the Bar Kochba and Theodor Herzl student societies, after the war the largest centre of interest in Zionism shifted from the universities to broadly oriented youth organisations. Particularly in the 1930s they grew even larger, especially the Czech ones. Among the best known and numerically strongest was Makkabi, whose activities often resembled those of Sokol, the Czech nationalist physical-education association.[191] Makkabi managed to found dozens of branches

---

[187] Sole, 'Modern Hebrew Education in Subcarpathian Ruthenia', 409.
[188] AHMP, SK IX/998.
[189] Borek, Židovské strany v politickém systému Československa 1918–1938, 119–20. Koeltzsch argues that the state's excuse for not financing the Jewish schools was that the Jews did not form a 'language minority' and so failed to meet this precondition for state support. See Koeltzsch, 'Geteilte Kulturen', 155.
[190] This demand was initially raised by Reisz in his first speech in the National Assembly, where he was a Jewish Party deputy. CZA, Oskar Rabinowicz Collection, A 87/384, copy of the minutes of the seventh session of the Chamber of Deputies, the National Council of the Slovak Republic, 21 December 1929, 30.
[191] For example, 'Der Sokol – ein Ziel', Selbstwehr, no. 27 (1938): 10.

Figure 5.3. Swimmers from Hagibor, who represented Czechoslovakia at international swim meets.

throughout Bohemia and Moravia, training thousands of members.[192] Makkabi members tended to be oriented more to physical education than Zionist education. The Hagibor sports organisation and, to a lesser extent, Hakoach established sections specialised in football, swimming, athletics and other sports. Among the top Hagibor competitors, it was swimmers in particular who excelled internationally, and in the 1920s and 1930s they represented Czechoslovakia in international competitions. In photographs from the period, the winners appear, with the Magen David on the breasts of their swimsuits, happily holding the Czechoslovak flag.[193]

Prague and Brno were also witness to two Makkabi world congresses. In 1933 Richard Pacovský, the head of the Makkabi Association in Czechoslovakia and also an active member of the Theodor Herzl Society, took charge of the opening of the Congress of the International Makkabi Association in a full hall of the Corn Exchange in Prague.[194] Two years later Makkabi representatives from all over western, central and eastern Europe,

---

[192] In 1921 Makkabi in Czechoslovakia had 31 societies with 2,000 members and, in 1936, 82 societies with 10,300 members. See Beda Brüll, 'Československý Makabi', *Židovský kalendář* (1937–1938), 101.

[193] Among the best Hagibor swimmers were Julius Balázs, František Getreuer, Pavel (Pali) Steiner, Kurt Epstein, František Schulz, Arnošt Reiner and Hanuš Abeles. See Joseph C. Pick, 'Sports', in *The Jews of Czechoslovakia*, vol. II, 207–11.

[194] NA, ministerstvo vnitra presidium, 225-809-52, report of 28 August 1933.

and also from Palestine, met in Brno. The gathering of more than 1,000 delegates was greeted by, among others, representatives of the Czechoslovak Ministry of Health.[195] Although on such occasions Makkabi members emphasised the organisation's roots in the Zionist programme, the true state of affairs was actually quite different in many branches. This is evident also from the minutes of the January 1931 meeting of the provincial committee of the Jewish National Fund. They mention that although the Makkabi organisation demands from its members that they pay the shekel fee for the Zionist organisation, 'many people go to Makkabi only for the physical exercise and are not interested in Zionism. Moreover, some sports clubs that have little or no interest in Zionism are associated with Makkabi'.[196] Nevertheless, part of the Makkabi Association was the Makkabi Hatzair youth club, whose activity was to a certain extent similar to that of the Tekhelet Lavan (Blau-Weiss, that is, Blue and White) movement. Particularly in the 1930s this society was oriented towards preparing young people for making *aliyah*.

At the universities in the First Republic the Theodor Herzl Society was dominant. There were, however, many other Zionist student societies, for example Hatikva (Hatikvah [The Hope]), Kartel - sdružení sionistických socialistických akademiků (Kartel - the Association of Zionist Socialist University Students), which was particularly active in 1935-1938, or the Lese- und Redehalle jüdischer Hochschüler in Prag, which was called 'the Halle' in short and whose members were called 'Hallenser'. The Halle was established as a moderate German counterweight to the Czech-Jewish societies. It is clear from the activities of the society and the contemporaneous letters of Kurt Blumenfeld, however, that the Lese- und Redehalle jüdischer Hochschüler had already become a society oriented to Jewish nationalism even before World War I.[197] In Brno, there was a similar society, the Jüdisch-akademische Lese- und Redehalle in Brünn, which became an exclusively Zionist student organisation shortly after World War I.[198] The Association of Zionist University Students (Svaz sionistických akademiků) was the umbrella organisation for all the Zionist student societies.[199]

---

[195] Ibid., č. 67.431/I, report of 19 September 1935.
[196] CZA, Keren Kayemeth Leisrael Collections, KKL 5/3763, Minutes of a Session of the Provincial Committee of the Jewish National Foundation, 28 January 1931.
[197] Blumenfeld, *Im Kampf um den Zionismus*, 42-43; S. Goschen, 'Zionist Students' Organisations', in *The Jews of Czechoslovakia*, vol. II, 180.
[198] Goschen, 'Zionist Students' Organisations', 181; See also the letter from Viktor Fischl to the author, of 22 November 2002.
[199] For a thorough description of Zionist student life, see *Židovský studente viz...*, published by the Sionistický svaz obvodový pro Čechy v Praze (Zionist District Association in Bohemia) and the Spolek židovských akademiků Theodor Herzl (Theodor Herzl Society of Jewish Students) (Prague, n.d. [probably 1937]). See also Goschen, 'Zionist Students' Organisations', 173-84.

At universities in Prague, however, there were also societies of Jewish nationalists from other parts of the country or from other countries. For instance, the Judea Society had Jewish nationalist members from Slovakia and He-Ḥaver included Zionist students from Poland and Romania;[200] also the Self-help (Svépomoc) society, originally for Polish students, became a society of Jewish nationalists, because only an insignificant proportion of its members was of a nationality other than Jewish.[201] Bar Giora, Hatḥiya, and Hasmonea were, on the other hand, so-called 'couleur' societies of eastern-European Jewish students, similar to the Barissia society. That meant that they accepted challenges to duels just like the Burschenschaften, and their members wore uniforms or national dress in society colours at their ceremonies.

It was, however, the Tekhelet Lavan, which played the decisive role among the Zionist youth in the Bohemian Lands. The movement developed out of the Blau-Weiss organisation after World War I. Present at the creation of Blau-Weiss were people close to the Bar Kochba Society and its secondary-school organisation Ha-Shaḥar (Hebrew for dawn).[202] One of the reasons for the creation of the Blau-Weiss movement was the endeavour to lighten up the overly intellectual and spiritual character of the Bar Kochba Society. Another reason for the creation of the Blau-Weiss was the spreading antisemitism in Wandervogel, a German youth organisation.[203] The extraordinarily successful Wandervogel movement was founded by Karl Fischer in the Steglitz district in Berlin in 1897. The main mottos of its members were romance, freedom and the simple life in the great outdoors. In Germany, Jews were admitted to the Wandervogel organisation without major problems until autumn 1913.[204] The case was different in the Austrian part of the Habsburg Monarchy. Although the first branch of Wandervogel was not founded in the Bohemian Lands till 1911, from the beginning membership was based on racial rules.[205]

---

[200] AHMP, SK X/343.
[201] NA, ZÚ pres., 207-419-49, 8/5/45/175.
[202] This Ha-Shaḥar organisation had nothing in common with the Polish youth group of Revisionist Zionists, which was not founded till 1922.
[203] George L. Mosse, *The Crisis of German Ideology: Intellectual Origins of the Third Reich* (New York, 1964), 183.
[204] Ibid., 180-84.
[205] CZA, Bar Kochba / Barissia Collection, A 317/3, Richard Karpe, 'Bar Kochba und Blau-Weiss. Die Entstehung des jüdischen Wanderbundes Blau-Weiss in Böhmen und seine Entwicklung während des ersten Weltkrieges', 3; for an abridged version, see Richard Karpe, 'The Beginnings of "Blau-Weiss" in Bohemia and its Development during the First World War', in *Rhapsody to Tchelet Lavan in Czechoslovakia*, ed. Amos Sinai (Israel, 1996), 16-20.

Figure 5.4. Footballers from Hagibor before a match against Slavia, one of the best football clubs in Czechoslovakia. Photograph from 1937.

Blau-Weiss members went hiking and camping together, played guitars and sang, and were only secondarily interested in Jewish history, Zionism and Eretz Israel. During World War I they also joined forces with the Bar Kochba members to help Galician refugees.[206] As early as during World War I, the number of Blau-Weiss members continuously increased. And from the beginning it was young people of German-speaking families who predominated there. Many families wanted to send their children to Blau-Weiss rather than worry about their safety in German organisations.[207] During World War I, the German organisations placed even greater emphasis on national character.

The movement kept founding new branches throughout Bohemia and Moravia. The most active Blau-Weiss centres were in the Sudeten-German towns of Teplice-Šanov (Teplitz-Schönau), Carlsbad, Varnsdorf (Warnsdorf), Děčín-Podmokly (Tetschen-Bodenbach) and Jablonec nad Nisou (Gablonz an der Neisse) and the Moravian towns of Brno, Moravská Ostrava, Olomouc and Prostějov.[208]

It was also important that Blau-Weiss in the Bohemian Lands developed as a movement strictly opposed to any militarism, even the military-like features of Scouting. That was clear from the beginning of the First

---

[206] Karpe, 'The Beginnings of "Blau-Weiss" in Bohemia and its Development during the First World War', 19.
[207] Philip Boehm, '"Tchelet-Lavan": A School for Practical Zionism (A Personal Story)', 23.
[208] Ibid., 24–25.

Republic, when the rank-and-file members of the organisation rejected the military discipline introduced on the German model by the new leaders Walter Moses and Heinz Nagler. (Moses even coined the slogan: 'Der Blau-Weiss ist eine Armee auf dem Marsch'.) In 1920 the opponents to militarism managed to make Blau-Weiss in Czechoslovakia completely independent from the similar movement in Germany.

Another impulse to the debate on the character of the movement was the encounter with the ideology of the Ha-Shomer ha-Tsa'ir organisation, which was established in Galicia and increasingly gained adherents in eastern Europe. Its adherents often had their own uniforms with epaulets, kerchiefs, hats and slogans, including the Scouting motto 'Be Prepared'. Ha-Shomer ha-Tsa'ir gradually developed into a distinctly left-wing movement that was almost communist.

The Blau-Weiss members did not adopt any of the features of the Ha-Shomer ha-Tsa'ir. The difference, however, went deeper. After World War I, Blau-Weiss became increasingly oriented to the instruction of Jewish history, Hebrew and Jewish traditions, in order to help the Jews of the Bohemian Lands to find their Jewish identity. Many of the Zionists from the eastern-European Ha-Shomer ha-Tsa'ir organisation had been brought up in Orthodox milieus and large Jewish communities. They needed no further education in traditions or Hebrew.[209]

Together with the organisational and ideological changes there were also changes in the name, statutes and by-laws of the Blau-Weiss. From 1923 onwards it was called Tekhelet Lavan (Blue White), and it was based firmly on the foundations of Zionism. The Tekhelet Lavan statutes and by-laws declare that its aim 'is to teach Scouting and civil virtues to Jewish youth, and thus to bring up a new generation of Jews strong and healthy in body and mind. It will achieve that aim by organising regular excursions and social meetings devoted to their cultural and moral up-bringing.'[210]

In periodicals for young people at the time, however, it is repeatedly stressed that the Scouting taught in Tekhelet Lavan is 'free of all things military'.[211] Moreover, an excessive emphasis on Scouting could, according to some leaders of Tekhelet Lavan, lead to 'internal assimilation': 'the spiritual basis of a young Jewish man is different from the foundations of spiritual activity of the youth of the nations surrounding us. For these reasons the activity of Tekhelet Lavan is first of all nationally conscious and culturally educational.'[212]

---

[209] Ibid., 26–28.
[210] AHMP, SK XIV/595, Statutes of 1923.
[211] For example, Karel Bruml, 'K sjezdu', *Listy židovské mládeže*, nos. 4–5 (1923): 40.
[212] R. Lederer, 'O židovský skauting', *Listy židovské mládeže*, no. 6 (1923): 54.

Figure 5.5. A girls' athletics team from Hagibor at a meet in Kolín, 1932.

In the early years after World War I many Tekhelet Lavan members also decided to make *aliyah*. The first farms were established where the future ḥalutsim toughened up by doing agricultural work. Socialist impulses from the Ha-Po'el Ha-Tsa'ir movement also made themselves strongly felt here. Most ḥalutsim from the Bohemian Lands were members of Tekhelet Lavan. In Palestine they founded the Beit Alfa (1922), Heftziba (1922), Sarid (1926), Givat Haim (1932), Maoz Haim (1937) and Ein Gev (1937) kibbutzim.[213]

In the mid-1920s, however, another shift took place. In his report on the youth movement Hans Lichtwitz (1906–1989), at a meeting of the Central Committee of the Zionist Organisation in 1927, said about Tekhelet Lavan:

> We can distinguish three stages in the Tekhelet Lavan movement. The first ended with the war. Typical of the second stage was the orientation to *aliyah*, to which they [the youth] found their way not so much through Zionism,

---

[213] Amos Sinai, 'Introduction', in *Rhapsody to Tchelet Lavan in Czechoslovakia*, 11. Czechoslovak ḥalutsim also settled in the villages Ness Ziona, Rehovot, Rishon LeTsion, Ben Shemen, Petah Tikva, Herzliya, Kfar Saba, Ra'anana, Gan Shmuel, Hadera, Binyamina, Nahalal, Ein Harod, Tel Yosef, Mishmar HaEmek, Degania Alef and Kfar Gun. See Oskar Aschermann, 'Českoslovenští Židé v Palestýně a styky obou zemí', *Židovský kalendář*, no. 35 (1934): 95.

but through Socialism. This stage is now finished. The movement is now of a general Zionist orientation. The leading figures are not ḥalutsim.[214]

Zionism – a German Jewish Matter?

The Tekhelet Lavan movement took hold chiefly among the German Zionist youth, both in the Bohemian borderlands and in the German-Czech linguistically mixed areas and in Moravia. Not until 1938 was a Czech alternative to Tekhelet Lavan formed – the El Al organisation. In the course of roughly one year, until the end of the Second Republic, it grew remarkably.[215] El Al began in January 1937, when Buber again gave a talk in Prague about Jewish identity. A young man by the name of Paul Kohn collected addresses of the young people in the audience and invited them to the first meeting of the future El Al society. At the time of registration, in early 1938, the organisation had about fifty members, yet it was already publishing the *El Al Revue* with a circulation of 200 copies. By the end of 1938 the movement had about 200 members, with branches in Brno and Hradec Králové. Considering the political situation, their programme was aimed mainly at *aliyah*, though few of its members ever made it to Palestine.[216]

The glaring difference between the organisational skills of the Zionist youth in the German and Czech milieus became the main topic of several Jewish youth congresses in 1923 and 1924. At the Second Congress of Jewish Youth, in May 1923, which was attended mainly by representatives of rural Bohemia, the participants decided on the wording of a resolution about their relationship to Tekhelet Lavan, particularly to their camps. They agreed that the Jewish youth from the Czech areas were just now beginning to organise and still felt a need 'to get close to nature, a stage that Tekhelet Lavan has already got beyond'. At the end of the statement it says: 'We are not separated from Tekhelet Lavan by language, but by our development.'[217]

Other documents clearly reveal that the Zionists faced difficulties in winning over the young generation of Czech Jews from Czech areas before 1938. In their confidential documents the representatives of the Central Zionist Association of Czechoslovakia made no secret of the fact that in some Czech areas there was a generational conflict. Whereas the older

---

[214] CZA, The Zionist Organisation - Central Office, London, Z4/3564, Minutes of a session of the Zionist Executive Committee, 23 May 1927, 3.
[215] AHMP, SK XXII/2705.
[216] Otto B. Kraus, 'The El Al Divertimento', in *Rhapsody to Tchelet Lavan in Czechoslovakia*, 256-58.
[217] 'II. sjezd žid. mládeže', *Listy židovské mládeže*, no. 6 (1923): 57.

German or utraquist generation still supported the Zionist programme, 'their children found themselves in an unstoppable stream of cultural assimilation, from which they could be extricated for the Jewish nation and Jewish culture only with the help of well-prepared and organised cultural and educational work'.[218]

The Zionists also endeavoured to promote Czech as their language.[219] Particularly in Moravia, Zionists campaigned for Czech 'out of tact and loyalty to the milieu in which they lived'.[220] The most active campaigning for Czech among Zionists took place at the beginning of the Czechoslovak Republic and then after Hitler took power in Germany. Even about six months before Czechoslovak independence, Ludvík Singer published a large article for *Židovské zprávy*, in May 1918, in which he stated that it was a scandal that Jews in a mostly Czech milieu did not know the Czech language and culture. Their responsibility, he said, was to learn Czech and not always to put themselves into the position of 'Servi Camerae' (that is, 'servants of the Royal Chamber', in German *Kammerknechtschaft*, a term commonly used to describe the legal position of Jews in the pre-emancipation period, when the Jewish community was totally dependent on the ruler). He added, '[i]f not as its members, let us at least be the friends of the nation in whose midst we live. It will be by way of tactful, dignified behaviour, not by intrusiveness, that we shall grow closer to each other.'[221]

Similarly, Zionists were careful not to use German in the 1930s. In protest of the Nazis in Germany, not a word of German was heard at the inaugural session of the Zionist Congress in Prague in August 1933.[222] At the Eleventh Congress of the Central Zionist Association of Czechoslovakia, in 1934, Rufeisen declared, 'with the revival of Hebrew as a living language the state language must be used in the Jewish circle with all that entails'.[223]

---

[218] CZA, The Zionist Organisation - Central Office, London, Z4/2338, a letter to local Zionist groups and trustees of the Zionist Working Committee for the Bohemian Region in the Central Zionist Association of Czechoslovakia (Ústřední svaz sionistický pro ČSR), 20 December 1926.

[219] See also Tatjana Lichtenstein, '"Making" Jews at Home: Zionism and the Construction of Jewish Nationality in Inter-war Czechoslovakia', in *East European Jewish Affairs* 36, no. 1 (2006): 57–58.

[220] František Friedmann, *Mravnost či oportunita? Několik poznámek k anketě akad. spolku 'Kapper' v Brně* (Prague, 1927), 38.

[221] Ludvík Singer, 'Menšiny', *Židovské zprávy*, no. 5 (1918): 2.

[222] AKPR, Židé D 6215/33: Various Jewish organisations (Různé židovské organizace), record of 22 August 1933.

[223] NA, ministerstvo vnitra presidium, 225-1323-1, X/Ž/6, 1936–40, Report from the Eleventh Congress of the Central Zionist Association of Czechoslovakia, held in Moravská Ostrava, 30–31 December 1934.

It is also true that whereas *Selbstwehr*, a weekly written in German, was losing readers, the circulation of *Židovské zprávy* was growing. According to Fischl, its last editor-in-chief before World War II, *Židovské zprávy*, rather than *Selbstwehr* (whose readers were mainly from the older generation), increasingly became the periodical of the young generation of the First Republic.[224]

Another sphere in which the Zionists considerably helped to promote Czech among the Jews was schooling. Although instruction at the Jewish National School in Brno was initially bilingual, from the mid-1920s onwards it was only in Czech. The same was true at the Mukachevo grammar school, where, next to Hebrew, emphasis was also on mastering Czech. And, in the mid-1930s, Zionists even taught Czech to the children of German refugees at the Jewish school in Prague. One of the teachers of Czech there was Stella Fischlová, the wife of Viktor Fischl.

In Bohemia, because of the Jews' considerable integration into the Czech milieu, the Zionist youth movement developed much more slowly than in Moravia. At a congress in Uherské Hradiště, Moravia, in 1924, coordination of the Zionist movement in the Czech areas was entrusted to the Theodor Herzl Society in Prague.[225] In the First Republic, the Theodor Herzl Society, rather than Bar Kochba, became the main Zionist students' society in Bohemia.[226] This cultural shift, where a Czech society came to lead the Zionist students, reflects the general trend of cultural integration into Czech society. The trend grew among the Jews throughout the Bohemian Lands, including the Zionists. For the Theodor Herzl Society, however, the shift towards Czech also meant a limitation. Whereas articles and books by Bar Kochba members could find readers throughout Europe, the articles and books of the Herzl Society remained known to only a limited number of Czech readers. This was pointed out to the Herzl Society leadership by Hans Kohn in a letter from Jerusalem in 1928. In it he called upon the members to carry on the tradition of the pre-war Bar Kochba Society, and to publish in German to become international again.[227] Kohn, who had lived abroad for many years, did not realize, however, that in the delicate nationalist situation in Bohemia, the Zionists were careful not to provoke anyone with German-language publications.

---

[224] See my interview with Fischl, 'Pak to ale dopadlo ještě jinak'.
[225] See *Listy židovské mládeže*, no. 2 (1924): 23.
[226] Concerning the shift in responsibility for the student Zionist movement from Bar Kochba to the Theodor Herzl Society, see Franz Kahn (of the Central Zionist Association of Czechoslovakia) in a letter to the Zionist executive body in London, of 21 March 1927, CZA, The Zionist Organisation - Central Office, London, Z4/3564.
[227] JNUL, Hugo Bergmann Archives, Arc. 4, 1502/1561, letter from Hans Kohn to the Theodor Herzl Society, 9 July 1928.

Zionists and Refugees in the 1930s

The political atmosphere of Czechoslovakia in the 1930s may be summarized as democracy in the shadow of Nazism. Czech-German tensions in the borderlands came increasingly to the fore, and the growing number of German refugees became a symbol of the difference in regimes in Germany and in Czechoslovakia. Many Jewish institutions and societies – the Jewish Centre for Social Care, the charitable societies (mostly women's) of the individual Jewish communities, and the Prague Lodge of B'nai B'rith – began to help the German Jews in Bohemia and Moravia. The most efficient in providing aid to Jewish refugees, however, were the Zionists, who became part of the leadership of the Prague branch of HICEM.[228] A worldwide organisation to help Jewish refugees, HICEM[229] was formed in 1927 by the merger of the Hebrew Immigrant Aid Society (HIAS), the Jewish Colonization Association (ICA) and Emigdirect (United Committee for Jewish Emigration). Jewish nationalists endeavoured to relieve the misery of the refugees by providing not only material support, but also education. The children of German Jews attended a Jewish primary school in Prague, where courses in Czech were also open to them.

Among the Zionists helping the German Jews, it was the members of the Women's International Zionist Organisation (WIZO), particularly Marie Schmolka and Hanna Steiner, who stood out. Together with Chaim Hoffmann (who later took the name Chaim Yahil) they were also in charge of the Prague branch of HICEM. In Bratislava, the local WIZO was run by Gisi Fleischmann, who helped hundreds of refugees in Slovakia to emigrate. The work of HICEM in Prague was supported partly by the individual Jewish communities and in particular by the Jewish Joint Distribution Committee, an American charitable organisation.[230]

In the First Republic, the WIZO went through an extremely dynamic development. In the Bohemian Lands after World War I, there was only a local Mädchenklub, which before the war had consisted mainly of sisters and wives of Bar Kochba members. It was Steiner who did the most to turn the Mädchenklub into a Czechoslovak branch of the WIZO. In

---

[228] For the context of Czechoslovak refugee policy towards Jews from Germany and the charitable institutions helping Jews, see Kateřina Čapková and Michal Frankl, *Nejisté útočiště: Československo a uprchlíci před nacismem 1933–1938* (Prague and Litomyšl, 2008); a German edition is forthcoming from Böhlau Verlag in 2012.

[229] The full name is the Hebrew Intergovernmental Committee for European Migration. In Czech: the Pomocný ústav pro židovské průchozí a vystěhovalce, 'Hicem' (the Aid Agency for Jewish Emigrants and Emigrants in Transit). See AHMP, SK II/1037.

[230] Chaim Yahil, 'Social Work in the Historic Lands', in *The Jews of Czechoslovakia*, vol. II, 397.

Figure 5.6. The departure for Palestine of Jewish refugees from the Reich. Photographed at Wilson Station, Prague, 1934.

Czechoslovakia in 1938 there were already 104 branches of the WIZO with about 12,000 members in all.[231] In the late 1920s and 1930s it was the WIZO that undertook the ambitious project of providing assistance to the Jews of Subcarpathian Ruthenia, which was funded by the Joint Distribution Committee. As early as the end of the 1920s the situation in Subcarpathian Ruthenia began to be charted out by Vally Waldsteinová, the wife of Emil Waldstein, a Lidové noviny correspondent in Užhorod at that time.[232] In her travels Waldsteinová found out the particular needs of the local Jews, most of whom lived below the poverty line. Schmolka and Steiner then took part directly in the distribution of assistance to inhabitants of the individual Subcarpathian Ruthenian villages. It was no coincidence that Steiner also presided over the Jewish Women's Aid Committee for Subcarpathian Ruthenia.[233]

WIZO aid to the Jews of Subcarpathian Ruthenia is a good illustration of the long-standing efforts of Zionist women to help the poor. They were thus well equipped with a variety of experience when later helping

---

[231] CZA, Irma Pollak Collection, A 439/3, 'Geschichte der zionistischen Frauenbewegung in der CSR', 5.
[232] Blätter für die jüdische Frau, no. 21 (1926): 3.
[233] AHMP, SK II/973.

refugees from Germany. Eventually, in the 1930s, Schmolka and Steiner devoted themselves to helping refugees to such an extent that they had no time left for the promotion of Zionist ideas. Irma Polak of the WIZO recalls:

> When Prague was being flooded with great masses of German refugees, Hanna Steiner and Marie Schmolka were there ready to protect and to help them. I was supposed to be the third one helping in that work, but I refused. When I realized what dimensions their work was growing to, and that it was taking up all their strength and energy, I decided to stand on guard in my work for Zionism.[234]

Presiding over the Czechoslovak Committee for Aid to Refugees from Germany, Schmolka also came into close contact with the Minister of the Interior, Josef Černý, who granted her requests for help.[235] The other members of the WIZO organised retraining courses for women and girls from Germany. German Jews were also looked after by the Palestine Office, which in the latter years was run by Jakob Edelstein. In view of the exemplary activity of the HICEM, however, the help of the Palestine Office was increasingly limited to obtaining visas and travel documents.[236] In 1938 in addition to Jews from Germany, Jewish refugees arrived from Austria and, throughout September, from the Sudetenland as well. The number of Sudeten Jews who moved to the interior is estimated at 17,000.[237]

For Zionists the annexation of the Sudetenland to Germany was of course a fundamental blow to the structure of their organisation. This is evident also from Franz Kahn's letter of October 1938 to the world Zionist Organisation. In it, Kahn analyzes the losses suffered by the Zionist Organisation after the annexation of the Sudetenland: in Bohemia the Zionists lost twenty-four local groups with 3,000 shekel-payers, and in Moravia and Silesia twenty-one groups with 1,000 shekel-payers. In Bohemia there thus remained only nine groups with about 2,600 payers, and in Moravia and Silesia twenty-eight groups with about 5,000 shekel-payers. Kahn's report also provides further evidence that Zionism in Bohemia took hold particularly in the border areas.[238]

---

[234] Irma Polak, 'Geschichte der zionistischen Frauenbewegung in der CSR', 7. For more on Steiner and Schmolka, see Bondy, *'Elder of the Jews'*.
[235] Erich Kulka, 'The Jews in Czechoslovakia between 1918 and 1968', 281.
[236] A letter from Růža Löwy (a WIZO member, who worked as Jakob Edelstein's secretary in the Palestine Office) to Karl Schwager. See CZA, Bar Kochba / Barissia Collection, A 317/13, of 15 February 1975.
[237] Kurt R. Grossmann, 'Refugees to and from Czechoslovakia', in *The Jews of Czechoslovakia*, vol. II, 571.
[238] CZA, Organisation Department Collection, S5/435, letter from Franz Kahn to Lauterbach, 14 October 1938.

The rescue of the Sudeten Jews then became the concern particularly of Emil Margulies and Bedřich Ullmann. Margulies became the chairman of the organisation that brought together the previous religious communities in the Sudetenland, and was also in charge of the Rechtshilfestelle für sudetendeutsche jüdische Flüchtlinge in Prag (Legal Aid Office for Sudeten-German Jewish Refugees in Prague). Ullmann, who founded the Ullmann-Komitee für sudetendeutsche Flüchtlinge (The Ullmann Committee for Sudeten German Refugees), endeavoured to get visas from the world Zionist Organisation and the British, Dutch and Swedish governments for at least half of the Sudeten Jews. This is evident from records of Ullmann's meetings with members of the former Jewish communities from the Sudetenland, in which he informed people attending the meetings of other possible ways to obtain visas, for example, for young people or for girls as servants in private homes.[239] An important role in working with the consulates of the individual countries and in obtaining information on exceptions for emigration was also played by the Makkabi sports organisation.[240]

In the period between the German invasion of the rump Czechoslovakia in mid-March 1939 and the outbreak of war a few months later, about 200 Jews from Czechoslovakia managed to receive visas thanks to the tireless efforts of Viktor Fischl and Leo Herrmann, who, in exile in London, founded the Self-aid Association of Jews from Czechoslovakia. Through this work, Fischl came into contact with Jan Masaryk, the Czechoslovak Foreign Minister in exile, who endeavoured to help the organisation as much as possible. Later, Fischl became the head of a department of the Ministry of Foreign Affairs and one of Masaryk's close collaborators.[241]

During the Second Republic, however, it was not only Jews from the Sudetenland who were in danger. It was also becoming clear to many Jews from the interior of the country that the situation was getting worse. Only now, feeling threatened, were some Zionists beginning to consider emigrating to Palestine. It was typical of Zionists in the Bohemian Lands that, among other things, they postponed making *aliyah* or did not take it seriously throughout the period of the First Republic. A popular joke about Zionists fits therefore also for the interwar Czechoslovakia: 'What is Zionism?

---

[239] NA, ministerstvo vnitra presidium, 225-979-12, X/Ž/6/2.
[240] NA, ministerstvo vnitra presidium, 225-979-12, X/Ž/6/2, report of a public meeting concerning emigration and Zionism, 21 February 1939.
[241] Čapková, 'Pak to ale dopadlo ještě jinak', 15. For Jan Masaryk's wartime recollections, see Viktor Fischl, *Hovory s Janem Masarykem* (Prague, [1952], 1991).

It is when one Jew is trying to convince another to fund a third one's journey to Palestine.'²⁴²

The vast majority of the ḥalutsim from Czechoslovakia came from poor areas of Slovakia and from Subcarpathian Ruthenia. By emigrating to Palestine, they were therefore often hoping to earn a better living. From the report of He-Ḥaluts, which together with the Palestine Office was in charge of the preparation and emigration of ḥalutsim, one learns that only 109 young people emigrated in 1935, mostly from the east of Czechoslovakia. The number of ḥalutsim who managed to make aliyah was, moreover, limited by the small number of certificates from the Jewish Agency.²⁴³

Also, in a November 1937 report about the state of Zionism in Czechoslovakia, Elias Auerbach (1882–1971), a German Zionist, biblical scholar and physician who founded the first modern hospital in Haifa in 1909, wrote to Kurt Blumenfeld in Jerusalem, after a week's sojourn in Prague, about the Prague Zionists: 'When I tell them that they should, in any event, make it possible for their children to emigrate to Palestine, they furtively nod their heads and suddenly get embarrassed that they have nodded.'²⁴⁴

After the signing of the Munich Agreement, however, the situation changed radically. Even many Czech and German Jews who had not been involved in Zionism now sought a way out of the country, to Palestine or elsewhere. Because of Czech antisemitism, thousands of Jewish secondary-school and university students from the Czech milieu began to be interested in the possibility of aliyah. Ruth Bondy writes about their change of attitude:

> Sometimes these young people felt as if all their lives they had in fact been striving for the impossible: to be accepted by Czech society as equals, as Czechs in every respect apart from a few minor, old-fashioned family customs. For many it was a revelation. They realized how comfortable it was to live among fellow Jews with whom there was no need to be on guard; how effortless, how unnecessary to make an impression. How many wonderful experiences derived from life in the youth movement: how good it was to hike through the woods (sometimes with restricted access to water, as training for the land of the desert), to camp out in tents, sit in parks, engage in stormy ideological debate or exercise drills, and to sing Hebrew songs with all one's heart.²⁴⁵

---

²⁴² Wilma Abeles Iggers, ed., *Die Juden in Böhmen und Mähren: Ein historisches Lesebuch* (Munich, 1986), 226; in English: *The Jews of Bohemia and Moravia: A Historical Reader*, trans. Wilma Abeles Iggers, Káča Poláčková-Henley and Katherine Talbot (Detroit, 1992).
²⁴³ AHMP, SK XXII/1099, minutes of the general meeting of 26 May 1936.
²⁴⁴ CZA, Organisation Department Collection, S5/434, Letter from Elias Auerbach to Kurt Blumenfeld, 17 November 1937, 2.
²⁴⁵ Bondy, 'Elder of the Jews', 135.

The number of available certificates was, however, extremely limited. It is therefore understandable that the Zionists at the head of the Palestine Office gave priority to people who had gone through the preparatory agricultural or trade courses (*hakhshara*) or who had somehow helped to advance the cause of Zionism in the Bohemian Lands.

The dispute between the Czech-Jews and the Zionists during the Second Republic thus assumed a dreadful form. The editors of *Židovské zprávy* reacted to the xenophobic statement of the Association of Czech-Jews that the government should evacuate German-Jewish and non-Jewish refugees from the Czech interior as quickly as possible in order to preserve the Czech character of the interior with an angry response. The editors assured the officials of the Association of Czech-Jews that when they requested visas for Palestine from the Zionists, they could be sure they would not be granted any.[246]

When they found themselves seriously threatened, the Jews of the Bohemian Lands realized that the Zionists were much better prepared for the new situation, thanks to their experience with the German-Jewish refugees, their extensive organisational structure and many supporters, their contacts with people abroad, and, last but not least, the ideology of Jewish nationalism. These advantages of Zionists, stemming particularly from their having a certain influence on the granting of some visas, also entailed, however, a great deal of responsibility and self-sacrifice.

On 15 March 1939, the day the Germans occupied the rump Czecho-Slovakia and the Protectorate of Bohemia and Moravia was established, the leading Czechoslovak Zionists (Kahn, März, Edelstein, Friedmann, Otto Zucker and Chaim Hoffmann) met in Kahn's flat to discuss the drastically changed situation. Some of them complained that leaders and instructors had not yet emigrated to Palestine because the Zionist movement was urging them to stay in Czechoslovakia where they were needed. Now they were in the Nazi trap and had to be helped. Edelstein opposed that view:

> for years the Zionists had claimed to be the true and responsible leaders of the Jewish people, and yet they had never really succeeded in reaching the Jewish masses. This was a historical moment: the Jewish population felt lost and were looking for someone to lead them. They could not be abandoned now. Mass emigration might have to be organised, or, if this too proved impossible, the Zionist leaders would have to face the problem of protecting the multitude until the storm had passed, and, whatever happened, their place was now at the head of Jewry.[247]

---

[246] Otta Stross, 'Válka židovská', *Rozvoj*, no. 47 (1938): 2.
[247] Bondy, *'Elder of the Jews'*, 119.

Conclusion

The Jews of Bohemia have often been seen as a community between Czechs and Germans.[1] This widespread conception is clearly an oversimplification of a complex situation and can easily lead to misinterpretation. First, it presupposes distinct groups of people with assumed clear lines between each other. This notion is inaccurate since bilingualism and indifference to nationality were common among the inhabitants of Bohemia, particularly in Prague, and were not specific to Jews.[2] Second, it assumes that Jews stood apart from the debates about national narratives, that they were only passive bystanders and mostly victims in the Czech-German conflict.[3] But many Jews, like many of their Christian neighbours, were active in a national movement; they became members of Czech or German

---

[1] Ruth Kestenberg-Gladstein, 'The Jews between Czechs and Germans in the Historic Lands, 1848–1918', in *The Jews of Czechoslovakia. Historical Studies and Surveys*, vol. I (Philadelphia, 1968), 21–71; Eduard Goldstücker, 'Jews between Czechs and Germans around 1848', *Leo Baeck Institute Year Book* 17 (1972): 61–71; Wilma A. Iggers, 'Juden zwischen Tschechen und Deutschen,' *Zeitschrift für Ostforschung* 37 (1988): 428–42; Jan Havránek, 'Židé mezi Čechy a Němci v Praze', in *Židé v české a polské občanské společnosti*, ed. Jaroslav Valenta (Prague, 1999), 27–35; Marek Nekula and Walter Koschmal, eds., *Juden zwischen Deutschen und Tschechen: Sprachliche und kulturelle Identitäten in Böhmen, 1800–1945* (Munich, 2006).
[2] See Zahra, *Kidnapped Souls*; Koeltzsch, 'Geteilte Kulturen'; Judson, *Guardians of the Nations*; Shumsky, 'Historiografiyah, le'umiyut ve-du-le'umiyut'; Martin Wein, 'Yehudim czecho-germanim ve-tu lo? T'guvah le-ma'amaro shel dimitry shumsky', *Zion* 70, no. 3 (2005): 383–92.
[3] That the Czech-German conflict should not be the key for understanding antisemitism in Bohemia was persuasively shown by Michal Frankl, *Emancipace od židů*, 246–71.

political parties; and they accepted the German or the Czech national narratives. Others followed the Zionist narrative.

Some historians interpret Zionism in Bohemia as an 'escape' from the Czech-German national conflict.[4] In contrast, Dimitry Shumsky argues that Prague Zionists not only did not want to escape the Czech-German conflict, but actually sought to profit from their Prague experience. The multilingual environment, which they were part of, led them, he argues, to criticize ethno-nationalism. This became even more evident in their involvement in Brit Shalom, an organisation which favoured the idea of a bi-national state in Palestine.[5] I share the view that cultural Zionism in Bohemia occupies a unique place in the history of Zionism.[6] As I have sought to demonstrate in my analysis of the interwar Zionist movement, the focus of many Bohemian Zionists changed after World War I, because of the opportunity to develop Jewish nationalism as a political movement with representatives at nearly all levels of the state administration. Nevertheless, many pre-war contacts and ideas remained, which I have endeavoured to demonstrate particularly by comparing the political activities of the Bohemian Zionists with those of Buber and of Weizmann.

Still, one has to be cautious in interpreting the ideas of Hugo Bergmann and other members of the Bar Kochba association. In contrast to Herzl or later revisionist Zionists, they did not see Zionism as the 'solution to the Jewish question' by Jews' emigrating to Palestine and creating an independent Jewish state. Influenced by Buber, they advocated a Jewish renascence and the search for their Jewish roots. Their criticism of political Zionism did not mean, however, that their ideas were not based on ethnocentric thinking. Manfred Voigts's thorough analysis clearly demonstrates that the cultural Zionists—Martin Buber and Hugo Bergmann in particular—were strongly influenced by the ideas of the Romantic German philosopher Johann Gottlieb Fichte (1762-1814), especially his *Reden an die deutsche Nation* (Addresses to the German Nation, 1808). Apart from the similarity of some of their writings, in which Germans were only substituted for by Jews, Buber and Bergmann also adopted Fichte's vocabulary, including the term *Blutgemeinschaft* (community of blood).[7] This at the end supports the idea that we should not understand Bohemian

---

[4] Most explicitly Rozenblit, *Reconstructing a National Identity*, 36-37, 124-25, 146.
[5] Shumsky, *Beyn prag li-yerushalayim*.
[6] Apart from the works of Shumsky see also Kieval, *The Making of Czech Jewry*, 93-154; Spector, *Prague Territories*, 135-59; Spector, 'Another Zionism'; Bruce, *Kafka and Cultural Zionism*.
[7] Manfred Voigts, „Wir sollen alle kleine Fichtes werden!" *Johann Gottlieb Fichte als Prophet der Kultur-Zionisten* (Berlin and Vienna, 2003). See also the analysis of Buber's *Three Addresses on Judaism* in Hillel Kieval, *Making of Czech Jewry*, 127-36.

Zionism as a smokescreen for nationally undecided Jews. Voigts's analysis puts the ideology of Bohemian Zionists into the context of other national movements that all claimed to be based on an ethnic understanding of nationalism. He shows that Zionists, like Czechs and Germans, were following a similar ideological pattern. The construction of the ethnic basis of the Jewish nation was a major concern of the interwar Zionists as well, as has been persuasively shown by Tatjana Lichtenstein, who has analysed the writings of the Zionist statistician František Friedmann.[8]

A key problem in interpreting the national identities of the Bohemian Jews lies in conflating three different perspectives on the matter. There were Jewish organisations which favoured different national narratives. These are the focus of my book. I have analysed the development of the ideology and organisational structure of the Czech-Jewish and the Zionist movements and also the reasons for the absence of a German national movement among Bohemian Jews in the interwar period. This is, from my point of view, the crucial perspective. The organised movements offered national narratives that were discussed in the Jewish as well as in the non-Jewish press. They shaped public opinion on the matter. Moreover, the national affiliation of Jews was also a political matter of state importance and the leaders of these two movements competed for privileged positions in negotiations with the state authorities regarding the Jews of the country.

The history of these movements does not, however, mirror the complex matter of the national identities of Jews who were not active members of any such movement. For instance, as we have seen, the organisational failure of the Czech-Jewish movement was actually caused primarily by the far-reaching integration into Czech-speaking society by Jews who no longer felt any need to organise in special Jewish organisations. National identities from the perspective of most Jews outside the organisational structure of nationally minded Jews have not been discussed in this book.

The third perspective is that of the state. The Czechoslovak state, like all other nation-states, tried to ascertain and to influence the national identities of its citizens. The state, by means of the census, claimed to be able to know the size of its national minorities and sought to force its citizens to choose one nationality only. Moreover, by means of the criteria it presented in the census, the state tried to diminish the role of minorities. In Czechoslovakia, this was most obvious in the state policy towards the Jews. Here, Czech politicians successfully combined all the favourable aspects in question: Jews could either choose their nationality according to their mother tongue or claim to be of Jewish nationality. In Bohemia, in

---

[8] Lichtenstein, 'Making Jews at Home', 105–12.

the Czech interior particularly, where the integration of Jews into Czech society proceeded very successfully, Jews could strengthen the 'Czechoslovak' nation. In Moravia, most Bohemian border regions, Slovakia and Subcarpathian Ruthenia, Jews who claimed to be Jewish by nationality weakened the German, Magyar and Ruthenian minorities. Moreover, because of extensive propaganda by the state and by the Zionists, the recognition of Jewish nationality in the census was also used to demonstrate the democratic character of Czechoslovakia. And, in addition to the pragmatic arguments of the Czech nationalists and the Zionists, the arguments for the recognition developed by the philosophers Masaryk, Rádl and Krejčí were indeed based on their democratic view that Jews should be given an opportunity to express their special national demands.

To confuse or conflate the perspective of the Jews with that of the state is misleading. The number of Jews (by religion) of a certain nationality as ascertained by the census tells us little about the subjective national identities of those people. One can only be sure that the Czech-Jews claimed to be 'Czechoslovaks' and the Zionists to be Jews. But otherwise a whole range of interpretations is possible. Many bilingual people of Jewish origin declared themselves as belonging to the 'Czechoslovak' nation, while many German, Magyar or Yiddish-speaking people chose Jewish nationality because they understood the strategy of the state and wanted to be loyal. Tens of thousands of Jews, in Slovakia and Subcarpathian Ruthenia in particular, declared Jewish nationality because they understood that religion played a crucial role in their lives but they did not understand Judaism as a national concept.

It is nevertheless true that the legal framework and the national propaganda of the state had an impact on all Jewish national movements. The first reason was that because of this framework Jewish nationalist organisations could count on state support, and their importance grew. The second reason was that all the national narratives were influenced by the Jews' loyalty to the Czechoslovak state. Consequently, the German-speaking Jews did not develop any pro-German propaganda among Jews and often switched to the Czech language or became Zionists. This development was accelerated after the Nazis came to power in Germany. And, unlike some Bohemian Germans of the *völkisch* movement, the Jews who decided for German nationality never questioned the sovereign rights of the Czechoslovak state over the whole territory of the Bohemian Lands, including the German-speaking border regions. They understood that they were now members of a national minority in a state that advocated the rights of Czechs and Slovaks. In contrast to the 'irredentists' or 'negativists', the 'activist' German political parties, which supported the Czechoslovak government until 1938, could therefore always count on a considerable number of votes from German-speaking Jews. This same respect for the Czechs' right to the territory of the Bohemian Lands was also evident amongst the Zionists. In contrast to the Bund in Poland, which advocated Jewish autonomist rights there, the Jewish nationalists in the Bohemian Lands operated with the conception of a Jewish homeland in Palestine (though most of them did not plan to emigrate there). It is obvious that Czech-Jews accepted the Czech 'historical' right to the Bohemian Lands.[9]

My book has endeavoured to trace the different national narratives that were developed by the Bohemian Jews in the interwar period. The question of the national identity of the Bohemian Jews must be understood in the wider cultural, political and social contexts. Highly urbanized, mostly middle class, turning away from Orthodox Judaism, and rapidly integrating culturally into the surrounding community, the Jews of Bohemia displayed all the features of 'western Jewry'. Moreover, before World War I the Bohemian Lands did not experience Jewish immigration from Galicia and Tsarist Russia. Those Jews, by contrast, increased the size of the Jewish communities elsewhere in central and western Europe. This phenomenon played a central role in the history of the Jews of the Bohemian Lands, because it was these eastern European Jewish migrants who formed the Jewish working classes of Berlin, Vienna, Paris and London, and added their Yiddish culture to the cultures of these capital cities. A considerable number of these refugees also swelled the ranks of the local Orthodox Jews. The Jews of Bohemia were almost more 'western' than the Jews of western Europe: neither Yiddish culture nor an important class of Jewish workers existed in Bohemia, and the absence of eastern European immigrants only confirmed the secular nature of the Jews of Bohemia. This state of affairs was not changed even by the Galician refugees, who came to Bohemia during World War I, since most of them soon left the country before the war's end. Indeed, even the Jews of Subcarpathian Ruthenia, though they had moved to the Bohemian Lands in considerable numbers, particularly to Prague, were soon largely integrated into the local Jewish community.

Two periods of relative political and social peace in Bohemia were key to the Jews' integration into the surrounding society. The first period began with the achievement of equal rights for the Jews in 1867 and lasted until the 1890s, which saw expanded suffrage in elections to the Reichsrat

---

[9] For a comprehensive analysis of Czech political conceptions of national territory, see Peter Haslinger, *Nation und Territorium im tschechischen politischen Diskurs 1880-1938* (Munich, 2010).

at Vienna, the Badeni Language Ordinances and the Hilsner Affair, all of which fanned the flames of nationalism and antisemitism. The second period was the years of the first Czechoslovak Republic. Though pogroms and antisemitic outbursts lasted for more than a year after the declaration of Czechoslovak independence in October 1918, the 1920s and most of the 1930s were a period of relative calm. Until the Second Republic, established right after the Munich Agreement of September 1938, antisemitism was largely suppressed in Bohemia.

The question remains, however, of why antisemitism during the First Republic was so much less palpable in the Czech parts of the country than it was in the German-speaking borderlands, Slovakia and Subcarpathian Ruthenia, where the situation was far more complicated. An important role in this was played primarily by the way in which the Czechoslovak Republic had been established. It was officially a state of Czechoslovaks, yet the 'Czechoslovak' nation was almost exclusively a creation of Czech politicians and it failed to satisfy most Slovaks as well as the German and Magyar inhabitants of the new country. The national and political aspirations of the Czechs, by contrast, had been met to the greatest possible extent. Moreover, at the Paris Peace Conference in Versailles Czechoslovakia came out on the side of the victors (even though the vast majority of its men had been in the Austro-Hungarian Army). Czechs could therefore allow themselves to act magnanimously towards the numerically insignificant Jewish community. Furthermore, many Czech politicians were fully aware of Czechoslovakia's dependence on the Allies for the very existence of the country. Consequently, they urged the public and deputies to the Czechoslovak National Assembly to act against antisemitism and to work to maintain Czechoslovakia's democratic reputation. Another factor that contributed to the relatively smooth integration of the Jews into Czech society during the First Republic was the high degree of secularization, not only of its Christians, but also of its Jews. This is reflected, for example, in the high proportion of mixed marriages.

Another reason for the lower incidence of overt antisemitism during the First Republic (and one that is usually given as the primary reason) is the role and authority of President Masaryk. He influenced the political atmosphere of the Bohemian Lands to such an extent that antisemitism was generally considered unacceptable in politics and society. During the Hilsner Affair, decades before Czechoslovak independence, Masaryk had rejected outright the accusation of blood libel (the legend of ritual murder) and antisemitism in general. Because of the Masaryk cult in the First Republic, antisemitism in politics and generally in public was considered an attack on the very foundations of Czechoslovak statehood. Consequently, antisemitism, particularly in the 1930s, was an ideological weapon of the irredentist movements of the German, Polish and Slovak national minorities. And Czech society returned to antisemitic rhetoric and antisemitic acts during the Second Republic, when the Masaryk cult and the idea of the Czechoslovak Republic were being subjected to harsh criticism.[10]

The foregoing would suggest that the Czech-Jews, who sought the Jews' integration into Czech society, were successful in finding support in the interwar period, unlike the Zionist movement, which emphasized the otherness of the Jews. But the situation was far more complicated than that, and, at the level of political organisations, one could well argue that the opposite was true. In matters related to the Jews of Czechoslovakia the institutions of the Jewish nationalists (mainly the Jewish National Council, the Jewish Party and the Zionist Organisation of Czechoslovakia) became the preferred partners of the government and the president. From the perspective of Jewish society as well, the Zionists, by means of their periodicals, *Selbstwehr* (Self-defence) and *Židovské zprávy* (Jewish News), which were subscribed to by many more people than just adherents of Zionism, shaped public opinion on Jewish affairs. The periodical of the Czech-Jews, *Rozvoj* (Development), could not compete with them in terms of circulation. Also, a comparison of the number of people in the First Republic buying shekels (the membership dues paid by Zionist Organisation members) with the number of members of the largest Czech-Jewish organisation, the Association of Czech-Jews (Svaz Čechů židů), leads one to the same conclusion. In 1938, the Association of Czech-Jews had slightly more than 2,000 members. The Zionists who paid dues numbered more than 12,500 in the Bohemian Lands in the same year. Even if the payment of shekel fees were a mere formality for many Jews, that would not sufficiently explain the six-fold difference in membership.

In no other European society into which most Jews had integrated did adherents of Jewish nationalism win greater social and political status and respect than in Bohemia. There are several explanations for the organisational success of Zionism and the failure of the organised Czech-Jewish movement. The main reason for the lack of interest in the Czech-Jewish movement during the First Republic was, we have seen, the high degree of Jewish integration into the Czech national and cultural community. Many sympathizers of the Czech-Jewish movement joined, for example, the Sokol gymnastics organisation instead of Czech-Jewish associations; they subscribed to Czech periodicals according to their political leanings; and they voted predominantly for Czech political parties.

---

[10] See also Michal Frankl, 'Antisemitism in Bohemian Lands', in *Antisemitism in Eastern Europe. History and Present in Comparison*, ed. Hans-Christian Petersen and Samuel Salzborn (Frankfurt am Main, 2010), 35-6.

The situation was different in other countries. In neighbouring Germany, for example, the Centralverein deutscher Staatsbürger jüdischen Glaubens, the umbrella organisation of the German Jewish integrationists, experienced its greatest boom during the Weimar Republic. With 72,500 members in 1924, it was the largest Jewish organisation in Germany.[11] This disproportion is convincingly explained by the different political situation and social climate in Germany, where the atmosphere was very tense after the humiliating terms of the peace agreement and then in the economic crisis beginning in 1923. Membership of the Centralverein grew because many integrated German Jews felt threatened by the high degree of antisemitism.

Although the Czech-Jews were surprised by the pogroms and outbursts at the beginning of the First Republic, the situation became so much calmer in the course of the 1920s that the Czech-Jewish organisations, unlike the 'assimilationist' organisations in Germany, did not have to play the role of the defenders of Jewish rights. Czechoslovak independence meant the fulfilment of the Czech-Jews' programme in another respect as well. Not only did integration into surrounding society continue, but the vast majority of the Jews of Bohemia and Moravia also reoriented from German culture to Czech. Compared to other 'assimilationist' movements in western Europe, the Czech-Jewish movement came into being in order to win over Jews from the Czech areas for Czech culture and Czech national consciousness. For that reason their adversaries initially were the Jews who had already integrated into the German-speaking population rather than the Zionists. The creation of the Czechoslovak Republic was thus understood as the crowning of the Czech-Jews' efforts, because it considerably accelerated the process of becoming Czech. German-language Jewish schools were closed down, Czech (next to Hebrew) easily became the language of religious service in the vast majority of synagogues, Jews increasingly subscribed to Czech periodicals, and the number of Jewish children at Czech schools increased rapidly.

Among those Jews who remained loyal to the organised Czech-Jewish movement in the interwar period, two quite different groups predominated. First of all there were the nationally oriented Jews, who were in control of the leadership of the Association of Czech-Jews. Their efforts to demonstrate to the surrounding population that Czechness was more important to them than Jewishness even led them to adopt a xenophobic position against refugees from Germany in the 1930s. At this time, the Kapper Students' Society (Akademický spolek Kapper) stood in opposi-

---

[11] Barkai, 'Wehr dich!', 120.

Conclusion • 249

Figure C.1. Eva Pokorná (on the left), a Shoah survivor, shown here in her Sokol uniform.

tion to the Association of Czech-Jews. It had a unique conception of the cultural symbiosis of the Czechs and the Jews, continuing the ideas of the leading Czech-Jewish thinker, Jindřich Kohn.

The Zionist movement developed its organisational structure during the First Republic, thus making itself far more visible. The largest bastions of Zionism were in German-speaking borderlands, Moravia, Silesia and Prague. By contrast, in the Czech-speaking interior of the country (except Prague), the Zionists met with a minimum of support. In 1938, 56 per cent of all Zionists from the Bohemian Lands lived in Moravia and Silesia; 24 per cent of them lived in the Sudetenland, 14 per cent in Prague, and 6 per cent in the remaining areas, which were mostly Czech.[12]

The Jews' lack of interest in the organised Czech-Jewish movement still does not explain the Zionists' success in talks with the Czechoslovak government and the strong position that Jewish nationalists won amongst the Jews of the Bohemian Lands, which was unparalleled in countries with predominantly western kinds of Jewish community. Among the many reasons that Jewish nationalists so surprisingly made their way into the political and cultural circles of the First Republic are the similarity of the demands of the Czech and Jewish politicians who sought to achieve the self-determination of their own nations (as expressed in Woodrow Wilson's Fourteen Points), the sympathies of leading public figures like Masaryk, Krejčí, Rádl and Novák, the great support for Zionism in Moravia in consequence of the special historical and demographic conditions of the Jews there, and the joining of Slovakia and Subcarpathian Ruthenia to the Bohemian Lands in October 1918.

The Czech-Jewish movement certainly increased the number of people with 'Czechoslovak' nationality in Bohemia. It was, however, the Zionist movement and its conception of Jewish nationality, which helped—from the perspective of the Czech politicians—to 'neutralize' the vast majority of Jews in other parts of the republic, who would otherwise, according to their mother tongue, decide for German, Magyar, or Ruthenian nationality during the census. The political strategies of the Zionists and the Czech politicians were therefore fully convergent.

A great advantage of the Jewish nationalists was that they had institutions that the Czech-Jews lacked for the promotion of their interests. As early as at the turn of the century the Czech-Jews were working, for example, with the Czech National Council. The archives of the Czech National Council (renamed the Czechoslovak National Council after the war) contain various Czech-Jewish petitions, statements and reports of antisemitic

---

[12] CZA, Organisation Department Collection, S5/435, Franz Kahn to Leo Lauterbach, letter of 14 October 1938.

outbursts. When they thought it necessary, the members of the Council passed these on to other political bodies. On 22 October 1918, Jewish nationalists set up the Jewish National Council, which aimed to represent all Jews who declared themselves part of the Jewish national minority. The Jewish National Council, the establishment of which the Czech-Jews had tried to prevent, then achieved a much more advantageous position for political talks with the Government and the National Assembly, because it was *de jure* on the same level as the Czechoslovak National Council and now communicated directly with the individual ministries and the police commissioner.

The Jewish Party was also of key importance. Though it did not win seats in the National Assembly till 1929, it won seats on municipal and town councils from the beginning of the 1920s. The importance and success of the Jewish Party is reflected by the number of votes they won in the Bohemian Lands, which was far larger than the number of people who in the censuses declared their nationality as Jewish. This can be explained mainly by the truly moderate programme of the Zionists of the Bohemian Lands. Their loyalty to Czechoslovakia was not seriously doubted by anyone and their political programme was essentially limited to the cultural revival of the Jewish part of the population and the fight against antisemitism.

Relations between the active Czech-Jews and the Zionists during the First Republic were marked by an irreconcilable struggle to gain a privileged position both in the Jewish Community and in relations with leading Czechoslovak politicians. Nevertheless, the two movements had certain features in common. Not only the Czech-Jews and the Zionists, but all Jews in the Bohemian Lands were closely tied to the cultures of their milieus, Czech, German, or both. The social integration of the Jews also proceeded apace in the Bohemian Lands.

Even though the Czech-Jews and the Zionists offered competing national programmes, a closer look at the national narratives of the two movements reveals many similarities in their arguments. A comparison of their two student organisations should help us to make this analogy clear. Wherein exactly lay the difference between the Czech-Jewish members of the Kapper Society, who in the 1930s took an intense interest in their Jewish roots, and, on the other hand, the Zionist students of the Theodor Herzl Society in this period? The members of both societies spoke Czech, lived with Czech culture, and were interested in their roots. The Czech-Jews sought to learn what they as Czechs of Jewish origin could contribute to the Czech nation. The Zionists sought to explain the basis of their Jewish national identity.

Moving to a particular, personal level, we may ask what the difference was between the writer-activists Egon Hostovský and Viktor Fischl, each of whom led one of these societies in the 1930s. Both men never denied their Jewish roots and both were brought up in the Czech cultural milieu. Both men's works are among the best in the Czech literature of their day. Fischl, however, was head of the Jewish national movement; Hostovský was a convinced Czech-Jew. Each man was distinguished by the national identity he preferred. The choice was not determined, however, by knowledge of either Czech or of Hebrew or by the religious convictions or the historical experiences particular to one or the other man or the movement he supported. Indeed, the basic arguments in the propaganda materials of the two national movements are so similar that the idea of their being in opposition to each other is almost risible. The only real difference was in how their programmes were interpreted. No one from either group denied that before emancipation the Jews had constituted a special community of people sharing a common fate, or that in the past the Jewish religion had clearly distinguished and shaped the Jewish people and that this state of affairs had recently changed. Nor did anyone deny that in the nineteenth century and early twentieth century the Jews of Bohemia had integrated into Czech or German society or both, and had previously coexisted with the dominant population for several centuries. In the states of western Europe, by contrast, such co-existence had been interrupted by long-lasting expulsions of Jews.

Czech-Jews as well as Bohemian Zionists were constructing their national narratives from the same 'building blocks'. One side, however, deduced that in terms of nationality they were Czechs, while the other side deduced that they were mainly Jews. Both groups, and we would add German Jews as well, could base their national narrative on a 'usable past' either as Czechs, Germans or Jews, because Bohemian history offered enough shared experiences and events for all three national narratives. What, then, led individual people to choose one interpretation over the other?

The key condition for integration was acceptance by the surrounding society. That is also why the situation in the interwar period seemed somewhat different in the German-speaking borderlands, where, particularly in the 1930s, the German *völkisch* movement was gaining strength and a much higher proportion of young Jews was joining the Zionist movement than elsewhere in the country. In Prague and in the Czech areas until the end of the First Republic the Czechs' and Germans' attitudes towards the Jews were more open and Jews could easily take part in the societies and social activities of the local dominant population. The often almost idyllic co-existence of Jews and Gentiles, however, was in most places brought to a brutal end by the Munich Agreement, the Reich's annexation of the Sudetenland, and the establishment of the Second Republic. These events made it possible for a wave of nationalist and antisemitic passions to appear among the non-Jewish Czechs in connection with the immediate military threat to the country and the disappointment that followed the political betrayal of Czechoslovakia by France and Great Britain. It was during the Second Republic that young Jews from the Czech areas of Bohemia began to join the Zionist movement in large numbers, whereas the movement had previously been dominated by Jews from German-speaking families.

The Zionists ranks were not filled only with Jews who felt discriminated against by dominant community. Yet it remains unclear, particularly with regard to Prague and the Czech areas, what compelled other individual Jews to join either Zionist or Czech-Jewish organisations. Clearly, rather than linguistic or other cultural differences it was relations in families, among friends, and at school and work, which were crucial. Hostovský and Fischl, for example, each adopted their own parents' national convictions. In other families, national identity differed from one family member to another. One's early school years, workplace, university life, or even simply a chance event putting an individual in the milieu of one or the other national persuasions were often decisive in the choice of nationality.

On the whole, the question of the national identity of the Jews of Bohemia was unique and complicated mainly because there were only small differences between the possible choices. The Jews of Bohemia were in most cases united by their love for their native land, Bohemia, which stemmed in part from a lack of substantial Jewish immigration. They were also bound by their lukewarm attitude to the Jewish religion and, except for Communists of Jewish origin, by their loyalty to the Czechoslovak state and its leading representatives, Masaryk and Beneš. Because of that shared basis, it was not at all unusual for individual Jews from Bohemia to adopt another national identity without making great changes in their everyday lives; nor was it unusual to be without any clearly defined national identity. Neither an individual's mother tongue nor the political programme of the various nationalist movements played much of a role in leading an individual to prefer one nationality over another. What was decisive, however, was one's social contacts with both the Jews and the Gentiles of the country.

BIBLIOGRAPHY

I. Primary Sources

a) Archival Collections

Czech Republic

Archiv hlavního města Prahy (Prague City Archives): Spolkový katastr.
Archiv Kanceláře prezidenta republiky (Archives of the [Czechoslovak] President's Office).
Archiv Univerzity Karlovy (Archives of Charles University): Všestudentský archiv, Akademický senát Německé univerzity.
Archiv Ústavu Tomáše G. Masaryka (Archives of the Tomáš Garrigue Masaryk Institute): fond TGM-R.
Archiv Židovského muzea v Praze (Archives of the Jewish Museum in Prague): Protokoly schůzí reprezentace ŽNOP, 1918–39; collections regarding Jewish associations.
Národní archiv, Praha (National Archives, Prague): Ministerstva vnitra presidium, 1918–38; Národní rada česká/československá, 1900–38; Presidium zemského úřadu, 1918–38; Emil Margulies Collection; Policejní presidium, 1918–38.
Památník národního písemnictví (Literature Archives, Museum of Czech Literature): Rudolf Fuchs, Otokar Fischer, Arne Novák Papers.

Israel

Central Archives for the History of the Jewish People: Gustav Sicher Papers.
Central Zionist Archives (Jerusalem): Bar Kochba / Barissia (A 317), Irma Pollak (A 439), Oskar Rabinowicz (A 87), Jirmejahu Oskar Neumann (A 331), Keren Kayemeth Leisrael (KKL 5), Leo Herrmann (A 145), Documents on the History of Zionism in Czechoslovakia (F 15), Organization Department (S5), The Zionist Organization – Central Office, London (Z4).
Jabotinsky Institute (Tel Aviv).
Jewish National & University Library (Jerusalem): Hugo Bergmann, Martin Buber Papers.

Austria
Österreichisches Staatsarchiv (Vienna): Neues Politisches Archiv, 1918-38.

b) Periodicals

Bar Kochba Zirkular, ed. Richard Pacovský. Tel Aviv, 1954-72.
B'nai B'rith: Monatsblätter der Grossloge für den Čechoslovakischen Staat, 1920-38.
Blätter für die jüdische Frau, 1926.
Jüdische Presse, 1930.
Jüdischer Almanach, 1918-38.
Juedisches Pressbureau Wien, 1918.
Kalendář česko-židovský, 1918-38.
Listy židovské mládeže, 1923-24.
Medina Iwrit, 1936-38.
Mitteilungsblatt der Hitachduth Olej Germania, 1938.
Rozhled, 1917-20.
Rozvoj, 1918-38.
Selbstwehr, 1918-38.
Tel Chaj, 1936-37.
Tribuna, 1919-24.
Věstník akademického spolku Kapper, later Kapper, 1932-36.
Věstník židovských náboženských obcí v českých zemích a na Slovensku, 1923-38.
Die Wahrheit, 1927-38.
Die Welt, 1897.
Židovské zprávy, 1918-38.
Židovský kalendář, 1918-38.
Židovský socialista, 1919-20.

c) Books, Pamphlets and Articles

Baum, Karl. 'Das jüdische Prag der Gegenwart in Zahlen'. Monatschrift für Geschichte und Wissenschaft des Judentums 73 (1929): 349-65.
Bericht über die Tätigkeit des Vereins der jüd. Hochschüler Bar Kochba in Prag während des 34. Vereinssemesters (Winter 1909-1910) erstattet... vom Obmanne Phil. Hugo Herrmann. Prague, 1910.
Boháč, Antonín. Hlavní město Praha. Studie o obyvatelstvu. Prague, 1923.
———. 'Národnost při druhém sčítání lidu'. Statistický obzor 12, nos. 1-2 (1931): 14-30.
———. 'Rádlův Sociologický rozbor naší národnostní statistiky'. Československý statistický věstník nos. 1-2 (1930): 1-22.
Born, Jürgen. Franz Kafka. Kritik und Rezeption zu seinen Lebzeiten 1912-1924. Frankfurt am Main, 1979.
Brod, Max. Die dritte Phase des Zionismus. Berlin, 1917.
———. Im Kampf um das Judentum. Vienna and Berlin, 1920.
———. Sozialismus im Zionismus. Vienna and Berlin, 1920.
Brody, Heinrich. Widerspricht der Zionismus unserer Religion? Leipzig, 1909.
Buber, Martin. At the Turning: Three Addresses on Judaism. New York, 1952.
———. Drei Reden über das Judentum. Frankfurt am Main, 1911.
———. Tři řeči o židovství. Prague, 1912.

Československá statistika, sv. 37, řada VI, vol. III (Sčítání lidu, sešit 6). Prague, 1927.
Československá statistika, sv. 9, řada VI, vol. I (Sčítání lidu, sešit 1). Prague, 1924.
Československá statistika, sv. 98, řada VI, vol. I (Sčítání lidu, sešit 7). Prague, 1934.
Dějiny českožidovského hnutí. Prague, 1932.
Donath, Oskar. 'Siegfried Kapper'. In *Jahrbuch der Gesellschaft für Geschichte der Juden in der Čechoslovakischen Republik* 6 (1934): 323-42.
——. *Židé a židovství v české literatuře 19. století.* Brno, 1923.
——. *Židé a židovství v české literatuře 19. a 20. století.* Prague, 1930.
Epstein, Oskar. *Proklamations- oder Tatsachen-Zionismus?* Prague, 1925.
Fousek, František. *Příručka ku čtení bursovních a obchodních zpráv v denním tisku.* Prague, 1922.
Friedmann, František. *Mravnost či oportunita? Několik poznámek k anketě akad. spolku 'Kapper' v Brně.* Prague, 1927.
——. 'Pražští Židé', *Židovský kalendář* 10 (1929-30): 148-207.
——. *Strana židovská.* Prague, 1931.
——. 'Židé v Čechách'. In *Die Juden und Judengemeinden Böhmens in Vergangenheit und Gegenwart*, ed. Hugo Gold. Brno, 1934: 729-30.
Fünfzig Semester 'Barissia'. Festschrift. Prague, 1928.
Goldelman, Salomon. *Das arbeitende Palästina: Zionistischer Sozialismus.* Prague, n. d.
[Guth, Otakar] dr. G. 'Úvodem'. In Viktor Vohryzek, *K židovské otázce: Vybrané úvahy a články.* Prague, 1923: 3-13.
——. *Podstata židovství a jiné úvahy.* Prague, 1925.
Herrmann, Hugo. *The First Five Years.* Johannesburg, n. d.
'Interpelacja koła żydowskiego i odpowiedź p. Ministra spraw wewnętrnych w sprawie rubryki „narodowość" na formularzu spisowym ludności oraz naruszania praw języka żydowskiego w instrukcji spisowej'. *Sprawy narododościowe* VI, no. 1 (1932): 91-93.
Das jüdische Prag: Eine Sammelschrift mit Texten von Max Brod [et al.]. Mit einer Einführung von Robert Weltsch. Kronberg, [1917] 1978.
Die jüdische Aktion: Programmschrift des Herdervereines in Prag. Prague, 1919.
Kafka, Franz. *Brief an den Vater.* Prague 1919.
——. *Letter to His Father*, trans. Ernst Kaiser and Eithne Wilkins. New York, 1996.
Klineberger, Bohdan. *Náboženský cit.* Prague, 1906.
Kohn, Jindřich. *Asimilace a věky*, vols. I-III. Prague, 1936.
Kraus, Mořic, ed. *České modlitby při veřejné bohoslužbě v synagoze spolku 'Or-Tomid' v Praze.* 2nd ed. Prague, 1899.
Kritika sionismu. Prague, n. d.
'Kwestja narodowościowa w programie drugiego powszechnego spisu ludności Rzeczypospolitej Polskiej. Wywiad z Generalnym Komisarzem Spisowym p. Dr. Rajmundem Buławskim'. *Sprawy narododościowe* VI, no. 1 (1932): 1-27.
Lederer, Edvard [Eduard]. *Epištola k Čechům-židům o tom, jak se dosud tajnosnubná panna 'Tribuna' šťastně provdala a co všechno tomu předcházelo.* Prague, 1927.
——. *Kapitoly o židovství a židovstvu*, vols. I-II. Prague, 1925.
Lederer, Viktor. *Českožidovské otázky.* Prague, 1899.
Margulies, Emil. *Zionismus und Deutsche Fortschrittspartei: Offener Brief an die Führer der Partei in Prag.* Teplitz-Schönau, 1904.
Masaryk, Tomáš Garrigue. *Světová revoluce.* Prague, 1930.
Mendes-Flohr, Paul R., ed. *A Land of Two Peoples: Martin Buber on Jews and Arabs.* New York, 1983.
Neue Wege: Festschrift. Prague, 1903.
Neumann, Ervín. *Práce, program a cíl Svazu Čechů židů v ČSR.* Prague, 1937.

Peroutka, Ferdinand. *Budování státu: Výbor 1918-1923*. Prague, 1998.
Příležitostné řeči pro českožidovské kazatele, trans. and ed. Josef Kraus. Prague, 1895.
Rádl, Emanuel. *Národnost jako vědecký problem*. Prague, 1929.
Rychnovsky, Ernst, Oskar Donath, and Friedrich Thieberger, eds. *Masaryk a židovství*. Prague, 1931.
Sionismus: Idea a skutečnost. Prague, 1926.
Stein, Maximilian. *Vorträge und Ansprachen von*. Frankfurt am Main, 1929.
Stross, Otta. *Vývoj židovské otázky po světové válce*. Prague, 1937.
Teytz, Viktor. *Několik poznámek k otázce českožidovské*. Prague, 1913.
Vohryzek, Viktor. *K židovské otázce: Vybrané úvahy a články*. Prague, 1923.
Vom Judentum. Leipzig, 1913.
Výroční zpráva Akademického spolku 'Kapper' v Praze za rok 1921-1922. Prague, 1922.
Waksman, Tsvi Hirsh. *In land fun maharal un masaryk*. Warsaw, 1936.
Weltsch, Felix. *Allgemeiner Zionismus: Eine ideologische Skizze*. Prague, 1936.
———. *Das Wagnis der Mitte*. Mährisch Ostrau, 1937.
Zaleski, Władysław Józef. *Międzynarodowa ochrona mniejszości*. Warsaw, 1932.
Židovský studente viz . . . Prague, n.d., c. 1937.
Zpráva z Jednoty pro péči hospodářskou a kulturní. Prague, 5 December 1920.

d) Letters, Memoirs and Diaries

Avni, Jizchak. 'Die zionistische Jugendbewegung in der ČSR'. In *Deutsche Jugend in Böhmen 1918-1938: Beiträge des Waldkraiburger Kolloquiums*, ed. Peter Becher. Benediktbeuern, 1993: 97-108.
Bergmann, Hugo. *Tagebücher und Briefe, 1901-1948*, vol. 1, ed. Miriam Sambursky. Königstein, 1985.
Blumenfeld, Kurt. *Erlebte Judenfrage: Ein Vierteljahrhundert deutscher Zionismus*. Stuttgart, 1962.
———. *Im Kampf um den Zionismus: Briefe aus fünf Jahrzehnten*, ed. Miriam Sambursky and Jochanan Ginat. Stuttgart, 1976.
Brod, Max, ed. *Franz Kafka. The Diaries 1910-1923*, trans. Joseph Kresh and Martin Greenberg. New York, 1976.
———. *Über Franz Kafka*. Frankfurt am Main, 1974.
———. *Der Prager Kreis*. Frankfurt am Main, 1979.
———. *Streitbares Leben*. Munich, 1960.
———. 'Zikhronot mi-t'kufat ha-hitbolelut'. In *Prag vi-yerushalayim*, ed. Felix Weltsch. Jerusalem, 1955: 52-56.
Čapková, Kateřina. 'Pak to ale dopadlo ještě jinak: Rozhovor s Viktorem Fischlem o českých sionistech, asimilantech a židovské politice'. *Věstník židovských náboženských obcí v českých zemích a na Slovensku*, no. 3 (2001): 6-7, 15.
Fischl, Viktor. *Hovory s Janem Masarykem*. Prague, 1991.
Fuchs, Rudolf. 'Erinnerungen an Franz Kafka'. In Max Brod, *Über Franz Kafka*. Frankfurt am Main, 1974: 367-69.
Gordon, Aaron David. 'Briefe aus Palästina'. *Der Jude* 1, no. 10 (January 1917): 643-49; no. 11 (February 1917): 728-36; no. 12 (March 1917): 794-801.
Guth, Otakar, ed. *Vzpomínky a úvahy 1876-1926*. Prague, 1926.
Haas, Willy. *Die literarische Welt. Erinnerungen*. Munich, 1958.
Herrmann, Leo. 'Erinnerungen eines sudetendeutschen Zionisten'. *Mitteilungsblatt der Hitachduth Olej Germania*, April 1938.

Hostovský, Egon. 'The Czech-Jewish Movement'. In *The Jews of Czechoslovakia*, vol. II. Philadelphia and New York, 1971: 148-54.
Kafka, Franz. *Briefe 1902-1924*. Frankfurt am Main, 1958.
——. *Letters to Felice*, ed. Erich Heller and Jürgen Born. Trans. James Stern and Elisabeth Duckworth. New York, 1973.
Kohn, Hans. *Martin Buber, sein Werk und seine Zeit: Ein Beitrag zur Geistesgeschichte Mitteleuropas 1880-1930*, 3rd ed. Cologne, 1961.
Kohner, Walter. 'Portrait einer Studentenverbindung'. *Zeitschrift für die Geschichte der Juden*, nos. 2-3 (1966): 125-32.
Kreutzberger, Max, ed. *Georg Landauer: Der Zionismus im Wandel dreier Jahrzehnte*. Tel Aviv, 1957.
Makovíni, Karol. *Svedectvo o Židoch na Slovensku*. Prague, 1936.
Mauthner, Fritz. *Prager Jugendjahre: Erinnerungen*. Frankfurt am Main, 1969.
Neumann, Jirmejahu. 'Zur Geschichte der zionistischen Jugendbewegung in der Slowakei'. *Zeitschrift für die Geschichte der Juden*, nos. 2-3 (1966): 133-42.
Peroutka, Ferdinand. *deníky … dopisy … vzpomínky*, compiled and ed. Slávka Peroutková. Prague, 1995.
Polak, Irma. 'The Zionist Women's Movement'. In *The Jews of Czechoslovakia*, vol. II. Philadelphia and New York, 1971: 137-47.
Rauchberg, Heinrich. *Der nationale Besitzstand in Böhmen*. Leipzig, 1905.
Rhapsody to Tchelet Lavan in Czechoslovakia. Israel, 1996.
Teytz, Viktor. *Několik poznámek k otázce českožidovské*. Prague, 1913.
Tramer, Hans, and Kurt Loewenstein, eds. *Robert Weltsch zum 70. Geburtstag von seinen Freunden*. Tel Aviv, 1961.
Weltsch, Robert. 'Looking Back Over Sixty Years'. *Leo Baeck Yearbook* 27 (1982): 379-90.

II. Secondary Works

Abramson, Henry. *A Prayer for the Government. Ukrainians and Jews in Revolutionary Times, 1917-1920*. Cambridge, 1999.
Anderson, Benedict R. *Imagined Communities. Reflections on the Origin and Spread of Nationalism*. 2nd ed. London, 1991.
Augustine, Dolores L. 'Arriving in the Upper Class: The Wealthy Business Elite of Wilhelmine Germany'. In *The German Bourgeoisie*, ed. David Blackbourn and Richard J. Evans. London and New York, 1991: 46-86.
Báar, Monika. *Historians and Nationalism: East-Central Europe in the Nineteenth Century*. Oxford, 2010.
Bahm, Karl F. 'Beyond the Bourgeoisie: Rethinking Nation, Culture, and Modernity in Nineteenth-Century Central Europe'. *Austrian History Yearbook* 29 (1998): 19-35.
Bakke, Elizabeth. 'The Making of Czechoslovakism in the First Czechoslovak Republic'. In *Loyalitäten in der Tschechoslowakischen Republik 1918-1938. Politische, nationale und kulturelle Zugehörigkeiten*, ed. Martin Schulze Wessel. Munich, 2004: 23-44.
Barkai, Avraham. *'Wehr dich!': Der Centralverein deutscher Staatsbürger jüdischen Glaubens (C.V.), 1893-1938*. Munich, 2002.
Bauer, Yehuda. 'In Search of a Definition of Antisemitism'. In *Approaches to Antisemitism. Context and Curriculum*, ed. Michael Brown. New York and Jerusalem, 1994: 10-23.
Becher, Peter, and Anna Knechtel, eds. *Praha - Prag 1900-1945. Literaturstadt zweier Sprachen*. Passau, 2010.

Beller, Steven. 'Germans and Jews as Central European and "Mitteleuropäisch" Elites'. In *Mitteleuropa: History and Prospects*, ed. Peter Stirk. Edinburgh, 1994: 61-85.
Berger, Natalia, ed. *Where Cultures Meet: The Story of the Jews of Czechoslovakia*. Tel Aviv, 1990.
Berger, Tilman. 'Böhmisch oder Tschechisch? Der Streit über die adäquate Benennung der Landessprache der böhmischen Länder zu Anfang des 20. Jahrhunderts'. In *Franz Kafka im sprachnationalen Kontext seiner Zeit: Sprache und nationale Identität in öffentlichen Institutionen der böhmischen Länder*, ed. Marek Nekula, Ingrid Fleischmann, and Albrecht Greule. Cologne, Weimar and Vienna, 2007: 167-82.
Bergson, Henri. *Œuvres*. Paris, [1889] 1970.
Biale, David, ed. *Cultures of the Jews: A New History*. New York, 2002.
Bihl, Wolfdieter. 'Die Juden'. In *Die Habsburgermonarchie 1848-1918*, vol. III, part 2. Vienna, 1980: 880-948.
Blau, Bruno. 'Nationality among Czechoslovak Jewry'. *Historia Judaica* 10 (1948): 147-54.
Bondy, Ruth. *'Elder of the Jews': Jakob Edelstein of Theresienstadt*, trans. Evelyn Abel. New York, 1989.
Borek, David. *Židovské strany v politickém systému Československa 1918-1938: Kapitoly z politického života státotvorné menšiny*, M.A. thesis, Faculty of Arts, Charles University, Prague, 2002.
Brod, Peter. *Die Antizionismus- und Israelpolitik der UdSSR: Voraussetzungen und Entwicklung bis 1956*. Baden-Baden, 1980.
———. 'Die Juden in der Nachkriegstschechoslowakei'. In *Judenemanzipation - Antisemitismus - Verfolgung in Deutschland, Österreich-Ungarn, den Böhmischen Ländern und in der Slowakei*, ed. Jörg K. Hoensch, Stanislav Biman, and Ľubomír Lipták. Essen, 1999: 211-28.
———. 'Židé v Československu'. In *Židé v Sudetech*. Prague, 2000: 277-83.
Brubaker, Rogers, and Frederick Cooper. 'Beyond "Identity"'. *Theory and Society* 29 (2000): 1-47.
Bruce, Iris. *Kafka and Cultural Zionism: Dates in Palestine*. Madison, 2007.
Bryant, Chad. *Prague in Black: Nazi Rule and Czech Nationalism*. Cambridge, MA, 2007.
———. 'Czech, or German? Nazi Occupation, Postwar Expulsions, and the Origins of the Central European Nation-State'. *European Studies Forum* 31, no. 1 (Spring 2008): 37-42.
Bubeník, Jaroslav, and Jiří Křesťan. 'Zjišťování národnosti a židovská otázka'. In *Postavení a osudy židovského obyvatelstva v Čechách a na Moravě v letech 1939-1945*, ed. Helena Krejčová, and Jana Svobodová. Prague, 1998: 11-39.
Čapková, Kateřina. 'Czechs, Germans, Jews - Where Is the Difference? The Complexity of National Identities of Bohemian Jews, 1918-1938'. *Bohemia* 46, no. 1 (2005): 7-14.
———. 'Jewish Elites in the 19th and 20th Centuries: The B'nai B'rith Order in Central Europe'. *Judaica Bohemiae* 36 (2000): 119-42.
———. 'kafka un der yidisher teater: di mizrakh-eyropeyishe yidn in di oygn fun proger yidn'. *yerusholaymer almanakh* 28 (2008): 362-71.
———. 'Mit *Tribuna* gegen das *Prager Tagblatt*: Der deutsch-tschechische Pressekampf um die jüdischen Leser in Prag'. In *Grenzdiskurse: Zeitungen deutschsprachiger Minderheiten und ihr Feuilleton in Mitteleuropa bis 1939*, ed. Sibylle Schönborn. Essen, 2009: 127-40.
———. 'Piłsudski or Masaryk? Zionist Revisionism in Czechoslovakia 1925-1940'. *Judaica Bohemiae* 35 (1999): 210-39.
———. 'Raum und Zeit als Faktoren der nationalen Identifikation der Prager Juden'. In *Praha-Prag 1900-1945*, ed. Peter Becher, and Anna Knechtel. Passau, 2010: 21-30.

———. 'Specific Features of Zionism in the Czech Lands in the Interwar Period'. *Judaica Bohemiae* 38 (2002): 106-59.

Čapková, Kateřina, and Michal Frankl, *Nejisté útočiště: Československo a uprchlíci před nacismem 1933-1938*. Prague and Litomyšl, 2008 (German edition forthcoming by Böhlau Verlag in 2012).

Cermanová, Iveta. 'Židovské osvícenství v Praze'. *Židovská ročenka* 5768 (2007-08): 42-63.

Claussen, Detlev, *Grenzen der Aufklärung. Die gesellschaftliche Genese des modernen Antisemitismus*. 2nd ed. (Frankfurt am Main, 1994).

Cohen, Gary B. 'Ethnicity and Urban Population Growth: The Decline of the Prague Germans, 1880-1920'. *Studies in East European Social History*, no. 2 (1981): 3-26.

———. 'Jews in German Liberal Politics: Prague, 1880-1914'. *Jewish History* 1, no.1 (1986): 55-74.

———. 'Jews in German Society: Prague, 1860-1914'. *Central European History* 10, no. 1 (1977): 28-54.

———. *The Politics of Ethnic Survival: Germans in Prague, 1861-1914*. 2nd ed. West Lafayette, Indiana, 2006.

Crhová, Marie. 'Sionistická volební politika na konci 20. let'. *Paginae Historiae* (1999): 166-88.

Cullman, Peter Simonstein. *History of the Jews of Schneidemühl: 1641 to the Holocaust*. Bergenfield, 2006.

Czajecka, Bogusława. *Archiwum Związku Żydowskich Stowarzyszeń Humanitarnych 'B'nei B'rith' w Krakowie (1892-1938): Zarys Dziejów Związku, Historia Zespołu i Inwentarz*. Cracow, 1994.

Dejmek, Jindřich, and František Kolář, eds. *Československá zahraniční politika a vznik Malé dohody 1920-1921*, vols. I-II. Prague, 2004-05.

Demetz, Peter. *Böhmen böhmisch: Essays*. Vienna, 2006.

Färber, Meir. 'Die jüdisch-nationale Bewegung in der Tschechoslowakei'. *Zeitschrift für die Geschichte der Juden in der Tschechoslowakei*, nos. 3-4 (1965): 149-55.

———. *Dr. Emil Margulies, ein Lebenskampf für Wahrheit und Recht*. Tel Aviv, 1949.

Fiedler, Jiří. *Židovské památky v Čechách a na Moravě*. Prague, 1992.

Fink, Carole. *Defending the Rights of Others: The Great Powers, the Jews, and International Minority Protection, 1878-1938*. Cambridge, 2004.

Fišer, Zdeněk. *Poslední pogrom: Události v Holešově ve dnech 3. a 4. prosince 1918 a jejich historické pozadí*. Kroměříž, 1996.

Frankl, Michal. 'Antisemitism in Bohemian Lands'. In *Antisemitism in Eastern Europe. History and Present in Comparison*, ed. Hans-Christian Petersen, and Samuel Salzborn. Frankfurt am Main, 2010, 29-45.

———. 'The Background of the Hilsner Case: Political Antisemitism and Allegations of Ritual Murder, 1896-1900'. *Judaica Bohemiae* 36 (2000): 34-118.

———. '*Emancipace od židů*': *Český antisemitismus na konci 19. století*. Prague and Litomyšl, 2007 (German edition: '*Prag ist nunmehr antisemitisch*': *Tschechischer Antisemitismus am Ende des 19. Jahrhunderts*, trans. Michael Wögerbauer. Berlin, 2011).

———. '"Sonderweg" of Czech Antisemitism? Nationalism, National Conflict and Antisemitism in Czech Society in the Late 19th Century'. *Bohemia* 46, no. 1 (2005): 120-34.

———. 'Tschechien'. In *Handbuch des Antisemitismus: Judenfeindschaft in Geschichte und Gegenwart*. Vol. 1. *Länder und Regionen*, ed. Wolfgang Benz. Munich, 2008: 364-69.

———. '"Židovstvo ztrácí své základy": Československo a rumunská uprchlická krize (1937-1938)'. *Terezínské studie a dokumenty* (2005): 297-309.

Gajan, Koloman. 'Masaryk a Max Brod: Židovská otázka v ČSR v letech 1918-1920'. *Židovská ročenka* (2000-01): 28-50.

——. 'Postoj T. G. Masaryka k židovství a sionismu za první republiky'. In *Hilsnerova aféra a česká společnost 1899-1999*. Prague, 1999: 129-37.
Gellner, Ernest. *Nations and Nationalism*, 2nd ed. Oxford, 2007.
Gitelman, Zvi, ed. *The Emergence of Modern Jewish Politics: Bundism and Zionism in Eastern Europe*. Pittsburgh, 2003.
Gold, Hugo, ed. *Gedenkbuch der untergegangenen Judengemeinden Mährens*. Tel Aviv, 1974.
——. *Die Juden und Judengemeinden Böhmens in Vergangenheit und Gegenwart*. Brno, 1934.
Goldstücker, Eduard. 'Jews between Czechs and Germans around 1848'. *Leo Baeck Institute Year Book* 17 (1972): 61-71.
Goschen, S. 'Zionist Student's Organizations'. In *The Jews of Czechoslovakia: Historical Studies and Surveys*, vol. II. Philadelphia and New York, 1971: 173-84.
Grossmann, Kurt R. 'Refugees to and from Czechoslovakia'. In *The Jews of Czechoslovakia: Historical Studies and Surveys*, vol. II. Philadelphia and New York, 1971: 565-81.
Hadler, Frank. '"Erträglicher Antisemitismus"? Jüdische Fragen und tschechoslowakische Antworten 1918/19'. *Jahrbuch des Simon-Dubnow-Instituts* 1 (2002): 169-200.
——, ed. *Weg von Österreich! Das Weltkriegsexil von Masaryk und Beneš im Spiegel ihrer Briefe und Aufzeichnungen aus den Jahren 1914 bis 1918: Eine Quellensammlung*. Berlin, 1995.
Hagen, William W. 'The Moral Economy of Ethnic Violence: The Pogrom in Lwów, November 1918'. *Geschichte und Gesellschaft* 31, no. 2 (2005): 203-26.
Hahn, Fred. 'The Dilemma of the Jews in the Historic Lands of Czechoslovakia, 1918-38'. *East Central Europe* 10, nos. 1-2 (1983): 24-39.
——. 'Němečtí Židé a politické strany'. In *Židé v Sudetech*. Prague, 2000: 100-04.
——. 'T. G. Masaryk and the Jews', manuscript in the Wiener Library London, sign. W 7.
Hall, Stuart. 'The Question of Cultural Identity'. In *Modernity: An Introduction to Modern Societies*, ed. Stuart Hall, David Held, Don Hubert, and Kenneth Thompson. Cambridge and Oxford, 1996: 595-634.
Hamáčková, Vlastimila. 'Débuts du mouvement assimilateur tchéco-juif'. *Judaica Bohemiae* 14, no. 1 (1978): 15-23.
Hanková, Monika. 'Klara Fischer-Pollak (1899-1970): (Po)válečné osudy židovské lékařky z Karlových Varů'. In *Židé v Čechách 2. Sborník příspěvků ze semináře konaného v září 2008 v Nýrsku*, ed. Vlastimila Hamáčková, Monika Hanková, and Markéta Lhotová. Prague, 2009: 50-70.
Haslinger, Peter. *Nation und Territorium im tschechischen politischen Diskurs 1880-1938*. Munich, 2010.
Havránek, Jan. 'Židé mezi Čechy a Němci v Praze'. In *Židé v české a polské občanské společnosti*, ed. Jaroslav Valenta. Prague, 1999: 27-35.
Haumann, Heiko. 'Das jüdische Prag (1850 bis 1914)'. In *Die Juden als Minderheit in der Geschichte*, ed. Bernd Martin, and Ernst Schulin. Munich, 1981: 209-30.
——, ed. *Der Erste Zionistenkongress von 1897: Ursachen, Bedeutung, Aktualität . . . in Basel habe ich den Judenstaat gegründet*. Basle, 1997.
Häusler, Wolfgang. 'Das österreichische Judentum zwischen Beharrung und Fortschritt'. In *Die Habsburgermonarchie, 1848-1918*, vol. IV. Vienna, 1985: 633-69.
Havránek, Jan. 'Sociální struktura pražských Němců a Čechů, křesťanů a Židů ve světle statistik z let 1890-1930'. *Český časopis historický*, no. 3 (1995): 470-79.
——. 'Structure sociale des Allemands, des Tchèques, des chrétiens et des juifs à Prague, à la lumière des statistiques des années 1890-1930'. In *Allemands, Juifs et Tchèques à Prague, 1890-1924/ Deutsche, Juden und Tschechen in Prag 1890-1924*, ed. Maurice Godé, Jacques Le Rider, and Françoise Mayer. Montpellier, 1996: 71-81.
Havránek, Jan, and Zdeněk Pousta, eds. *Dějiny Univerzity Karlovy 1918-1990*, vol. IV. Prague, 1998.

Hazoni, Yoram. *The Jewish State: The Struggle for Israel's Soul*. New York, 2000.
Hecht, Louise. *Ein jüdischer Aufklärer in Böhmen: Der Pädagoge und Reformer Peter Beer (1758–1838)*. Cologne, 2008.
Heřman, Jan. 'The Development of Bohemian and Moravian Jewry'. *Papers in Jewish Demography*. Jerusalem, 3–11 August 1969.
Hermann, Tomáš, and Anton Markoš, eds. *Emanuel Rádl – vědec a filosof: Sborník z mezinárodní konference konané u příležitosti 130. výročí narození a 60. výročí úmrtí Emanuela Rádla / Emanuel Rádl – Scientist and Philosopher: Proceedings of the International Conference Commemorating the 130th Anniversary of the Birth and 60th Anniversary of the Death of Emanuel Rádl*. Prague, 2004.
Herzog, Andreas. 'Vom Judentum: Anmerkungen zum Sammelband des Vereins Bar Kochba'. In *Kafka und Prag*, ed. Kurt Krolop, and Hans Dieter Zimmermann. Berlin and New York, 1994: 45–58.
Hickmann, A. L. *Geographish-statistischer Taschen-Atlas von Österreich-Ungarn*. Vienna, 1900.
Hirschler, Gertrude. 'The History of Agudath Israel in Slovakia (1918–1939)'. In *The Jews of Czechoslovakia. Historical Studies and Surveys*, vol. II. Philadelphia and New York, 1971: 155–72.
Hlaváčková, Ludmila, Alena Míšková, and Jiří Pešek, 'Německá univerzita v Praze 1882–1918'. In *Dějiny Univerzity Karlovy 1802–1918*, vol. III, ed. Jan Havránek. Prague, 1997: 305–30.
Hobsbawm, Eric J. *Nations and nationalism since 1780. Programme, Myth, Reality*. 2nd ed. Cambridge, 1990.
Hödl, Klaus. 'Zum Wandel des Selbstverständnisses zentraleuropäischer Juden durch Kulturtransfer'. In *Kulturtransfer in der jüdischen Geschichte*, ed. Wolfgang Schmale, and Martina Steer. Frankfurt and New York, 2006: 57–82.
Holeczek, Heinz. 'The Jews and the German Liberals'. *Leo Baeck Institute Yearbook* (1983): 77–91.
Hollinger, Robert. *The Dark Side of Liberalism: Elitism vs. Democracy*. London, 1996.
Horak, Stephan. *Poland and Her National Minorities, 1919–39*. New York, [1961].
Housková, Hana. *Česlicí času: Život a dílo Karla Fleischmanna*. Prague, 1998.
Hradská, Katarina. 'Židovská komunita počas prvej ČSR: Vzťah slovenskej majoritnej spoločnosti voči židovskej menšine'. *Česko-Slovenská historická ročenka* (2001): 49–58.
Hroch, Miroslav. *Social Preconditions of National Revival in Europe*. Cambridge, 1985.
Hurwic-Nowakowska, Irena. *Żydzi polscy (1947–50): Analiza więzi społecznej ludności żydowskiej*. Warsaw, 1996.
Iggers, Wilma. *Die Juden in Böhmen und Mähren: Ein historisches Lesebuch*. Munich, 1986.
———. 'The Flexible National Identities of Bohemian Jewry'. *East Central Europe* 7, no. 1 (1980): 9–48.
———. 'Juden zwischen Tschechen und Deutschen', *Zeitschrift für Ostforschung* 37 (1988): 428–41.
———. *Zeiten der Gottesferne und der Mattheit: Die Religion im Bewußtsein der böhmischen Juden in der ersten Tschechoslowakischen Republik*. Leipzig, 1997.
Janowsky, Oscar. *The Jews and Minority Rights, 1898–1919*. New York, [1933] 1966.
Jelinek, Yeshayahu A. *The Carpathian Diaspora: The Jews of Subcarpathian Rus' and Mukachevo, 1848–1948*. New York, 2007.
———. 'Prevrat v rokoch 1918–1919 a Židia (poznámky a úvahy)'. In *'Spoznal som svetlo a už viac nechcem tmu…': Pocta Jozefovi Jablonickému*. Bratislava, 2005: 29–43.
Jenkins, Richard. *Rethinking Ethnicity: arguments and exploration*, 2nd ed. London, 2008.
———. *Social Identity*, 3rd ed. Abingdon, New York, 2008.

The Jews of Czechoslovakia: Historical Studies and Surveys, vols. I-III. Philadelphia and New York, 1968, 1971, 1984.

Judson, Peter. *Exclusive Revolutionaries: Liberal Politics, Social Experience, and National Identity in the Austrian Empire, 1848-1914*. Ann Arbor, 1996.

——. *Guardians of the Nations: Activists on the Language Frontiers of Imperial Austria*. Cambridge, MA, and London, 2006.

Kaiser, Vladimír. 'Židovská komunita v Ústí nad Labem v 19. a 20. století'. In *Židé v Sudetech*. Prague, 2000: 217-24.

Kamenec, Ivan. *Po stopách tragédie*. Bratislava, 1991.

Karady, Victor. *Gewalterfahrung und Utopie: Juden in der europäischen Moderne*. Frankfurt am Main, 1999.

Katz, Jacob. *A House Divided: Orthodoxy and Schism in Nineteenth-Century Central European Jewry*. Hanover and London, 1998.

Kestenberg-Gladstein, Ruth. 'Athalot Bar Kochba'. In *Prag vi-yerushalayim*, ed. Felix Weltsch. Jerusalem, 1954: 86-110.

——. 'The Internal Migration of Jews in 19th Century Bohemia'. *The Field of Yiddish* (1969): 305-09.

——. 'The Jews between Czechs and Germans in the Historic Lands, 1848-1918'. In *The Jews of Czechoslovakia*, vol. I. New York and Philadelphia, 1968: 21-71.

——. *Neuere Geschichte der Juden in den böhmischen Ländern: Das Zeitalter der Aufklärung 1780-1830*, vol. I. Tübingen, 1969.

Kieval, Hillel J. 'Choosing to Bridge. Revisiting the Phenomenon of Cultural Mediation'. *Bohemia* 46, no. 1 (2005): 15-27.

——. *Languages of Community: The Jewish Experience in the Czech Lands*. Berkeley, Los Angeles and London, 2000.

——. *The Making of Czech Jewry: National Conflict and Jewish Society in Bohemia, 1870-1918*. New York and Oxford, 1988.

——. 'Negotiating Czechoslovakia: The Challenges of Jewish Citizenship in a Multiethnic Nation-State'. In *Insiders and Outsiders: Dilemmas of East European Jewry*, ed. Richard I. Cohen, Jonathan Frankel, and Stefani Hoffman. Oxford and Portland, OR 2010: 103-19.

King, Jeremy. *Budweisers into Czechs and Germans: Local History of Bohemian Politics, 1848-1948*. Princeton and Oxford, 2002.

——. 'The Nationalization of East Central Europe: Ethnicism, Ethnicity, and Beyond'. In *Staging the Past. The Politics of Commemoration in Habsburg Central Europe, 1848 to the Present*, ed. Maria Bucur, and Nancy M. Wingfield, West Lafayette, IN, 2001: 112-52.

Kisch, Guido. 'Linguistic Conditions among Czechoslovak Jewry: A Legal-Historical Study'. *Historia Judaica* 8 (1946): 19-32.

Klein-Pejšová, Rebekah. '"Abandon Your Role as Exponents of the Magyars": Contested Jewish Loyalty in Interwar (Czecho)Slovakia'. *Association for Jewish Studies Review* 33, no. 2 (November 2009): 341-62.

——. 'Among the Nationalities: Jewish Refugees, Jewish Nationality, and Czechoslovak Statebuilding', Ph.D. thesis, Columbia University 2007.

Koeltzsch, Ines. 'Antijüdische Straßengewalt und die semantische Konstruktion des "Anderen" im Prag der Ersten Republik', *Judaica Bohemiae* 46, no. 1 (2011): 73-99.

——. 'Die gezählte Stadt. Tschechen, Juden und Deutsche im Prager Zensus (1900-1930)'. In *Praha - Prag 1900-1945. Literaturstadt zweier Sprachen*, ed. Peter Becher, and Anna Knechtel. Passau, 2010: 9-20.

——. 'Geteilte Kulturen. Eine Geschichte der tschechisch-jüdisch-deutschen Beziehungen in Prag (1918-1938)', Ph.D. thesis, Freie Universität Berlin, 2010.

———. 'Gustav Flusser: Biographische Spuren eines deutschen Juden in Prag vor dem Zweiten Weltkrieg'. *Flusser Studies: Multilingual Journal for Cultural and Media Theory* 5 (November 2007): 1-13.
Kohn, Hans. *The Idea of Nationalism: A Study in its Origins and Background*. New York, 1967.
———. *Nationalism: Its Meaning and History*. Princeton, 1955.
Kosatík, Pavel. *Ferdinand Peroutka, život v novinách (1895-1938)*. Prague and Litomyšl, 2003.
Koschmal, Walter. *Der Dichternomade: Jiří Mordechai Langer – ein tschechisch-jüdischer Autor*. Cologne, Weimar, and Vienna, 2010.
Kovtun, Jiří. *Tajuplná vražda: Případ Leopolda Hilsnera*. Prague, 1994.
Krejčová, Helena. 'Nástin spolkové činnosti českožidovského asimilačního hnutí'. In *Sborník k problematice multietnicity*, ed. Zdeněk Kárník. Prague, 1996: 85-109.
———. 'Publikační činnost akademického spolku Kapper', *Documenta Pragensia* X, no. 2 (1990): 503-19.
———. 'Židovská komunita v moderní české společnosti'. In *Židé v novodobých dějinách*, ed. Václav Veber. Prague, 1997: 17-27.
Krolop, Kurt. 'Ein Manifest der "Prager Schule"'. *philologica pragensia* 7, no. 4 (1964): 329-36.
———. 'Herder-blätter'. *philologica pragensia* 6, no. 2 (1963): 211-22.
———. 'Zu den Erinnerungen Anna Lichtensterns an Franz Kafka'. *Acta Universitatis Carolinae – Philologica* 5 (1968): 21-60.
Krolop, Kurt, and Hans Dieter Zimmermann, eds. *Kafka und Prag*. Berlin and New York, 1994.
Křen, Jan. *Konfliktní společenství: Češi a Němci 1780-1918*. Prague, 1990.
Křesťan, Jiří, Alexandra Blodigová, and Jaroslav Bubeník. *Židovské spolky v českých zemích v letech 1918-1948*. Prague, 2001.
Kuchenbecker, Antje. *Zionismus ohne Zion: Birobidžan. Idee und Geschichte eines jüdischen Staates in Sowjet-Fernost*. Berlin, 2000.
Kučera, Jaroslav. 'Politický či přirozený národ? K pojetí národa v československém právním řádu meziválečného období'. *Český časopis historický* 99, no. 3 (2001): 548-68.
Kuděla, Jiří. 'Galician and East European Refugees in the Historic Lands: 1914-16'. *Review of the Society for the History of Czechoslovak Jews* IV (1991-92): 15-32.
Kulka, Erich. 'The Jews in Czechoslovakia between 1918 and 1968'. In *Czechoslovakia: Crossroads and Crises, 1918-1988*, ed. Norman Stone, and Eduard Strouhal. London, 1989: 271-96.
Kulka, Otto Dov. 'History and Historical Consciousness. Similarities and Dissimilarities in the History of the Jews in Germany and the Czech Lands 1918-1945'. *Bohemia* 46, no. 1 (2005): 68-86.
Kvaček, Robert. 'The Birth of Czechoslovakia and Considerations Leading Up to It'. *The Prague Yearbook of Contemporary History* (1998): 1-18.
———. 'Ke vzniku Československa'. *Český časopis historický*, no. 4 (1998-96): 717-35.
Langer, František. 'My Brother Jiri'. In Jiri Langer, *Nine Gates to the Chassidic Mysteries*, trans. Stephen Jolly. New York, 1961: 148-64.
Láníček, Jan. 'The Czechoslovak Government-in-Exile and the Jews during the World War 2 (1938-1948)', Ph.D. thesis, University of Southampton, 2010.
Levene, Mark. 'Nationalism and its Alternatives in the International Arena: The Jewish Question at Paris, 1919'. *Journal of Contemporary History* 28 (1993): 511-31.
Levý, Otakar. *Baudelaire, jeho estetika a technika*. Brno, 1947.

Lichtenstein, Tatjana. '"Heja, Heja Hagibor!" - Jewish Sports, Politics, and Nationalism in Czechoslovakia, 1923-1930'. In *Leipziger Beiträge zur jüdischen Geschichte und Kultur*, vol. II, ed. Dan Diner. Munich, 2004: 191-208.

———. 'Making Jews at Home: Jewish Nationalism in the Bohemian Lands, 1918-1938', Ph.D. thesis, University of Toronto, 2009.

———. '"Making" Jews at Home. Zionism and the Construction of Jewish Nationality in Inter-war Czechoslovakia'. *East European Jewish Affairs* 36, no. 1 (2006): 49-71.

Liekis, Sarunas. *A State within a State? Jewish Autonomy in Lithuania 1918-1925*. Vilnius, 2003.

Lipscher, Ladislav. 'Die soziale und politische Stellung der Juden in der ersten Republik'. In *Die Juden in den böhmischen Ländern*, ed. Ferdinand Seibt. Munich and Vienna, 1983: 269-80.

Loewenstein, Bedřich. 'Ein tschechischer Denker der Krise Emanuel Rádl (1873-1942)'. *Bohemia* 46, no. 1 (2005): 135-51.

———. 'Motivy antisemitismu'. In *Antisemitismus v posttotalitní Evropě*. Prague, 1993: 19-25.

———. 'Überlegungen zum tschechischen Antisemitismus'. In Loewenstein, *Wir und die anderen: Historische und kultursoziologische Betrachtungen*. Dresden, 2003: 399-412.

Lorencová, Anna and Anna Hyndráková, 'Die tschechische Gesellschaft und die Juden in den Erinnerungen von Zeitzeugen'. *Theresienstädter Studien und Dokumente* (1999): 141-67.

Lowenstein, Steven M. 'Decline and Survival of Rural Jewish Communities'. In *In Search of Jewish Community: Jewish Identities in Germany and Austria, 1918-1933*, ed. Michael Brenner, and Derek J. Penslar. Bloomington and Indianapolis, 1998: 223-42.

———. 'Die Gemeinde'. In *Deutsch-jüdische Geschichte in der Neuzeit*, vol. III, *Umstrittene Integration 1871-1918*. Munich, 1997: 123-50.

———. 'Das religiöse Leben'. In *Deutsch-jüdische Geschichte in der Neuzeit*, vol. III, *Umstrittene Integration 1871-1918*, ed. Steven M. Lowenstein et al. Munich, 1997: 101-22.

Luft, Robert. 'Nationale Utraquisten in Böhmen: Zur Problematik "nationaler Zwischenstellungen" am Ende des 19. Jahrhunderts'. In *Allemands, Juifs et Tchèques à Prague, 1890-1924*, ed. Maurice Godé, Jacques Le Rider, and Françoise Mayer. Montpellier, 1996: 37-51.

Mařan, Ctibor. *Kniha o Alfredu Fuchsovi*. Prague, 1946.

Marcus, Marcel R. '"Der Jude" - gibt es ihn eigentlich? Über die Arten, Jude zu sein'. In *'Judenklischees' und jüdische Wirklichkeit in unserer Gesellschaft*, ed. Jörg Albertz. Berlin, 1989: 31-44.

Maurer, Trude. *Die Entwicklung der jüdischen Minderheit in Deutschland (1790-1933): Neuere Forschungen und offene Fragen*. Tübingen, 1992.

———. 'Juden im Prager deutschen Bürgertum'. *Judaica* 58, no. 3 (September 2002): 172-87.

McCagg, William O., Jr. 'The Jewish Position in Interwar Central Europe: A Structural Study of Jewry at Vienna, Budapest, and Prague'. In Yehuda Don, and Victor Karady, *A Social and Economic History of Central European Jewry*. New Brunswick and London, 1990: 47-81.

Mendelsohn, Ezra. *The Jews of East Central Europe between the World Wars*. Bloomington, 1983.

———. *On Modern Jewish Politics*. New York, 1993.

———. 'Zionist Success and Zionist Failure: The Case of East Central Europe between the Wars'. In *Essential Papers on Zionism*, ed. Jehuda Reinharz, and Anita Shapira. New York, 1996: 171-90.

Meyer, Peter. 'Czechoslovakia'. In *The Jews in the Soviet Satellites*, ed. Peter Meyer et al., Westport, CT, 1971: 49-206.
Miller, Michael Laurence. *Rabbis and Revolution: The Jews of Moravia in the Age of Emancipation*. Stanford, CA, 2010.
Míšková, Alena. 'Od Schönerera ke genocidě?'. In *Židé v Sudetech*. Prague, 2000: 47-64.
Mišovič, Ján. *Víra v dějinách zemí koruny české*. Prague, 2001.
Mittleman, Alan L. *The Politics of Torah: The Jewish Political Tradition and the Founding of Agudat Israel*. Albany, NY, 1996.
Mosse, George L. *The Crisis of German Ideology: Intellectual Origins of the Third Reich*. New York, 1964.
Nečas, Jaromír. *Politická situace na Podkarpatské Rusi (rok 1921)*. Prague, 1997.
Nekula, Marek. 'Česko-německý bilingvismus'. In Walter Koschmal, Marek Nekula, and Joachim Rogall, *Češi a Němci: Dějiny – kultura – politika*, trans. Václav Maidl. Prague and Litomyšl, 2002: 152-57.
——. *Franz Kafkas Sprachen: '... in einem Stockwerk des innern babylonischen Turmes ...'*. Tübingen, 2003.
Niewyk, Donald L. 'The Impact of Inflation and Depression on the German Jews'. *Leo Baeck Institute Yearbook* (1983): 19-36.
——. *The Jews in Weimar Germany*. Manchester, 1980.
Nižňanský, Eduard. 'Majorita a židovská minorita v období holokaustu: Poznámky k problematike sociálneho prostredia holokaustu'. In *Národ a národnosti na Slovensku v transformujúcej sa spoločnosti: Vzťahy a konflikty*, ed. Štefan Šutaj. Prešov, 2005: 184-95.
Orzoff, Andrea. *Battle for the Castle: The Myth of Czechoslovakia in Europe, 1914-1948*. Oxford, 2009.
——. '"The Literary Organ of Politics": Tomáš Masaryk and Political Journalism, 1925-1929'. *Slavic Review* 63, no. 2 (2004): 275-300.
Pařík, Arno. 'Z dějin židovských náboženských obcí v Čechách a na Moravě'. In Jiří Fiedler, *Židovské památky v Čechách a na Moravě*. Prague, 1992: 5-24.
Pěkný, Tomáš. *Historie Židů v Čechách a na Moravě*, rev. and expanded 2nd ed. Prague, 2001.
Pešek, Jiří. 'Jüdische Studenten an den Prager Universitäten, 1882-1939'. In *Franz Kafka im sprachnationalen Kontext seiner Zeit: Sprache und nationale Identität in öffentlichen Institutionen der böhmischen Länder*, ed. Marek Nekula, Ingrid Fleischmann, and Albrecht Greule. Weimar and Cologne, 2007: 213-228.
Pešek, Jiří, Alena Míšková, Petr Svobodný, and Jan Janko. 'Německá univerzita v Praze v letech 1918-1939'. In *Dějiny Univerzity Karlovy 1918-1990*, vol. IV, ed. Jan Havránek, and Zdeněk Pousta. Prague, 1998: 181-212.
Petrášová, Markéta, and Jarmila Skochová. *Karel Fleischmann: Life and Work*. Prague, 1987, exhibition catalogue.
Pick, Joseph C. 'Sports'. In *The Jews of Czechoslovakia*, vol. II. Philadelphia and New York, 1971: 185-228.
Pickhan, Gertrud. *"Gegen den Strom": Der allgemeine jüdische Arbeiterbund "Bund" in Polen, 1918-1939*. Stuttgart, 2001.
Pynsent, Robert. 'The Literary Representation of the Czechoslovak "Legions" in Russia'. In *Czechoslovakia in a Nationalist and Fascist Europe 1918-1948*, ed. Mark Cornwall, and R. J. W. Evans. Oxford, 2007: 63-88.
Rabinowicz, Aharon Moshe K. 'The Jewish Minority'. In *The Jews of Czechoslovakia*, vol. I. New York and Philadelphia, 1968: 155-266.
——. 'The Jewish Party'. In *The Jews of Czechoslovakia*, vol. II. Philadelphia and New York, 1971: 253-346.

Rabinowicz, Oskar K. 'Czechoslovak Zionism: Analecta to a History'. In *The Jews of Czechoslovakia. Historical Studies and Surveys*, vol. II. Philadelphia and New York, 1971: 19-136.
Rataj, Jan. 'Český antisemitismus v proměnách let 1918-1945'. In *Židé v české a polské občanské společnosti*, ed. Jerzy Tomaszewski, and Jaroslav Valenta. Prague, 1999: 45-64.
Ratzabi, Shalom. *Between Zionism and Judaism: The Radical Circle in Brith Shalom, 1925-1933*. Leiden, 2002.
Rechter, David. *The Jews of Vienna and the First World War*. London and Portland, 2001.
———. 'A Nationalism of Small Things: Jewish Autonomy in Late Habsburg Austria'. *Leo Baeck Institute Yearbook* 52 (2007): 87-109.
Reinharz, Jehuda, and Anita Shapira, eds. *Essential Papers on Zionism*. New York, 1996.
Reiterer, Albert. *Die unvermeidbare Nation: Ethnizität, Nation und nachnationale Gesellschaft*. Vienna, 1988.
Řezníčková, Kateřina. *Študáci a kantoři za starého Rakouska. České střední školy v letech 1867-1918*. Prague, 2007.
Riff, Michael Anthony. 'The Ambiguity of Masaryk's Attitudes on the 'Jewish Question'. In *T.G. Masaryk (1850-1937)*, vol. 2. *Thinker and Critic*, ed. Robert B. Pynsent. London, 1989: 77-87.
———. 'Assimilation and Conversion in Bohemia: Secession from the Jewish Community in Prague 1868-1917'. *Leo Baeck Institute Yearbook* 26 (1981): 73-88.
Roshwald, Aviel. 'Jewish Identity and the Paradox of Nationalism'. In *Nationalism, Zionism and Ethnic Mobilization of the Jews in 1900 and Beyond*, ed. Michael Berkowitz. Leiden, 2004: 11-24.
Rothkirchen, Livia. 'Czechoslovak Jewry: Growth and Decline. Part I - 1918-1939'. In *Where Cultures Meet: The Story of the Jews of Czechoslovakia*, ed. Natalia Berger. Tel Aviv, 1990: 151-64.
———. *The Jews of Bohemia and Moravia: Facing the Holocaust*. Lincoln, NE, 2005.
———. 'Slovakia: I., 1848-1918'. In *The Jews of Czechoslovakia*, vol. I. New York and Philadelphia, 1968: 72-84.
———. 'Slovakia: II., 1918-1938'. In *The Jews of Czechoslovakia*, vol. I. New York and Philadelphia, 1968: 85-124.
Różański, Przemysław. 'Pogrom lwowski 22 listopada 1918 roku w świetle zeznań Organizacji Syjonistycznej złożonych przed komisją Morgenthaua'. *Kwartalnik Historii Żydów*, no. 211 (2004): 347-58.
Rozenblit, Marsha L. *The Jews of Vienna, 1867-1914: Assimilation and Identity*. Albany, NY, 1983.
———. *Reconstructing a National Identity: The Jews of Habsburg Austria during World War I*. Oxford, 2001.
Rybár, Ctibor, ed. *Židovská Prague: Glosy k dějinám a kultuře*. Prague, 1991.
Saß, Anne-Christin. 'Berlin - Ir VaEm BeIsrael: Osteuropäisch-jüdische Migranten in der Hauptstadt der Weimarer Republik', Ph.D. thesis, Freie Universität Berlin, 2011.
Schenker, Anatol. *Der Jüdische Verlag 1902-1938: Zwischen Aufbruch, Blüte und Vernichtung*. Tübingen, 2003.
Schnitzler, Leopold. *Prager Judendeutsch: Ein Beitrag zur Erforschung des älteren Prager Judendeutsch in lautlicher und insbesondere in lexikalischer Beziehung*. Gräfeling bei Munich, 1966.
Schulze-Wessel, Martin. 'Die Politik gegenüber den Juden in der Ersten Tschechoslowakischen Republik: Entwürfe und Wirklichkeiten (1918-1938)'. In *Zwischen großen Erwartungen und bösem Erwachen: Juden, Politik und Antisemitismus in Ost- und Südosteuropa 1918-1945*, ed. Dietmar Dahlmann, and Anke Hillbrenner. Paderborn, 2007: 121-36.

———, ed. *Loyalitäten in der Tschechoslowakischen Republik 1918–1938. Politische, nationale und kulturelle Zugehörigkeiten*. Munich, 2004.
Shimoni, Gideon. *The Zionist Ideology*. Hanover and London, 1995.
Shumsky, Dimitry. *Beyn prag li-yerushalayim: tsiyonut prag ve-ra'yon ha-medinah ha-du-le'umit be-erets-yisrael*. Jerusalem, 2010.
———. 'Czechs, Germans, Arabs, Jews: Franz Kafka's "Jackals and Arabs" between Bohemia and Palestine'. *Association for Jewish Studies Review* 33, no. 1 (2009): 71–100.
———. 'Historiografiyah, le'umiyut ve-du-le'umiyut: yahadut czecho-germanit, zionei prag u-mekorot ha-gisha ha-du-leumit shel Hugo Bergmann'. *Zion* 69, no. 1 (2004): 45–80.
———. 'Introducing Intellectual and Political History to the History of Everyday Life: Multiethnic Cohabitation and Jewish Experience in Fin-de-Siècle Bohemia'. *Bohemia* 46, no. 1 (2005): 39–67.
———. 'On Ethno-Centrism and its Limits: Czecho-German Jewry in Fin-de-Siècle Prague and the Origins of Zionist Bi-Nationalism'. *Jahrbuch des Simon-Dubnow-Instituts* 5 (2006): 173–88.
Silberstein, Laurence J., ed. *Mapping Jewish Identities*. New York and London, 2000.
Smith, Anthony. 'The "Golden Age" and National Renewal'. In *Myths and Nationhood*, ed. Geoffrey Hosking, and George Schöpflin. London, 1997: 36–59.
Sole, Aryeh. 'Modern Hebrew Education in Subcarpathian Ruthenia'. In *The Jews of Czechoslovakia: Historical Studies and Surveys*, vol. II. Philadelphia and New York, 1971: 401–39.
Sorkin, David. 'The Impact of Emancipation on German Jewry: A Reconsideration'. In *Assimilation and Community: The Jews in Nineteenth-Century Europe*, ed. Jonathan Frankel, and Steven J. Zipperstein. Cambridge, 1992: 177–98.
———. *The Transformation of German Jewry, 1780–1840*. Oxford, 1987.
Spector, Scott. 'Another Zionism: Hugo Bergmann's Circumscription of Spiritual Territory', *Journal of Contemporary History*, 34, no. 1 (January 1999): 85–106.
———. 'Die Konstruktion einer jüdischen Nationalität – die Prager Wochenschrift Selbstwehr', *brücken: Germanistisches Jahrbuch. Neue Folge* 92 (1991): 37–44.
———. *Prague Territories: National Conflict and Cultural Innovation in Franz Kafka's Fin de Siècle*. Berkeley, Los Angeles, and London, 2000.
Šrámková, Barbora. *Max Brod und die tschechische Kultur*. Wuppertal, 2010.
Steiner, Jan. 'Národnost při sčítání lidu v roce 1930 a její zjišťování na Ostravsku'. *Slezský sborník* 85, no. 2 (1987): 113–32.
Stillschweig, Kurt. 'Nationalitätenrechtliche Stellung der Juden in der Tschechoslowakei'. *Historia Judaica*, no. 1 (1938–39): 39–49.
Stölzl, Christoph. 'Die "Burg" und die Juden: T. G. Masaryk und sein Kreis im Spannungsfeld der jüdischen Frage: Assimilation, Antisemitismus und Zionismus'. In *Die 'Burg': Einflußreiche politische Kräfte um Masaryk und Beneš*, vol. 2, ed. Karl Bosl. Munich and Vienna, 1974: 79–110.
———. *Kafkas böses Böhmen: Zur Sozialgeschichte eines Prager Juden*. Munich, 1975.
Suny, Ronald Grigor, and Michael D. Kennedy, eds. *Intellectuals and the Articulation of the Nation*. Ann Arbor, 1999.
Szabó, Miloslav. 'National Conflict and Anti-Semitism at the Beginning of the Twentieth Century. The Case of the Czech Slovakophiles Karel Kálal and Eduard Lederer'. *Judaica Bohemiae* 44, no. 1 (2009): 49–81.
———. '"Židovská otázka" na Slovensku v prvých rokoch Československej republiky'. *Střed*, no. 2 (2011): 59–81.
Tauš, Karel. *Slovník cizích slov, zkratek, novinářských šifer, pseudonymů a časopisů pro čtenáře novin*, 2nd ed. Blansko, 1947.

Tenenboym, Josef. *Tsvishn milchome un sholem: yidn oyf der shlus konferents noch der ershter veltmilchome.* Buenos Aires, 1956.
Thiesse, Anne-Marie. *La création des identités nationales.* Paris, 1999.
Tomaszewski, Jerzy. 'Naród żydowski w Europie środkowej'. In *Józef Chlebowczyk – badacz procesów narodotwórczych w Europie XIX i XX wieku,* ed. Marie Wanda Wanatowicz. Katowice, 2007: 56–74.
——. 'Spisy ludności w Czechosłowacji 1921, 1930 jako źrodło do badania stosunków narodowościowych'. *Slezský Sborník. Acta Silesiaca* 96, no. 2 (1998): 95–105.
——. 'Židovská otázka na Slovensku v roku 1919'. In *Historik v čase a priestore. Laudatio Ľubomírovi Liptákovi,* ed. Ivan Kamenec, Elena Mannová, and Eva Kowalská. Bratislava, 2000: 173–86.
Toury, Jacob. 'Defense Activities of the Österreichisch-Israelitische Union before 1914'. In *Living with Antisemitism: Modern Jewish Responses,* ed. Jehuda Reinharz. Hanover, 1987: 167–92.
Tramer, Hans. 'Die Dreivölkerstadt Prag'. In *Robert Weltsch zum 70. Geburtstag von seinen Freunden,* ed. Hans Tramer and Kurt Loewenstein. Tel Aviv, 1961: 138–206.
Triendel-Zadoff, Mirjam. *Nächstes Jahr in Marienbad. Gegenwelten jüdischer Kulturen der Moderne.* Göttingen, 2007.
Tůma, Oldřich, and Jiří Jindra, eds. *Czechoslovakia and Romania in the Versailles System.* Prague, 2006.
Urban, Otto. 'Bürgerlichkeit und das tschechische Bildungsbürgertum am Ende des 19. Jahrhunderts'. In *'Durch Arbeit, Besitz, Wissen und Gerechtigkeit': Bürgertum in der Habsburgermonarchie,* vol. 2, ed. Hames Stekl, Peter Urbanitsch, Ernst Bruckmüller, and Hans Heiss. Vienna, Cologne, and Weimar, 1992: 203–09.
——. *Česká společnost 1848–1918.* Prague, 1982.
——. 'Zur Fragen der Formierung der neuzeitlichen nationalen Gesellschaft: Die Modellsituation der tschechischen Gesellschaft'. In *Formen des nationalen Bewußtseins im Lichte zeitgenössischer Nationalismustheorien,* ed. Eva Schmidt-Hartmann. Munich, 1994: 255–62.
Urbanitsch, Peter. 'Die politischen Judengemeinden in Mähren nach 1848'. In *Moravští Židé v rakousko-uherské monarchii (1780–1918). XXVI. Mikulovské symposium.* Brno, 2003: 39–53.
Vassogne, Gaëlle. *Max Brod in Prag: Identität und Vermittlung.* Tübingen, 2009.
Vobecká, Jana. 'Populační vývoj Židů v Čechách v 19. a první třetině 20. století: Společenské a hospodářské souvislosti'. *Studie Národohospodářského ústavu Josefa Hlávky* 3 (2007).
Voigts, Manfred. *"Wir sollen alle kleine Fichtes werden!" Johann Gottlieb Fichte als Prophet der Kultur-Zionisten.* Berlin and Vienna, 2003.
Volkov, Shulamit. *Germans, Jews, and Antisemites: Trials in Emancipation.* Cambridge, 2006.
——. *Jüdisches Leben und Antisemitismus in 19. und 20. Jahrhundert.* Munich, 1990.
Vondrášková, Iveta. 'The Czech-Jewish Assimilation Movement and Its Reflection of Czech National Traditions'. *Judaica Bohemiae* 36 (2000): 143–59.
Vyskočil, Josef. 'Die tschechisch-jüdische Bewegung: Zum 90. Jahrestage der Gründung des Verbandes tschechisch-jüdischer Akademiker'. *Judaica Bohemiae* 3, no. 1 (1967): 36–56.
Wein, Martin J. 'Czechoslovakia's First Republic, Zionism and the State of Israel'. M.A. thesis, Emory University, Atlanta, 2001.
——. 'Jüdisch-tschechischer Gedächtnistransfer im Schatten Deutschlands und Polens'. In *Die Destruktion des Dialogs: Zur innenpolitischen Instrumentalisierung negativer Fremdbilder und Feindbilder: Polen, Tschechien, Deutschland und die Niederlande im Vergleich, 1900*

bis heute, ed. Dieter Bingen, Peter Oliver Loew, and Kazimierz Wóycicki. Darmstadt and Wiesbaden, 2007: 103–13.

———. 'Yehudim czecho-germanim ve-tu lo? T'guvah le-ma'amaro shel dimitry shumsky'. *Zion* 70, no. 3 (2005): 383–92.

———. 'Zionism in Interwar Czechoslovakia: Palestino-Centrism and Landespolitik'. *Judaica Bohemiae* 44, no. 2 (2009): 5–47.

Weinbaum, Laurence. *A Marriage of Convenience: The New Zionist Organization and the Polish Government 1936–1939*. New York, 1993.

Weiss, Yfaat. 'Central European Ethnonationalism and Zionist Binationalism'. *Jewish Social Studies* 1 (2004): 93–117.

Wiechmann, Dietmar. *Traum vom Frieden: Das bi-nationale Konzept des Brith-Schalom zur Lösung des jüdisch-arabischen Konfliktes in der Zeit von 1925–1933*. Schwalbach/Ts, 1998.

Wingfield, Nancy M. 'Czech, German or Jew: The Jewish Community of Prague during the Interwar Period'. In *The Czech and Slovak Experience: Selected Papers from the Fourth World Congress for Soviet and East European Studies, Harrogate, 1990*, ed. John Morison. Basingstoke and London, 1992: 219–29.

———. *Minority Politics in a Multinational State: The German Social Democrats in Czechoslovakia, 1918–1938*. New York, 1989.

Wladika, Michael. *Hitlers Vätergeneration. Die Ursprünge des Nationalsozialismus in der k.u.k. Monarchie*. Vienna, 2005.

Wlaschek, Rudolf M. *Juden in Böhmen: Beiträge zur Geschichte des europäischen Judentums im 19. und 20. Jahrhundert*, 2nd rev. and expanded ed. Munich, 1997.

Yahil, Chaim. 'Social Work in the Historic Lands'. In *The Jews of Czechoslovakia: Historical Studies and Surveys*, vol. II. Philadelphia and New York, 1971: 393–99.

Zahra, Tara. *Kidnapped Souls. National Indifference and the Battle for Children in the Bohemian Lands, 1900–1948*. Ithaca and London, 2008.

Zimmermann, Mosche. *Die deutschen Juden 1914–1945*. Munich, 1997.

Zimmermann, Volker. *Die Sudetendeutschen im NS-Staat: Politik und Stimmung der Bevölkerung im Reichsgau Sudetenland (1938–1945)*. Essen, 1999.

INDEX

A
Abeles, Hanuš, 226
Abeles, Otto, 172
Adler, Egon, 86
Adler, Friedrich, 50
Adler, Norbert, 29n10
Agudas Yisroel (Agudat Yisra'el), 53, 195, 222
Aḥad Ha'Am (Asher Hirsch Ginsberg), 34, 181, 207, 216
    and Tomáš G. Masaryk, 35
Akademický spolek Kapper. *See* Kapper Students' Society
aliyah, 227, 231, 232, 238-39
Alliance Israélite Universelle, 29, 190
Altenberg, Peter, 79
Anderson, Benedict, 47
antisemitism, 15
    after Munich Agreement, 239
    Czech-ews on, 113-20, 134, 137, 144, 148, 153, 159-60
    immediately after WWI, 110-13
    in interwar Czechoslovakia, 24-25, 246-47
    in Wandervogel, 228
    See also Czech Progressive Party
    See also Hilsner affair
    See also Holešov
    See also Jan Herben
Arabs in Palestine, 184, 210, 214, 220
Arbes, Jakub, 96
Argentina, 209
Arlosoroff, Chaim, 185, 209
Arnstein, Ignát, 101, 129n123
Aronowitsch, Israel (Aharoni), 176, 180
Association of Czech-Jews (Svaz Čechů židů), 92, 134
    and work with Jews in other countries, 157
    and Jews in Moravia, 138-40
    and Jews in Slovakia, 141-43
    attempt to revise its nationalist programme, 157-60
    clash with Kapper Society, 144-45, 149
    on Birobidzhan, 164-65
    on Czech and German antisemitism, 153
    on Nazism, 156-57
    on refugees from Sudetenland, 165-68
    on *yishuv* in Palestine, 115
    origins of, 131-33
    pressure from Czech administration on, 155-56
    See also Ervín Neumann
    See also Maxim Reiner
    See also Otto Stross
Association of Jewish Slovak Students of Bratislava (Sdruženie židovských akademikov Slovákov v Bratislavě), 142-43
Association of Progressive Czech-Jews (Svaz českých pokrokových židů), 102-4, 110, 120-24, 127, 130-33, 137-38, 146
Association of Slovak-Jews (Zväz slovenských židov), 142
Auerbach, Elias, 239
Auerhan, Jan, 43
Augustine, Dolores, 78
Aussig. *See* Ústí nad Labem
Australia, 166
Austria, 14, 31, 58, 87, 197, 218
    B'nai B'rith in, 75-76, 78-79
    crisis of liberalism in, 67-68
    Jewish integrationists in, 93, 97-98
    Jewish parliamentary group in, 27-28

B
B'nai B'rith Order, 69, 73-74
    and Zionists, 88-90

272 • Index

in Bohemian Lands, 76-78
on arts and sciences, 78-83
on restratification, 115
origins of, 74-75
See also Herderverein
See also Sigmund Freud
See also Vienna
Badeni, Casimir, 64
Balázs, Julius, 226
Balfour Declaration, 27, 187
Bar Giora (association), 228
Bar Kochba Society, 15, 64, 88-89, 201,
    203, 228, 234-35, 242
    and Chaim Weizmann, 213
    and Emil Margulies, 216
    and Galician refugees, 184-87
    and Martin Buber, 181-84
    and socialism, 204-5, 207
    opposition to Barissia, 177-81
    origins of, 173-177
Barák, Josef, 98
Barissia (association), 177-79, 216, 219, 228
Basch, Antonín, 128, 129n123
Baťa, Tomáš, 130
Baum, Oskar, 79, 82-83
    on status of women, 204
Bäumel, Richard, 137
Baxa, Karel, 102
    and Emil Margulies, 217-18
Beck, Josef, 159, 167
Beer, Peter, 57
Beer-Hofmann, Richard, 79
Beilis, Mendel, 102
Belgium, 15, 209
Beller, Steven, 68
Beneš, Edvard, 31, 34, 107, 156, 253
    on 'Jewish clauses', 30-31
Benešov, 110
Bergmann, Arthur, 174, 180, 201, 215
Bergmann, Johanna, 179
Bergmann, Samuel Hugo, 18, 29n10, 174,
    202, 218
    and Johann Gottlieb Fichte, 242
    and Tomáš G. Masaryk, 175
    Bar Kochba and, 174-81
    Brit Shalom and, 184, 214
    ethno-nationalism and, 242-43
    Ha-Po'el Ha-Tsa'ir and, 207-8
    his criticism of pre-war Zionism in
        Bohemia, 203
    Hit'aḥadut and, 208-9
    Jüdischer Verlag and, 213
    on 'Ostjuden', 177
    on Hebrew, 176
    on 'Jewish clauses', 30-31

socialism and, 204
Bergmann, Siegmund, 179
Bergson, Henri, 149
Berlin, 14-16, 57, 74, 77-78, 84, 86-87,
    89, 111, 155, 177, 181, 200, 245
Bezruč, Petr, 40, 86
Biale, David, 2
Bielsko (Bielitz), 74
Birnbaum, Nathan, 177n29
Birobidzhan, 164-65
Bisenz. *See* Bzenec
Blau-Weiss. *See* Tekhelet Lavan
Blumenfeld, Kurt, 170, 183, 191, 227, 239
Boháč, Antonín, 42-43
Bohemia (newspaper), 71-72
Böhm, Adolf, 180
Bondy, Bohumil, 51
    Czech-Jewish Students' Society
        and, 98
    his nationality in census, 51-2
Bondy, Filip, 96
Bondy, Josef, 159
    on autonomous Jewish region in
        Subcarpathian Ruthenia, 165
    on Birobidzan, 164
    on Romanian Jewish refugees, 164
Bondy, Leon, 128-30
Bondy, Max, 132n138
Bondy, Otto
    on alcoholism, 114
    on Jewish vices, 116
Bondy, Ruth, 239
Borchardt, Rudolf, 79
Borochov, Ber, 207
Boskovice (Boskowitz), 22
Boskowitz. *See* Boskovice
Brandeis, Louis, 29
Bratislava (Pressburg), 141-3, 196, 222, 235
Březnovský, Václav, 100, 146
Brit Trumpeldor (association), 220
Brit Shalom (association), 184, 214, 242
Brno (Brünn), 20, 39, 62n17, 89, 90, 128
    Czech-Jewish movement in, 137-40
    Zionist movement in, 172, 193,
        206-7, 210, 217, 219, 226-27,
        229, 232, 234
Brod, Elsa, 185
Brod, Karel, 132n139
Brod, Max, 28, 36, 50, 70, 72, 79, 174, 180,
    189, 191, 200, 205
    and Tomáš G. Masaryk, 38-40, 104
    and Yiddish theatre, 177
    B'nai B'rith and, 82, 87
    Die dritte Phase des Zionismus, 204
    Galician refugees and, 185

Ha-Po'el Ha-Tsa'ir and, 204–5, 207
  Herder-Blätter and, 83
  Hit'aḥadut and, 208
  Jüdischer Volksheim (Berlin) and, 185
  on Herderverein manifesto, 85n82
  Sozialismus im Zionismus, 204
Brod, Petr, 49
Brody, Heinrich (Jindřich), 90
  biographical sketch, 196
  Mizraḥi and, 196
  Sinai association and, 195
  Widerspricht der Zionismus unserer Religion?, 196
Brünn. See Brno
Brüx. See Most
Bryant, Chad, 6
Buber, Martin 15, 17, 88–89, 172, 184, 204, 208, 242
  and Chaim Weizmann, 212–13
  and Johann Gottlieb Fichte, 242
  Bar Kochba and, 178, 181–84
  Brit Shalom and,184
  El Al association and, 232
  ethno-nationalism and, 242–43
  Ha-Po'el Ha-Tsa'ir and, 209
  Jüdischer Volksheim (Berlin), 185
  Jugendmeeting, 183–84, 208
  on socialism, 209
  parallel with Jindřich Kohn, 148–49
  Three Addresses on Judaism, 181–83, 203n117, 208
Budivoj (association), 8, 192
Budweis. See České Budějovice
Bukovina, 119
Bulgaria, 157
Bund, the (Algemeyner Yidisher Arbeter Bund in Lite, Poyln un Rusland), 170, 208, 245
Business and Arts League (Jednota pro péči hospodářskou a kulturní), 127–30
Bzenec (Bisenz), 22n31, 110

C
Carlsbad, 17, 62, 74, 209, 216, 229
Čas (periodical), 109, 125
Čáslav, 110
Census:
  comparison with Poland, 47–49
  determination of nationality in, 7
  Jewish nationality in, 26, 33, 40–47
  pitfalls of results of, 47–55
Centralverein deutscher Staatsbürger jüdischen Glaubens (association), 93, 190, 248

Centralverein zur Pflege jüdischer Angelegenheiten (association), 88
Černošice, 111
Černý, Josef, 237
Česká strana pokroková. See Czech Progressive Party
České Budějovice (Budweis), 3, 62, 110
Českožidovské listy (periodical), 99, 101–2
Českožidovské společenské sdružení (The Czech–Jewish society), 135–36
Chlum, Johann, 82
Chomutov (Komotau), 216
Cohen, Gary, 51–52, 69–70
Cracow, 74, 76
Crimea, 190
Czech Progressive Party (Česká strana pokroková), 107–9
Czech-Jewish Students' Society (Spolek českých akademiků židů), 104, 174
  and František Ladislav Rieger, 101–2
  in interwar period, 133–35
  on antisemitism, 113–14
  origins of, 93–99

D
Dagan, Avigdor. See Fischl, Viktor
Dante, Alighieri, 86
Děčín (Tetschen), 17, 210, 216, 229
Dědic, Karel, 100, 146
Der Jude (periodical), 77, 208
Der jüdische Sozialist (periodical), 206
Deutsche demokratische Freiheitspartei, 71
Deutsche nationalsozialistische Arbeiterpartei, 64
Die jüdische Aktion, 84–85
Die Wahrheit, Prague (periodical), 66, 71–73, 91
Die Wahrheit, Vienna (periodical), 72–73
Dollfuss, Engelbert, 91
Donath, Oskar, 79
Dostál-Lutinov, Karel, 101
Drachovský, Josef, 128
Drtina, František, 108
Dux, Luděk, 101, 115, 128, 129n123, 130

E
Eckstein, Friedrich, 210
Edelstein, Jacob, 171n8, 206, 237, 240
Ehrenfeld, Nathan, 196
Ehrenfeld, Salomon, 195
Eisner, Leopold, 129n123
Eisner, Pavel (Paul), 50, 71, 81–82
El-Al (association), 232
Engel, Alfred, 39, 185, 219
Engel, Emanuel, 99

Engliš, Karel, 128
Epstein, Kurt, 226
Epstein, Oskar, 176
    Ha-Po'el Ha-Tsa'ir and, 207, 209
    Zionist Realists and, 210-11

F
Faktor, Emil, 71
Fanta, Otta, 86n85
Feder, Richard, 154
Feig, Alex, 207
Feiwel, Berthold, 172, 181-82, 212-13
Fichte, Johann Gottlieb, 242
Fischer, František, 159
Fischer, Karl, 228
Fischer, Otokar, 50, 82
Fischer, Otto, 129n123, 133
Fischl, Karl, 28
Fischl, Viktor (Avigdor Dagan), 86, 192, 200-1, 234
    and Jan Masaryk, 238
    parallel to Egon Hostovský, 252-53
    Self-aid Association of Jews from Czechoslovakia and, 238
Fischlová, Stella, 255
Fleischmann Gisi, 171n8, 235
Fleischmann, Karel, 8, 192
Fousek, František, 108
Fraenkl, Jakob, 178
France, 25, 105, 190, 253
Freud, Sigmund, 76, 79-80
Freud, Viktor, 176, 181, 203n117, 216
Freund, Ervín, 144, 149-50
Freund, Oswald, 29n10
Friedmann, František, 174, 201, 221, 240, 243
Frischer, Arnošt, 206, 224
Fuchs, Alfréd, 8, 125, 138
Fuchs, Rudolf, 50, 70, 82-84, 86

G
Gablonz an der Neisse. See Jablonec nad Nisou
Galicia, 15-16, 119, 177, 184-87, 245
Galician refugees, 15-16, 245
    Czech-Jews on, 119
    Zionists and, 177, 184-87, 219, 229
Gerad, Arnošt, 157-58
German Casino (Deutsches Casino, association), 69-70, 91, 111
German university in Prague, 43, 61, 65-66, 72, 173
Germania (association), 65
Germany, 15, 17, 23, 61, 67-68, 72, 78, 196

B'nai B'rith in, 76-79, 90
Jewish integrationists in, 93, 97-98, 105, 190, 248
refugees from, 110, 150, 156, 235-37
rural Jews in, 19
Wandervogel in, 228
Getreuer, František, 226
Goethe, Johann Wolfgang, 81, 176
Goga, Octavian, 163
Goldfaden, Abraham, 15
Goldmann, Nahum, 217, 219
Goldstein, Angelo, 39, 90, 200, 202, 210-12
    Jewish Party and, 223-25
    Theodor Herzl Society and, 175
Gordon, David, 207-10
Gottlieb, František, 201
Great Britain, 25, 77, 212, 217, 220-21, 253
Grégr, Julius, 98
Grünbaum, Karel, 86n85
Grünbaum, Yitshak, 218
Gurion, David Ben, 213
Gutfreund, Pavel, 116
Guth, Otakar, 121
    and Tomáš G. Masaryk, 36, 102
    Business and Arts League and, 128, 129n123
    on Czech-Jewish daily, 124n101
    on Polish Jews, 119-20
    on religion, 103
Gütig, Ernst, 178, 182

H
Haas, Willy, 70, 79, 81, 87
    Die jüdische Aktion and, 84-85
    Herder-Blätter and, 83
    Herderverein and, 83-84, 86
    on Jewish religion, 20
Hadina, Emil, 66
Hadler, Frank, 28
Hagibor (association), 198n107, 226, 229, 231
Hajn, Alois, 125
Hajn, Antonín, 100
Hakoakh (association), 98, 226
Hamburg, 89
Hammerschlag, Moritz, 74-75
Ha-Po'el Ha-Tsa'ir (association), 85n82, 204-9, 231
Hart, Jan, 162
Hašek, Jaroslav, 50, 126, 192
Hashachar (association), 181
Ha-Shomer ha-Tsa'ir (association), 230

Haskalah, 56–58
Hasmonea (association), 228
Hathiya (association), 228
Hatikva (association), 227
Hauner, Vilém, Julius, 126
Hegel, Georg Wilhelm Friedrich, 211
He-Ḥaluts (association), 190, 239
He-Ḥaver (association), 228
Hejduk, Adolf, 96
Heller, Kurt, 160n241, 160n242
    on refugees from Sudetenland, 166
Henlein Party, 72, 162
Henlein, Konrad, 64
Herben, Jan, 108–10, 120–21
Herder-Blätter (periodical), 83
Herderverein (association), 83–87, 90
Heřmanův Městec, 110
Herrmann, Hugo, 176–77, 202, 210
Herrmann, Leo, 64, 88, 176, 179, 181–82, 201–2, 238
Herrnheiser, Julian, 175
Herzl, Theodor, 172, 178, 182, 189, 191, 202, 207, 212, 242
HICEM (association), 235, 237
Hilsner Affair, 25, 33–34, 70, 100, 102, 113, 151, 217, 246
Hirsch, Ervín, 134
Hirsch, Mořic, 124, 131
Hirschler, Simon, 222
Hit'aḥadut (association), 208–11
Hlaváč, Bedřich, 125
Hnídek, František, 32
Hoffmann, Antonín, 196
Hoffmann, Camill, 50
Hoffmann, Chaim (Chaim Yahil), 235, 240
Hohenwart, Karl, 67
Holešov (Holleschau), 22, 193
    pogrom in, 110
Holland, 15
Holleschau. *See* Holešov
Homberg, Herz, 57
Hořovice (Horschowitz), 110
Horschowitz. *See* Hořovice
Hostovský, Egon, 127, 144
    parallel to Viktor Fischl, 252–53
Housková, Hana, 192
Hradec Králové (Königgrätz), 94, 232
Hungary, 58
Hvězda (association), 131
Hyndráková, Anna, 20

I

Iggers, Wilma, 61
Iglau. *See* Jihlava
Ikhud, 184

J

Jablonec nad Nisou (Gablonz an der Neisse), 62, 229
Jabotinsky, Vladimir, 219–20
Janáček, Leoš, 50
Janowitz, Franz, 83
Jednota pro péči hospodářskou a kulturní. *See* Business and Arts League
Jeiteles, Berthold, 24
Jeiteles, Isidor, 195
Jenkins, Richard, 6
Jerusalem, 184, 196, 202, 213, 234
Jesenská, Milena, 125, 192
Jewish National Council (Židovská národní rada), Prague:
    and Galician refugees, 185–87
    and Jews in Moravia, 193
    and Jews in Slovakia, 197
    and orthodox Jews, 195
    and Po'ale Tsiyon, 199, 205
    and 'Jewish clauses', 29–31
    and Tomáš G. Masaryk, 37–39
    origins of, 27–28, 148, 172, 188–89
Jewish Party, 43–44, 54–55, 71, 90, 107, 136, 171, 174, 192, 199–202, 217, 221–25
Jihlava (Iglau), 20
    Czech-Jewish movement in, 137–38
    Zionist movement in, 193
Jindřichův Hradec (Neuhaus), 110
Jirásek, Alois, 176, 190
Joyce, James, 79
Jüdische Lese- und Redehalle in Brünn (association), 219, 227
Jüdische Rundschau (newspaper), 202, 209
Jüdische Volksstimme (periodical), 182, 219
Jüdischer Volksverein Zion (association), 88, 179
Judson, Peter, 6n21
Jung Juda (periodical), 179
Jungbunzlau. *See* Mladá Boleslav

K

Kadeřávek, František, 190
Kafka, Franz, 50, 79, 81, 83, 125, 191
    Brief an den Vater, 19–20
    Herderverein and, 84
    Jüdischer Volksheim (Berlin), 185
    Toynbee Hall and, 89
    Yiddish theatre and, 16, 177
Kafka, Herrmann, 50
Kahn, Franz, 90–91, 202, 234n226, 237, 240
Kalendář česko-židovský (periodical), 94, 96, 99, 156

Kamenice nad Lipou (Kamnitz and der
    Linde), 110
Kamnitz an der Linde. See Kamenice nad
    Lipou
Kaplan, Eliezer, 208
Kapper (periodical), 144, 148
Kapper Students' Society (Akademický
    spolek Kapper), 83, 133-35, 248, 251
    and Jews in Moravia, 138-39
    and Jews in Slovakia, 141-43
    and Jindřich Kohn, 148-49
    revolt against Association of
        Czech-Jews, 143-50
Kapper, Siegfried, 50, 104, 133
Kartel (association), 227
Kaschau. See Košice
Kaznelson, Siegmund, 85, 176, 179-80, 213
Kellner, Leon, 89
Kellner, Viktor, 176, 180-81
Kestenberg-Gladstein, Ruth, 58, 61
Kettner, Hynek, 129n123
Kettner, Leopold, 86n85
Kieval, Hillel, 8, 11, 58
King, Jeremy, 3
Kisch, Egon Erwin, 70-71
Klaar, Alfred, 71
Klatovy (Klattau), 110, 129n123
Klattau. See Klatovy
Klein, Arthur, 173
Kleiner, Kamil, 132
Klein-Pejšová, Rebekah, 52
Kleist, Heinrich, 89
Klement, Václav, 130
Klíma, Ladislav, 126
Klineberger, Bohdan, 100-1, 103-4, 126,
    132
    Business and Arts League and,
        129n123
    Náboženský cit, 103
    on assimilation, 122
Kodíček, Josef, 125
Koeltzsch, Ines, 6, 127n115, 225n189
Kohn, Edmund, 75, 79
Kohn, Hans, 1, 29n10, 176, 179, 209, 234
    Brit Shalom and, 184, 214
Kohn, Jindřich, 83, 100, 107, 114, 121,
    132, 158, 160, 250
    and Henri Bergson, 149
    and Tomáš G. Masaryk, 36, 102, 211
    Business and Arts League and, 129
    Kapper Society and, 148-49, 160,
        168
    on Nazism and its localization, 156
    Tribuna and, 126
Kohn, Josef, 173

Kohn, Paul, 232
Kohn, Rudolf, 36-37
Kohner, Hugo, 219
Kohner, Walter, 171, 178n36
Kolín (Kolin), 62n17, 110, 231
Kolman, Arnošt, 183
Komotau. See Chomutov
Königgrätz. See Hradec Králové
Kopecký, Josef, 190
Kornfeld, Felix (Ben Jomtov), 134
Kornfeld, Paul, 79
Košice (Kaschau), 47, 141, 142
Kostelec nad Černými lesy
    (Schwarzkosteletz), 59
Kouša, Josef, 190
Kralupy nad Vltavou (Kralup and der Mol-
    dau), 110, 129n123
Kramář, Karel, 38n39, 107, 112
Kramerius, Václav Matěj, 94
Kraus, Josef, 96
Kraus, Mořic, 96
Krejčí, František, 41, 43, 189, 244, 250
Kremsier. See Kroměříž
Kříženecký, Jaroslav, 128
Kroměříž (Kremsier), 63n17, 110, 193
Kučera, Jaroslav, 46
Kugel, Chaim, 90, 171n8, 223-25
Kutná Hora (Kuttenberg), 110, 111
Kuttenberg. See Kutná Hora
Kvapil, Jaroslav, 190

L

L'viv (Lemberg, Lwów), 15
Landau, Ezechiel, 58
Landauer, Gustav, 185
Landes, Zdeněk, 201
Langer, František, 81-82, 192
Langer, Herbert, 159-60
Langer, Jiří Mordechai, 83, 146, 177n30
Laurin, Arne (Arnošt Lustig), 71-72
    Tribuna and, 125-27
Lauterbach, Leo, 90
League against Antisemitism (Liga proti
    antisemitismu), 160
Lebenhart, Philipp, 179
Lederer, Eduard, 100, 138, 224n186
    and Emanuel Rádl, 122-23
    and Tomáš G. Masaryk, 103
    Kapitoly o židovství a židovstvu, 103
    on Birobidzhan, 165
    on Czech antisemitism, 114n70
    on Czech-Jewish integration, 120-22
    Realist party and, 107-8
    Tribuna and, 125-26
Lederer, Franz, 91

Lederer, Josef, 129n123
Lederer, Max, 100-1, 132, 138
　　on Czech antisemitism, 153
Lemberg. *See* L'viv
Lese- und Redehalle der deutschen Studenten in Prag (association), 65
Lese- und Redehalle jüdischer Hochschüler in Prag (association), 227
Lessing, Theodor, 70
Levý, Otakar, 141-42
Liberec (Reichenberg), 17, 62, 65, 66, 74, 216
Lichtenstein, Tatjana, 243
Lichtwitz, Hans, 86, 231
Lieben, Eugen, 195
Lieben, Salomon Hugo, 24, 195
Lodgman von Auen, Rudolf, 216
Lorencová, Anna, 20
Loria, Felix, 206
Löwy, Alfréd, 173-4
Löwy, Julius, 178
Löwy, Růža, 180, 237n236
Lwów. *See* L'viv

M

Machar, Josef Svatopluk, 96, 108
Mader, Julius, 66
Mährisch Ostrau. *See* Moravská Ostrava
Makkabi, 192, 225-27, 238
Mannheimer, Georg, 71-72
Manning, Philipp, 182
Marburg, 196
Marek, Ferdinand, 91
Mareš, Michal, 125
Margulies, Emil, 171n8, 180, 197, 201-2, 214-23
　　and Karel Baxa, 217-18
　　Radical Zionists and, 217-19
　　rescue of Sudeten Jews and, 238
　　Revisionist movement and, 219-20
　　Jewish Party and, 221-23
　　Zionismus und Deutsche Fortschrittspartei, 215
Margulies, Isidor, 214
Mariánské Lázně (Marienbad), 17, 216
Marienbad. *See* Mariánské Lázně
Markus, Vítězslav, 124n101, 135
März, Paul, 219, 240
Masaryk, Jan, 238
Masaryk, Tomáš Garrigue, 25, 31, 72, 99-100, 102-5, 107, 123, 191, 224n186, 225, 253
　　and Eduard Lederer, 103
　　and Jindřich Kohn, 102
　　and Max Brod, 38-40, 189

　　and Otakar Guth, 36
　　Bar Kochba and, 175, 179
　　on antisemitism, 112, 246-47
　　recognition of Jewish nationality and, 33-41
　　Tribuna and, 125-27
　　Zionist Realists and, 210-11
Matzke, Frank, 66
McCagg, William O., 15
Medina Ivrit (periodical), 220
Mělník (Melnik), 110
Mendelsohn, Ezra, 9
Mendelssohn, Moses, 57, 152
Menorah Brith Hanoar. *See* Herderverein
Minařík, Stanislav, 123
Mittler, Liese, 86
Mizraḥi (association), 90, 196, 199, 211
Mladá Boleslav (Jungbunzlau), 63n17, 130
Moller, Jörn, 86n85
Moravia, 3, 8, 17, 23, 54, 65, 98, 106, 137
　　Czech-Jewish movement in, 137-40, 143, 159
　　religious situation in, 22
　　specifics of Jewish settlement in, 20, 22
　　Zionist movement in, 172, 193-95, 197, 206, 224n186, 229, 233-34, 237, 250
Moravská Ostrava (Mährisch Ostrau), 20, 63n17, 90
　　Czech-Jewish movement in, 138, 140
　　Zionist movement in, 197, 199, 218, 219, 229
Morawetz, Richard, 128, 129n123, 138
Moses, Walter, 230
Most (Brüx), 17, 216
Motzkin, Leo, 77
Mráz, Josef, 43
Mukačevo. *See* Mukachevo
Mukachevo (Munkács, Mukačevo), 171
　　grammar school in, 224-25, 234
Müller, Viktor, 143n189
Munich Agreement, 10, 25, 72, 165, 239, 246, 253
Munkács. *See* Mukachevo
Münzer, Egmont, 86
Musil, Josef, 137
Musil, Robert, 83

N

Náchod (Nachod), 62n17, 110, 196
Nagler, Heinz, 230
Napajedla (Napajedl), 140n175
Národní jednota českožidovská. *See* National Union of Czech-Jews

Národní listy (newspaper), 45, 98, 108-9, 167
National Union of Czech-Jews (Národní jednota českožidovská), 99, 102, 130, 137, 139
Němec, Bohumil, 155-56
Němec, Václav, 190
Neruda, Jan, 176
Neubauer, Robert, 178
Neuhaus. *See* Jindřichův Hradec
Neumann, Ervín, 115-16, 151-53, 157
Neumann, Kamil, 134, 141
Neumann, Oskar, 211
Neuzerekwe. *See* Nová Cerekev
Nimburg. *See* Nymburk
Nordau, Max, 174, 178n36
Nová Cerekev (Neuzerekwe), 110, 113
Novák, Arne, 189, 250
Nymburk (Nimburg), 110

O
Obernik, Grete, 180
Olmütz. *See* Olomouc
Olomouc (Olmütz), 20, 63n17
    Czech-Jewish movement in, 137-40
    Zionist movement in, 193, 206, 229
Oplatka, Emil, 175
Or Tomid (association), 96-97, 131
Orzoff, Andrea, 31
Österreichisch-Israelitische Union (association), 93
Oxford, 89, 196

P
Pacovský, Karel, 18
Pacovský, Richard, 226
Palacký, František, 151
Palestine, 27, 75, 90, 185, 187, 197, 200, 207-10, 213, 220
    aliya to, 170, 180-81, 232, 238-40
    Czech-Jews on, 115, 158, 164-65
    Jewish-Arab conflict in, 184, 210, 220, 242
    kibbutzim founded by Zionists from Bohemian Lands in, 231
Pardubice (Pardubitz), 102, 104, 144
Paris Peace Conference, 26-30, 105, 246
Pečky (Peček), 110
Pelikán, Ferdinand, 129
Pelikán, Jan, 22
Penížek, Josef, 129
Peroutka, Ferdinand, 112, 123
    Tribuna and, 124-25
Peters, Gustav, 42
Philipp Lebenhart, 179

Pibrans. *See* Příbram
Pick, Arnošt, 144
Pick, Otto, 50, 71-72, 81, 83
Pilsen (Plzeň), 62, 74, 188
Písek (Pisek), 76, 94, 110
Pitter, Přemysl, 189
Pleschner, Max, 100, 125-26, 127n115, 132
Po'ale Tsiyon (association), 190, 199, 204-10
Podbořany (Podersam), 216
Poděbrady (Podiebrad), 83, 110
Podersam. *See* Podbořany
Podiebrad. *See* Poděbrady
Podlipný, Jan, 102
Poláček, Karel, 125
Polak, Arthur, 206
Polak, Irma, 237
Poland, 14, 29, 31-32, 38, 45, 68, 170, 190, 195, 218, 220, 228
    B'nai B'rith in, 75-76
    census in, 47-49
    pogroms in, 187
Popper, Ernst, 84-85
Popper, Josef, 35, 75, 90
Popper, Rudolf, 90
Postelberg. *See* Postoloprty
Postoloprty (Postelberg), 216
Považská Bystrica, 147n201
Prager Tagblatt (newspaper), 42, 46, 70-72, 91, 123
Prager, Vilém, 139
Prague, 6, 9, 23-24, 50, 63, 99, 102, 128, 131, 135, 152-53, 172-73, 237
    Czech-German conflict in, 242
    demography of Jewish community in, 14-19
    German-Jewish elite in, 69-73, 118
    language of Jews in, 50, 53n81, 234
    Orthodox Jews in, 195-97
    Po'ale Tsiyon in, 206
    riots in 1918, 110-11
    tensions between borderlands and, 63-67, 214-16
    Zionist movement in, 173-91, 199-200, 208, 226, 228, 232, 239
Preissová, Gabriela, 96, 191
Prerau. *See* Přerov
Přerov (Prerau), 22n31, 140, 193
Pressburg. *See* Bratislava
Příbram (Pibrans), 94, 110
Prößnitz. *See* Prostějov
Prostějov (Prößnitz), 22, 62n17, 139, 193, 206, 229
Pštross, Zdeněk, 129n123

R

Rabinowicz, Oskar, 211
Radical Zionists, 199, 212n152, 217–20
Rádl, Emanuel, 41, 122, 129, 189, 244, 250
    on Czech-Jewish movement, 36, 122
    on nationality, 42–43, 45
Rakous, Vojtěch, 18, 107–8, 122, 126, 129n123, 135
    and Rudolf Fuchs, 82
    Czech Progressive Party and, 108
    on German-speaking Jews, 118
Rauchberg, Heinrich, 17n11, 42–43
Realists, the. *See* Czech Progressive Party
Reichenberg. *See* Liberec
Reiner, Arnošt, 226n193
Reiner, Josef, 125
Reiner, Maxim, 24, 101, 124n101, 129n123, 131
    on Czech antisemitism, 153
    on refugees from Germany, 162
Reiss, Jakub, 206–7
Reisz, Julius, 43, 171n8, 222–25
Reitler, Julius, 99
Resek, Felix, 179
Resek, Karl, 179
Revisionist Zionism, 199, 219–21
Richter, Ota, 116, 160
Rie, Oskar, 76
Rieger, Ladislav, 101–2, 152
Riff, Michael, 69
Romania, 31, 54, 68, 136, 157, 190, 228
    B'nai B'rith in, 74
    Jewish refugees from, 163–64
Rosen, Arthur, 84–85
Rosen, Lia, 182
Rosenblüth, Martin, 183
Rosenzweig, Arthur, 155–56
Roubíček, Gustav, 138
Rozhled (periodical), 36, 108, 113, 119, 121, 123, 128, 131, 133
Rozsypal, Antonín, 222
Rozvoj (periodical), 72, 102, 104, 121, 131, 133, 149–50, 157, 162, 247
Rufeisen, Josef, 28n8, 90, 199–200, 209, 211, 218–19, 223, 224n186
    and Chaim Weizmann, 212
    on Czech language, 233
Russia, 15, 26–27, 103, 173, 245
Růžička, Heřman, 129n123, 132n139
Růžička, Josef, 129n123

S

Saaz. *See* Žatec
Sadská (Sadska), 110
Šalda, F.X., 126
Salten, Felix, 182
Salus, Hugo, 82, 88
Šámal, Přemysl, 108
Saudek, Emil, 82
Scharf, Jakub, 100–1, 129n123, 148
Scheuer, Fritzi, 180
Scheuer, Miriam, 219
Schick, Marta, 180
Schleissner, Paul, 86n85
Schmolka, Marie, 235–37
Schnitzler, Arthur, 79
Schnitzler, Leopold, 211
Schönbaum, Emil, 43
Schönerer, Georg, 64, 67
Schulhof, Stanislav, 100, 122
Schulz, František, 226n193
Schulz, Lev, 86n85
Schulze-Wessel, Martin, 25
Schur, Hans, 86
Schuster, Václav, 128, 130
Schwager, Karl, 185
Schwarzkosteletz. *See* Kostelec nad Černými lesy
Sdruženie židovských akademikov Slovákov v Bratislavě. *See* Association of Jewish Slovak Students of Bratislava
Seidl, Walter, 66
Sekanina, František, 190
Selbstwehr (periodical), 110, 171, 176n26, 179, 210, 217, 219, 234
Self-aid Association of Jews from Czechoslovakia, 238
Shumsky, Dimitry, 49, 175n22, 242
Sicher, Gustav, 196–97
Silesia, 17, 40, 54, 65, 74, 188, 223, 237
    Czech-Jewish movement in, 137, 139
Šimonek, Josef, 127
Šimsa, Jaroslav, 147
Sinai (association), 194–95
Sinclair, Upton, 79
Singer, Ludvík, 28–29, 36, 174, 292, 210, 218, 223–24
    and Chaim Weizmann, 212
    and Karel Baxa, 217
    on Czech language, 233
    on Jewish nationality during census, 43–44
    Paris Peace Conference and, 29–31
Slovakia, 22, 31, 47, 54, 105, 192, 195, 228, 235
    Agudas Yisroel in, 53
    anti-Jewish outbursts, 112
    Czech(oslovak)-Jewish movement in, 140–43, 165

Jewish nationality in, 52-53
Jewish Party and, 55
national campaign in, 39, 189
Zionism in, 170-72, 188, 207, 221-23
Šmeral, Bohumír, 165
Smith, Anthony, 4-5
Sobotka, Josef, 156
Sokol (association), 110, 225, 247, 249
Sokolow, Nahum 30-31
Soloweitschik, Max, 217
Sonnenfeld, Karl, 193
Sorkin, David, 9
Soukup, František, 28, 112
Soviet Union, 115, 164, 190
Spolek českých akademiků židů. See Czech-Jewish Students' Society
Sprinzak, Joseph, 208, 211
Šrámek, Fráňa, 86
Srdínko, Otakar, 28
Staněk, Alois, 40
Štědrý, František, 86n85
Stein, August, 35, 128, 129n123, 146-47
Steiner, Hanna, 211, 235-37
Steiner, Pavel (Pali), 226
Steinherz, Samuel, 65-66, 82
Stránský, Adolf, 98, 104, 107
Stránský, Rudolf, 195
Stříbrný, Jiří, 28n5
Stricker, Robert, 172, 217
Stross, Jindřich, 129n123
Stross, Karel, 159
Stross, Otto, 115, 155-56, 159, 161-63
    on refugees from borderlands, 166-67
Subcarpathian Ruthenia, 16, 22, 47, 54-55, 105, 171-72, 192, 194, 207, 221-25, 236, 239
    Czech-Jews on, 141, 164-65
    Jewish nationality in, 53, 106, 170, 188-89, 244
Svaz Čechů židů. See Association of Czech-Jews
Svaz českých pokrokových židů. See Association of Progressive Czech-Jews
Švehla, Antonín, 28n5, 127
Sweden, 77
Switzerland, 77

T

Taaffe, Eduard, 67
Tábor (Tabor), 63n17, 94, 110
Taussig, Richard, 181
Taussik, Otto, 128, 129n123
Tekhelet Lavan (Blau-Weiss), 227-30

Teplice-Šanov (Teplitz-Schönau), 17, 62, 88, 155, 229
Teplitz-Schönau. See Teplice-Šanov
Terezín (Theresienstadt), 8, 104, 121, 202n115, 206
Tetschen. See Děčín
Teytz, Viktor, 97, 100, 102, 122, 131
    Tribuna and, 125-26
Theodor Herzl Society, 18, 147, 175-76, 183, 192, 200-3, 226-27, 234, 251
Theresienstadt. See Terezín
Thieberger, Friedrich, 87, 201
Tochten, Eugen, 147
Tohn, Zdeněk, 156
Toman, Karel, 86
Tomášek, František, 43
Torberg, Friedrich, 70-71
Toynbee Hall, 89, 181
Toynbee, Arnold, 89
Trautenau. See Trutnov
Tribuna (newspaper), 71, 82, 124-27, 130
Trutnov (Trautenau), 64,215
Tse'ire Tsiyon (association), 208

U

Uherské Hradiště (Ungarisch Hradisch), 172n10, 193, 234
Uherský Brod (Ungarisch Brod), 22n31, 193
Uherský Ostroh (Ungarisch Ostra), 22n31
Ukraine, 45, 54
Ullmann, Bedřich, 238
Ungar, Markus, 29, 189, 195, 222
Ungarisch Brod. See Uherský Brod
Ungarisch Hradisch. See Uherské Hradiště
Ungarisch Ostra. See Uherský Ostroh
United States, 17, 34, 74, 187
Urania (association), 66, 91
Urban, Otto, 59
Ústí nad Labem (Aussig), 62, 63n18, 215
Utitz, Emil, 71
Užhorod, 192, 196, 236

V

Varnsdorf (Warnsdorf), 229
Veith, Karel, 128
Verunáč, Václav, 128
Vienna, 9, 14-17, 43, 52, 65-66, 72-73, 86, 98, 140, 188, 191, 206, 214, 245
    B'nai B'rith in, 75-79, 89
    conversions in, 69
    Moravian Zionists and, 172
Vizovice (Wisowitz), 140n175
Vobecká, Jana, 17
Vogl, Erwin, 210

Vohryzek, Lev, 107, 132
    Kapper society and, 146
    Tribuna and, 125-27
Vohryzek, Viktor, 100-4, 107, 130
    and Ferdinand Peroutka, 123
    and Jan Herben, 109
    on Czech-Jewish newspaper, 123
    on Czechness with a Jewish tinge, 121
    on Jewish religion, 103
    Realists and, 108-9
Volksverband der Juden für die Slowakei (association), 197
Vraný, Josef, 127
Vrchlický, Jaroslav, 96
Vyškov (Wischau), 140n175

W

Waldes, Jindřich, 128, 129n123
Waldstein, Emil, 174, 191-92, 201, 236
Waldsteinová, Vally, 236
Warnsdorf. *See* Varnsdorf
Warsaw, 14
Weber, Koloman, 222
Wechsberg, Joseph, 70
Wein, Martin, 172
Weiner, Arnim, 90
Weiner, Oldřich, 121
Weininger, Otto, 81
Weizmann, Chaim, 172, 211-14, 242
    and Emil Margulies, 202, 217-18
    Bar Kochba and, 181, 213
    Hit'aḥadut and, 210-11
    Revisionists and, 219-20
Weltsch, Felix, 79, 82-83, 87, 176, 179, 200-1, 204, 209
    Das Wagnis der Mitte, 211-12
Weltsch, Frieda, 180
Weltsch, Robert, 88, 176, 179-80, 184, 199-200, 202, 214
    and Chaim Weizmann, 213
Weltsch, Theodor, 88
Werfel, Franz, 83, 86, 104, 191
Wertheimer, Max, 104
Westphalia, 78
Wiegler, Paul, 84
Wiesmeyer, Emil, 75, 77
Winter, Lev, 104
Winter, Zikmund, 96
Winternitz, Alfred, 129n123
Wischau. *See* Vyškov
Wise, Stephen, 29
Wisowitz. *See* Vizovice
WIZO (association), 235-7
Wolf, Hermann, 64-65

Y

Yahil, Chaim. *See* Hoffmann, Chaim
YMCA, 115, 147
Young Czechs (Mladočeši), 98-102, 104n41, 107, 132
Yugoslavia, 31, 136, 157
Yushchinsky, Andrei, 102

Z

Zahra, Tara, 6
Žalud, Josef, 99
Žatec (Saaz), 62, 215
Zíbrt, Čeněk, 146
Židovské zprávy (periodical), 134-35, 154, 174, 191-92, 200, 219, 234
Židovský kalendář (periodical), 200-1
Zionist Realists, 210-11
Živanský, Bohdan, 128
Zlín (Zlin), 130
Zucker, Alois, 99
Zucker, Otto, 240
Zweig, Arnold, 79
Zweig, Hans, 211n146

www.ingramcontent.com/pod-product-compliance
Lightning Source LLC
Chambersburg PA
CBHW072146100526
44589CB00015B/2115